Expo

Higher Teacher's Guide

Tracy Traynor

www.heinemann.co.uk

✓ Free online support
✓ Useful weblinks
✓ 24 hour online ordering

01865 888058

Heinemann Educational Publishers
Halley Court, Jordan Hill, Oxford OX2 8EJ
Part of Harcourt Education

Heinemann is the registered trademark of
Harcourt Education Limited

First published 2006

10 09 08 07 06
10 9 8 7 6 5 4 3 2 1

British Library Cataloguing in Publication Data is available
from the British Library on request.

10-digit ISBN: 0 435717 89 8
13-digit ISBN: 978 0 435717 89 6

Publisher: Trevor Stevens

Editor: Charonne Prosser

Produced by Ken Vail Graphic Design, Cambridge

Printed by Ashford Colour Press

Cover photo: Image State

Every effort has been made to contact copyright holders of material reproduced in this book. Any omissions will be rectified in subsequent printings if notice is given to the publishers.

Tel: 01865 888058 www.heinemann.co.uk

Running the CD-ROM

To run this CD-ROM you require Microsoft® Internet Explorer 5 or above, Microsoft® Word and Adobe® Acrobat® Reader® 5 or above.

For further details please see the readme.txt file on the CD-ROM.

To run on Microsoft® Windows® 2000, XP:
- Insert the CD into your CD-ROM drive: the CD-ROM should run automatically.

To run on Microsoft® Windows® 98, NT:
- Insert the CD into your CD-ROM drive. In the window that appears click on **index.htm**.

If your PC does not support autorun:
- Go to **Start**, select **Run**, type in **D:\index.htm** (substitute D with the letter of your CD-ROM drive), click OK.

Contents

Introduction

Expo offers a lively, communicative approach, underpinned by clear grammatical progression. The course is suitable for a wide ability range and includes differentiated materials and differentiated Workbooks in *Expo 1* and differentiated Student Books and Workbooks in *Expo 2* and *3*.

Expo 4 exists in three different versions, each of which is differentiated to provide complete coverage of the GCSE specifications as follows:

Expo 4 for AQA Higher (GCSE Grades A*–C)
Expo 4 for Edexcel Higher (GCSE Grades A*–C)
Expo 4 for OCR Higher (GCSE Grades A*–C)

Expo 4 for AQA Foundation (GCSE Grades C–G)
Expo 4 for Edexcel Foundation (GCSE Grades C–G)
Expo 4 for OCR Foundation (GCSE Grades C–G)

NB This Teacher's Guide accompanies **all three Higher Student Books** and contains all the information you require to help you use them. Where appropriate there are clearly-marked separate sections for each examination board.
(There is a separate Teacher's Guide to accompany the Expo 4 Foundation Student Books.)

Expo 4 is designed to continue from *Expo 1, 2* and *3*, but is also suitable for students who have followed a different course at Key Stage 3.

Expo 4 Higher: the components

***Expo 4 Higher:* the components**		*Also available: Expo 4 Foundation components*
Student Book	3 versions – AQA, Edexcel, OCR	*3 versions – AQA, Edexcel, OCR*
CDs (x 4)	1 set – accompanies all 3 Higher Student Books	*1 set – accompanies all 3 Foundation Student Books*
Workbook	1 – accompanies all 3 Higher Student Books	*1 – accompanies all 3 Foundation Student Books*
Teacher's Guide	1 – accompanies all 3 Higher Student Books	*1 – accompanies all 3 Foundation Student Books*
Teacher's Guide CD-Rom	1 – accompanies Higher Teacher's Guide (included as part of Higher Teacher's Guide)	*1 – accompanies Foundation Teacher's Guide (included as part of Foundation Teacher's Guide)*
Assessment pack	3 versions, each covering both Higher and Foundation books for the appropriate exam board – AQA, Edexcel, OCR	

Student Book
There are three separate Student Books (AQA, Edexcel and OCR). The Student Book is designed to last for two years and contains all the language required for preparation for the GCSE examination. There are ten Modules: it is expected that Modules 1–6 will be completed in the first year of the course and Modules 7–10 in the second.

Audio CDs
There are four CDs. These accompany all three Student Books. They contain listening material for both presentation and practice. The material includes texts, dialogues and interviews, all recorded using native speakers.

Workbook
The Workbook accompanies all three Student Books. It provides self-access reading and writing tasks, which are ideal for homework. At the end of each module there is a page of grammar revision and a two-page *Mots* section (as given in the SB), to be used for reference and revision. All Workbook pages are referred to at the end of the appropriate module in the Teacher's Guide, with solutions to the activities.

Teacher's Guide
The Teacher's Guide contains:

- overview grids for each module
- clear teaching notes for all activities
- solutions for Student Book and Workbook activities
- full transcripts of the recorded material

Teacher's Guide CD-Rom
The CD-Rom accompanying the Teacher's Guide provides a separate customisable scheme of work for each specification (AQA (Specification A and Specification B), Edexcel and OCR). It also contains matching charts for AQA, Edexcel and OCR examinations. This information is listed separately for each examination board and presented in two different ways: first by topic/theme/context and then unit by unit for each module in the book.

Assessment pack
There are three separate Assessment Packs available to accompany *Expo 4*. These cover both Higher and Foundation books for the appropriate exam boards.

Expo 4 for AQA assessment pack
Expo 4 for Edexcel assessment pack
Expo 4 for OCR assessment pack

Each pack has been written by an experienced examiner from the appropriate examination board (AQA/Edexcel/OCR). The design and type of questions follow the examination boards' own papers and give much-needed practice in developing examination skills.

Each of the main assessment blocks represents two Modules. It is suggested that one assessment block be used at the end of each term of the two-year course, and that the final assessment be used at the end of the course as a pre-examination test.

The Expo 4 Assessment Packs include the following important features:

- assessments have clear and concise mark schemes for Listening, Speaking, Reading and Writing
- Speaking assessments contain pages for students and for teachers
- rubrics reflect the language used by the examining bodies, familiarising students with GCSE-style questions throughout Years 10 and 11

How the course works

Progression

The first one or two double-page spreads of each Module (*Déjà vu*) are devoted to language that should already be familiar to students from Key Stage 3. The *Déjà vu* pages in later modules also contain a small number of items of vocabulary and grammatical structures that have been taught in earlier modules in *Expo 4*. The rest of the Units continue to revise earlier material but new grammar and structures are built into the activities to ensure steady progression.

As well as the clear progression within each Module, language is constantly recycled through all Modules in a systematic spiral of revision and extension. What is covered is clearly shown in the Teacher's Guide in the planning summary at the beginning of each Module, to help teachers plan a programme of work appropriate for the ability group that they teach.

Core units

In each module the *Déjà vu* section is followed by the core units.

The objectives for each core unit are clearly listed at the start of the unit. These generally consist of a topic objective (e.g. *Talking about your friends*) and a grammar objective (e.g. *Adjective agreement*).

Expo-langue boxes

The key structures introduced in a Unit in the Student Book are presented in an *Expo-langue* box, providing support for speaking and writing activities. Reminders of grammar points previously introduced are also included in separate boxes in the Unit. *Expo-langue* boxes contain page references to the comprehensive *Grammaire* section at the back of the Student Book, where the structures are explained more fully. For further details of the grammar covered in *Expo 4 Higher* see **Grammar coverage** on p. 8.

Lesson starters

For all *Déjà vu* and core units in the Student Book there are two lesson starters, the first at the beginning of the unit, the second approximately halfway through the unit, where a second lesson is likely to begin. All starters are given in the Teacher's Guide.

The starters are simple activities that allow you to recap on previous knowledge or to prepare the pupils for new language to be learnt in the unit. They are designed to get the lesson off to a brisk start, focusing the pupils' attention and promoting engagement and challenge.

Plenaries

For all *Déjà vu* and core units in the Student Book there is also a plenary session. All plenaries are given in the Teacher's Guide.

Again, plenaries are simple activities, aiming to draw out the key learning points. Pupils are actively involved and are expected to demonstrate and explain what they have learned in the unit. They identify links with what the pupils have learnt so far and what they will learn later in the course.

Skills and strategies

Tip boxes appear throughout *Expo 4* to help students improve their language-learning skills and to equip them with strategies that will enhance their performance in the examination. These are easily recognised by the tip box symbol.

Throughout the Teacher's Guide, the following symbol ☑ is used to highlight further useful techniques and also targeted activities to help improve exam performance. This applies to activities in the Student Book and to starter and plenary activities.

Practice for written coursework/the speaking test

Contrôle continu

This section is designed to help students prepare for the written coursework part of their examination. It provides regular guided practice, helping them to structure what they have learned over the previous Modules into a relevant piece of work. Students are given support in the form of a model text (with activities), a suggested structure to use and hints on language and grammar (including references to the relevant parts of the Module) to help them raise the level of their writing.

When using the *Contrôle continu* to help your students prepare for their coursework tasks, it is essential that you refer to the guidance given for preparing and producing coursework assignments in the specification for the examining board you are using.

In particular, please note the relevant guidance for:

- use of stimulus material
- correction of mistakes in initial drafts
- submission of final pieces of work
- the amount of work to be produced under controlled conditions

It is necessary you follow this guidance to comply with the exam regulations.

À l'oral

On pp. 176–185 of the Student Book is the *À l'oral* section, which provides for each module a single page of practice to help students prepare for the GCSE Speaking test. This is designed to enable students to become familiar with and practise answering questions in the style of the final examination.

This section is different for each of the three GCSE specifications: each Student Book contains practice role-plays, presentations and general conversation questions appropriate to the relevant exam board. To support these materials, the Teacher's Guide contains a separate set of notes for each *À l'oral* section: these can be found at the end of the relevant Module.

Expo 4 for AQA
The *À l'oral* for each module contains:
- one or more practice Higher level roleplays
- a topic for presentation and discussion with a model cue card
- a number of general conversation questions likely to be asked on the subject matter of the module.

Each module also contains specific tips and general advice to help students prepare for their speaking test.

Expo 4 for Edexcel
The *À l'oral* for each module contains:
- one or more practice Higher level roleplays: both types of roleplay used in the Higher exam (*Roleplay Type B* and *Roleplay Type C*) are covered where appropriate
- a topic for presentation and discussion with a model cue card
- a number of general conversation questions likely to be asked on the subject matter of the module.

Each module also contains specific tips and general advice to help students prepare for their speaking test.

Expo 4 for OCR
The *À l'oral* for each module contains:
- one or more practice Higher level roleplays: both types of roleplay used in the Higher exam (*Roleplay Type 2* and *Roleplay Type 3*) are covered where appropriate
- a topic for presentation and discussion with a model cue card
- a number of general conversation questions likely to be asked on the subject matter of the module.

Each module also contains specific tips and general advice to help students prepare for their speaking test.

Further support

À toi

Also at the back of the Student Book is the *À toi* section: this provides a double-page spread of further reading and writing practice for each Module, supplying a variety of types of 'authentic' texts to work on.

Reference material

The Student Book also contains essential reference material:

- At the end of each Module a summary of the vocabulary covered, arranged by subject. This section, entitled *Mots*, will serve as a valuable examination revision tool.
- At the end of the book, the *Grammaire* section explains the grammar points introduced in *Expo 4* in more detail. It also contains page references back to the core unit(s) in which the relevant grammar point is covered, to enable students to review the point in context.
- Also at the end of the book is the *Vocabulaire*, a comprehensive French–English wordlist and a shorter English–French wordlist.

Incorporating ICT

Appropriate use of Information and Communication Technology (ICT) to support modern foreign language learning is a requirement of the National Curriculum.

Word-processing and desktop publishing skills will be particularly useful for students preparing for the coursework option for the writing part of the GCSE examination. References to e-mail and websites occur within the course, as they do in the GCSE examination papers. Students should be encouraged to e-mail contemporaries in French-speaking countries and to research authentic information in French on the internet.

Suggestions for ICT activities have been included in the Teacher's Guide. The following grid shows the location in *Expo 4 Higher* and nature of these activities.

Useful websites

We've collected together links to useful websites to help you and your pupils get the best from the web. Each of the sites includes interactive pupil activities or articles in the target language that will help your pupils to practise and improve their French.

- All the sites are chosen for their educational content.
- Each is checked by teachers to ensure relevance and suitability.
- Each link comes with a short description to help guide you.

In order to ensure that the links are up-to-date, that the links work, and that the sites aren't inadvertently linked to sites that could be considered offensive, we have made the links available on the Heinemann website at www.heinemann.co.uk/hotlinks. When you access the site, the express code is 7898T.

Unit	Activity type
M1 U1	Making contact with French students using e-mail or video-conferencing
M1 U4	Using a word-processing or DTP package to create a holiday journal
M2 U1	Using a word-processing or DTP package to create adverts for entertainments
M2 U3	Making contact with French students using e-mail or video-conferencing
M2 U4	Making contact with French students using e-mail or video-conferencing
M2 U5	Researching films in French on the internet
M3 U3	Researching the geography of francophone countries on the internet
M4 U3	Using a word-processing package to write about a disastrous trip and to redraft their texts
M4 U4	Researching shopping vocabulary using French websites
M5 DV2	Researching school uniform on the internet
M5 U2	Using a word-processing package to keep a journal about daily activities
M6 U3	Using a word-processing package to write a letter of application for a job; researching job opportunities on the internet
M6 U4	Using a word-processing or spreadsheet package to create and use a vocabulary notebook
M6 U5	Using a word-processing package to write a letter about work experience
M7 U1	Using a word-processing or DTP package to write an advertisement for a hotel
M7 U2	Using a word-processing package to write a letter enquiring about accommodation
M7 U5	Researching types of holidays on the internet
M8 U1	Researching sportspeople on the internet
M8 U4	Researching a major sports event on the internet
M9 U3	Making contact with French students using e-mail or video-conferencing
M10 DV	Researching the work of Médecins Sans Frontières on the internet
M10 U5	Researching endangered animals on the internet

Grammar coverage

Grammar is fully integrated into the teaching sequence in *Expo* to ensure that pupils have the opportunity to learn thoroughly the underlying structures of the French language. Most units have a grammar objective so that the pupils can see clearly which grammar structures they are learning in each unit. The key grammar points are presented in the *Expo-langue* boxes on the Student Book pages with short explanations. Fuller explanations are provided in the *Grammaire* section at the back of the Student Book. In addition there are units in the *Higher Workbook* which specifically focus on grammar.

Grammar points explained and practised in *Expo 4 Higher:*

1 Nouns and pronouns
Gender
Singular/plural
The definite article
The indefinite article
The partitive article
Subject pronouns
Direct object pronouns
Indirect object pronouns
Relative pronouns: **qui**, **que** and **dont**
lequel and **celui**
Emphatic pronouns
y
en

2 Adjectives and adverbs
Position of adjectives
Agreement of adjectives
Possessive adjectives
Comparatives and superlatives
Demonstrative adjectives: **ce/cette/ces**
Adverbs

3 Verbs
The infinitive
The present tense
The perfect tense
The imperfect tense
Mixing past tenses
The perfect infinitive
The pluperfect tense
The near future tense
The future tense
The conditional
The imperative
The passive voice
Negatives
Question forms
Reflexive verbs
Verbs with the infinitive
si clauses

4 Structural features
Prepositions
Question words
Intensifiers
Connectives
depuis
Impersonal verbs
Expressions with **avoir**
Time expressions

5 Extras
Numbers
Days
Dates
Times

List of grammar points practised on the ***Grammaire*** *pages in the Higher Workbook:*

Workbook	Grammar	Teacher's Guide
p. 9	Present, perfect and near future tenses	p. 28
p. 18	Direct object pronouns	p. 49
p. 27	Agreement of adjectives Comparatives	p. 72
p. 37	Impersonal verbs Demonstrative adjectives	p. 98
p. 47	Reflexive verbs	p. 122
p. 56	Indirect object pronouns Relative pronouns	p. 145
p. 67	Irregular verb: **aller** Imperative	p. 171
p. 76	Perfect infinitive Pluperfect tense	p. 194
p. 84	**en** Adverbs	p. 214
p. 93	Present, perfect, imperfect, future, and conditional tenses	p. 236

Module 1: Moi (Student Book pages 6–23)

Unit	Main topics and objectives	Grammar
Déjà vu 1 **Moi ... et quelques autres** (pp. 6–7)	Talking about yourself and other people Revising key present tense verb forms	Present tense – **je** form of verbs – **aimer** (full paradigm) – **être, avoir, faire** (full paradigms) **mon, ma, mes** Adjective agreement (nationalities, singular)
Déjà vu 2 **Les choses que j'aime faire ...** (pp. 8–9)	Saying what you like and don't like doing **aimer** + infinitive	**quel** (all forms) **aimer** + infinitive Negatives – **ne ... pas/jamais** – **du/de la/des** changing to **de** (**de l'** to **d'**) after negative
1 Moi, moi et encore moi! (pp. 10–11)	More about yourself Reflexive verbs	Reflexive verbs (present tense)
2 Mes parents (pp. 12–13)	Talking about your parents and what they do Using masculine and feminine nouns	Masculine/Feminine forms of jobs No article with jobs (**il est ingénieur**)
3 Mes copains et mes copines (pp. 14–15)	Talking about your friends Adjective agreement	Adjective agreement (singular)
4 Centre de loisirs (pp. 16–17)	Saying what you have done The perfect tense	Perfect tense (formation with **avoir** and **être**)
5 Ma passion (pp. 18–19)	Talking about your main hobby The near future tense	Near future tense **aller** (present tense) **depuis** + present tense
Contrôle continu **Ma passion** (pp. 20–21)	*Coursework* Writing about a favourite leisure activity	*All main grammar points of the module*
À l'oral (p. 176)	*Exam speaking practice* Leisure activities (in the past, present and future) Talking about yourself and your family	*All main grammar points of the module*
À toi (pp. 186–187)	Self-access reading and writing	

Déjà vu 1: Moi ... et quelques autres

(Student Book pages 6–7)

Main topics and objectives

- Talking about yourself and other people
- Revising key present tense verb forms

Grammar

- Present tense
  - **je** form of verbs
  - **aimer** (full paradigm)
  - **être, avoir, faire** (full paradigms)
- **mon, ma, mes**
- Adjective agreement (nationalities, singular)

Key language

Personal details (name, age, etc.)

Resources

CD1, tracks 2–4
Cahier d'exercices, page 2
Grammaire 2.2

The *Déjà vu* sections are designed to give students a quick and focused review of vocabulary areas and topics relevant to the module. The vocabulary/topics have been previously covered at KS3 or (for later modules) earlier in *Expo 4*.

Starter 1

Aim
To revise giving basic information about yourself.

Present yourself to the class using the following structures:

Je me présente. Je m'appelle ... J'ai ... ans. J'ai ... sœur(s)/... frère(s). Ma sœur/Mon frère a ... ans.

Ask one or two confident students to present themselves in the same way. Then ask students in groups to introduce themselves to each other.

1 Écoutez et lisez les textes. Répondez aux questions.

Reading. Students listen to three people introducing themselves and read the text at the same time. They then answer the questions in French, identifying the person/people referred to in each.

You could stop the recording at random points and ask students to say the next word, to check that they are following.

Audioscript 2

Je m'appelle Laurent. J'ai quinze ans et j'ai une sœur jumelle, Amélie. J'habite à Bruxelles en Belgique, et je parle français. J'aime les chiens, mais nous n'avons pas d'animal parce que ma sœur ne les aime pas. Physiquement, je suis assez grand, mince, brun et beau! Ma passion est le cinéma, mais j'adore aussi les BD.

Je me présente. Je m'appelle Pascal, j'ai quatorze ans et mon anniversaire est le 15 août. Je suis français et j'habite en France, à Lyon. Mes deux sœurs s'appellent Lydie et Sophie et nous avons un chat, qui s'appelle Ludo. J'ai aussi un demi-frère, qui s'appelle Antoine, mais il a dix-neuf ans et habite à Paris chez son père. Je suis assez grand aux cheveux bruns et aux yeux bleus. Je suis sportif: je fais du basket et du VTT.

Mon nom est Karima. J'habite à Marseille dans le sud de la France et je suis grande et brune. Mon anniversaire est le 10 novembre et j'ai seize ans. Mon frère a dix ans et s'appelle Hakim. J'ai aussi un demi-frère, Kévin, qui a seize ans, mais il habite chez sa mère à Paris. Nous avons également un chien et un oiseau.

Answers

1 Pascal
2 Antoine, le demi-frère de Pascal
3 Pascal, Lydie, Sophie, Antoine, Karima, Hakim, Kévin
4 Laurent, Amélie
5 Pascal
6 Karima
7 Pascal, Lydie, Sophie, Antoine, Karima, Hakim, Kévin
8 Laurent, Amélie
9 Antoine, Kévin
10 Karima

2 Comment s'appellent-ils? (10)

Listening. Students listen to 10 first names being spelled out and note the names.

Before you start, run through the French alphabet as a class. A list giving the phonetic pronunciation of each letter is given in the Student Book (p. 6). You could then write up letters or show them on cards as prompts to test students at random.

Audioscript 3

– *Dans notre groupe, nous sommes dix. ... Il y a* ***Mathieu*** *M–A–T–H–I–E–U ...*
– ***Jérémie*** *J–É–R–É–M–I–E ...*
– ***Agathe*** *A–G–A–T–H–E ...*
– ***Hakim*** *H–A–K–I–M ...*
– ***Berthe*** *B–E–R–T–H–E ...*
– ***Guillaume*** *G–U–I–L–L–A–U–M–E ...*
– ***Jean-Pascal*** *J–E–A–N - –P–A–S–C–A–L ...*
– ***Françoise*** *F–R–A–N–Ç–O–I–S–E ...*
– ***Faustine*** *F–A–U–S–T–I–N–E ...*
– *Et moi,* ***Nolwène*** *... et ça s'écrit ... N–O–L–W–È–N–E.*

Answers

See bold in audioscript

3 À deux. Épelez les noms des personnes et des villes.

Speaking. In pairs: students take it in turn to pretend to be the people featured in the prompts. They ask and answer questions about their names and where they are from, spelling out the answers. A sample exchange is given.

Starter 2

Aim
To revise the vocabulary for nationalities. To revise adjective agreement.

Write up the following and ask students in pairs to come up with a sentence on the nationality of each. Do the first as a model.

Jack Black – **Il est américain.**

Sean Connery

J. K. Rowling

Kim Clijsters

Paula Radcliffe

Thierry Henry

Angelina Jolie

Roger Federer

Ask students to summarise the rule for making adjectives of nationality agree (for the feminine, add an **-e** but adjectives ending in **-e** unchanged).

4 Copiez et remplissez la carte d'identité de chaque personne. (1–3)

Listening. Students make three copies of the identity card shown. They then listen to three people introduce themselves and note the details for each person on a separate identity card.

For support, you could go through the headings on the identity cards before playing the recording and ask students to predict the kind of language they need to listen out for.

⊞ Ask students to note the additional details given by each person (i.e. information not covered by the headings on the identity cards).

Audioscript 4

1 *Bonjour. Je m'appelle Didier. Ça s'écrit D–I–D–I–E–R.*

J'ai quinze ans et mon anniversaire est le 8 janvier.

Je suis belge et j'habite à Waterloo, en Belgique. Waterloo, ça s'écrit W–A–T–E–R–L–O–O.

J'ai une sœur, qui s'appelle Lydie, L–Y–D–I–E, et nous avons un grand chien, qui s'appelle Maximus. Je suis de taille moyenne, j'ai les yeux bruns et les cheveux noirs et courts. Ce que j'aime, c'est le vélo. ... Ce que je n'aime pas? Je n'aime pas du tout faire mes devoirs.

2 *Bonjour. Mon prénom? Céline. Ça s'écrit C–É–L–I–N–E.*

J'ai quatorze ans et mon anniversaire est le 25 avril.

Je suis suisse et j'habite à Lausanne, en Suisse.

Je n'ai ni frère ni sœur, mais nous avons deux chats. Je suis grande et blonde et j'ai les yeux verts. Ce que j'aime, c'est la musique. Je joue de la guitare et je fais de la danse. Je n'aime pas les maths.

3 *Bonjour. Je m'appelle Ambre. Ça s'écrit A–M–B–R–E.*

Je suis française. J'habite à Bordeaux, dans le sud-ouest de la France.

J'ai quinze ans et mon anniversaire est le 3 mars. Ma sœur s'appelle Sabine, S-A-B-I-N-E et mon chat s'appelle Kaline, K–A–L–I–N–E. J'ai une demi-sœur, qui s'appelle Karo, K–A–R–O, mais on se dispute tout le temps. Heureusement, elle habite chez sa mère et on ne la voit pas souvent. Ce que j'aime bien faire?? euh ... c'est envoyer des textos à mes amis et jouer aux Sims sur l'ordinateur. Je n'aime pas le sport.

Answers

1

Prénom	Didier
Âge	15 ans
Date d'anniversaire	8 janvier
Nationalité	belge
Domicile	Waterloo, Belgique
Famille	sœur (Lydie)
Animaux	chien (Maximus)

Additional information
il est de taille moyenne et il a les yeux bruns, les cheveux noirs et courts; il aime le vélo; il n'aime pas faire ses devoirs

2

Prénom	Céline
Âge	14 ans
Date d'anniversaire	25 avril
Nationalité	suisse
Domicile	Lausanne, Suisse
Famille	–
Animaux	deux chats

Additional information
elle est grande et blonde et elle a les yeux verts; elle aime la musique (la guitare, la danse); elle n'aime pas les maths

3

Prénom	Ambre
Âge	15 ans
Date d'anniversaire	3 mars
Nationalité	française
Domicile	Bordeaux, France
Famille	sœur (Sabine), demi-sœur (Karo)
Animaux	chat (Kaline)

Additional information
elle aime envoyer des textos à ses amis et jouer aux Sims sur l'ordinateur; elle n'aime pas le sport

Three **Expo-langue** boxes are supplied to support students in doing exercises 5, 6 and 7.

Expo-langue: the present tense

Use this grammar box to remind students that the ***je*** form of regular –**er** verbs ends in –**e** in the present tense and to revise the full paradigms of **aimer** and the key irregular verbs **être**, **avoir** and **faire**. There is more information on p. 212 of the Student Book.

Expo-langue: *mon, ma, mes*

Use this grammar box to review the possessive adjectives **mon**, **ma**, **mes**. There is more information on p. 211 of the Student Book.

Expo-langue: adjective agreement

Use this grammar box to review adjective agreement in the singular with nationalities. You could consolidate the point by prompting students in English with a range of nationalities: they respond with the masculine and feminine versions. There is more information on p. 210 of the Student Book.

5 Imaginez que vous êtes François ou Françoise. Écrivez un paragraphe sur vous.

Writing. Using the details on the identity card supplied, students pretend to be either François or Françoise and write a paragraph about themselves. Draw their attention to the tip box on connectives, which they should always try to include to add interest and variety to their texts.

6 Parlez de vous.

Speaking. In pairs: students introduce themselves to each other, using the text they wrote in exercise 5 as a model. A sample structure is given. Encourage them to read through this first and to make notes to help them: they should not write out a complete answer but just use key words to remind them, along the lines of those listed.

7 Présentez-vous. Écrivez un paragraphe sur vous-même.

Writing. Students write a paragraph introducing themselves in detail. Encourage them to use the key words from exercise 6 to structure their texts, and to include connectives and intensifiers (**un peu, assez, très,** etc.).

Plenary

Get a few students to adopt the identity of someone famous or someone in the class. They present themselves using the structures in exercise 6 (but omitting their name) and the rest of the class has to guess who they are.

Cahier d'exercices, page 2

1

Answers

1 F **2** F **3** PM **4** V **5** V **6** V **7** F **8** PM

2

Answers

Example:
Je suis David et je suis suisse. J'ai 15 ans et mon anniversaire, c'est le 11 décembre. Je suis né en 1992 à Geneve en Suisse. Je parle anglais, allemand et français. J'habite avec mon père et mon grand frère qui a 18 ans. Moi, j'aime les sports mais ma passion, c'est la musique R&B.

Déjà vu 2: Les choses que j'aime faire ...

(Student Book pages 8–9)

Main topics and objectives

- Saying what you like and don't like doing
- **aimer** + infinitive

Grammar

- **quel** (all forms)
- **aimer** + infinitive
- Negatives
  - **ne ... pas/jamais**
  - **du/de la/des** changing to **de** (**de l'** to **d'**) after negative

Key language

Sports and activities
Expressions of time and frequency

Resources

CD1, tracks 5–7
Cahier d'exercices, page 3
Grammaire 3.13, 3.16

Starter 1

Aim
To revise the vocabulary for sports and other activities. To revise the structure **aimer** + infinitive.

Write up: **Le week-end, j'aime ...**

and beneath this **faire du vélo, jouer au football, jouer de la guitare, ...**

Give students in pairs two minutes to come up with a list of activities they like doing at the weekend, using the verbs you have supplied and any others they can think of (e.g. **aller à la piscine, regarder la télévision**, etc.). Which pair can make the longest list? Can they come up with an example no one else has thought of?

After listening to students' answers, ask the class to explain the structure they have been using: what is **aimer** followed by?

1 Écoutez et lisez le texte. Répondez aux questions.

Reading. Students listen to Louis talking about the activities he likes/doesn't like and read the text at the same time.

Audioscript 5

J'aime le sport. Mon sport préféré, c'est le basket. Je m'entraîne trois fois par semaine dans un club, et on joue contre un autre club de la région le week-end. J'aime également faire du vélo et du judo, mais je déteste le jogging et la natation. Le soir, je fais mes devoirs en écoutant de la musique. J'ai un ordinateur et des jeux, mais c'est mon petit frère qui y joue toujours. Moi, je trouve ça ennuyeux. Mon frère aime aussi regarder des séries à la télé, mais elles sont vraiment nulles. Je préfère sortir avec mes copains, mais je sors rarement parce que mes parents travaillent souvent le soir et que je dois m'occuper de mon petit frère. J'aime envoyer des textos à mes copains et lire des BD.

Answers

1. Le sport préféré de Louis est le basket.
2. Il aime aussi faire du vélo et du judo.
3. Il déteste le jogging et la natation.
4. Il aime sortir avec ses copains et envoyer des textos à ses copains et lire des BD.
5. Il trouve jouer à l'ordinateur ennuyeux.

Expo-langue: *quel*

Use the questions in exercise 1 to introduce this grammar box on **quel?** ('which?'). Point out that while students need to be careful to use the four different forms correctly in their writing, all four are pronounced the same. There is more information on p. 215 of the Student Book.

Expo-langue: *aimer* + the infinitive; *jouer à/jouer de*

This covers a range of useful structures to use when talking about activities. You can use it first of all to consolidate **aimer** + the infinitive, then move on to focus on how **faire** and **jouer** are used when talking about activities:

– **faire** + the relevant form of **de** for sports which you do or go (e.g. horse-riding)

– **jouer** + the relevant form of **à** for sports you play (e.g. football)

– **jouer** + the relevant form of **de** for playing an instrument

There is more information on p. 216 of the Student Book.

2 Écoutez et notez en français. (a) Qu'est-ce qu'ils aiment faire? (b) Qu'est-ce qu'ils n'aiment pas faire? (c) Pourquoi n'aiment-ils pas le faire? (1–4)

Listening. Students listen to the four conversations. For each person, they note: (**a**) what he/she likes doing (**b**) what he/she doesn't like doing (**c**) why he/she doesn't like the particular activity.

Audioscript 6

1 *– Bonjour, Nathan. Dis-moi, quel est ton sport préféré?*
– Le sport, c'est ma passion. J'adore le foot et le tennis.
– Et qu'est-ce que tu n'aimes pas?
– Je n'aime pas le volley et la natation.
– Aimes-tu jouer à l'ordinateur?
– Non, je n'aime pas jouer à l'ordinateur, c'est ennuyeux.

2 *– Bonjour, Sandrine. Quel est ton sport préféré?*
– Je n'aime pas trop le sport sauf l'équitation.
– Tu n'aimes pas jouer au tennis?
– Non, pas vraiment.
– Et la natation?
– Beurk! Je déteste la natation ... euh ... parce que je n'aime pas l'eau froide.

3 *– Bonjour, Delphine. Tu aimes le sport?*
– Oh oui! J'adore.
– Quel est ton sport préféré?
– Le ski en hiver, et ... euh, en été le canoë.
– Tu aimes jouer au tennis?
– Ah oui!
– Qu'est-ce que tu n'aimes pas faire?
– Le volley, je n'aime pas jouer au volley.
– Pourquoi?
– Parce que c'est fatigant et les garçons gagnent toujours.

4 *– Et toi, Michel? Quel est ton sport préféré?*
– Le cyclisme ... J'aime faire du vélo, moi.
– Et que penses-tu des autres sports?
– Lesquels?
– Le foot, par exemple?
– Non, je n'aime pas jouer au foot.
– Le tennis?
– Non plus, c'est ennuyeux.

Answers

1 (a) le foot, le tennis **(b)** le volley, la natation, l'ordinateur **(c)** l'ordinateur – c'est ennuyeux
2 (a) l'équitation **(b)** le tennis, la natation **(c)** la natation – elle n'aime pas l'eau froide
3 (a) le ski, le canoë, le tennis **(b)** le volley **(c)** le volley – c'est fatigant, les garçons gagnent toujours
4 (a) le cyclisme **(b)** le foot, le tennis **(c)** le tennis – c'est ennuyeux

Starter 2

Aim
To review expressions of time and frequency.

Write up:

1	2
souvent	on Sundays
deux fois par mois	once a week
d'habitude	in winter
jamais	on Monday mornings
en été	at the weekend
presque tous les jours	
le samedi après-midi	

Ask students in pairs to come up with an English translation for each French expression in **1**. They should then translate the English phrases in **2** into French (referring back to **1** to help them with the structures as necessary).

3 Lisez le texte et complétez les phrases.

Reading. Students read Charlotte's text on the activities she likes/doesn't like doing and complete the eight sentences about it.

Answers

1. Elle n'aime pas **le foot/les jeux d'équipe**.
2. Elle **déteste** le VTT.
3. Elle **joue/aime jouer** à l'ordinateur.
4. Elle y joue **deux ou trois fois par semaine**.
5. Elle **n'aime pas** la télé.
6. Elle préfère **écouter de la musique (et chanter en même temps) et lire**.
7. Sa passion, c'est **le surf**.
8. Elle en fait **presque tous les jours quand elle est au bord de la mer** en été.

4 Qui fait quoi et quel jour? Prenez des notes en français. (1–3)

Listening. Students listen to the three conversations and fill in the grid, noting for each person which activities they do on which day.

Audioscript 7

1 *Le soir quand je rentre, je fais tout d'abord mes devoirs. Après, je vais à la piscine pour nager ... J'y vais trois fois par semaine, le lundi, le mercredi et le samedi. Une fois par semaine, je joue au squash avec mon grand frère, ... le jeudi soir. Le samedi, je vais en ville avec mes copains et le dimanche, on fait souvent du vélo. Voilà, c'est tout.*

2 *Le mercredi, je vais à un cours de GRS ... GRS, ça veut dire gymnastique, rythmique et sportive. C'est entre la gymnastique et la danse, et j'aime bien ça. Je fais aussi un cours de taekwando une fois par semaine, le lundi soir ... Et le week-end, ... le samedi après-midi je fais de* *la musique ... c'est-à-dire que j'apprends à jouer de la guitare. Le samedi soir, je vais souvent au cinéma avec ma meilleure copine et le dimanche, normalement, on dîne chez ma grand-mère.*

3 *Ben, ... d'habitude, le soir, il y a toujours des devoirs à faire, mais le lundi soir, j'ai entraînement de judo. Le mercredi, je prends des cours de plongée ... à la nouvelle piscine olympique, ... le mercredi on fait de la plongée ... Et le vendredi soir, je sors avec mes copains. Le samedi, ben, ... le samedi après-midi après le collège, on se retrouve en ville avec mes copains et on fait du skate. Et puis le dimanche, euh ... en été, je fais du VTT et en hiver, du ski de fond.*

Answers

	lundi	mardi	mercredi	jeudi	vendredi	samedi	dimanche
1	nage	–	nage	joue au squash	–	nage va en ville	fait du vélo
2	taekwando	–	GRS	–	–	joue de la guitare va au cinéma	dîne chez sa grand-mère
3	fait du judo	–	fait de la plongée	–	sort avec ses copains	retrouve en ville avec ses copains et fait du skate	fait du VTT/du ski de fond

5 Imaginez que vous êtes Isabelle. Complétez le texte pour elle.

Writing. Using the picture prompts supplied, students pretend they are Isabelle and write a paragraph saying what activities they do and their opinion of them. A sample structure is given. Encourage them to include some of the expressions of time and frequency covered on this page in their writing.

Expo-langue: negatives

Before students do exercise 6, read through this grammar box together. It covers the position of negative structures such as **ne ... pas** and **ne ... jamais** (round the verb). Ask students how they would make statements like **J'aime faire du sport** negative.

It also reviews how **du/de la/des** change to **de** (and **de l'** changes to **d'**) after a negative. There is more information on pp. 214 and 208 of the Student Book.

6 À deux. Quelle est ton activité préférée? Posez-vous des questions et répondez-y.

Speaking. In pairs: students take it in turn to ask and answer questions about the activities they do/don't do. The questions and the beginnings of some responses are supplied for support. You could model an example with a confident student.

7 Décrivez: (a) ce que vous aimez faire et (b) quand vous en faites; (c) ce que vous n'aimez pas faire et (d) pourquoi vous n'aimez pas en faire.

Writing. Students write a paragraph on what activities they like to do and when, and what activities they don't like to do, including reasons why they're not keen.

Plenary

Ask students to summarise the grammar relating to activities that they have covered in this unit. How is **aimer** used? When do you use **faire de**? Which structure do you use to say you play a sport? To say you play an instrument?

Then use various time expressions as prompts, in English or French, (e.g. every day/**tous les jours**) for students to respond with an appropriate activity (e.g. **J'écoute de la musique tous les jours**).

Cahier d'exercices, page 3

1a

Answers

quatre exemples d'aimer + infinitif: j'aime également faire du snowboard; j'aime faire du vélo; j'aime jouer de la guitare; j'aime lire.
trois exemples d'aimer + nom: j'aime surtout les sports d'hiver; je n'aime pas beaucoup la télé; j'aime la musique; j'aime les magazines de sport.

1b

Answers

J'aime faire du snowboard. → J'aime le snowboard.
J'aime faire du vélo. → J'aime le vélo.
J'aime jouer de la guitare. → J'aime la guitare.
J'aime lire. → J'aime la lecture.
J'aime surtout les sports d'hiver. → J'aime faire les sports d'hiver.
Je n'aime pas beaucoup la télé. → J'aime beaucoup regarder la télé.
J'aime la musique. → J'aime écouter de la musique.
J'aime les magazines de sport. → J'aime lire les magazines de sports.

2

Answers

a tous les week-ends **b** presque tous les jours **c** en été
d d'habitude **e** souvent **f** une fois par semaine
g le soir **h** en hiver **i** chaque semaine **j** parfois

3

Answers

Pupil's own work

1 Moi, moi et encore moi!

(Student Book pages 10–11)

Main topics and objectives

- More about yourself
- Reflexive verbs

Grammar

- Reflexive verbs (present tense)

Key language

un frère cadet/aîné
une sœur cadette/aînée
un demi-frère
une demi-sœur
un beau-père
une belle-mère
séparé(e)
divorcé(e)
célibataire
remarié(e)
On s'entend bien.
Elle m'embête/m'énerve.
Je dois m'occuper d'elle.
Il se moque toujours de moi.
On s'amuse bien.
Je m'ennuie.
Il ne s'ennuie jamais.

Resources

CD1, tracks 8–10
Cahier d'exercices, page 4
Grammaire 3.15

Starter 1

Aim
To reintroduce reflexive verbs. To revise vocabulary to describe daily routines.

Write up the following in random order (correct order given here for reference). Ask students to put them in chronological order, according to what they would do on a typical day.

je me réveille
je me lève
je me douche
je m'habille
je prends mon petit déjeuner
je me brosse les dents
je vais au collège
je m'amuse avec mes copains
je rentre chez moi
je me repose un peu avant de faire mes devoirs
je me couche

After checking answers, ask students what kind of verbs **je me réveille**, etc., are. Can they remember how they work and think of any other examples? (**me présenter** and **m'appeler** both came up earlier in the module.)

1 Écoutez et lisez le texte. Écrivez V (Vrai), F (Faux) ou PM (Pas Mentionné) à côté de chaque phrase.

Listening. Students listen to Camille talking about herself and her family, and read the text at the same time. They then read the ten statements on the text and decide whether each is true or false or not mentioned in the text.

Audioscript 8

Je me présente. Je m'appelle Camille et j'ai seize ans. Mon anniversaire est le 28 novembre. Je suis de taille moyenne (je mesure 1,66 mètre), j'ai les cheveux bruns et les yeux verts. Je suis française. J'habite en France dans un petit village de montagne en Haute-Savoie, d'où on peut voir le Mont-Blanc toujours couvert de neige.

J'ai une sœur cadette qui a neuf ans, et qui s'appelle Louise. Normalement, on s'entend bien, mais de temps en temps elle m'énerve, surtout quand elle ne veut pas aider à la maison et que c'est moi qui dois ranger sa chambre. Elle vient dans ma chambre quand je fais mes devoirs, elle m'embête et puis on se dispute. Quand mes parents sortent le soir, je dois m'occuper d'elle. J'ai aussi un grand demi-frère qui habite chez sa mère. Quand il nous rend visite, il se moque toujours de moi, mais si on va à la piscine ou au cinéma ensemble on s'amuse bien.

Je ne sais pas ce que je veux faire dans la vie. J'aime dessiner et travailler à l'ordinateur. Je suis assez timide et plutôt sérieuse, mais je suis aussi travailleuse. Si je n'ai rien à faire je m'ennuie. Ma sœur est complètement différente, elle est bavarde et rigolote. Elle ne s'ennuie jamais et elle est gâtée par tout le monde! Nous n'avons pas d'animal. J'en voudrais un, mais je suis allergique aux poils de chat.

Answers
1 F **2** PM **3** F **4** F **5** PM **6** V **7** F **8** F **9** F **10** PM

Expo-langue: Reflexive verbs (present tense)

Use this grammar box to consolidate the present tense of reflexive verbs before students do exercise 2. There is more information on p. 215 of the Student Book.

2 Relisez le texte de Camille et trouvez les mots.

Reading. Students reread the text in exercise 1 and find the French for six reflexive verbs.

The activity includes a note suggesting students focus on learning those verbs which they think might be useful when talking about their own experience. Explain that identifying the most relevant language is a useful technique at this level, where students will encounter a lot of new vocabulary.

Answers

1 s'amuser **2** se disputer **3** s'ennuyer
4 s'entendre bien **5** se moquer de **6** s'occuper de

Starter 2

Aim

To revise possessive adjectives (**mon, ma, mes,** etc.) in the singular (my/your/his/hers/its). To revise vocabulary for members of the (extended) family.

Write up the following grid:

	singular		plural
	masculine	feminine	
my	**mon**		
your		**ta**	
his/her/ its			**ses**

Ask students in pairs to copy and complete the grid and then to come up with nine phrases, each including one of these words and a different family member, e.g. **mon frère**, etc.

When checking answers, ask for the French for any family members not covered (see the list in the *Mots* section on p. 22 for reference).

3 Écoutez et complétez la grille. (1–4)

Listening. Students copy out the grid. They then listen to four people talking about how they get on with other family members and note the details.

Audioscript 9

1 – Pascal, tu t'entends bien avec ta famille?

– Pendant les vacances, je fais du vélo et de la pêche avec mon père ... Il est cool, mon père, et on s'amuse bien ensemble. C'est ma petite sœur qui m'énerve. Nous nous disputons tout le temps. En revanche, je m'entends bien avec mes grands-parents. Mon grand-père est vraiment sportif. On joue au tennis et c'est toujours lui qui gagne!

2 – Et toi, Lydie? Comment tu t'entends avec ta famille?

– C'est ma mère qui m'énerve car on se dispute toujours. Elle dit toujours: «Fais ceci, fais cela!» ... mais je m'entends bien avec mon beau-père. On joue au squash ensemble. D'habitude, mon demi-frère et moi, nous nous amusons bien, nous jouons au ping-pong ou au baby-foot et il m'aide à faire mes devoirs surtout ceux de maths.

3 – Vincent, comment tu t'entends avec tes frères?

– Je m'entends très bien avec mon frère aîné .... et moins bien avec ma sœur parce qu'elle vient toujours dans ma chambre. Je préfère être avec mon copain. On s'amuse bien ensemble parce qu'on aime la même musique.

4 – Delphine, tu t'entends bien avec ta famille?

– Je me dispute toujours avec mes parents. Je dois rester à la maison au lieu de sortir avec mes copains. Pendant les vacances, je vais chez mes grands-parents. Je m'entends bien avec eux et quand je suis là, je joue avec mes cousins. On s'amuse bien ensemble.

Answers

	s'amuse avec	se dispute avec	s'entend bien avec	autres informations
Pascal	son père	sa petite sœur	ses grands-parents	Il fait du vélo et de la pêche avec son père. Il joue au tennis avec son grand-père.
Lydie	son demi-frère	sa mère	son beau-père	Elle joue au squash avec son beau-père. Elle joue au ping-pong et au baby-foot avec son demi-frère et il l'aide à faire ses devoirs.
Vincent	son copain	sa sœur	son frère aîné	Vincent et son copain aiment la même musique.
Delphine	ses cousins	ses parents	ses grands-parents	Elle doit rester à la maison au lieu de sortir avec ses copains.

4 Qui écrit? Pascal, Lydie, Vincent ou Delphine?

Reading. Students read the four texts and use the information noted in exercise 3 to identify the writer for each one.

Answers

1 Vincent **2** Lydie **3** Delphine **4** Pascal

5 Faites un résumé. Utilisez vos réponses à l'exercice 3 et les textes ci-dessus.

Writing. Students write a summary of how Pascal, Lydie, Vincent and Delphine get on with people in their families, using the information and structures from exercises 3 and 4. A box reminding them of the forms of **son, sa, ses** is supplied for support.

R Explain to students how important it is to identify useful vocabulary in texts in the Student Book and to note this down and learn it as they go along. Ask students to identify the vocabulary and structures in these texts that they could use when going on to talk about their own family relationships.

6 Vidéoconférence avec le lycée de Camille. Elle vous invite à parler de vous. Préparez un dialogue.

Speaking. Students imagine that they are going to have a videoconference with the students at the school attended by Camille (from exercise 1). They prepare a dialogue to include the same sort of information covered by Camille's text and including details of how they get on with the members of their families.

The Vidéoconférence presentation is a regular feature throughout the course.

If you have links with a school in France, use these activities as a cue for students to make contact with French students in their year. This could be done as an actual videoconference (if you have the technology in place) or as an exchange of e-mails, with students asking and answering questions in French (and then reciprocating by doing the activity in English).

Draw attention to the tip box on how to tackle this as an activity: students should make notes (in the form of single words or pictures) and work from these rather than prepared answers. A box listing fillers – French expressions they can use to buy themselves time while they think about what they want to say next – is also supplied for support. If they can learn to use these, it will really help them in their exams: it will not only give them time to think, it will also help them sound more authentic.

If you have time, give students the opportunity to practise their dialogue in pairs and then choose a few pairs to perform in front of the class.

7 Reliez l'anglais et le français.

Reading. Students read six English expressions that can be used to get help if you are having trouble understanding and match them to the correct French versions.

Point out that using expressions like these is another useful strategy to make you sound fluent and one that students should practise and use when speaking French: it enables you to get help while still remaining in control in the conversation.

Answers

1 e **2** a **3** b **4** f **5** c **6** d

8 Écoutez et notez. C'est quelle phrase? (1–6)

Listening. Students listen to the six expressions in French from exercise 7 and note the relevant letter for each (from **a–f**).

Audioscript 10

1 *Comment est-ce qu'on dit en français ... ?*

2 *Je n'ai pas compris ce que vous avez dit.*

3 *Pourriez-vous l'épeler, s'il vous plaît?*

4 *Pourriez-vous parler plus fort, s'il vous plaît?*

5 *Pourriez-vous parler plus lentement, s'il vous plaît?*

6 *Pourriez-vous répéter, s'il vous plaît?*

Answers

1 b **2** d **3** a **4** c **5** f **6** e

Plenary

Ask students to tell you two useful tips they have picked up so far that would help them in the speaking part of the exam (preparing for the speaking test by working from notes; using fillers such as **ben ...** to buy time and sound more authentic). Ask for examples in both areas.

Explain that there will be suggestions throughout **Expo 4** to help students tackle the exam. Suggest that students keep a list of these techniques and try to implement them as much as possible in their work. The more familiar they become, the better prepared students will be for the exam.

Cahier d'exercices, page 4

1

Answers

Any two out of: 15 yr old boy; lives in Strasbourg with family; gets on with brother; does not get on with sister; dad lives in Nantes; does lots of things with best friend.

2

Answers

I get on very well with him.
... the same kind of music
We don't have the same tastes.
She annoys me all the time.
I see him sometimes at the weekend.
When I'm at his house ...
very close to where I live in Paris
Sometimes, at the weekend ...

3

Answers

1 Nathan est français de nationalité et il a quinze ans.
2 Dans la famille de Nathan il y a sa mère, sa sœur, son frère et son père qui a une nouvelle femme.
3 À part son père, Nathan s'entend bien avec son frère parce qu'il aime le même genre de musique.
4 Nathan ne s'entend pas très bien avec sa sœur parce qu'ils n'ont pas les mêmes goûts.
5 Le weekend, il va parfois chez son père qui habite à Nantes.
6 Chez son père, il fait du sport; il joue au tennis ou au golf ou il va au cinéma.
7 Vincent habite à Paris, tout près de chez Nathan.
8 Nathan et Vincent sont inséparables.

2 Mes parents

(Student Book pages 12–13)

Main topics and objectives

- Talking about your parents and what they do
- Using masculine and feminine nouns

Grammar

- Masculine/Feminine forms of jobs
- No article with jobs (**il est ingénieur**)

Key language

Il/Elle est ...
coiffeur/euse
comptable
cuisinier/ère
infirmier/ère
informaticien(ne)
ingénieur
instituteur/trice
kinésithérapeute
maçon
mécanicien(ne)
menuisier
nourrice
plombier
secrétaire
serveur/euse
sapeur-pompier
vendeur/euse
Il/Elle travaille ...
dans un bureau
dans une grande surface
dans un hôpital
dans une école primaire
dans un garage
dans une cantine
dans une garderie
sur un chantier
Je m'entends bien avec mes parents.
Je ne m'entends pas bien avec lui/eux.
Je ressemble plutôt à ma mère qu'à mon père.
Mes parents sont séparés.

Resources

CD1, track 11
Cahier d'exercices, page 5
Grammaire 1.1

Starter 1

Aim
To use strategies to work out vocabulary (cognates).

Write up the following. Give students two minutes to work out the English for each word. To get them started, tell them that these words fall into a single vocabulary topic. Students can work in pairs for support.

informaticien
vétérinaire
instituteur
cuisinière
ingénieur
maçon
infirmière
comptable
plombier

When checking answers, ask students how they worked out the answers. What didn't they know and how did they work it out? (Re)introduce the word **cognate** and remind students that they will find cognates not just in English (e.g. **plombier** - plumber), but also in French, especially as their French vocabulary expands (e.g. **compter** = to count). If they are studying other languages, they may also find these a useful resource (e.g. in Spanish **enfermero** = nurse).

Go on to read through the tip box on strategies for dealing with unknown words at the bottom of p. 12 before students tackle exercise 1. These should be familiar to students from KS3 work. Can they add any techniques to those listed? (e.g. using the context (either the topic, as they did in the Starter, or the detail of a text), using a process of elimination to narrow down the options, etc.)

1 Lisez. Que font-ils dans la vie? Où travaillent-ils?

Trouvez les images et les mots qui correspondent.

Reading. Students read the three texts in which the speakers talk about what jobs members of their family do and where they work. They identify the relevant pictures for each.

Answers

1	2	3
père – f maçon, chantier	père – c cuisinier, restaurant	mère – i serveuse, restaurant
mère – h secrétaire, bureau	mère – a coiffeuse, salon de coiffure	père – d ingénieur, usine
oncle – g menuisier, atelier	tante – e kinésithérapeute, clinique	grand-mère – j comptable, bureau

2 Complétez les deux phrases pour chaque personne.

Writing. Student write two sentences for each of the people mentioned in exercise 1, saying what they do and where they work. A sample structure is given.

Starter 2

Aim
To review the vocabulary for jobs and how to say what job someone does.

Write up: **Il/Elle est ...** Ask students to identify the job you are going to mime, using the structure you have written up. Then mime one of the jobs covered on p. 12 or in Starter 1. The first student to answer correctly then takes a turn miming another job for the rest of the class to identify, and so on. Make sure students are clear that no article is used in this structure.

3 Que font-ils et où travaillent-ils? Choisissez la bonne image et la bonne phrase. (1–4)

Listening. Students listen to four people being interviewed about what their mothers and fathers do. They identify the correct picture and phrase for each.

Audioscript 11

1 – *Que fait ton père dans la vie?*
– *Il est informaticien. Il travaille dans un bureau.*
– *Et ta mère? Elle travaille?*
– *Elle travaille dans un hypermarché, une grande surface. Elle est vendeuse.*

2 – *Et toi? Que fait ton père?*
– *Il travaille à son compte ... Il travaille sur un chantier. Il est plombier.*
– *Et ta mère?*
– *Elle travaille dans un hôpital. Elle est infirmière.*

3 – *Et toi? Ah, je sais, ton père est instituteur, n'est-ce pas?*
– *Oui. Il travaille dans une école primaire.*
– *Et ta mère?... Elle travaille aussi?*
– *Elle travaille à mi-temps. Elle est cuisinière. Elle fait les repas pour la cantine de l'école.*

4 – *Et toi? Ton père est mécanicien, n'est-ce pas?*
– *Oui, il travaille dans un garage. Il répare les autos.*
– *Et ta mère? Elle travaille?*
– *Oui, elle est nourrice. Elle travaille dans une garderie. Elle s'occupe de petits enfants.*

Answers

1 *c, dans un bureau* f, dans une grande surface
2 b, sur un chantier g, dans un hôpital
3 e, dans une école primaire h, dans une cantine
4 a, dans un garage d, dans une garderie

4 Qui parle?

Reading. Students read the four texts and the six statements which follow and identify who said each of the statements.

These texts could also be used for reading aloud practice, with the focus on correct pronunciation and intonation.

Answers

1 Sophie **2** Sophie **3** Yannick **4** Yannick **5** Bruno **6** Aminta

5 À deux. Vos parents. Posez et répondez aux questions. Préparez vos réponses.

Speaking. In pairs: students take it in turn to ask and answer questions about their parents. The questions are supplied for reference. Give them time to prepare their answers first.

6 Écrivez un court texte sur vos parents.

Writing. Students write a short text about their parents. Some phrases are supplied for support.

➕ For homework, ask students to make a list of jobs not covered in this unit, using a dictionary or other resources. Encourage them to work in pairs/groups of three or four and to pool their information.

Plenary

Ask students what techniques were suggested in this unit for tackling unknown vocabulary (see the Tip box on p. 12 and the suggestions in Starter 1). Suggest students add these strategies to their list of exam techniques.

Point out that making connections between words can also help students memorise vocabulary. Ask them to suggest connections that might help them remember the vocabulary for jobs (e.g. **infirmière** + English 'infirm'; **informatique** + **informaticien**, etc.).

Cahier d'exercices, page 5

1

Answers

1 kinésitherapeute **2** coiffeuse **3** ingénieur
4 mécanicien **5** serveuse **6** sapeur-pompier
7 secrétaire **8** infirmière **9** maçon **10** cuisinier
11 institutrice **12** comptable

2

Answers

Pupil's own work

3 Mes copains et mes copines

(Student Book pages 14–15)

Main topics and objectives

- Talking about your friends
- Adjective agreement

Grammar

- Adjective agreement (singular)

Key language

Mon (petit) copain est ...
Ma (petite) copine idéale est ...
actif/ve
bavard(e)
branché(e)
bruyant(e)
décontracté(e)
drôle
égoïste
généreux/euse
gentil(le)
insupportable
intelligent(e)
nerveux/euse
organisé(e)
paresseux/euse
rigolo(te)
sportif/ve
sympa
timide
travailleur/euse

Resources

CD1, track 12
Cahier d'exercices, page 6
Grammaire 2.2

Starter 1

Aim
To review adjectives to describe people.

Make a series of statements about famous people (real or fictional) or people in/known to the class, using the adjectives introduced in exercise 1 on p. 14, e.g.

Mr Bean est bavarde.
Serena Williams est active.
Magic Johnson n'est pas de taille moyenne etc.

Ask students to do a thumbs up if they agree with the statement and a thumbs down if they disagree. Choose someone who disagrees to give you a correct statement about the person.

1 Écoutez et attribuez les mots à la bonne personne. (13)

Listening. Students copy out the grid. They listen to the descriptions of the three people and note the details in the grid, using the labelled pictures supplied for reference.

Audioscript 12

Mélinda est de taille moyenne et blonde. Elle est bonne élève en classe. Elle est toujours bien organisée, elle a de bonnes notes et elle est travailleuse. Elle n'est pas bavarde, disons qu'elle est ... ben ... plutôt timide. Elle déteste le foot et le tennis, mais elle aime la musique.

Guillaume, ... lui, il est grand et brun. Il est intelligent. Il n'est pas, euh, bavard. Il n'aime pas faire de sport, mais comme il se passionne pour la danse, il faut dire qu'il est assez actif. Il fait de la danse latino-américaine, alors il n'est pas paresseux, il est plutôt travailleur. Et il est rigolo.

Valentine, euh, elle est plutôt petite. Elle a les cheveux noirs et les yeux bleus. Elle fait de l'équitation: elle monte très bien à cheval. Elle est aussi très bonne en maths et en physique. Elle est gentille, elle m'aide souvent à faire mes exos de maths. Elle est la première à aider une vieille dame à traverser la rue.

Answers

Mélinda	Guillaume	Valentine
de taille moyenne	grand	petite
organisée	intelligent	sportive
travailleuse	actif	intelligente
timide	travailleur	gentille
	rigolo	

Expo-langue: adjective agreement (singular)

Read through this grammar box after exercise 1 to review agreement of adjectives in the singular. There is more information on p. 210 of the Student Book.

R Students could rewrite the last paragraph of Camille's text on p. 10 as though it had been written by Matthieu, who has a brother called Luc.

2 Reliez le français et l'anglais.

Reading. Students read the eight French adjectives and match each to the correct English translation.

Answers

branché(e) – trendy/switched on
bruyant(e) – noisy
généreux/euse – generous
décontracté(e) – relaxed/laid back
insupportable – dreadful/unbearable
drôle – funny
nerveux/euse – nervous
sympa – nice

3 À deux. Choisissez trois personnes et posez la question.

Speaking. In pairs: students choose three celebrities each and discuss their opinions of them. They should take it in turn to start off the dialogue by asking **Qu'est-ce que vous pensez de ... ?** A sample exchange and a list of useful expressions are supplied. Encourage students to use a dictionary for any additional adjectives they want to use.

Starter 2

Aim
To revise adjectives used to describe what people look like.

Describe what a student in the class or a teacher in the school looks like using the structures below. The class has to guess who it is. The student who first correctly identifies the person then describes another student, and so on.

Il/Elle est (assez/très) grand(e)
Il/Elle a les cheveux ... et les yeux ...

4 Lisez les textes rapidement et trouvez l'essentiel.

Reading. ☑ Students read the four texts in order to identify the people being described in the eight questions. Point out that they should not be trying to understand the texts in detail: the aim is to skim-read them, concentrating on identifying only the information necessary to complete the exercise. Explain that this is a useful technique to develop for the exam: they will save valuable time by concentrating on what is important.

Answers

1 Sarah **5** Frédéric
2 Arthur **6** Maryse
3 Sarah **7** Frédéric
4 Arthur **8** Maryse

5 À deux. Décrivez les copains.

Speaking. In pairs: students take it in turn to describe the four teenagers pictured (doing two each). Some sample structures are supplied for support.

6 Faites la description d'un petit copain/une petite copine idéal(e).

Writing. Students write a paragraph on the ideal boyfriend/girlfriend. Some sample structures are supplied for support.

R Students could swap texts and check their partner's work for accuracy and interest.

Plenary

Give students two minutes in pairs to do the following quiz on adjectives without looking at their books. Tell them they cannot use the same adjective twice. They need to come up with:

- 3 adjectives which end in **-euse** in the feminine form (giving both the masculine and feminine)
- 2 adjectives where the feminine form ends **-te**
- 2 negative adjectives
- 1 adjective which doesn't change in the feminine form.

Cahier d'exercices, page 6

1

Answers

Example:
1 bavarde (chatty); active (active); énervant (annoying); généreuse (generous); heureuse (happy); petite (small); timide (timid); gentille (kind); travailleuse (hard-working); intelligente (intelligent); sportif (sporty); adorable (adorable); organisé (organised); extraverti (extravert); bruyant (noisy); paresseux (lazy); moyenne (average); gentil (kind); rigolo (fun)
2 Underlined: timide; adorable.

2

Answers

Answers open to interpretation
1 Nicolas **2** Amandine **3** Amandine **4** Julien
5 Julien **6** Valentin **7** Élodie

3

Answers

Pupil's own answers

4 Centre de loisirs

(Student Book pages 16–17)

Main topics and objectives

- Saying what you have done
- The perfect tense

Grammar

- Perfect tense (formation with **avoir** and **être**)

Key language

Lundi, je suis allé(e) ...
au centre de loisirs
J'ai fait ...
du karaté
du judo
du théâtre
de la natation
de la danse
de l'entraînement
de l'escrime
des arts martiaux
J'ai nagé.
J'ai bavardé avec mes copains.
J'ai lu des BD.
J'ai écouté de la musique.
Nous avons mangé une pizza.
C'était super/fantastique/cool/génial!
Bof./C'était pas mal.
C'était nul.
Ce n'est pas mon truc.

Resources

CD1, tracks 13–14
Cahier d'exercices, page 7
Grammaire 3.3

Starter 1

Aim
To review times using the 12- and 24-hour clocks.

Write up the following times (using the 12-hour clock). Students in pairs take it in turn to respond with the corresponding time using the 24-hour clock. Model the first one (**deux heures et demie – quatorze heures trente**).

2.30 p.m.	4.00 p.m.
6.00 p.m.	9.30 p.m.
10.30 p.m.	11.00 p.m.
7.15 p.m.	5.45 p.m.
3.30 p.m.	

If you wanted to extend the activity, you could include other times such as 8.05, 3.10, 4.50, etc.

1 C'est quelle activité? Complétez les phrases.

Reading. Students read the brochure for the leisure centre. Using the details in the brochure, they complete a sentence for each picture **1–8** to say what they did, using the perfect tense. The exercise introduces the perfect tense, but students do not need to revise it in order to complete the activity. It is covered in detail in the next lesson.

Answers

1 J'ai fait de la natation.
2 J'ai fait de la danse.
3 J'ai fait de l'escrime.
4 J'ai fait de la plongée.
5 J'ai fait du théâtre.
6 J'ai fait du judo.
7 J'ai fait du karaté.
8 J'ai fait de l'aérobic.

2 Écoutez. Relisez le dépliant dans l'exercice 1 et notez les détails. (1–4)

Listening. Students copy out the grid. They listen to four people talking about the activities they do at the leisure centre and note the details in the grid.

Audioscript 13

1 *La semaine dernière, je suis allé à la piscine mercredi et vendredi pendant une heure, de 19h00 à 20h00. Puis, je suis allé au gymnase ... euh ... jeudi de 17h00 à 19h00 parce que je veux garder la forme.*

2 *Mercredi dernier, je suis allée à la salle polyvalente comme tous les mercredis. On a eu un cours de 10h30 à 12h00, et puis l'après-midi, on a joué ensemble de 15h00 à 17h00.*

3 *Lundi, je suis allé au gymnase à 17h00. Le cours a duré ... ben ... une heure, comme toujours, mais quelquefois on reste encore une demi-heure de plus. Puis mercredi, ... mercredi j'ai voulu essayer un nouveau sport! Ce sport a lieu au gymnase de 15h30 à 17h00, mais il faut avoir l'équipement et le costume, et tout cela coûte cher et ... ben ... ce n'est pas mon truc. Je préfère les arts martiaux.*

4 *La semaine dernière, je suis allée au gymnase pour une heure le lundi, de 18h00 à 19h00, mais on reste encore une demi-heure s'il n'y a pas de classe après. Et puis mercredi, il y a un cours toute la matinée au gymnase ... une heure pour nous et puis, nous aidons les petits. Et vendredi soir, on fait encore deux heures de 18h00 à 20h00.*

Answers

	Où?	Quel jour?	À quelle heure?	Quel cours?
1	piscine; gymnase	mercredi et vendredi; jeudi	19h00–20h00; 17h00–19h00	natation; aérobic
2	salle polyvalente; salle polyvalente	mercredi	10h30–12h00; 15h00–17h00	musique; orchestre
3	gymnase; gymnase	lundi; mercredi	17h00–18h00; 15h30–17h00	karaté; escrime
4	gymnase; gymnase; gymnase	lundi; mercredi; vendredi	18h00–19h00; 9h00–12h00; 18h00–20h00	danse; danse; danse

Starter 2

Aim

To revise the perfect tense. To remind students to associate certain time phrases with specific tenses.

Write up the following, with the second column in random order (in correct order here for reference only).

1 Lundi dernier, il	**est allé au centre de loisirs.**
2 Maintenant, je	**joue au foot.**
3 L'après-midi, j'	**ai bavardé avec ma copine.**
4 Hier soir, nous	**avons mangé un pizza.**
5 L'année dernière, elle	**est allée en France.**
6 Le samedi, nous	**écoutons des CD chez moi.**

Ask students to match the columns. When checking answers, ask how they worked each one out (covering the use of time phrases as well as how the perfect tense is formed). The **Expo-langue** box at the top of p. 17 gives a framework for then consolidating this.

Expo-langue: perfect tense (formation with *avoir* and *être*)

Use this grammar box to review how the perfect tense is formed before students do exercise 3. There is more information on p. 212 of the Student Book.

3 Qu'est-ce qu'ils ont joué ou fait? Quel jour et à quelle heure?

Speaking. In pairs: using the grid supplied (and working out details of activities from the brochure in exercise 1), students say what each person/ group did at the leisure centre, giving details of when and where.

4 Copiez le texte et remplissez les blancs avec les mots à droite.

Reading. Students read the gapped text and complete it using the words supplied. The text consolidates the perfect tense: all the missing words are past participles.

Answers

1 allé **2** fait **3** bavardé **4** lu **5** écouté **6** joué **7** rentrés **8** nagé **9** mangé **10** vu

5 Qu'est-ce qu'ils ont fait? C'était comment? (1–5)

Listening. Students listen to five people talking about what they did on particular days and their opinions of the activities. They write a sentence on each activity and a sentence giving an opinion. A box summarising the language used for opinions is supplied.

With a higher ability class, you might want to contrast the use of different past tenses in this activity: perfect to describe a completed event, imperfect for descriptions.

Audioscript 14

1 *Mercredi dernier? J'ai joué au basket. C'était un match. C'était un désastre! Nous avons perdu 7 à 0. C'était nul … complètement nul.*

2 *Mercredi … Alors, le matin … euh, non … l'après-midi, j'ai fait une balade en vélo avec mon copain et il a plu. Et tu sais, le vélo, ce n'est pas mon truc. En plus, je suis tombée et alors non, … ce n'était pas fantastique, plutôt le contraire, c'était nul.*

3 *Qu'est-ce que j'ai fait le mercredi? Ah, oui … le matin je suis allé à la piscine. On apprend à faire de la plongée … Si c'était bien? Bof … le moniteur dit «Respirez par le nez», mais moi, je n'y arrive pas. C'est difficile, tu sais!*

4 *Ben, mercredi … j'ai fait un cours de danse. D'habitude, j'aime bien, mais le prof n'était pas là et la remplaçante n'était pas assez stricte. On a fait des bêtises … c'était nul!*

5 *La semaine dernière, j'ai fait un stage d'équitation. Je suis montée à cheval pour la première fois de ma vie. Ça s'est bien passé. Ah oui, super bien. J'ai adoré.*

Answers

1 *Il a joué au basket. C'était nul.*
2 Elle a fait une balade en vélo. C'était nul.
3 Il est allé à la piscine/a fait de la plongée. C'était pas mal.
4 Elle a fait un cours de danse. C'était nul.
5 Elle a fait un stage d'équitation. C'était super/fantastique/ génial.

6 Imaginez: vous êtes allé(e)s en vacances en France chez votre corres avec votre famille. Qu'est-ce que vous avez fait? C'était comment?

Writing. Students imagine they went with their family to visit their French penpal for a holiday. They write a paragraph about what they did each day and give their opinions of these activities. Sample structures are supplied for support.

Students could do this activity on computer, adding in photos and pictures to make a holiday journal.

Plenary

Play a chain game round the class to consolidate talking about activities in the past. Each student repeats the chain so far and adds their own expression. If he/she makes a mistake, misses an item out or can't add an item, he/she is out. Start it off: **Le week-end dernier, j'ai fait de la natation, ...**

Cahier d'exercices, page 7

1

Answers

Samedi dernier, je suis allé au centre de loisirs avec mes copains, Luc, Sarah et Vincent. Le matin, on a fait beaucoup de sport. D'abord, j'ai joué au tennis puis nous avons joué au volley. C'était bien, mais fatigant! Luc a joué au basket et au badminton parce qu'il n'aime pas le tennis.
L'après-midi, vers deux heures, nous sommes allés à la piscine où nous avons nagé pendant deux heures. C'était génial. Plus tard, nous sommes rentrés chez moi et on a mangé une pizza et on a bavardé.
Finalement, quand mes copains sont partis, j'ai écouté de la musique et j'ai regardé un DVD avec ma famille. Le film était nul et moi, j'étais très fatigué!

2

Answers

Example:
Lundi dernier, je suis allé à la piscine avec mes copains, puis l'après-midi, j'ai fait du ski.
Le soir, j'ai fait du taï chi et ensuite, j'ai écouté de la musique.
Mardi matin, j'ai joué au foot d'abord, puis deux heures plus tard, j'ai joué au basket avec mes copains. L'après-midi, j'ai fait de la danse, puis le soir j'ai fait du judo et du théâtre.
Mercredi matin, je suis allé à la piscine et j'ai fait de la plongée. Plus tard, l'après-midi, je suis allé au parc où j'ai fait du skate.
Le soir, je suis allé au cinéma où j'ai vu un bon film comique.

5 Ma passion

(Student Book pages 18–19)

Main topics and objectives

- Talking about your main hobby
- The near future tense

Grammar

- Near future tense
- **aller** (present tense)

Key language

Je me passionne pour le sport.
Ma passion, c'est le foot.
Je joue au foot depuis cinq ans.
J'en fais depuis deux ans.
Je l'ai choisi parce que …
J'en fais parce que …
c'est bon pour la santé
j'aime la camaraderie
j'ai gagné
je suis devenu(e) accro
je me suis inscrit(e) au club
L'année prochaine, …
je vais prendre part aux compétitions
je vais être dans la première équipe

Resources

CD1, tracks 15–16
Cahier d'exercices, pages 8–9
Grammaire 3.8, 4.5

Starter 1

Aim

To reintroduce the near future tense. To revise grammar points/language from earlier in the module.

Write up the following and ask students in pairs to identify the errors in the sentences and write them out correctly and to translate them. (Correct versions shown in italics in brackets for reference only.) Which pair can spot and correct most errors?

1 **Je vais écouter du musique avec mon frere cadet.**
(Je vais écouter *de la* musique avec mon *frère* cadet.)

2 **Le semaine prochaine, nous allons jouer au piano.**
(*La* semaine prochaine, nous allons jouer *du* piano.)

3 **Il va travaillé dans un grand surface.**
(Il va *travailler* dans *une grande* surface.)

4 **Elle ne vais pas rentre chez moi parce que ma sœur est trop bavarde.**
(Elle ne *va* pas *rentrer* chez moi parce que ma sœur est trop bavarde.)

1 Écoutez et lisez le texte.

Reading. Students listen to Sascha talking about her passion for football and read the text at the same time.

Audioscript 15

J'ai une passion pour le foot. J'y joue deux fois par semaine et je m'entraîne une fois par semaine.

Je joue au foot depuis toujours. J'ai commencé quand j'avais six ans. D'abord, j'ai joué avec mes frères dans la rue. Plus tard, je me suis inscrite au club des jeunes et maintenant, on joue des matchs amicaux le mercredi et le dimanche. Jusqu'à présent, j'ai seulement joué sur le terrain de notre club.

La semaine dernière, j'ai joué dans l'équipe junior B contre l'équipe A et nous avons gagné 2-0. C'est moi qui ai marqué le premier but.

Cette année, je vais passer dans la première équipe. On va jouer des matchs contre des équipes d'autres villes de notre région, donc on va prendre le bus avec les seniors quand on va jouer ailleurs.

Pour jouer dans la première équipe, j'ai besoin d'un nouveau maillot à rayures rouges et noires, un short noir, des chaussettes rouges et des chaussures de foot noires. Pour gagner de l'argent pour les acheter, je vais faire la vaisselle dans le café de mon village pendant les vacances l'été prochain.

J'aime le foot parce que c'est bon pour la santé, et j'aime l'ambiance et la camaraderie, on est entre amis. Je préfère jouer plutôt que de regarder les matchs, mais il faut aussi en regarder pour apprendre. Quelquefois, l'entraîneur nous filme et puis, il nous critique. C'est bien parce que comme ça, on apprend à mieux jouer. Je vais continuer à jouer aussi longtemps que possible, mais je sais que pour les footballeurs le plus grand risque, c'est un accident, surtout au genou.

2 Trouvez les mots ou les expressions dans le texte.

Reading. Students reread the text to find the French translations of the nine English time phrases listed.

+ Ask students to group the expressions according to whether they are used in the text to talk about the past, the present or the future.

Answers

1 quand
2 d'abord
3 plus tard
4 maintenant
5 jusqu'à présent
6 la semaine dernière
7 cette année
8 l'été prochain
9 quelquefois

Expo-langue: near future tense

Read through this grammar box which covers the near future tense. You could ask students to find examples of this tense in the text in exercise 1.

3 À deux. Discutez en anglais.

Speaking. In pairs: students discuss Sascha's text in English, using the questions supplied.

Starter 2

Aim
To consolidate the near future tense.

Write up the following:

aller regarder jouer faire manger écouter

Ask students in pairs to write six sentences using the near future tense. Each sentence must use a different part of **aller** (e.g. **je vais, tu vas,** etc.) and a different infinitive from the list you have supplied.

Listen to sample answers. Ask students to summarise how the near future is formed.

4 Traduisez en anglais les mots et les phrases en bleu dans le texte de l'exercice 1. Utilisez un dictionnaire, si nécessaire.

Reading. Students reread the text in exercise 1 and translate the words and phrases highlighted there in blue. They can use a dictionary, but encourage them first to use the strategies highlighted earlier in the module for working out new words.

Answers

je me suis inscrite – I joined
matchs amicaux – friendly matches/friendlies
seulement – only
ailleurs – somewhere else
j'ai besoin – I need
l'ambiance – the atmosphere
mieux – better
surtout – especially

5 Copiez le texte en remplissant les blancs.

Writing. Students copy and complete the gap-fill text using the words supplied. Before they begin, they should read the tip box, which lists strategies for approaching activities like this (reading the whole text first so that they can use the verbal context to work things out and the topic to make guesses more focused; using grammar to work out the function of words in a sentence, etc.). Stress that they should aim to practise this approach whenever they face a gap-fill activity as it will help them when they have to tackle activities of this sort in the exam.

You might want to point out that the answers contain 'distractors' – i.e. there are more answers than gaps. This is often a feature of exam tasks too.

R Go through the answers to exercise 5 as a class, discussing why each one is correct and why other options don't work.

Answers

1 depuis **2** fin **3** inscrit **4** entraînement **5** sauf
6 piscine **7** allons **8** fait **9** compétitions **10** régional
11 forme **12** coucher

Expo-langue: *depuis* + present tense

Use this grammar box to cover **depuis** + the present tense before students do exercise 6. Point out the usefulness of this structure when talking about their own experience.

6 Que font-ils? Depuis quand? Qu'est-ce qu'ils vont faire? (1–4)

Listening. Students copy out the grid. They listen to four people talking about which activities they like doing and note the details in the grid.

Audioscript 16

1 *Ma passion, c'est l'équitation. Je vais au centre hippique tous les mercredis. Je m'occupe des chevaux. Je le fais depuis plus de six ans. J'ai commencé depuis toute petite. J'ai toujours adoré les chevaux. Cette année, je vais avoir mon propre cheval. Je suis si contente!*

2 *Je fais du cyclisme depuis deux ans. Je sors tous les dimanches avec mon père et je m'entraîne deux ou trois fois par semaine. Cette année, je vais m'inscrire au club de cyclisme et puis, je vais faire des courses contre la montre.*

3 *Ma passion, c'est le rugby. Je joue depuis trois ans. Ma mère ne m'a pas permis de jouer avant parce qu'elle trouve ce sport trop dangereux, mais moi, j'adore. Je vais à l'entraînement tous les mercredis et l'année prochaine, je vais être dans l'équipe junior.*

4 *Ma passion, c'est le cinéma. J'ai beaucoup de DVD de vieux films en noir et blanc. Je les collectionne depuis deux ans. J'en ai une bonne vingtaine. J'adore les films de Woody Allen. L'année prochaine, je vais m'inscrire au club de cinéma et apprendre à tourner un film.*

Answers

	passion	depuis quand	au futur
1	*l'équitation*	*plus de six ans*	*Elle va avoir son propre cheval.*
2	du cyclisme	deux ans	Il va s'inscrire au club de cyclisme et il va faire des courses contre la montre.
3	le rugby	trois ans	Il va être dans l'équipe junior.
4	le cinéma	deux ans	Elle va s'inscrire au club du cinéma et apprendre à tourner un film.

7 Écrivez une réponse à Sascha. Répondez aux questions.

Writing. Students write responses to a list of questions from Sascha, who wants to know what they like doing. The beginning of each response is supplied for support.

8 Vidéoconférence. Préparez un dialogue. Vous allez parler de votre passion. Puis vous allez poser deux questions à votre partenaire sur sa passion.

Speaking. Students imagine that they are going to have a videoconference with students at a French school. They prepare a dialogue in which they talk about what they like doing. They also prepare two questions to ask the person they are speaking to about what he/she likes doing. Suggest students reduce their notes to just a short list (of around six key words) to use as a prompt when they are actually doing the dialogue.

See p. 18 for suggestions on actually linking up with a partner school in France to exchange information.

Plenary

Get two or three pairs to perform the dialogue they prepared in exercise 8 in front of the class. Invite constructive feedback in the following areas:

- pronunciation
- intonation (Did the questions sound like questions?)
- authenticity. (Did the pairs use words such as **euh, et alors**, etc., to buy them thinking time?)

Cahier d'exercices, page 8

Answers

Underlined:
on va enregistrer
on va faire
on va l'envoyer
on va avoir
on va être

Answers

1 Danièle a seize ans.
2 Elle aime le rock et le Nu Metal.
3 Elle chante depuis quatorze ans.
4 Dans le groupe, il y a une guitare électrique, une guitare basse, une batterie et un clavier.
5 Ils chantent les chansons de Danièle.
6 On va enregistrer deux chansons de Danièle.
7 Elle veut être célèbre un jour.

Cahier d'exercices, Grammaire, page 9

Answers

Je me présente. Je m'appelle Thomas et j'ai seize ans. J'habite à Lyon en France. Mes deux frères s'appellent Luc et Valentin. Nous avons un chat qui s'appelle Sophie. Je suis assez grand et j'ai les yeux bleus.
Samedi dernier, je suis allé à la piscine avec mon frère. Après, nous avons bu un coca et nous avons mangé une pizza. Ensuite, on a joué au basket puis on est allés au parc et on a joué au foot.
Le soir, nous sommes allés dans un restaurant avec nos parents. Mon père a bu du vin et ma mère a mangé un steak-frites.
Demain, je vais jouer au tennis avec mon copain, Vincent. Puis on va aller chez lui et on va écouter de la musique. L'après-midi, je vais aller en ville avec ma sœur. Elle va acheter un nouveau jean. Nous allons rentrer vers quatre heures. Le soir, je vais regarder un film au cinéma.

Answers

Example:
1 J'adore le sport. J'aime faire du vélo et j'adore le basket mais je n'aime pas le football.
2 Samedi dernier, je suis allé(e) à la piscine puis après ça, je suis allé(e) au café où j'ai mangé une pizza puis j'ai écouté de la musique chez moi.
3 Le week-end prochain, je vais faire du roller puis l'après-midi, je vais jouer au tennis et le soir, je vais regarder un DVD chez moi avec des copains.

Contrôle continu: Ma passion

(Student Book pages 20–21)

Topics revised

- Writing about a favourite leisure activity

1 Trouvez les mots ou les phrases dans le texte.

Students read Lucy's text on her favourite leisure activity, judo. They then find the French versions of the eleven English words/phrases in the text.

Answers

martial arts – les arts martiaux
(judo) kit – la tenue (de judo)
level – le niveau
black belt – la ceinture noire
very talented – très doué
beginners – les débutants
one of the best – l'un des meilleurs
disadvantage – l'inconvénient
advantage – l'avantage
everybody – tout le monde
at the same time – en même temps

2 Imaginez que vous êtes Lucy. Répondez aux questions en français.

Students reread the text. They imagine they are Lucy and answer the ten questions in French from Lucy's perspective.

Answers

1 C'est un sport/un art martial.
2 J'ai commencé à faire du judo l'année dernière.
3 Je l'ai choisi parce que c'est le plus connu des arts martiaux, mes amis en font et c'est bon pour la forme.
4 J'en fais le lundi et le mercredi soir.
5 J'en fais avec un moniteur/avec mes amis.
6 Il faut avoir une tenue.
7 La couleur de la ceinture signifie le niveau qu'on a atteint.
8 L'avantage, c'est qu'on garde la forme et qu'on se fait de nouveaux amis facilement.
9 Oui, l'inconvénient, c'est qu'il faut s'entraîner tous les jours si on veut devenir vraiment très bon, et quelquefois, c'est difficile surtout quand on a beaucoup de devoirs.
10 Oui, je vais passer dans le groupe des seniors l'année prochaine (et je voudrais obtenir la ceinture marron).

3 Décrivez votre passe-temps préféré.

Using Lucy's text and the **Boîte à outils** section to help them, students write their own text on their favourite leisure activity.

The **Boîte à outils** section gives students the support they need to structure their own writing.

Encourage students to adopt the kind of approach taken in this section to all extended writing activities.

It would be good to create model answers together for this first module. Focus on the key points that need to be included for a student to get the best grade:

- reference to the past, present and future using the appropriate tenses
- opinions with justifications
- varied sentence structures, including connectives and intensifiers.

À l'oral (AQA edition)

(Student Book page 176)

Topics revised

- leisure activities you usually do/have done
- leisure activities you plan to do
- talking about yourself and your family

1 You are talking to a French friend about your hobbies. Your partner will play the part of the friend and will begin the conversation.

Roleplay. In roleplays, students work in pairs, taking it in turn to ask and answer the questions.

Students practise talking about the activities they like doing and when they do them; they then move on to talking about activities they have done in the past.

☑ Draw students' attention to the **!** symbol before they start: this means that they will have to give a response which they have not prepared. This is a feature of all AQA Higher-level roleplays. As the tip box in the Student Book outlines, students need not be entirely *unprepared*. By looking at the other questions and thinking about the situation, they should be able to think about possible questions that might come up and work out how to respond to them.

2 You are discussing what you might do this evening with your French friend. Your partner will play the part of the friend and will begin the conversation.

Roleplay. Students practise talking about what they are doing this evening/did on Saturday/are going to do tomorrow.

3 Prepare a ninety-second presentation called *Je me présente*.

Make yourself a cue card to help you remember what to say. Keep it as simple as possible. When you have practised the presentation, see if you can reduce the number of words you need on the cue card.

Presentation. Students prepare a ninety-second presentation on themselves and their families.

☑ Look together at the cue card supplied and ask students to use this to reconstruct what they might say. Students should then prepare their own talk, using a similar cue card for support, and give their talk to a partner or group. Emphasise that cue cards need to be very simple, both to comply with the exam rules and to be effective as prompts.

Listen to one or two talks and/or have students record them for reference. Ask questions to elicit more information, highlighting areas that students might have overlooked. Suggest they look at their presentation again bearing these in mind. Stress the importance of redrafting and improving work at this level.

4 Possible conversation questions

Conversation. ☑ These are key questions to practise for the speaking exam, taken from the module as a whole. It would be useful to work first on model answers together at this stage. Students can then practise asking and answering the questions in pairs. They should be encouraged to include in their responses:

- as much detail as possible
- a variety of tenses (past, present and future to achieve the highest grades)
- opinions
- connectives and intensifiers.

Encourage them to refer to this checklist routinely until they get into the habit of including this kind of detail every time.

À l'oral (Edexcel edition)

(Student Book page 176)

Topics revised

- leisure activities you usually do/have done
- leisure activities you plan to do
- talking about yourself and your family

1 You are staying with your penfriend in France and are discussing what you are going to do. Your partner will play the part of your penfriend and will begin the conversation.

Roleplay Type B. In roleplays, students work in pairs, taking it in turn to ask and answer the questions using the text and picture prompts.

Roleplays throughout the **À l'oral** sections are identified as *Roleplay Type B* or *Roleplay Type C* in line with the Edexcel exam specification.

Students practise talking about what they are doing this evening and what they usually do, and make arrangements to go out.

☑ Draw students' attention to the ! symbol before they start: this means that they will have to give a response which they have not prepared. This is a feature of all Edexcel roleplays. As the tip box in the Student Book outlines, students need not be entirely *unprepared*. By looking at the other questions and thinking about the situation, they should be able to think about possible questions that might come up and work out how to respond to them.

2 You and your penfriend are discussing plans for the weekend. Your partner will play the part of your penfriend and will begin the conversation.

Roleplay Type B. Students practise making arrangements for what they are doing this weekend.

3 Presentation and general conversation

Presentation. Students prepare a one-minute presentation on themselves and their families.

Make sure students read through the tip box in the bottom right-hand corner of the page before starting work on this section. They need to clearly understand that they should not use everything they know in the presentation – they need to keep something back for the conversation. The tip box also gives advice on structuring their material.

☑ Look together at the cue card supplied and ask students to use this to reconstruct what they might say. Students should then prepare their own talk, using a similar cue card for support, and give their talk to a partner or group. Emphasise that cue cards need to be very simple, both to comply with the exam rules and to be effective as prompts.

Listen to one or two talks and/or have students record them for reference. Ask questions to elicit more information, highlighting areas that students might have overlooked. Suggest they look at their presentation again bearing these in mind. Stress the importance of redrafting and improving work at this level.

Possible conversation questions. These are key questions to practise for the speaking exam, taken from the module as a whole.

☑ It would be useful to work first on model answers together at this stage. Students can then practise asking and answering the questions in pairs. They should be encouraged to include in their responses:

- as much detail as possible
- a variety of tenses (past, present and future to achieve the highest grades)
- opinions
- connectives and intensifiers.

Encourage them to refer to this checklist routinely until they get into the habit of including this kind of detail every time.

Mai 1

À l'oral (OCR edition)

(Student Book page 176)

Topics revised
- leisure activities you usually do/have done
- leisure activities you plan to do
- talking about yourself and your family

1 You are talking to a French friend about your hobbies. Your partner will play the part of the friend and will begin the conversation.

Roleplay Type 2. In roleplays, students work in pairs, taking it in turn to ask and answer the questions.

Roleplays throughout the **À l'oral** sections are identified as *Roleplay Type 2* or *Roleplay Type 3* in line with the OCR exam specification.

☑ Draw students' attention to the prompt 'Answer a question' before they start: this means that they will have to give a response which they have not prepared. This is a feature of all OCR Type 2 Roleplays. Tell students that they need not be entirely *unprepared*. By looking at the other questions and thinking about the situation, they should be able to think about possible questions that might come up and work out how to respond to them.

Students practise talking about the activities they like doing and when they do them; they then move on to talking about activities they did last night.

2 You are discussing what you might do this evening with your French friend. Your partner will play the part of the friend and will begin the conversation.

Roleplay Type 2. Students practise suggesting things to do this evening, and talking about what they would like to do tomorrow and what they usually do. They take it in turn to play themselves/a French friend.

3 Prepare a one-minute presentation called *Je me présente*.

Presentation. Students prepare a one-minute presentation on themselves and their families.

☑ The tip box summarises how students should use cue cards in a task like this. Look together at the cue card supplied and ask students to use this to reconstruct what they might say. Students should then prepare their own talk, using a similar cue card for support, and give their talk to a partner or group. Emphasise that cue cards need to be very simple, both to comply with the exam rules and to be effective as prompts. Once they have practised what they want to say, students should aim to reduce the prompts on their card.

The tip box also emphasises two other important elements students need to bear in mind when doing presentations:

1 They should aim to include the full range of tenses, even in topics like this where it is more difficult. Encourage students to plan for how they might do this.

2 They need also to include a variety of opinions and to justify these.

Listen to one or two talks and/or have students record them for reference. Ask questions to elicit more information, highlighting areas that students might have overlooked. Suggest they look at their presentation again bearing these in mind. Stress the importance of redrafting and improving work at this level.

4 *Mes loisirs*: possible conversation questions

Conversation. These are key questions to practise for the speaking exam, taken from the module as a whole.

☑ It would be useful to work first on model answers together at this stage. Students can then practise asking and answering the questions in pairs. They should be encouraged to include in their responses:

- as much detail as possible
- a variety of tenses (past, present and future to achieve the highest grades)
- opinions
- connectives and intensifiers.

Encourage them to refer to this checklist routinely until they get into the habit of including this kind of detail every time.

À toi

(Student Book pages 186–187)

- Self-access reading and writing

1 Qui est ... ? Trouvez le métier de chaque personne.

Reading. Students read the seven short texts and identify which job each person does.

Answers

1 médecin **2** journaliste **3** hôtesse de l'air
4 photographe **5** coiffeuse **6** architecte **7** standardiste

2 Trouvez les mots/les phrases dans les textes.

Reading. Students reread the texts and find the French expressions for the five pictured items.

Answers

1 le journal **2** l'imprimante **3** mises en plis **4** les plans des bâtiments

3 Décrivez la famille de Théo.

Writing. Using the family tree, students write two sentences on each person in Théo's family, giving their nationality and their job.

Answers

Le grand-père de Théo est suisse. Il est agriculteur.
La grand-mère de Théo est française. Elle est comptable.
Le père de Théo est français. Il est mécanicien.
La mère de Théo est suisse. Elle est professeur/institutrice.
La sœur de Théo est française. Elle est étudiante.
La tante de Théo est française. Elle est médecin.
L'oncle de Théo est espagnol. Il est mécanicien.
Le cousin de Théo est espagnol. Il est informaticien.
La cousine de Théo est espagnole. Elle est coiffeuse.

4 Lisez le texte et mettez les images dans le bon ordre.

Reading. Students read the text and put the pictures (**a–f**) in the order they are mentioned.

Answers

b, a, d, c, f, e

5 Trouvez la bonne définition.

Reading. Students reread the text in exercise 4 and work out the meaning of the seven French expressions from the multiple-choice options.

Answers

1 c **2** b **3** c **4** a **5** b **6** c **7** b

6 Qu'est-ce que tu as fait la semaine dernière?

Writing. Students write a paragraph saying what they did each day last week. A sample beginning is given for support.

Module 2: On sort? (Student Book pages 24–39)

Unit	Main topics and objectives	Grammar
Déjà vu **Qu'est-ce qu'on fait?** (pp. 24–25)	Discussing TV and cinema Using articles and object pronouns	Pronouns – direct object pronouns – y
1 Ça te dit? (pp. 26–27)	Arranging to go out Using pronouns after prepositions	Emphatic pronouns
2 Désolé, je ne peux pas (pp. 28–29)	Explaining why you can't do something Using modal verbs	Modal verbs (**vouloir**, **pouvoir**, **devoir**) + the infinitive
3 Ce n'était pas mal (pp. 30–31)	Describing what you did Using the perfect and imperfect tenses	Perfect tense (formation of past participles)
4 C'est la fête! (pp. 32–33)	Describing special occasions Imperfect tense of **avoir** and **être**	Imperfect tense for descriptions (**être**/**avoir**)
5 Il s'agit de quoi? (pp. 34–35)	Describing what you saw or read Expressing complex ideas in a simple way	**mieux, pire(s)** **le/la/les meilleur(e)(s), le/la/les plus mauvais(e)(s)**
Contrôle continu **Un de mes films préférés** (p. 36–37)	*Coursework* Writing a review of a film or book	*All main grammar points of the module*
À l'oral (p. 177)	*Exam speaking practice* Arranging to go out Talking about your favourite TV programme and books/films you like Talking about celebrations in the past	*All main grammar points of the module*
À toi (pp. 188–189)	Self-access reading and writing	

Déjà vu: Qu'est-ce qu'on fait?

(Student Book pages 24–25)

Main topics and objectives

- Discussing TV and cinema
- Using articles and object pronouns

Key language

Television programmes
Types of films
Responses to invitations
Expressions of opinion

Resources

CD1, track 17
Cahier d'exercices, page 12
Grammaire 1.7

Grammar

Pronouns
- direct object pronouns
- y

Starter 1

Aim
To revise vocabulary for talking about television programmes.

Give students three minutes *working strictly on their own* to come up with an example of a programme on British television for each of the following. When they have completed their lists, they check their answers with a partner. Each time they have the same answer in a category, the pair wins one point. The pair with the most points wins.

1 une série policière
2 une émission de science-fiction
3 une comédie
4 un jeu télévisé
5 une émission de télé-réalité
6 une émission musicale
7 une série médicale
8 un dessin animé

1 Écoutez et lisez la conversation. Notez les mots qui manquent.

Listening. Students listen to the conversation and read the gap-fill text at the same time. They complete the text using the words supplied.

After checking answers, draw students' attention to the tip box reminding them to use the definite article with likes and dislikes (**j'aime *les* films d'horreur**).

Audioscript 17

– *Salut, Thomas! C'est Julie. Tu veux aller au cinéma avec moi ce soir?*
– *Ça dépend. Qu'est-ce qu'on passe?*
– *Il y a* Star Wars épisode 3: La Revanche des Sith.
– *Ça ne me dit rien. Je* ***n'aime pas*** *beaucoup les films de science-fiction. Je les trouve* ***ennuyeux****.*
– *Bon, qu'est-ce qu'on fait, alors? Tu* ***veux*** *regarder la télé chez moi?*
– *Oui, je veux bien. Qu'est-ce qu'il y a à la télé* ***ce soir****?*
– *Euh… il y a* Joey.
– *Qu'est-ce que c'est?*
– *C'est* ***une comédie*** *comme* Friends.
– *Ah, non! Pas ça! Je* ***déteste*** *les comédies américaines.*
– ***Il y a*** *aussi* La Nouvelle Star*, à 20h50. Tu veux regarder ça?*
– *Chouette! J'adore les* ***émissions*** *musicales! Alors, je viens chez toi à 20h15. D'accord?*
– *D'accord. À bientôt!*

Answers

Also shown in bold in the audioscript.
1 n'aime pas **2** ennuyeux **3** veux **4** ce soir
5 une comédie **6** déteste **7** il y a **8** émissions

2 À deux. Adaptez la conversation ci-dessus. Utilisez vos propres idées et des mots ci-dessous si vous voulez.

Speaking. In pairs: students adapt the conversation in exercise 1, using their own ideas and/or the prompts supplied. A sample exchange is given.

Starter 2

Aim
To review expressing likes and dislikes. To practise justifying opinions.

Write up the following and ask students to complete the sentences with an appropriate reason. Students could work in pairs for support.

Je n'aime pas les dessins animés. Je les trouve …
Les histoires d'amour? Bof! Elles sont un peu …
J'adore les films d'épouvante parce que …
D'habitude, j'aime les films d'action, mais quelquefois …
Je déteste les westerns parce que …

When listening to answers, ask students to spell out any adjectives used and get the class to give feedback on the accuracy of agreements.

Expo-langue: direct object pronouns; the pronoun *y*

Use this grammar box to introduce direct object pronouns and the indirect pronoun **y** before students do exercise 3. There is more information on p. 208 of the Student Book.

3 Lisez le quiz et répondez aux questions. Puis regardez la solution. Vous êtes comme ça?

Reading. Before they do the activity, ask the students what they think the exercise is about. If they are struggling, draw their attention to the structure (questions plus multiple choice answer options) and the cartoon illustrating it. Where would they find a text like this? (in a magazine) Remind them that non-verbal clues like this can help them work out the context of a text, which can be very useful for tackling new vocabulary. Using the details here, can they translate the title?

Students do the quiz on whether they are a TV/cinema addict or not, reading the text and answering the multiple choice questions. They then work out their score and read the appropriate result.

R Ask students to identify all the direct object pronouns in the quiz text and to say what nouns/ phrases they replace.

4 À deux! Interviewez votre partenaire en utilisant les questions de l'exercice 3.

Speaking. In pairs: students interview each other, taking it in turn to ask and answer the questions in the quiz in exercise 3.

Before they start, draw students' attention to the tip box on including expressions of frequency and opinions in their French to make it more interesting. Give them time to identify useful phrases of this sort on the page and to list any others they remember for reference.

5 Écrivez un paragraphe sur votre famille, la télé et le cinéma.

Writing. Students write a paragraph about themselves and their families, detailing their television and film preferences and how often they watch both.

They should use their list of useful time expressions and opinions in this activity too.

+ Students could include justifications of the opinions expressed in their texts, along the lines of those in Starter 2.

Plenary

Write up:
Je regarde ...
le DVD, la télévision, les films

Ask students to give you a sentence for each of these, replacing the noun (**le DVD**, etc.) with the appropriate direct object pronoun.

Ask them to do the same for
J'écoute ...
le Podcast, la radio, les CD

Ask for a summary of the forms of the direct object pronoun. Can they remember another pronoun covered in this unit? See if they can give you a few examples of sentences incorporating **y**.

Cahier d'exercices, page 12

1

Answers

Possible answers:
Group 1:
Star Wars Épisode III, H2G2 Le guide du voyageur galactique, (Justification – sci-fi films)
Group 2:
Madagascar, Wallace et Gromit, le mystère du lapin-garou, (Justification: animated films)
Group 3
Harry Potter et la coupe de feu, Le monde de Narnia, La légende de Zorro, (Justification – fantasy films)
Group 4
Charlie et la chocolaterie, Chicago, (Justification – comedy / musical comedy)

2

Answers

1 Chicago **2** Charlie et la chocolaterie **3** Star Wars Épisode III **4** Madagascar **5** Le monde de Narnia **6** Harry Potter et la coupe de feu

3

Answers

Possible answers
1. More complex than most Hollywood films. Good entertainment with cabaret music.
2. Thinks this film is really good. He adores the Oompa-loompas and Johnny.
3. Likes it; thinks Anakin is cool and funny. Is a fan of Hayden.
4. Loved it; including the jokes and the song 'I like to move it'. Likes the animals.
5. Is about a lion and a white witch. Thinks film is great.
6. Film is super cool but not allowed for the under 12s because of violent scenes. Story becoming more terrifying.

1 Ça te dit?

(Student Book pages 26–27)

Main topics and objectives

- Arranging to go out
- Using pronouns after prepositions

Grammar

- Emphatic pronouns

Key language

Il y a une séance à ...
L'entrée, c'est combien?
Ça coûte combien?
un concert
une pièce (de théâtre)
un spectacle (de danse)
un billet
avec la carte d'étudiant
complet
tarif réduit
C'est gratuit.
Ça commence à ... ?
On se retrouve où/à quelle heure?
chez moi/toi
chez lui
À bientôt/demain/samedi!

Resources

CD1, tracks 18–19
Cahier d'exercices, page 13
Grammaire 1.11

Starter 1

Aim
To practise reading for gist. To practise taking notes effectively.

Tell students you are going to test them on how quickly they can pick up information in French. You will give them one minute to look at the texts in exercise 1 on p. 26 before asking them questions about the texts. They can make notes in that time, which they can later refer to. After one minute, ask them to close their books and ask the following questions to test their gist understanding:

- What type of texts are they?
- What are the entertainments advertised?

Did they have time to get the information required? Ask students if they found making notes helpful. How did they do it? Did they use the time effectively? Point out the usefulness of (1) focusing on understanding the main points when time is short and (2) devising shortcuts for noting information (symbols/abbreviations, etc.).

1 Lisez les annonces, puis reliez le français et l'anglais.

Reading. Students read the five adverts and then match the six English expressions with the correct French versions.

They then identify the two *faux amis* in the adverts.

Answers
1 e **2** c **3** f **4** a **5** d **6** b

2 Relisez les annonces. Écrivez V (Vrai), F (Faux) ou PM (Pas Mentionné) à côté de chaque phrase.

Reading. Students read the adverts again. They then read the ten statements on the text and decide whether each is true or false or not mentioned in the text.

Answers
1 F **2** V **3** V **4** PM **5** F **6** V **7** PM **8** V **9** F **10** V

Starter 2

Aim
To practise listening for numbers.

In pairs: ask students each to write out eight prices without showing the list to their partner. All prices should be under 100€ and some should include cents (e.g. 45,50€). Students then take it in turn to read out their prices for their partner to write them down. They swap their answers and check who got the most correct.

3 Écoutez. On parle de quelle annonce dans l'exercice 1? Notez les bonnes lettres. (1–4)

Listening. Students listen to four conversations and decide which advert each refers to.

Audioscript 18

1
– Salut, Farida! Écoute, il y a un spectacle de danse intéressant ce soir. Tu veux y aller avec moi?
– Tu sais, j'aime bien la danse, mais je n'ai pas beaucoup d'argent en ce moment. Les billets coûtent combien?
– Ce n'est pas cher. C'est 7 euros avec la carte d'étudiant. Ça va?
– OK, ça va. C'est à quelle heure?
– Ça commence à 19 heures.
– On se retrouve où et à quelle heure?
– Chez moi, à 18h30. D'accord?
– D'accord. À bientôt!

2
– Salut, Hugo! Tu es fan de Moby, n'est-ce pas?
– Oui, je l'aime beaucoup. Pourquoi?
– Parce qu'il joue au concert de la Fête de la Musique demain, au Palais de Versailles. Tu veux y aller?

– Super! Je veux bien, mais c'est combien, l'entrée? Ça doit coûter cher.
– Non, pas du tout. C'est gratuit!
– Gratuit! Chouette! Il faut y aller de bonne heure, alors?
– Oui, on se retrouve chez toi, vers midi?
– D'accord. À demain, alors!

3 *– Dis, Ahmed, tu veux aller au théâtre samedi? Il y a une pièce de Marivaux au Théâtre de Jouy.*
– Désolé, je n'aime pas beaucoup les pièces de théâtre. Je préfère aller au cinéma.
– D'accord. Qu'est-ce qu'on passe en ce moment?
– Il y a Crazy kung-fu, *au Ciné-cité. Ça te dit?*
– Oui, j'aime bien les films d'arts martiaux. C'est à quelle heure?
– Attends, je vais regarder dans le journal. Euh … il y a une séance à 20h20. Ça va?
– Ça va. On se retrouve où et à quelle heure?
– On se retrouve au cinéma à 20h. OK?
– D'accord. À samedi!

4 *– Bonjour, Claire, c'est moi. Écoute, il y a un grand festival de musique le week-end prochain. J'y vais avec Sébastien. Ça t'intéresse?*
– Bof. Ça dépend. Qui joue?
– Il y a Kyo, *par exemple. C'est un de mes groupes préférés!*
– D'accord. Ça coûte combien?
– Les billets coûtent 26€ pour la journée ou 52€ pour trois jours.
– 52€, c'est un peu trop cher pour moi, mais 26€, ça va.
– D'accord, je prends trois billets pour samedi, alors.
– On se retrouve où et à quelle heure?
– Ça commence à 14h30, donc on se retrouve chez Sébastien, vers 13 heures?
– D'accord. Chez lui, vers 13 heures. Au revoir!

Answers
1 E **2** B **3** D, A **4** C

4 Écoutez encore. On se retrouve où et à quelle heure? Trouvez les paires. (1–4)

Listening. Students listen to the recording again and find for each conversation the two relevant phrase for each (from **a–h**).

Audioscript 19

As for exercise 3.

Answers
1 e, d **2** g, b **3** c, h **4** a, f

Expo-langue: emphatic pronouns

Use this grammar box to introduce emphatic pronouns, pointing out the phrases in exercise 4 (e.g. **chez lui**, etc.) as illustrations. You could also give a few examples of emphatic pronouns used for emphasis, e.g.

Moi, je n'aime pas les spectacles de danse
Qui a mangé les gâteaux? Lui!

There is more information on p. 209 of the Student Book.

5 À deux. Complétez le dialogue. Choisissez ou inventez les détails.

Speaking. In pairs: students use the framework supplied, choosing from the options given or making up their own details, to create a dialogue in which they make arrangements to go out.

6 Écrivez deux ou trois annonces comme celles de l'exercice 1. Inventez les détails.

Writing. Using the adverts in exercise 1 as a model, students write two or three adverts of their own. Encourage them to be as inventive as they like and to use reference resources such as dictionaries or magazines to come up with ideas and vocabulary.

This could be done on computer using a word-processing or DTP package, with students incorporating pictures into their texts.

7 À deux. Faites un dialogue en utilisant une des vos annonces.

Speaking. In pairs: students make up a dialogue along the same lines as the one in exercise 5, this time using the information from one of the adverts they created for exercise 6.

Plenary

Ask the class to recap on what emphatic pronouns are and to tell you the forms. Then ask them to come up with four phrases, each featuring a different emphatic pronoun and a different preposition.

Cahier d'exercices, page 13

1

Answers
1 Casse-Noisette **2** Deftones **3** Star Wars l'Expo
4 Casse-Noisette **5** Casse-Noisette
6 Star Wars l'Expo **7** Deftones **8** Casse-Noisette

2

Answers
1 Pendant 4 mois. **2** Non, ça ferme le dimanche à 19 heures. **3** 3 concerts. **4** C'est 18€. **5** Parce que la réservation est conseillée

3

Answers
Pupil's own answers

2 Désolé, je ne peux pas

(Student Book pages 28–29)

Main topics and objectives

- Explaining why you can't do something
- Using modal verbs

Grammar

- Modal verbs (**vouloir, pouvoir, devoir**) + the infinitive

Key language

Désolé(e)./Excuse(z)-moi.
Je ne peux pas parce que ...
C'est trop cher pour moi.
Ma mère/Mon père dit que je dois ...
Mes parents disent que je dois ...
faire mes devoirs
garder mon petit frère
laver la voiture (de ma mère)
promener le chien (des voisins)
ranger ma chambre
rentrer avant 22 heures
rester à la maison
sortir avec mes parents
On doit aller voir ma grand-mère.
Mes parents doivent sortir.

Resources

CD1, track 20
Cahier d'exercices, page 14
Grammaire 3.16

Starter 1

Aim
To revise vocabulary for activities.

Write up the following and ask students to match the sentence halves, putting the second column in random order (in correct order here for reference). They should then translate them.

1 Tu veux	**aller au cinéma ce soir?**
2 On veut aller	**à la piscine.**
3 Je dois	**garder ma petite sœur.**
4 Il ne peut pas parce qu'	**il doit faire ses devoirs.**
5 Nous devons promener	**le chien.**
6 Elles ne peuvent pas	**venir à ma fête.**

When checking answers, ask students how they worked out the correct pairings.

1 Écoutez et regardez les images. Qui parle? (1–8)

Listening. Students listen to eight conversations in which people make excuses and use the labelled pictures to identify who is speaking in each one.

Audioscript 20

1 *Bonjour, Nicolas. Je suis désolé, mais je ne peux pas aller en ville avec toi cet après-midi parce que ma mère dit que je dois ranger ma chambre.*

2 *Salut, Anna! Je veux bien aller au cinéma ce soir, mais mes parents disent que je dois rentrer avant 22 heures. Est-ce qu'il y a une séance vers 18 heures?*

3 *Salut! Merci, mais je ne peux pas venir chez toi parce que mes parents doivent sortir et je dois garder mon petit frère. Désolé!*

4 *Coucou, c'est moi! Merci pour l'invitation, mais je dois rester à la maison ce week-end parce que j'ai beaucoup de devoirs à faire.*

5 *Bonjour, Emma. Excuse-moi, mais je ne peux pas sortir aujourd'hui. Je dois promener le chien des voisins parce qu'ils sont en vacances.*

6 *Salut, c'est moi. Je suis vraiment désolée, mais dimanche on doit aller voir ma grand-mère, donc je ne peux pas aller au concert.*

7 *Coucou, Malik. Merci pour l'invitation, mais on ne peut pas venir à ta fête parce qu'on doit sortir avec nos parents. Désolé!*

8 *Bonjour! Excuse-moi, mais je ne peux pas aller au bowling parce que je dois laver la voiture de ma mère. C'est pour gagner mon argent de poche, tu sais!*

Answers

1 Karim **2** Claire **3** Vincent **4** Mathilde **5** Adrien **6** Yasmina **7** Théo **8** Lisa

Expo-langue: modal verbs

Use this grammar box to introduce the modal verbs **vouloir, pouvoir** and **devoir** + the infinitive. There is more information on p. 216 of the Student Book.

2 À deux. Regardez les images et les mots et faites des dialogues.

Speaking. In pairs: students use the sample dialogue, the picture prompts and the support grid supplied to make up dialogues.

☑ Make sure that students know that the production of questions at this level is very important. They will have to identify situations in which they will need to know how to ask questions as well as how to give the answers and to learn the language for both sides of the exchange.

3 Inventez de nouvelles excuses. Utilisez un dictionnaire, si vous voulez.

Writing. Students make up their own excuses for refusing or being unable to accept an invitation, using a dictionary as necessary.

Starter 2

Aim
To revise modal verbs.

Tell students you are going to read out a range of excuses mothers have been given as reasons why teenagers cannot tidy their bedrooms. Students should raise their hand if they think the excuse is reasonable or put both hands on their head if it is unreasonable.

Je ne peux pas ranger ma chambre parce que ...
je dois aller à l'école
je veux bien surfer sur Internet
je me suis cassé le bras
je veux envoyer des textos à mes copains
je ne veux pas le faire
je dois garder le chien des voisins
j'ai beaucoup de devoirs à faire
je dors
je peux le faire demain
je l'ai déjà fait

4 Lisez les e-mails et répondez aux questions.

Reading. ☑ Students read the three e-mails and answer the seven questions on them, identifying the correct person in each case.

Give students time to read the tip box on reading complex texts before they tackle the activity.

Answers

1 Hakim **2** Lola **3** Lola **4** Julie **5** Hakim **6** Julie **7** Lola

5 Répondez aux questions en français.

Writing. Students reread the text and then write answers in French to the six questions on it.

Answers

1. *parce qu'elle doit faire son travail scolaire*
2. parce que ses grands-parents viennent en visite
3. parce qu'il doit aller en Bretagne avec ses parents
4. parce qu'il dit qu'elle ne peut pas aller au concert/doit bosser tout le week-end
5. parce que sa mère dit que Julie et son frère doivent aider à la maison
6. parce qu'il veut aller à la fête de Clément

6 Choisissez un des textos ci-dessous. Préparez et apprenez par cœur un message sur répondeur comme ceux de l'exercice 1, en donnant vos excuses. Donnez votre message et enregistrez-le, si possible.

Speaking. Students choose one of three text messages. They prepare an excuse for refusing the invitation, memorising it as a response that they would leave on a telephone answering machine, along the lines of the messages in exercise 1. They should then give their message to a partner and, if possible, record it.

Go to www.heinemann.co.uk/hotlinks and enter the express code 7898T for a link to a glossary of French text messaging abbreviations.

7 Écrivez un e-mail d'excuse comme ceux de l'exercice 4. Inventez les détails.

Writing. Students write an e-mail making an excuse for refusing an invitation or for being unable to attend an event. They should make up their own reasons, drawing on the language they have covered in the unit. Encourage them to be imaginative.

Plenary

Play a game round the class. Each student has to give a reason why he/she cannot come to a party, using **parce que je veux/je dois/je ne veux pas/je ne peux pas/je ne dois pas** + infinitive. Reward the most imaginative excuse.

Cahier d'exercices, page 14

1

Answers

1. Je ne peux pas parce que je dois garder ma petite souris.
2. Désolé! Je dois ranger la cage de mon hamster.
3. D'accord, mais je dois rentrer avant 21 heures pour promener mon crocodile.
4. Mes parents disent que je dois rester à la maison pour laver le chat!
5. Je ne peux pas parce que je dois sortir avec mon éléphant.
6. Excuse-moi, mais je dois promener le tigre de mes voisins.
7. Désolée, je dois laver le vélo de ma tortue.
8. Je voudrais bien, mais je ne peux pas. Je dois faire un gâteau aux rats pour mon serpent.

2

Answers

Pupil's own answers

3 Ce n'était pas mal

(Student Book pages 30–31)

Main topics and objectives

- Describing what you did
- Using the perfect and imperfect tenses

Grammar

- Perfect tense (formation of past participles)

Key language

Qu'est-ce que tu as fait?
J'ai/On a ...
acheté des CD
écouté de la musique
fait les magasins
fini le livre
mangé une pizza
lu des BD
regardé un film en DVD
vu King Kong
Je suis/On est ...
allé(e) au cinéma
rentré(e)
resté(e) à la maison

Les opinions
Il y avait ...
Il (n')y avait (pas) ...
C'était/Ce n'était pas ...
assez/tout à fait/très/trop/un peu
affreux
amusant
barbant
bien
émouvant
ennuyeux
formidable
génial
intéressant
lent
long
marrant
nul
pas mal
passionnant
(peu) original
plein d'action

Resources

CD1, tracks 21–22
Cahier d'exercices, page 15
Grammaire 3.3, 3.4

Starter 1

Aim
To practise linking tenses and time phrases.

Write up the following:
1 ... , j'ai regardé *I, Robot* en DVD.
2 ... , j'écoute des CD dans ma chambre.
3 ... , je vais aller au bowling.

Give students two minutes in pairs to come up with as many time phrases as possible to complete each of the three sentences.

When listening to answers, ask students to identify the tenses used.

1 Écoutez et lisez les textes. Puis regardez les phrases ci-dessous. Qui parle? Choisissez la bonne réponse. (1–4)

Listening. Students listen to four people talking about various activities they/their friends/their family have done. They then read eight statements and identify the speaker for each from the options listed.

Audioscript 21

1 *Dimanche dernier, je suis resté à la maison et j'ai regardé* Tigre et dragon *en DVD. Je suis fan des films d'arts martiaux. C'est un de mes films préférés parce que c'est plein d'action.*

2 *Hier soir, ma copine Mathilde et moi sommes allées au cinéma. Nous avons vu* King Kong. *Après, nous avons mangé une pizza et nous sommes rentrées à la maison vers 22 heures.*

3 *Mes deux sœurs adorent la lecture, surtout les livres de Harry Potter. Le week-end dernier, elles ont acheté toutes les deux* Harry Potter et le prince de sang mêlé. *Elles ont lu tout le week-end et elles ont fini le livre dimanche soir!*

4 *Samedi matin, mon petit copain a fait les magasins et il a acheté six CD avec l'argent qu'il a reçu comme cadeau d'anniversaire. Dimanche, il est resté à la maison et il a écouté du hip-hop et du rap dans sa chambre toute la journée.*

Answers

1 Nathalie
2 le petit copain de Liane
3 Farid
4 les sœurs de Damien
5 Nathalie
6 le petit copain de Liane
7 Nathalie
8 les sœurs de Damien

Expo-langue: the perfect tense (past participles)

Use this grammar box to continue work on the perfect tense: it focuses on how past participles are formed. There is more information on p. 212 of the Student Book.

R You could write up the infinitive of the verbs used in exercise 1 and ask students to give the past participle of each.

2 À deux. Faites un dialogue, en utilisant les détails dans la grille.

Speaking. In pairs: students make up a dialogue about what they did last weekend using the perfect tense and the word and picture prompts in the grid supplied. A sample exchange is given.

Starter 2

Aim
To revise past participles.

Put students into small teams. Tell them they have three minutes to come up with examples of past participles from the following verb types:

- 4 regular **-er** verbs
- 3 regular **-ir** verbs
- 2 regular **-re** verbs
- 5 irregular verbs

The team with the most correct answers is the winner.

The teaching notes throughout *Expo 4* suggest a variety of Starters and Plenaries which involve students working in teams. You may want to allocate teams at this stage which students can stay in throughout the year. This will save time whenever a team activity comes up. You could also keep an ongoing tally of points won in these activities and award a prize to the team with the highest score at the end of each term/ half-term.

3 Reliez les opinions en français et en anglais. Utilisez le glossaire ou un dictionnaire, si nécessaire.

Reading. Students match the French and English versions of the adjectives used for opinions. Encourage them to use the various strategies they have learned to work out unknown words and then to check their answers/any they are still unsure of in the Vocabulaire at the back of the Student Book or in a dictionary.

You may want to warn students that there are fewer English words than French as some of the French words are synonyms.

Answers

affreux – terrible
amusant – amusing/entertaining
barbant – boring
bien – good
chouette – brilliant/fantastic/great
émouvant – moving
ennuyeux – boring
formidable – brilliant/fantastic/great
génial – brilliant/fantastic/great
intéressant – interesting
lent – slow
long – long
marrant – funny
nul – rubbish
pas mal – not bad
passionnant – exciting
(peu) original – (un-)original
plein d'action – full of action

4 Écoutez ce qu'on a fait le week-end dernier. Pour chaque personne, notez en français: (a) l'activité et (b) l'opinion. (1–6)

Listening. Students listen to six people talking about what they did last weekend. For each speaker, they note in French (a) the activity and (b) the opinion expressed.

Audioscript 22

1 *Hier, je suis allée en ville avec ma copine, Marine. Elle est fan du groupe* Scissor Sisters, *donc elle a acheté leur dernier CD. Après, on a écouté le CD chez elle. Elle l'a trouvé génial, mais c'était un peu ennuyeux pour moi parce que je préfère la techno.*

2 *Samedi soir, mon frère et moi sommes restés à la maison et nous avons regardé* Les Indestructibles *en DVD. D'habitude, je n'aime pas beaucoup les dessins animés, mais c'était chouette. Je l'ai trouvé assez original et très marrant.*

3 *Ma sœur adore lire les BD, surtout les albums de* Tintin *et d'*Astérix. *Il y a deux jours, elle a acheté* Astérix chez les Bretons *et elle l'a lu dans le jardin. Elle a dit que ce n'était pas mal, mais elle préfère* Astérix et Cléopâtre.

4 *Dimanche après-midi, mes parents sont allés au cinéma. Ils ont vu le film français* Papa. *Ils ont dit que c'était bien et très émouvant.*

5 *Vendredi soir, je suis allé chez mon copain Thierry et on a regardé* La ferme célébrités *à la télé. C'est une émission de télé-réalité et c'était nul! Mais après, on a regardé une série policière, qui était assez passionnante et intéressante.*

6 *La semaine dernière, on a fait une sortie scolaire. On est allés au théâtre. On a vu une pièce de Molière. À mon avis, c'était barbant. C'était trop lent et beaucoup trop long.*

Answers

1 (a) écouter un CD (b) génial, un peu ennuyeux
2 (a) regarder un DVD **(b)** chouette – assez original, très marrant
3 (a) lire un BD **(b)** pas mal
4 (a) voir un film au cinéma **(b)** bien, très émouvant
5 (a) regarder la TV **(b)** nul; assez passionnant et intéressant
6 (a) voir une pièce du théâtre **(b)** barbant – trop lent, beaucoup trop long

Expo-langue: the imperfect (opinions)

Use this grammar box to remind students that **c'était** (the imperfect of **c'est**) is used for expressing opinions in the past. There is more information on p. 213 of the Student Book.

Ask students to read through the pronunciation box on **-ant/-ent** and **-on** sounds before they do exercise 5. Ask a few students to demonstrate the words featured by saying them to the class and give feedback on pronunciation.

R Students could then practise this in pairs using the following words: **amusant, éducation, émouvant, lent, long, passionnant, mon, comment.**

5 Vidéoconférence. Interviewez votre partenaire. Qu'est-ce que vous avez fait le week-end dernier? C'était comment?

Speaking. Students imagine that they are going to have a videoconference with students at a French school. They prepare a dialogue in which they talk about what they did last weekend and give their opinion of the activities. Draw their attention to the tip box reminding them to include intensifiers and time phrases in their French.

See p. 18 for suggestions on actually linking up with a partner school in France to exchange information.

6 Qu'est-ce que vous avez fait le week-end dernier? Mentionnez aussi votre famille ou vos copains. Regardez et adaptez les textes de l'exercice 1, en ajoutant des opinions.

Writing. Students write a paragraph saying what they did last weekend, including details of what their family or friends did too. They should reread the texts in exercise 1 and use these as models.

✓ Ask students to read through the tip box before they start. Remind them that it is very important to use a mixture of tenses (ideally past, present and future) in the speaking and writing parts of the exam if they want to attain the highest grades.

Plenary

Put the class into teams. Give each group an event, e.g. **une émission musicale, les vacances, un match de foot, une fête, une journée au collège**, etc. Each person in the group has to come up with a sentence to describe the event in the past, using **C'était** + an appropriate adjective. Each correct phrase wins a point; two points will be given if a negative or an intensifier is used. The team with the most points wins.

See Starter 2 on p. 42 for ideas on organising teams for activities like these.

Cahier d'exercices, page 15

1

Answers

Samedi matin, je suis restée à la maison. J'ài écouté de la musique sur mon Ipod. J'ai reçu mon Ipod pour mon anniversaire. C'est super cool! Puis l'après-midi, ma copine Marine est arrivée et nous sommes allées en ville ensemble. Nous avons pris le train; c'est rapide et ce n'est pas cher. Nous avons fait les magasins; j'ai acheté un nouveau jean avec l'argent que j'ai reçu comme cadeau d'anniversaire et Marine a acheté des boucles d'oreilles et un magazine. Elle est venue chez moi où nous avons mangé une pizza et de la salade. Puis à vingt heures, deux autres copains sont arrivés et on est allés ensemble au cinéma voir une comédie, Chicken Little. C'était chouette: très amusant et original. Je suis rentrée à la maison vers 22 heures trente. C'était une journée pleine d'action!

2

Answers

1 PM **2** F **3** V **4** V **5** V **6** PM **7** F **8** F

3

Answers

Pupil's own answers

4 C'est la fête!

(Student Book pages 32–33)

Main topics and objectives

- Describing special occasions
- Imperfect tense of **avoir** and **être**

Grammar

- Imperfect tense for descriptions (**avoir**/**être**)

Key language

On a fait une grande fête.
On a dansé.
J'ai reçu beaucoup de cadeaux.
On a fait une pique-nique.
Il y avait des feux d'artifice.
On a fêté Noël en famille.
On s'est offert des cadeaux.
On a mangé le grand repas traditionnel.
L'année prochaine, je vais ...
avoir un scooter
y retourner
aller chez mon oncle

Resources

CD1, tracks 23–24
Cahier d'exercices, pages 16–17
Grammaire 3.4

Starter 1

Aim
To practise identifying tenses. To work out one of the uses of the imperfect tense.

☑ Ask students in pairs to read the third text in exercise 1, p. 32 (beginning **L'année dernière ...**) and to list and identify all the verb tenses used.

When checking answers, ask students why each tense was used in the context it appeared.

Point out to students that this use of tenses is a good model to follow in their own writing and speaking, as reference to the past, present and future using the appropriate tenses is essential to gain the highest marks in the exam.

1 Écoutez et lisez les textes. (1–3)

Listening. Students listen to three people describing different celebrations and read the text at the same time.

Audioscript 23

1 *La semaine dernière, c'était mon anniversaire. J'ai eu quinze ans, donc samedi soir, on a fait une grande fête chez nous et j'ai invité une trentaine de mes copains. Mes parents étaient un peu nerveux, mais ça s'est bien passé. J'ai reçu beaucoup de cadeaux et il y avait aussi un délicieux gâteau d'anniversaire. Une copine qui est DJ a apporté ses CD et on a dansé jusqu'à minuit. C'était extra! Une de nos voisines n'était pas très contente du bruit, mais on s'est bien amusés quand même. L'année prochaine, je vais fêter mes seize ans et je vais avoir un scooter!*

2 *Il y a deux ans, j'étais à Nice pour la fête nationale, le quatorze juillet. Nous étions là en vacances, ma famille et moi, et il y avait beaucoup de monde, puisque c'est un jour de congé en France. Il y avait un grand défilé tout le long de la Promenade des Anglais. C'était assez drôle parce que tout le monde était déguisé en clown, en animal, etc. Après, il y avait un bal en plein air. Le soir, il n'y avait pas de place dans les restaurants, donc on a fait un pique-nique sur la plage, en regardant les magnifiques feux d'artifice, ce qui était bien agréable. Je vais y retourner avec mon frère l'année prochaine.*

3 *L'année dernière, comme d'habitude, on a fêté Noël en famille. La veille de Noël, on s'est offert des cadeaux et, puisqu'on est catholiques, ma mère est allée à la messe de minuit avec mes grands-parents. Moi, j'étais trop fatigué pour ça et j'avais un peu mal à la tête, donc je me suis couché de bonne heure. Puis, le jour de Noël, on a mangé le grand repas traditionnel: il y avait des huîtres, du foie gras, de la dinde et comme dessert la bûche de Noël. C'était délicieux. Mais cette année, on va faire quelque chose de différent à Noël. On va aller chez mon oncle au Québec! C'est génial, non?*

Expo-langue: the imperfect for descriptions (*avoir/être*)

Use this grammar box to review using the imperfect for descriptions in the past. The full paradigms of **avoir** and **être** are given and the imperfect of **il y a** (**il y avait**).

2 Traduisez en anglais les mots et les phrases en bleu dans le texte. Utilisez un dictionnaire, si nécessaire.

Reading. Students translate the words and phrases which appear in blue in the texts in exercise 1. They can use a dictionary if necessary, but encourage them first of all to try and work the words out using the various strategies they know: the tip box at the bottom of the page suggests using the context of the material and logic to help you.

Answers

une trentaine – around 30
ça s'est bien passé – it went really well
J'ai reçu beaucoup de cadeaux – I got lots of presents
jusqu'à minuit – until midnight
n'était pas très contente du bruit – (she) wasn't very happy about the noise
on s'est bien amusés – we really enjoyed ourselves
un scooter – a moped
il y avait beaucoup de monde – there were lots of people
un jour de congé – a (public) holiday
un grand défilé – a big/long procession
C'était assez drôle – It was quite funny
un bal – a dance/ball
les feux d'artifice – the fireworks
agréable – pleasant
on a fêté – we celebrated
La veille de Noël – Christmas Eve
on s'est offert – we exchanged/gave each other
la messe de minuit – Midnight mass
des huîtres – (some) oysters
du foie gras – (some) foie gras (paté)
de la dinde – (some) turkey
la bûche de Noël – Yule log

Starter 2

Aim

To consolidate the imperfect tense of **avoir** and **être**.

In pairs: students test each other on the imperfect tense of **avoir** and **être**, taking it in turn to prompt and respond. Only the student prompting has his/her Student Book open. Model an exchange: **avoir/nous – nous avions.**

3 Relisez les textes. Écrivez V (Vrai), F (Faux) ou PM (Pas Mentionné) à côté de chaque phrase.

Reading. Students reread the texts in exercise 1. They then read the ten statements on the texts and decide whether each is true or false or not mentioned in the text.

Answers

1 F **2** PM **3** V **4** F **5** V **6** PM **7** F **8** V **9** PM **10** V

➕ Students could research some French festivals, summarising when and how they are celebrated, such as Epiphany, Easter, Toussaint, etc.

4 Écoutez et complétez les phrases. (1–3)

Listening. Students listen to three people talking about special occasions and complete the three gap-fill sentences for each.

Audioscript 24

– *Thierry, quelle est ta fête préférée et pourquoi?*
– *Je crois que ma fête préférée, c'est le quatorze juillet. Moi, j'habite dans un petit village en Bretagne et tous les ans, pour la fête nationale, il y a une fête de campagne. Je l'aime bien comme fête parce que j'y vais avec mes copains et on peut se coucher plus tard que d'habitude.*
– *Qu'est-ce qu'on fait pour la fête?*
– *Beaucoup des habitants du village s'habillent en costume breton traditionnel, surtout les gens plus âgés. On mange des crêpes, on boit du cidre et le soir, il y a un bal folklorique. Tout le monde danse et on s'amuse bien jusqu'à une heure ou deux heures du matin!*

– *Laure, comment vas-tu fêter Noël cette année?*
– *Bof, on va faire la même chose que tous les ans, c'est-à-dire qu'on va aller chez ma grand-mère, qui habite à Toulouse. On va y arriver vers la fin de l'après-midi la veille de Noël et on va y rester deux ou trois jours.*
– *Qu'est-ce que vous allez faire là-bas?*
– *On va s'offrir des cadeaux, bien sûr. Je vais acheter des chocolats pour ma grand-mère parce qu'elle adore ça. Puis, le jour de Noël, on va manger le repas de Noël traditionnel: de la dinde et une bûche de Noël que mon père, qui est pâtissier, va préparer. C'est toujours pareil, mais c'est agréable quand même.*

– *Arthur, qu'est-ce que tu as fait pour fêter ton dernier anniversaire?*
– *C'était chouette parce que j'ai eu seize ans et mes parents m'ont donné la permission de sortir avec mes copains. D'abord, on est allé au bowling et après, on a mangé chez McDonald. Ensuite, on est allés en boîte et on a dansé jusqu'à minuit. Il y avait trop de monde et on avait très chaud, mais c'était marrant. Je suis rentré vers une heure du matin et j'étais très fatigué.*
– *Qu'est-ce que tu as reçu comme cadeau d'anniversaire?*
– *J'étais très content parce que j'ai reçu une chaîne hi-fi de mes parents et mon frère m'a offert un jeu d'ordinateur.*

Answers

Thierry

a Le quatorze juillet, il y a **une fête** dans son **village** en Bretagne.
b Ce soir-là, Thierry et ses **copains** peuvent **se coucher** plus tard que d'habitude.
c On **mange** des crêpes, **boit** du cidre et tout le monde **danse**.

Laure

d À Noël, elle va aller chez **sa grand-mère**, qui **habite à** Toulouse.
e Comme **cadeau**, Laure va acheter **des chocolats** pour sa grand-mère.
f On va manger de **la dinde** et le père de Laure, qui est pâtissier, va préparer une **bûche**.

Arthur

g Pour fêter **son anniversaire**, d'abord, il est allé au **bowling** avec **ses copains**.
h Le soir, en boîte **il y avait** trop de monde et **on avait** très chaud, mais c'était **marrant**.
i Arthur a **reçu** une chaîne hi-fi de ses parents et un **jeu d'ordinateur** de son frère.

5 Vidéoconférence. Préparez vos réponses aux questions suivantes:

Speaking. Students imagine that they are going to have a videoconference with students at a French school. They prepare their replies to the questions supplied (on the topic of celebrating birthdays/ other special occasions in the past). As before, suggest students work out what they want to say and then produce a short list of key words as a reminder when they are speaking.

See p. 18 for suggestions on actually linking up with a partner school in France to exchange information.

6 À deux. Interviewez votre partenaire. Si possible, enregistrez la conversation.

Speaking. In pairs: students interview each other as though doing a videoconference. If possible, allow them to record their conversations and play them back. They should comment constructively on each other's performance.

7 Décrivez une fête ou une occasion spéciale. Écrivez au présent, au passé composé, à l'imparfait et au futur proche.

Writing. ☑ Students write a description of a special occasion, such as a birthday or Christmas, etc. Before they start, ask them to think about how they are going to work in examples of four tenses: the present, the perfect, the imperfect and the near future. Encourage them to look back at the unit for ideas.

Plenary

Ask students to tell you how the imperfect was used in this unit. (for descriptions) Then go round the class asking students each to give you a sentence about a party using a verb in the imperfect (e.g. **il y avait, j'avais, j'étais, c'était,** etc.). Ask the class to feedback on each sentence – a thumbs up if the imperfect has been used correctly; a thumbs down if not.

Cahier d'exercices, pages 16–17

See unit 5 for answers.

5 Il s'agit de quoi?

(Student Book pages 34–35)

Main topics and objectives

- Describing what you saw or read
- Expressing complex ideas in a simple way

Grammar

- **mieux, pire(s)**
- **le/la/les meilleur(e)(s), le/la/les plus mauvais(e)(s)**

Key language

C'est l'histoire de …
L'histoire se déroule …
Le film est plein d'action.
À mon avis, la meilleure partie du film/livre, c'est …
l'acteur/l'actrice
l'ambiance

Resources

CD1, tracks 25–26
Cahier d'exercices, pages 16–18
Grammaire 2.4

Starter 1

Aim
To use context to work out new vocabulary.

Write up the following and give students three minutes in pairs to work out the English versions. Tell them these are all in the same category: they should start by looking for obvious clues to work out what the category is.

Harry Potter à l'École des sorciers
Le lion, la sorcière blanche et l'armoire magique
Rock academy
La guerre des mondes
Le seigneur des Anneaux
L'âge de glace

1 Écoutez et lisez les textes. (1–2)

Listening. Students listen to two people talking about a film/a book they have enjoyed recently and read the text at the same time.

Audioscript 25

– *Qu'est-ce que tu as vu ou lu récemment, Nathan?*

– *J'ai regardé* Batman begins *en DVD. C'est l'histoire de l'origine du super-héros Batman. Alors que Bruce Wayne est toujours enfant, un voleur tue ses parents. Plus tard comme adulte, Bruce revient à Gotham City, où il décide de se déguiser en chauve-souris pour lutter contre la criminalité. Le film est plein d'action et de personnages extraordinaires, comme «The Scarecrow», un méchant qui se déguise en épouvantail! À mon avis, c'est le meilleur film Batman et Christian Bale est excellent dans le rôle principal, mieux que les autres acteurs qui ont joué ce rôle.*

– *Et toi, Marine? Qu'est-ce que tu as vu ou lu récemment?*

– *J'ai lu* Harry Potter et le prisonnier d'Azkaban. *C'est le troisième livre de la série et à mon avis, c'est le meilleur. Dans cette histoire, Harry apprend que son parrain, Sirius Black, s'est échappé de la prison d'Azkaban et il pense que Sirius veut le tuer. Mais avec l'assistance de ses copains Ron et Hermione, il découvre la vérité et réussit à combattre ses vrais ennemis. Harry tombe amoureux aussi d'une jolie fille qui s'appelle Cho Chang. À mon avis, la meilleure partie du livre, c'est la partie dans le train, où Harry est attaqué par les Dementors. Ils sont les plus mauvais monstres de la série – pires que les vampires!*

Expo-langue

Use this grammar box to introduce the irregular comparative and superlative forms of **bon** and **mauvais**. There is more information on p. 211 of the Student Book.

2 Trouvez le français.

Reading. Students find the French for the 14 English expressions listed.

Answers

1 C'est l'histoire
2 un voleur tue ses parents
3 il décide de se déguiser en
4 pour lutter contre la criminalité
5 personnages extraordinaires
6 un échant
7 le rôle principal
8 le troisième livre de la série
9 Harry apprend que
10 avec l'assistance de ses copains
11 il découvre la verité
12 réussit a combattre ses vrais ennemis
13 Harry tombe amoureux
14 la meilleure partie du livre

3 Décrivez un film ou un livre de votre choix (ou choisissez un des titres ci-dessous), en adaptant des phrases de l'exercice 1.

Writing. Students describe a film or book, either of their own choice or using one of the suggestions given.

Students could research another film in French on the Internet, using (for example) the

Allo Ciné website (go to www.heinemann.co.uk/hotlinks and enter the express code 7898T) or keying the film name in English after clicking French preferences in your search engine. Ask them to summarise the details of the plot and to write a list of at least ten new words that they have worked out from the site (relating to the film or to the instructions on the site).

Starter 2

Aim
To practise using the superlative forms of **bien** and **mauvais.**

Write up the following in two columns, replacing the scored-through words with .... Ask students in pairs to complete the French translation with the correct comparative/superlative. If they need support, tell them to look back at the Expo-langue box on p. 34 of the Student Book.

1 the best Harry Potter DVD	**le ~~meilleur~~ DVD Harry Potter**
2 the worst song on the CD	**la ~~plus mauvaise~~ chanson du CD**
3 the best part of the film	**la ~~meilleure~~ partie du film**
4 the best American comedies	**les ~~meilleures~~ comédies américaines**
5 the worst monsters in the world	**les ~~plus mauvais~~ monstres du monde**

4 À deux. Préparez trois ou quatre phrases sur un autre film ou livre. Lisez-les à votre partenaire. Il/Elle doit deviner quel film ou quel livre c'est.

Speaking. In pairs: students write down three or four statements about another film or book, without saying the name. They read these out to their partner, who has to identify it.

Before they start, read together through the tip box, which focuses on keeping the text simple. Emphasise the importance of using what you know how to say and the resources available to you (in the form of texts, activity questions, etc.), rather than starting in English and trying to find the French for more complicated expressions. Developing this as a technique will make them more confident and more fluent language learners.

5 Écoutez et complétez le texte.

Listening. Students listen to the review of the French film *Les Choristes* and read through the gap-fill version of the recording. They work out what the ten missing words are (these are supplied in random order for support).

Alert students to the fact that when answers are given in this way, they often contain 'distractors', i.e. words which aren't used. It is worth bearing this in mind when they are checking their answers.

Audioscript 26

Les Choristes *est un des* ***meilleurs*** *films français des dernières années. Il s'agit de quoi?* ***L'histoire*** *se déroule en 1948, au Pensionnat de Fond de l'Étang, une* ***école*** *pour des garçons délinquants au cœur de la campagne française. Clément Mathieu,* ***professeur*** *de musique, mais qui est au chômage (rôle interprété par Gérard Jugnot), y arrive pour* ***travailler*** *comme surveillant. Malgré l'intimidation des élèves* ***difficiles*** *et les méthodes sévères que le directeur, Monsieur Rachin, utilise pour les discipliner, Clément* ***décide*** *d'essayer quelque chose de nouveau. Il décide d'apprendre la* ***musique*** *aux garçons et d'organiser une chorale. Il* ***découvre*** *que ses élèves ont des dons musicaux, mais l'arrivée d'un* ***garçon*** *très difficile met en péril ce projet. C'est par la magie du chant que Clément réussit à changer la vie de ses élèves. C'est un film sympa, émouvant et très bien joué.*

Answers

Also in bold in the audioscript
1 meilleurs **2** l'histoire **3** école **4** professeur **5** travailler
6 difficiles **7** décide **8** musique **9** découvre **10** garçon

6 Relisez le texte et répondez aux questions en anglais.

Reading. Students read the text in exercise 5 again and then answer the eight questions on it in English.

Answers

1 It takes place in 1948.
2 It's a school for delinquent boys.
3 He can't find work as a teacher.
4 He is very strict.
5 He teaches them music/to sing.
6 A very difficult boy arrives at the school.
7 It changes their lives.
8 He likes it – he thinks it's nice, moving and very well acted.

\+ Students could write a more detailed synopsis of a film they have seen recently and that they would recommend.

Plenary

Ask students to summarise the comparative and superlative forms of **bon** and **mauvais.** Then ask students in turn to recommend a film/book/CD to you using **À mon avis, le meilleur film/livre/CD, c'est ...**

Cahier d'exercices, pages 16–17

1

Answers

Possible answer:
Film (Le monde de Narnia) tells of the battle between good and evil. Review tells the story of the film. Section B: Sophie tells of a visit to the cinema with her family to see Narnia and they all say what they thought of the film. They all liked it.

2

Answers

This film tells about the battle between good and evil.
Jadis, the white witch puts a curse on Narnia.
The magical world is plunged into a bitter winter for a century.
Narnia is going to be saved by the four children.
The four children are evacuated to London during the bombings of the 2nd World War.
Lucy discovers a magic wardrobe.
The children get to know numerous incredible creatures.
You see 23 different types of creatures.
The Pevensie family meets the lion.
Aslan frees Narnia from the curse.

3

Answers

French word	Clue/How I worked it out	Meaning
fascinant	think of the English	fascinating
jeté une malédiction	*think of the French word* ***mal***	cast a spell
sorcière	think of the English	witch
faire la connaissance de	*verb –* ***connaître***	to get to know
incroyable	*verb –* ***croire***	unbelievable
suivant	*verb* ***suivre*** *– ending –****ant***	following
réfugiés	think of the English	evacuated
émerveillement	*think of* ***merveilleux***	amazement
nombreuses	*think of* ***nombre***	numerous
une partie de cache-cache	*think of* ***cacher***	game of hide and seek
la Seconde Guerre Mondiale	*think of* ***monde***	2nd World War

4

Answers

1 Sophie & Antoine **2** Alexandre **3** Charlotte
4 Alexandre **5** Charlotte

Cahier d'exercices, Grammaire, page 18

1

Answers

1 J'y vais souvent.
2 Je la regarde souvent le soir.
3 Toutes les semaines, je le fais.
4 J'y vais rarement.
5 Je les regarde en DVD.
6 Je les trouve super!

2

Answers

Start of answers given – endings according to pupil's opinions.
1 Je les trouve super.
2 Je (ne) les regarde (pas) …
3 Je les fais …
4 J'y vais …
5 J'y vais …
6 Je (ne) les regarde (pas) …

3

Answers

Je veux bien aller au cinéma mais je ne peux pas parce que mes parents veulent sortir.
Tu veux aller au centre sportif samedi ou est-ce que tu dois garder ta petite sœur? Samedi, normalement, mon frère et moi, nous devons promener les chiens, puis mon frère doit laver la voiture.
Alors, si tu peux venir samedi, je vais demander à Claire et Mathilde si elles veulent venir aussi. Je pense que Claire peut venir, mais Mathilde, ce n'est pas sûr. On doit être au centre sportif avant 11 heures.
Sébastien

Contrôle continu: Un de mes films préféré[s]

(Student Book pages 36–37)

Topics revised

- Writing a review of a film

1 Copiez les phrases en bleu dans le texte et trouvez l'équivalent en anglais ci-dessous.

Students copy out all the phrases shown in blue in the text and find the English phrase from those listed (**1–12**).

Answers

réalisé par
8 directed by
le film raconte l'histoire
5 the film tells the story
après la mort de
12 after the death of
la vedette du film
4 the star of the film
est tuée par
7 is killed by
tout finit bien
1 everything ends happily
tout à fait original
6 completely original
très bien joué
10 very well acted
doué comme acteur
9 a really talented actor
Une des meilleures scènes
3 one of the best scenes
l'ambiance du film
2 the atmosphere of the film
Je vais recommander le film à tous mes copains
11 I am going to recommend the film to all my friends

2 Imaginez que vous êtes Mathis. Répondez aux questions en français.

Students reread the text. They imagine they are Mathis and reply to the ten questions in French from his perspective.

Answers

1. J'ai vu ce film il y a deux ans.
2. Je l'ai vu en anglais (sous-titré en français).
3. C'est une comédie, un film d'action et un film d'horreur.
4. C'est l'histoire des orphelins Baudelaire et leur oncle qui veut le tuer pour hériter leur fortune.
5. Les personnages principaux sont les enfants Baudelaire – Violet, Klaus et Sunny – et leur oncle, le Comte Olaf.
6. Jim Carrey est la vedette du film – il joue le rôle du Comte Olaf.
7. Il est vraiment doué comme acteur: il peut être sinistre et drôle en même temps.
8. C'est un film tout à fait original, passionnant, amusant et très bien joué. Jim Carrey est doué comme acteur et le film a une ambiance très intéressante, avec des personnages et des événements extraordinaires.
9. Je vais recommander ce film à tous mes copains.
10. Je voudrais lire les livres de Lemony Snicket pour découvrir la suite de l'histoire.

3 Décrivez un film que vous avez vu ou un livre que vous avez lu en donnant votre opinion.

Using Mathis's text and the **Boîte à outils** section to help them, students write their own review of a film or a book.

À l'oral (AQA edition)

(Student Book page 177)

Topics revised

- making arrangements to go out
- booking tickets for the theatre
- talking about your favourite TV programme
- talking about books/films you like
- talking about celebrations in the past

☑ Introduce students to the **Tu parles!** feature: this comes up in the **À l'oral** section throughout the course. It introduces more colloquial language that students can use in the speaking tests to sound more authentic.

1 You are arranging to go out with your French friend. Your partner will play the part of your friend and will speak first.

Roleplay. Students practise making arrangments to go out to the cinema. Remind them that they should take it in turn to play each role in roleplays.

Before they begin, ask students what difference they note between the questions in exercise 1 and exercise 2. Ask them to summarise when **tu** is used and when **vous** is used, drawing their attention to the tip box at the end of the roleplays.

☑ Remind them what the **!** symbol signifies: they will have to give a response which they have not prepared. How can they get themselves ready for this?

2 You go to a theatre in France to book tickets. Your partner will play the booking clerk and will speak first.

Roleplay. Students practise booking tickets for the theatre, taking it in turn to be the customer and the theatre employee.

3 Prepare a ninety-second presentation called *Mon émission de télé préférée.*

Presentation. Students prepare a ninety-second presentation on their favourite television programme.

☑ Point out the tip box, which reminds students to use what they know and to keep the content simple. Students are also encouraged to make sure they include examples of verbs in the present, past and future to gain the highest grades.

Look together at the cue card supplied and ask students to use this to reconstruct what they might say. What do they need to remember when putting cue cards together? Students should then prepare their own talk, using a similar cue card for support, and give their talk to a partner or group.

4 Possible conversation questions:

Conversation. These are key questions to practise for the speaking exam, taken from the module as a whole. Students can practise asking and answering the questions in pairs.

☑ Tell them to look at the questions carefully before they structure a response, as this will tell them what tense they need to use.

À l'oral (Edexcel edition)

(Student Book page 177)

Topics revised

- making arrangements to go out
- booking tickets for the theatre
- talking about your favourite TV programme
- talking about books/films you like
- talking about celebrations, including celebrations in the past and future

1 You are arranging to go out with your French friend. Your partner will play the part of your friend and will begin the conversation.

Roleplay Type B. Students practise making arrangments to go out to the cinema. Remind them that they should take it in turn to play each role in roleplays.

Before they begin, ask students what difference they note between the questions in exercise 1 and exercise 2. Ask them to summarise when **tu** is used and when **vous** is used, drawing their attention to the tip box at the end of the roleplays.

2 You are on holiday in France and go to the theatre to book tickets. Your partner will play the part of the employee and will begin the conversation.

Roleplay Type B. Students practise booking tickets for the theatre, taking it in turn to be the customer and the theatre employee.

3 Presentation and general conversation

Presentation. Students prepare a one-minute presentation on their favourite television programme.

☑ Point out the tip box, which reminds students not to use all they know in the presentation, but to keep something back for the conversation.

Look together at the cue card supplied and ask students to use this to reconstruct what they might say. What do they need to remember when putting cue cards together? Students should then prepare their own talk, using a similar cue card for support, and give their talk to a partner or group.

Possible conversation questions. These are key questions to practise for the speaking exam, taken from the module as a whole. Students can practise asking and answering the questions in pairs.

☑ Tell them to look at the questions carefully before they structure a response, as this will tell them which tense they need to use.

À l'oral (OCR edition)

(Student Book page 177)

Topics revised

- talking about celebrations in the past
- talking about your favourite TV programme
- talking about books/films you like

1 Last year you were in France on your birthday. Use the notes below to describe what you did.

Roleplay Type 3. Students practise describing a celebration in the past, using the text and picture prompts supplied.

☑ Tell students that they can gain extra marks when doing *Type 3 Roleplays* in the exam by doing the following:

- developing the story (i.e. adding details in addition to those required by the specific prompts)
- responding appropriately to interruptions by the examiner (e.g. by confirming or adding details)
- expressing and justifying their opinions.

2 Prepare a one-minute presentation called *Mon émission de télé préférée.*

Presentation. Students prepare a one-minute presentation on their favourite television programme.

☑ Point out the tip box, which reminds students to use what they know and to keep the content simple. Students are also encouraged to include a wide variety of opinions and justifications to gain the highest grades.

Look together at the cue card supplied and ask students to use this to reconstruct what they might say. What do they need to remember when putting cue cards together? Students should then prepare their own talk, using a similar cue card for support, and give their talk to a partner or group.

3 *Qu'est-ce qu'on fait/a fait/va faire?*: possible conversation questions

Conversation. These are key questions to practise for the speaking exam, taken from the module as a whole. Students can practise asking and answering the questions in pairs.

☑ Tell them to look at the questions carefully before they structure a response, as this will tell them what tense they need to use.

2 À toi

(Student Book pages 188–189)

- Self-access reading and writing

1 Lisez les annonces et trouvez les abréviations.

Reading. Students read the four adverts and find the abbreviations for the eight French expressions listed.

☑ Before they start, students should read the tip box, which reminds them of useful strategies to use when working out unknown vocabulary.

Answers

1 *Ven* **2** Dim **3** Pl **4** gpes **5** résa **6** 1er **7** – de 12 ans **8** Mº

2 Relisez les annonces et répondez aux questions en anglais.

Reading. Students read the adverts in exercise 1 again and answer the ten questions in English.

Answers

1 8.30 pm **2** Monday **3** Abba **4** age 4 **5** *any 4 from:* tigers, elephants, ostriches, zebras, camels, dogs **6** 6€ **7** in the castle **8** around 10.30 pm **9** Bastille **10** tickets are sold out

3 Écrivez une annonce en utilisant les détails suivants. Utilisez des abréviations appropriées.

Writing. Students write their own advert based on the details supplied and using the appropriate abbreviations.

4 Lisez les phrases. Notez la lettre de la bonne annonce de l'exercice 1.

Reading. Students read the texts and note for each the letter of the advert referred to (from exercise 1).

Answers

1 D **2** B **3** A **4** D **5** C **6** B **7** A **8** C

5 Trouvez la seconde partie de chaque phrase.

Students match the sentence halves to produce complete sentences.

Answers

1 b **2** f **3** d **4** g **5** e **6** a **7** c

6 Écrivez une description d'une visite à un des divertissements de l'exercice 1. Utilisez des phrases des exercices 4 et 5 ci-dessus, si vous voulez.

Writing. Students write a description of a trip to one of the events advertised in exercise 1, using phrases from exercises 4 and 5.

Module 3 Là où j'habite (Student Book pages 40–55)

Unit	Main topics and objectives	Grammar
Déjà vu 1 **Ma maison** (pp. 40–41)	Talking about where you live More about adjectives	Position of adjectives – generally after – exceptions before (**grand/petit**)
Déjà vu 2 **Ma chambre** (pp. 42–43)	Talking about your own room **plus** and **moins**	The comparative – **plus/moins ... que** – **meilleur**
1 J'habite en ville (pp. 44–45)	Talking about the advantages and disadvantages of where you live **beau, nouveau** and **vieux**	**beau, vieux, nouveau** – before the noun – special forms (**bel, vieil, nouvel**)
2 Aujourd'hui et autrefois (pp. 46–47)	Comparing where you used to live and where you live now Using the imperfect tense	Imperfect tense – usage ('used to'; descriptions) – formation
3 La France métropolitaine (pp. 48–49)	The geography of France The superlative	The superlative – **le/la plus/moins ...** – **le/la meilleur(e)**
4 Ma ville (pp. 50–51)	Talking about a town **on peut/on pourrait** + infinitive	**pouvoir** + infinitive
Contrôle continu **Lyon** (pp. 52–53)	*Coursework* Advertising the local area	*All main grammar points of the module*
À l'oral (pp. 178)	*Exam speaking practice* Talking about your house Talking about the area you live in	*All main grammar points of the module*
À toi (pp. 190–191)	Self-access reading and writing	

Déjà vu 1: Ma maison

(Student Book pages 40–41)

Main topics and objectives

- Talking about where you live
- More about adjectives

Grammar

- Position of adjectives
  - generally after
  - exceptions before (**grand**/**petit**)

Key language

House locations
Rooms in a house

Resources

CD1, tracks 27–29
Cahier d'exercices, page 21
Grammaire 2.1

Starter 1

Aim
To revise vocabulary to talk about the rooms in a house.

Use exercise 1 on p. 40 as the starter.

1 Écoutez et lisez. Écrivez des titres sur l'image.

Listening. Students listen to Arthur talking about where he lives and read the text at the same time. They then use the text to write captions for each of the eight pictures shown.

Audioscript 27

– *J'habite un grand appartement dans un immeuble moderne en ville. Nous y habitons depuis cinq ans. Notre appartement se trouve au cinquième étage. Nous avons une petite entrée, une grande cuisine, un grand salon, deux grandes chambres et une petite chambre, une salle de bains, une douche et des toilettes. Mes parents ont la plus grande chambre et mes deux sœurs partagent l'autre. La petite chambre est à moi, et gare à ne pas y entrer quand je ne suis pas là!*

Answers

1 *l'immeuble où j'habite*
2 une (petite) entrée
3 une (grande) cuisine
4 un (grand) salon
5 une salle de bains
6 la chambre de mes sœurs
7 la (petite) chambre/ma chambre
8 des toilettes

2 Choisissez la bonne réponse.

Reading. Students read the eight sentences and choose the correct ending for each from the three options given (**a**, **b** or **c**).

Answers

1 b **2** b **3** a **4** a **5** b **6** b **7** a **8** a

Expo-langue: position of adjectives

Use this grammar box to review the position of adjectives in French before students do the extension activity: most adjectives come after the noun; certain exceptions (many of them very common/useful adjectives) come before the noun, e.g. **petit** and **grand**. Suggest students keep a list of adjectives that come before the noun and/or find some way of distinguishing these in their vocabulary notebooks/lists.

There is more information on p. 210 of the Student Book.

➕ Using the text in exercise 1 as a model, students write a description of their own home.

3 Écoutez et notez: masculin (M) ou féminin (F)?

Listening. Students listen to 10 phrases on the recording and note whether the adjective in each is masculine (M) or feminine (F).

Before playing the recording, ask students to recap on when the feminine form of an adjective is pronounced differently (only when the masculine form ends in a consonant; if it ends in a vowel, it has no effect on pronunciation).

Audioscript 28

1 des grandes villes
2 des petits villages
3 des grandes cathédrales
4 des petites églises
5 des grands châteaux
6 des petites maisons
7 des grandes rivières
8 des petits bateaux
9 des petits champs
10 des grandes forêts

Answers

1 F **2** M **3** F **4** F **5** M **6** F **7** F **8** M **9** M **10** F

4 À deux. Complétez les phrases avec *grand(e)* et *petit(e)* et puis prononcez les phrases.

Speaking. In pairs: students complete the 12 phrases supplied, using first **grand(e)** and then **petit(e)**, taking care to supply the adjective in the correct form in each case. Can they work out what **chienne** means?

Before students begin, read through the pronunciation box together. It focuses on the sound of the letter **p**, contrasting its pronunciation in English and French. Ask a few students to find and say aloud examples of French words featuring **p** and give feedback on pronunciation.

R Students make up further examples of their own to test each other.

Starter 2

Aim
To practise adjective agreement.

Write up the following:

maison – grand – depuis 2 ans – troisième étage
cuisine (petit) – salon (grand) – 4 chambres (petit/grand)

Ask students to write a description of a house using the details supplied.

When checking answers, ask students to summarise the rules for adjective agreement and position.

5 Trouvez la bonne définition.

Reading. Students find the correct definition (from **a–d**) for the four French words (**1–4**).

Answers
1 d **2** a **3** c **4** b

6 Où habitent-ils? (1–4)

Listening. Students listen to four people describing where they live. For each they identify the type of house, what is in the house/flat using the appropriate pictures (from **a–l**) and the length of time the person has lived there.

Audioscript 29

1 Notre maison est petite. Nous y habitons depuis dix ans. La maison est en ville. C'est une maison à trois étages … Il y a cinq chambres. Ma chambre est au deuxième … dans les combles. Au rez-de-chaussée, il y a l'entrée, la cuisine et la salle de séjour … Nous avons une cave au sous-sol, mais nous n'avons pas de jardin.

2 J'habite un bungalow neuf avec un grand jardin tout autour … Il y a trois chambres, une pour mes parents, une pour mon frère et une pour moi, c'est tout. Nous avons déménagé il y a quatre ans.

3 Nous habitons un grand immeuble en banlieue. Notre appartement est au sixième étage. Il y a quatre chambres. Nous n'avons pas de jardin, mais nous avons un grand balcon … On y habite depuis cinq ans.

4 Ma mère et moi habitons un appartement … dans un immeuble en ville. L'appartement n'est pas grand. Il y a deux chambres: une pour moi et une pour ma mère … Il y a un garage … Nous y habitons depuis deux ans.

Answers

1 *b, h, i, 10 ans*	**3** d, k, g, 5 ans
2 a, f, l, 4 ans	**4** c, j, e, 2 ans

7 Vidéoconférence. Où habitez-vous? Préparez une présentation.

Speaking. Students imagine that they are going to have a videoconference with students at a French school. They prepare a presentation on their house/flat using the grid supplied for support. As before, suggest students work out what they want to say and then produce a short list of key words as a reminder when they are speaking.

8 Décrivez votre maison idéale.

Writing. Students write a paragraph describing their ideal house. They can use the grid in exercise 7 for support as well as their imagination. A sample structure is provided.

Plenary

Choose a good response to exercise 8 and display it to the class. Ask students to identify why it is a good answer. Cover accuracy, use of detail, inclusion of connectives, etc.

Cahier d'exercices, page 21

1

Answers

1. J'habite à la campagne.
2. J'habite une maison.
3. J'y habite depuis 3 ans.
4. Au rez-de-chaussée, il y a une salle de bains et trois chambres; la chambre de mes parents, la chambre de moi et mon frère et la chambre de ma sœur.
5. Au premier étage, il y a un garage, une grande cuisine, un grand salon, une petite salle à manger et des toilettes.

Answers
Pupil's own answers

Déjà vu 2: Ma chambre

(Student Book pages 42–43)

Main topics and objectives

- Talking about your own room
- **plus** and **moins**

Grammar

- The comparative
  - **plus/moins ... que**
  - **meilleur**

Key language

Furniture

Resources

CD1, tracks 30–31
Cahier d'exercices, page 22
Grammaire 2.4

Starter 1

Aim
To revise the comparative.

Write up:

Tintin est moins haut que Shrek.

Lisa Simpson est plus intelligente que Bart Simpson.

Ask students if they agree with these statements. Recap on the comparative, then ask them, working in pairs, to come up with six statements of their own using **moins ... que** and **plus ... que**. The statements can be about celebrities, fictional characters and/or themselves and their friends.

1 Écoutez et lisez. Complétez les phrases ci-dessous.

Listening. Students listen to Coralie and Hervé discussing Hervé's bedroom and how it compares to the one in the picture. They then complete the eight sentences with the relevant details.

Before students start work on the sentences, read through the grammar box on the comparative.

Audioscript 30

- *Ta chambre est comme la chambre sur l'image?*
- *Non, elle est nettement plus petite.*
- *As-tu un lit comme ça?*
- *Non, il est plus grand que mon lit.*
- *Et la chaise?*
- *Elle est plus confortable que ma chaise.*
- *Et l'étagère?*
- *Elle est plus moderne que mon étagère.*
- *Et la commode?*
- *C'est plus pratique que ma commode. Les tiroirs sont plus grands.*
- *L'ordinateur?*
- *C'est plus cher que mon ordinateur.*
- *La télé?*
- *Ma télé est moins grande.*
- *L'armoire?*
- *C'est plus jolie que mon armoire. Mon armoire est démodée.*
- *Et la table?*
- *Ma table est moins haute.*

Answers

1 La chambre d'Hervé est **plus petit** que celle du catalogue.
2 Son lit est moins **grand/plus petit**.
3 Sa chaise est **moins confortable**.
4 Son étagère est **moins moderne**.
5 Sa commode est **moins pratique**.
6 Son ordinateur est **moins cher**.
7 Sa télé est **moins grand/plus petit**.
8 Son armoire est **moins jolie**.

Expo-langue: the comparative

Use this to review how the comparative is formed. There is more information on p. 211 of the Student Book.

R Students could identify all the instances of the comparative in the text for exercise 1.

2 Comparez votre chambre avec la chambre ci-dessus. À deux, posez et répondez aux questions.

Speaking. In pairs: students compare their own bedroom to the one pictured in exercise 1, taking it in turn to ask and answer questions. A sample exchange is given.

Starter 2

Aim
To revise vocabulary for items of furniture.

Write up the following as anagrams (answers in brackets for reference only). Tell students they are all items you would find in a bedroom. Which pair can solve them most quickly, writing them out with the correct indefinite article and an English translation?

apécan	(canapé)
dinaretour	(ordinateur)
mocodem	(commode)
retagéè	(étagère)
ireroma	(armoire)

3 Où mettent-ils les meubles? Ils font des bêtises. Écoutez et notez.

Listening. Students listen to two boys playing on the computer. They are moving the furniture about a virtual house, choosing unexpected locations. Students need to note each item of furniture and where it ends up.

Audioscript 31

- *Je peux jouer?*
- *Oui, bien sûr.*
- *Qu'est-ce qu'il faut faire?*
- *Tu n'as jamais joué aux Sims?*
- *Non … Tu sais que je n'ai pas d'ordinateur…*
- *Ah … Bon, on fait une maison … comme ça … et puis, on clique pour choisir des meubles … Et on fait glisser les meubles dans les pièces … comme ça, avec la souris. Bon, qu'est-ce qu'on a?*
- *Ben … il y a une armoire …*
- *Une armoire … Mettons-la dans la cuisine … derrière la table … Fais-la glisser … Oui, voilà.*
- *OK. Et le frigo?*
- *Le frigo? Mets-le dans la salle de bains … devant la baignoire.*
- *Frigo … Salle de bains … Et le grand lit?*
- *Mets-le dans … le salon, devant la fenêtre.*
- *Et le canapé?*
- *Dans la salle de bains … dans la baignoire.*
- *Et la commode?*
- *La commode?… Mets-la dans le garage.*
- *Et les chaises?*
- *Euh … dans le jardin.*
- *Et la lampe?*
- *Mets-la dans le frigo.*
- *Dans le frigo? Bon … Et qu'est-ce qu'on fait maintenant?*
- *Il faut choisir une famille …*
- *Les enfants! Venez manger!*

Answers

armoire – *cuisine*
frigo – salle de bains
grand lit – salon
canapé – salle de bains
commode – garage
chaises – jardin
lampe – frigo

4 Faites la liste. Où est-ce qu'ils ont mis les meubles?

Writing. Students use their answers to exercise 3 to write out sentences saying where the boys put the items of furniture.

Answers

Ils ont mis l'armoire dans la cuisine.
Ils ont mis le frigo dans la salle de bains.
Ils ont mis le grand lit dans le salon.
Ils ont mis le canapé dans la salle de bains.
Ils ont mis la commode dans le garage.
Ils ont mis les chaises dans le jardin.
Ils ont mis la lampe dans le frigo.

5 À deux. Vous allez jouer. Faites des suggestions bizarres!

Speaking. In pairs: students pretend they are playing the same computer game as the boys in exercise 3 and make up weird suggestions for where to put the ten items pictured. A sample exchange is given.

Before students begin, read through the tip box on the direct object pronoun together. Ask students if they also remember the plural form (**les**). Ask students what they notice about the position of the pronoun. Explain that although the direct object pronoun usually comes before the verb, when it is used with an imperative, it comes after.

6 Lisez et choisissez la bonne réponse.

Reading. Students read Luc's text. They then read the eight sentences and choose the correct ending for each from the three options given (**a**, **b** or **c**).

Answers

1 b **2** b **3** a **4** b **5** b **6** b **7** a **8** b

7 Ma chambre. Décrivez votre chambre.

Writing. Students write a paragraph describing their own bedroom. Encourage them to use the *Vocabulaire* section or a dictionary as necessary.

Plenary

Ask the class to tell you the forms of the direct object pronoun, using **le vélo**, **la chaise** and **les livres**. Then prompt with (e.g.) **les livres – la chambre** for a student to respond **Mets-les dans la chambre**. That student then prompts another in the same way, and so on.

Déjà vu 2: Ma chambre

Cahier d'exercices, page 22

1

Answers

1 à l'aise
2 seuls
3 lorsqu'
4 ton bureau
5 l'endroit
6 ils se sentent

2

Answers

1 *The number of young people who say* that their bedroom is where they feel most at ease.
2 14% find that the most personal objects are their music and their bed.
3 49% listen to music as the main activity they do in their bedroom.
4 31% think their desk and the contents are the most personal object in their room.
5 44% think homework is the main activity they do in their bedroom.
6 16% think their posters and artwork are their most personal objects in their room.
7 28% think reading is their main activity.

3

Answers

My bedroom is the only place where I feel calm. In it I have my books, my computer, posters, photos, my magazines and my love letters. My parents respect this privacy and in exchange, I do the household chores in my room. I also invite my friends to my room but I like being alone too. It relaxes me.

1 J'habite en ville

(Student Book pages 44–45)

Main topics and objectives

- Talking about the advantages and disadvantages of where you live
- **beau, nouveau** and **vieux**

Grammar

- **beau, vieux, nouveau**
  - before the noun
  - special forms (**bel, vieil, nouvel**)

Key language

beau/bel/belle
nouveau/nouvel/nouvelle
vieux/vieil/vieille
ancien(ne)
joli(e)
moderne
neuf/neuve
pittoresque
récent(e)
traditionel(le)
Chez nous, le problème, c'est ...
Il y a trop de ...
C'est à cause du/de la/des ...
la circulation
la pollution
les gaz d'échappement
le véhicule
le poids lourd
le périphérique
la place de stationnement
la station-service
le transport en commun
La pollution est devenue épouvantable.
Le pire, ce sont les poids lourds.
C'est tout le temps bruyant.
Il y a de plus en plus souvent des inondations.
On a construit une nouvelle autoroute tout près de chez nous.

Resources

CD1, tracks 32–33
Cahier d'exercices, page 23
Grammaire 2.1, 2.2

Starter 1

Aim
To introduce some of the language required to talk about advantages and disadvantages.

Give students working in pairs three minutes to come up with a list of adjectives they could use when talking about the advantages and disadvantages of where they live: they should aim to list six to eight in each category. Encourage them to use a dictionary as necessary. Write up their appropriate adjectives and suggest students copy this list down as useful vocabulary for the topic.

1 Écoutez et lisez. Trouvez les images et les phrases qui correspondent à chaque texte.

Listening. Students listen to Clément and Karel talking about where they live and read the text at the same time. They then choose the appropriate pictures (from **1–6**) and phrases (from **a–f**) to go with each person.

If students find this challenging, you could play the recording twice and suggest they identify the pictures on first listening and then focus on the phrases in the second.

R Ask students to choose one of the texts and list in English all the advantages and all the disadvantages mentioned.

Audioscript 32

– *Où habites-tu, Clément?*

– *J'habite dans une vieille maison en ville. Notre appartement est au cinquième étage. C'est un bel immeuble du 19e siècle. La maison est plein d'histoire, mais les pièces sont petites, les sanitaires sont vieux et les marches de l'escalier sont abîmées. Ma chambre est dans les combles et nous n'avons pas de chauffage central. Il fait très chaud en été et très froid en hiver. Heureusement, nous sommes à deux minutes des commerces et du cinéma. La maison est dans le vieux quartier de la ville près de la place du Marché. Les rues sont étroites et le soir, il y a de l'ambiance, mais pendant la journée, il y a trop de circulation et c'est trop bruyant. Le soir en été, tout le monde sort, les adultes jouent à la pétanque sur la place et nous faisons du skate. On s'amuse bien.*

– *Où habites-tu, Karel?*

– *Nous habitons un nouvel appartement dans la banlieue. C'est joli parce qu'il y a un grand et bel espace vert autour des immeubles où l'on peut jouer. Mais notre appartement est au huitième étage et l'ascenseur tombe souvent en panne. Pour moi ça va, cela m'aide à garder la forme, mais ma mère doit monter le bébé, la poussette et toutes les courses par l'escalier si je ne suis pas là pour l'aider. De plus, nos voisins d'à côté mettent de la musique très fort le soir. Nous avons du double-vitrage contre le bruit, mais ça ne sert à rien s'il fait chaud et qu'on veut ouvrir les fenêtres. Les gens qui habitent au-dessus passent leurs soirées à traîner des chaises par terre et cela fait un bruit épouvantable chez nous. C'est difficile quand on veut faire nos devoirs!*

Answers

Clément: 3, 2, 6; b, d, e
Karel: 4, 5, 1; f, c, a

Expo-langue: *beau, vieux, nouveau*

Before students do exercise 2, use this grammar box to present **beau, vieux** and **nouveau**: these adjectives go before the noun and have a special form before a vowel sound (**bel, vieil, nouvel**).

There is more information on p. 210 of the Student Book.

2 Copiez et complétez les mots.

Writing. Students copy out the gap-fill text about where various people live, using the correct forms of **beau/vieux/nouveau** to complete it.

Answers

Osman habite un **bel** appartement dans un **nouvel** immeuble. La **nouvelle** maison de Damien est dans un **beau** quartier où il y a de **vieux** bâtiments. Notre maison est **vieille**. Elle est située dans le **vieux** quartier sur les hauteurs de la ville, près du **vieux** château. Nous avons toujours eu une **belle** vue sur la ville, mais l'année dernière, on a construit un **nouvel** hôtel juste devant nous.

Starter 2

Aim
To practise the position of adjectives.

Write up the following sentences. [Answers below in brackets for reference only.] Give students three minutes to decide (1) whether the adjective is in the correct position or not and (2) to correct any errors of agreement.

1 **J'habite une maison vieille** [vieille maison].
2 **C'est un belle** [beau] **quartier.**
3 **Il habite un grand appartement.**
4 **C'est une beau** [belle] **maison blanche.**
5 **Le nouveau** [nouvelle] **ascenseur tombe souvent en panne.**
6 **C'est un appartement moderne.**

3 Écoutez et notez. Selon eux, c'est un avantage (A) ou un inconvénient (I)? (1–2)

Listening. Students copy out the grid. They listen to two people talking about the area they live in and note the details in the grid, identifying each as an advantage (A) or a disadvantage (I).

You might want to remind students that a person's tone of voice can give clues about what he/she is saying.

Audioscript 33

– *Où habites-tu, Victorien? C'est comment?*
– *On est bien situé. On est tout près de la place du Marché … Et aussi … ben, … nous sommes près des commerces. La boulangerie est juste en bas et le matin, on se réveille avec l'odeur du pain frais. L'ambiance est sympa. En été le soir, tout le monde sort … On joue à la pétanque sur la place … Nous, nous faisons du skate … On s'amuse … C'est pratique d'habiter en ville, mais notre rue est étroite, et on ne peut pas ouvrir les fenêtres pendant la journée parce qu'il y a trop de bruit et trop de pollution. La maison? Elle est vieille. Il n'y a pas de chauffage. Alors, en hiver, il fait froid … vraiment froid. Et ma chambre est dans les combles! D'habitude, en hiver, il gèle et en été, c'est comme un four … C'est comme ça …*
– *Et toi, Alizée? Où habites tu? Quels sont les avantages et les inconvénients?*
– *Ben, … où j'habite … On est dans la banlieue. Il y a un grand espace vert autour des immeubles où l'on peut jouer, mais ça manque d'ambiance, c'est trop tranquille … Il n'y a rien à faire pour les jeunes … Mais il y a moins de circulation et de pollution qu'en ville. L'appartement est neuf, il manque de caractère. Euh … l'appartement, il est au cinquième étage … et l'ascenseur tombe souvent en panne. Ma chambre est à côté de la cuisine des voisins et ils font un bruit épouvantable le soir! C'est difficile quand il faut faire ses devoirs. Les inconvénients? … Il faut prendre le bus pour aller en ville. Et nos voisins, bien sûr!*

Answers

	Victorien	Alizée
situation	A – *près du marché et des commerces*	A – grand espace vert
ambiance	A – bonne	I – trop tranquille
environs	I – étroite, trop de bruit et de pollution	A – moins de circulation et de pollution
maison	I – vieille; pas de chauffage	I – neuf; manque de caractère
chambre	I – en hiver, il gèle; en été, comme un four	I – à côté de la cuisine des voisins; trop de bruit

4 Quel est l'inconvénient? Reliez les textes aux bonnes images.

Reading. Students read the four texts and then match each to the appropriate picture.

Before they start, draw their attention to the tip box. This introduces another useful reading strategy – using other information supplied (here the details in the pictures) to predict and confirm the meaning of unknown words.

Answers

1 b **2** e **3** f **4** a

5 Imaginez que vous habitez dans une grande ville. Quels sont les avantages et les inconvénients? Est-ce qu'il y a un problème particulier?

Utilisez les phrases dans les textes ci-dessus pour vous aider.

Writing. Students imagine they live in a big town (or they can describe from their own experience if they do) and write a paragraph on the advantages and disadvantages of living there, giving more detail about one particular problem. They should use the texts in exercise 4 to help them.

6 Vidéoconférence. Là où j'habite. Préparez une présentation.

Speaking. Students imagine that they are going to have a videoconference with students at a French school. They prepare a presentation on the area they live in. A list of points to cover is supplied to help them structure it. They could use these as headings on their cue cards

Plenary

Ask the class to recap the rule on the position of adjectives and then tell you all the adjectives they have learned so far which go *before* the noun (**petit**, **grand**, **beau**, **nouveau**, **vieux**).

Get one or two students to perform their presentations from exercise 6. Ask the rest of the class comprehension questions on what they have heard.

Cahier d'exercices, page 22

1

Answers

1 Quand il pleut, la rivière monte et l'eau entre dans la maison.
2 Il y a des déchets dans la rue après le marché le samedi.
3 Il y a trop de bruit à cause des poids lourds.
4 J'habite une vieille maison; les sanitaires sont vieux aussi.
5 En hiver, on a froid parce qu'il n'y a pas de chauffage central.
6 Les pièces sont assez petites et il n'y a pas de place pour faire mes devoirs.
7 Il y a beaucoup d'espaces verts où les enfants peuvent jouer.
8 L'appartement est au huitième étage et souvent, l'ascenseur tombe en panne.
9 Les voisins sont bruyants; ils mettent de la musique trop fort.
10 On est près de commerces; les magasins sont à cinq minutes.

2

Answers

Pupil's own answers

2 Aujourd'hui et autrefois

(Student Book pages 46–47)

Main topics and objectives

- Comparing where you used to live and where you live now
- Using the imperfect tense

Grammar

- Imperfect tense
  - usage ('used to'; descriptions)
  - formation

Key language

Quand j'étais petit(e), …
J'habitais …
C'était pratique.
La maison était près de l'école/ loin des commerces.
Je faisais du judo.
Je préfère habiter …
Il me manque l'ambiance.
Ils me manquent mes copains.

Resources

CD2, tracks 2–3
Cahier d'exercices, page 24
Grammaire 3.4

Starter 1

Aim
To introduce the imperfect tense. To recognise language patterns and use them to predict other forms.

Write up the following grid and give students three minutes to complete it.

je portais	I used to wear
il habitait	
	she used to be
nous aimions	
	they used to have
vous faisiez	
il y avait	
tu téléphonais	

When checking answers, ask students to use their completed grids to summarise the endings for the imperfect tense.

1 Lisez et écoutez. Écrivez V (Vrai), F (Faux) ou PM (Pas Mentionné).

Reading. Students read the text and listen to the recording at the same time. They then read the ten statements on the text and decide whether each is true or false or not mentioned in the text.

Audioscript 2

– *Quand j'étais petit, nous habitions en ville, mais quand j'ai eu douze ans, nous avons déménagé et maintenant, nous habitons à la campagne depuis quatre ans déjà.*

– *Quand nous habitions en ville, je pouvais aller dans le centre-ville à pied. Notre maison était à deux minutes de l'école et je pouvais rentrer à midi déjeuner à la maison. Le soir, j'allais à la piscine ou à la bibliothèque avec mes copains. Je faisais du judo et je prenais des cours de guitare. C'était pratique.*

– *Maintenant, pour aller au collège, je prends le car de ramassage qui passe à sept heures. Il me faut trois quarts d'heure pour y aller. Si je veux aller à la piscine ou au cinéma, je dois rester en ville après la fin des cours et maman vient me chercher en voiture parce qu'il n'y a pas de bus. La nouvelle maison est plus grande et plus jolie et nous avons un grand jardin, mais je n'ai pas de copains dans le village et mes copains d'avant, ils me manquent.*

Answers
1 F **2** V **3** F **4** V **5** PM **6** V **7** V **8** F **9** F **10** F

Expo-langue: the imperfect tense (usage and formation)

Use this grammar box to cover the imperfect in more detail before students do exercise 2. It reminds students the imperfect is used for descriptions in the past and goes on to show how it is also used to talk about things which 'used to' happen (i.e. things which went on over a period of time, rather than single completed events).

Go over how the imperfect is formed (the **nous** form minus the **–ons** ending + the imperfect endings). **pouvoir** is used as the model. Draw student's attention to the single exception to this rule – **être**, which adds the imperfect endings to the stem **ét–**.

There is more information on p. 213 of the Student Book.

R Students could write out the complete paradigm for **être** and **habiter** in the imperfect tense.

2 Copiez et complétez les mots.

Writing. Students copy and complete the 10 gap-fill sentences with the correct form of the verb, either imperfect or present tense.

Answers

1 Quand il **était** jeune, il **habitait** en ville.
2 Maintenant, il **habite** à la campagne.
3 L'ancienne maison **était** près de l'école.
4 La nouvelle maison **est** dans un village.
5 Il **allait** à l'école à pied.
6 Maintenant, il y **va** en car.
7 En ville il **avait** beaucoup de copains.
8 Dans le village il n'**a** pas de copains.
9 Il **faisait** du judo.
10 Maintenant il n'en **fait** plus.

Starter 2

Aim
To consolidate the imperfect tense of **avoir** and **être**. To encourage students to use reference resources to check their work.

Write up the following verbs:
aller, finir, envoyer, venir, faire, s'appeler, dire, manger

Give students two minutes to write out the **je** form of each verb in the imperfect. When they have finished, they swap and check their partner's answers using the verb tables in the Grammar section of the book.

3 Où habitaient-ils et où habitent-ils maintenant? Copiez et complétez la grille.

Listening. Students copy out the grid. They listen to three people talking about where they used to live and where they live now and note the details in the grid.

Audioscript 3

– *Je m'appelle Siana. Quand j'étais petite, nous habitions à Paris … en banlieue parisienne, dans un grand immeuble … On était tout près des commerces. Pour aller au collège, je devais prendre le métro. Je détestais ça. Il y avait du monde et il me fallait une demi-heure. Maintenant, j'habite à la campagne depuis deux ans. C'est beaucoup plus tranquille. Pour aller au collège, je dois prendre le car de ramassage et il me faut toujours une demi-heure pour y aller, mais c'est l'atmosphère parisienne qui me manque.*

– *Je m'appelle Damien. Quand j'étais petit, j'habitais dans une grande ville, Lyon. J'allais à l'école à pied. C'était à deux minutes de la maison … Mais notre appartement était dans un grand immeuble où il y avait trop de bruit et mes parents se disputaient tout le temps. Maintenant, … j'habite dans un petit village à la campagne … avec ma mère et mes sœurs … depuis six mois. La maison est trop petite, mais je peux jouer au foot avec mes nouveaux copains. Tout le monde a un scooter …. C'est mon père qui me manque!*

– *Je m'appelle Claire. Quand j'étais plus jeune, j'habitais à la Martinique … Il faisait très chaud … Notre maison était au bord de la mer et j'avais plein de copains qui habitaient tout autour. Notre maison était petite et je devais partager ma chambre avec mes frères et mes sœurs. Ici on habite en banlieue … La maison est plus grande … Nous sommes arrivés ici il y a trois ans … J'ai une chambre pour moi toute seule, mais nous sommes trop loin des commerces et mes copains me manquent énormément.*

Answers

Siana:

	où	avantage	inconvénient	autres détails
avant	Paris, en banlieue	près des commerces	loin de l'école	prenais le métro au collège
maintenant	à la campagne	beaucoup plus tranquille	loin de l'école	depuis deux ans; prends le car de ramassage; manque: l'ambiance

Damien:

	où	avantage	inconvénient	autres détails
avant	dans une grande ville/Lyon	près de l'école	trop bruyant	ses parents se disputaient tout le temps
maintenant	dans un village	jouer au foot avec ses nouveaux copains	maison trop petite	depuis six mois; manque: le père

Claire:

	où	avantage	inconvénient	autres détails
avant	Martinique, au bord de la mer	plein de copains	maison trop petite	devait partager sa chambre
maintenant	en banlieue	maison plus grande/ chambre à lui	trop loin des commerces	depuis trois ans; manque: les copains

4 À deux. Imaginez que vous êtes Siana, Damien ou Claire. Posez-vous des questions et répondez-y.

Speaking. In pairs: students imagine they are Siana, Damien or Claire and take it in turn to ask questions and to answer them from those people's perspectives. The questions are supplied for support.

➕ Students write a description of a place where they used to live, which was either very good or very bad.

5 Écrivez un texte: Où j'habite: les avantages et les inconvénients

Writing. Students write a paragraph on the advantages and disadvantages of where they live. Draw their attention to the tip box on including modifiers. Can students think of any others? (e.g. **vraiment**, **un peu**, etc.).

6 Vidéoconférence. Vous allez vous informer sur le quartier où habitent vos camarades et sur les avantages et les inconvénients à y habiter.

Speaking. Students imagine that they are going to have a videoconference with students at a French school. Their aim is to find out about the area the person/people they are speaking to lives/live in. Prompts for the questions are supplied for support. Students also need to prepare their own response to these questions.

The tip box includes some useful phrases to use when giving opinions. Encourage students to work these into their presentations.

Give students the chance to practise their presentations in pairs, and to record themselves if possible.

Plenary

Ask students to recap on the imperfect tense: when it is used and how it is formed.

Then put the class into teams. The first person in the team prompts the second, using an infinitive and a subject pronoun (e.g. **aimer – il**). The second responds with the correct version of the imperfect (e.g. **il aimait**). The second in turn prompts a third member of the team, and so on. Each correct answer wins a point. They should keep going until the allocated time is up. The team with the most points wins.

Cahier d'exercices, page 24

1

Answers

Maria, 13 ans

J'habite en Indonésie. Avant le tsunami, j'habitais pas loin de la plage. Mon frère et moi, nous allions dans une école à cinq minutes de la plage. Je pouvais aller au collège à pied et je pouvais rentrer chez moi à midi. Tous les soirs, mes copains et moi, nous retrouvions près de la plage. C'était génial.

Mon père est commerçant et il avait une boutique près de la mer.

J'étais sur la plage quand le tsunami est arrivé. J'ai couru, mais ma maison était déjà en ruines.

Après le tsunami, tout a changé.

Maintenant, nous habitons avec mon oncle dans une petite maison. Moi, je vais dans un nouveau collège qui n'est pas si près de la mer. C'est difficile parce que je suis loin de mes copains et ils me manquent. Si je veux retrouver mes copains, je dois prendre le bus ou quelquefois mon père m'emmène en voiture. On ne se retrouve plus près de la plage. On se retrouve en ville.

2

Answers

1 Avant le tsunami, Maria habitait pas loin de la plage.
2 Maria et son frère allaient à une école cinq minutes de la plage.
3 Elle pouvait rentrer chez elle à midi.
4 Maria se retrouvait ses copains près de la plage tous les soirs.
5 Son père avait une boutique près de la mer.
6 Maintenant, ils habitent la maison de son oncle.
7 Son oncle a une petite maison.
8 Pour voir ses copains, elle doit prendre le bus.

3 La France métropolitaine

(Student Book pages 48–49)

Main topics and objectives

- The geography of France
- The superlative

Grammar

- The superlative
  - **le/la plus/moins ...**
  - **le/la meilleur(e)**

Key language

une grande ville
un centre administratif/ve
historique
industriel(le)
touristique
une station balnéaire
une station de ski
un port commercial
un port de pêche
un port de plaisance
C'est le site touristique le plus connu de France.
le/la plus ensoleillé(e)
le/la plus haut(e)
le/la plus long(ue)
le/la plus peuplé(e)
le/la plus proche

Resources

CD2, tracks 4–5
Cahier d'exercices, page 25
Grammaire 2.4

Starter 1

Aim
To work out the meaning of vocabulary in context.

Write up the following. Ask students where they might find these labels used. (on a map)
Give them three minutes working in pairs to come up with an example of an appropriate place in Britain for each of the labels.

une ville touristique
une ville historique
une ville industrielle
une station de ski
une station balnéaire
un port commercial
un port de pêche
un port de plaisance

When listening to their answers, ask students to translate each of the phrases into English.

1 De quelle ville s'agit-il? Écoutez et trouvez le nom des villes sur la carte. (a–h)

Listening. Students listen to two people doing some geography homework. Using the map and the details for each place on the recording, they identify the eight places discussed (referred to on the recording as **a–h**).

Audioscript 4

- *Alors, **a** se trouve au nord-ouest, c'est un grand port.*
- *C'est un port de pêche ou un port commercial?*
- *C'est un ancien port de pêche, mais aujourd'hui, c'est un grand port en plein développement et il y a un centre nucléaire très important. ... J'ai trouvé! ... **b** se trouve dans le sud, sur la côte méditerranéenne. C'est une station balnéaire et un port de plaisance ... Euh, c'est une ville connue pour son festival de cinéma qui y a lieu chaque année.*
- *Ça y est, j'ai trouvé!*
- ***c** ... se trouve dans les Alpes. C'est une station de ski. On y fait de l'alpinisme.*
- *Je crois que j'ai trouvé.*
- ***d**, c'est dans le sud, dans le sud-ouest exactement, dans le golfe de Gascogne. C'est une station balnéaire et un haut-lieu du surf.*
- *Bon ... **e**?*
- ***e** se trouve également dans le sud-ouest, sur la côte atlantique ... et c'est une grande ville entourée de vignobles. Elle est surtout connue pour son vin.*
- *OK. Et **f**?*
- ***f**, c'est dans le sud, en allant vers l'Espagne. C'est une ancienne ville médiévale fortifiée. C'est une ville historique et touristique.*
- *C'est sur la côte?*
- *Non.*
- *Ah oui, d'accord! Et **g**?*
- ***g**, c'est là où on fabrique les pneus... c'est une ville industrielle, dans le centre de la Franc e.*
- *J'ai trouvé! Et **h**?*
- *C'est un port de pêche.*
- *En Bretagne?*
- *Non, dans le nord, dans le Pas-de-Calais.*
- *J'ai aussi trouvé.*
- *Voilà! C'est tout!*

Answers
a Le Havre **b** Cannes **c** Chamonix **d** Biarritz **e** Bordeaux **f** Carcassonne **g** Clermont-Ferrand **h** Boulogne-sur-mer

+ In pairs: taking it in turn, students use the map to make a statement about each of the towns in exercise 1, e.g. **Le Havre – c'est un grand port au nord-ouest.**

Starter 2

Aim

To practise listening for numbers.

Tell students you are going to read out eight numbers for them to note. Read out the following in French.

342, 109, 726, 555, 1420, 3910, 5400, 690

After checking answers, point out the usefulness of this kind of exercise: listening tasks in the exam will certainly feature numbers. Suggest students find time to practise listening for numbers in pairs.

2 Écoutez et notez les détails qui manquent.

Listening. Students listen to the descriptions of six landscape features in France and note the words missing in the gap-fill version of the text.

Before playing the recording, get students to read through the sentences in the Student Book. Can they predict what kind of words they need to listen out for?

Audioscript 5

*La mer de Glace, dans le massif du Mont-Blanc, avec une longueur de **14**km, est le plus long glacier de France.*

*La Loire, qui prend sa source en Ardèche et mesure **1175**km, est le plus long fleuve de France.*

*Le lac du Bourget, avec une superficie de **45**km², est le plus grand lac de France.*

*La dune du Pilat, qui se trouve dans les Landes et qui mesure plus de **100**m de haut, est la plus haute montagne de sable d'Europe.*

*La plus grande île de France est la Corse, qui se trouve dans la mer Méditerranée et qui mesure **158**km de long.*

*Le Mont-Blanc (altitude **4808,45**m), qui se trouve dans les Alpes à la frontière de la France et de l'Italie, est le plus haut sommet d'Europe.*

Answers

See bold in the audioscript.

Expo-langue: the superlative

Use this grammar box to cover the superlative (how it is formed and used, and the irregular forms of **bon – le/la meilleur(e)**) before students do exercise 3. There is more information on p. 211 of the Student Book.

3 Lisez et complétez les phrases.

Writing. Students complete the eight gap-fill sentences using an appropriate superlative. When they have finished, ask them to swap answers and to check their partner's, focusing in particular on agreement.

Answers

1 Le Mont-Blanc est la **plus haute** montagne.
2 La Loire est le **plus long** fleuve.
3 La tour Eiffel est le site touristique **le plus connu**.
4 Paris est la **plus grande** ville.
5 Carcassonne est le **meilleur** exemple d'une ville fortifiée dans le Midi de la France.
6 Marseille est le **plus grand** port de France.
7 La Provence est la **plus belle** région de France.
8 La région Pas-de-Calais est la région la **plus proche** d'Angleterre.

4 À deux. Discutez. Chez vous, c'est quoi?

Speaking. In pairs: using the prompts supplied, students discuss what is the highest mountain, etc., in their own country.

Students use the internet to research the answers to these questions for a francophone country of their choice. They could then present the answers to the class.

5 Écrivez trois ou quatre phrases sur votre ville ou sur la grande ville la plus proche.

Writing. Students write a short paragraph on their own town or a city nearby, describing what it used to be like and what it's like now. A model text is supplied, with the language which needs to change shown in brackets.

6 Vidéoconférence. Préparez une présentation de votre ville ou votre région.

Speaking. Students imagine that they are going to have a videoconference with students at a French school. They prepare a presentation on their town or region. (They may find it useful to look back at the work they did for the Vidéoconférence exercise at the end of Unit 2, on p. 47, as well as using the text they wrote for exercise 5 here.)

Encourage them to use the language they know to structure the presentation and, as usual, to create a cue card to use as a prompt.

Give students the chance to practise their presentation in pairs, recording themselves if possible.

Plenary

Ask students to recap how the superlative is formed.

Then have a quiz on the superlative. This can be done orally or you could write up the questions. (Answers below in brackets for reference only.) Put the class into teams. Each team notes down their answers. The team with the most correct answers at the end is the winner.

Ask students to identify (in English):

1 **la plus grande ville d'Italie** (Rome)
2 **la plus haute montagne d'Écosse** (Ben Nevis)
3 **les sites touristiques les plus connus d'Égypte** (pyramids)
4 **l'immeuble le plus connu de France** (Eiffel Tower)
5 **le plus long fleuve du monde** (Nile)
6 **la plus grande ville d'États-Unis** (New York)

Cahier d'exercices, page 25

1

Answers

La population de la France est de 62,9 millions.
La plus peuplée ville, c'est Paris (9,928 millions)!
La plus grande ville dans le sud, c'est Marseille. Marseille a aussi le plus grand port de la France.
La plus visitée ville de France, c'est Paris.
La France est le plus visité pays du monde (plus de soixante-dix-millions de touristes par an).
La France est divisée en régions. Il y a 22 régions françaises.
La région qui a la plus grande superficie, c'est le Midi-Pyrénées avec 45,348 km2.
La région avec la plus élevée population, c'est l'Île-de-France avec 11,291 millions.
Chaque région est divisée en département. Il y a 96 départements français.
Il y a en plus quatre départements d'outre-mer (les DOM); la Martinique, la Guadeloupe, la Réunion, et la Guyane. La Réunion, c'est le département d'outre-mer le plus peuplé avec 600.000 habitants.
L'endroit le plus populaire pour les vacances chez les Français, c'est la France! Neuf Français sur dix passent leur vacances en France.

2

Answers

1 62.9 million
2 Marseilles
3 Over 70 million
4 France!
5 22
6 Île-de-France
7 96 départements
8 4 overseas areas; they are in the West Indies.

4 Ma ville

(Student Book pages 50–51)

Main topics and objectives

- Talking about a town
- **on peut/on pourrait** + infinitive

Grammar

- **pouvoir** + infinitive

Key language

Il y a ...
un centre commercial
un château
un musée
une cathédrale
des commerces
un espace vert (m)
l'aéroport (m)
Ma ville préférée, c'est ...
C'est une ville historique.
Elle se situe ...
en Écosse
dans le sud de l'Angleterre
Les touristes peuvent visiter des monuments/des sites.
On peut aussi faire du shopping/du sport.
On pourrait aussi aller au parc (d'attractions).
le park relais
le parking souterrain
la zone piétonne
le couloir réservé au bus
la route périphérique
On pourrait construir ...
On est en train d'ouvrir ...

Resources

CD2, tracks 6–7
Cahier d'exercices, pages 26–27
Grammaire 3.16

Starter 1

Aim
To revise modal verbs.

Write up **on peut** and ask what it means and what kind of verb it is. Ask for an example of it being used in a sentence, confirming/reminding students it is followed by an infinitive.

Ask students working in pairs to come up with six suggestions for things a visiting French friend could do in their town, using **On peut ...**

1 Écoutez et notez les mots qui manquent.

Listening. Students listen to the recording and note the missing words in the gap-fill version in the book.

With a good class, you could ask students to read through the text first and work out what kind of word is required to fill the gap (noun? verb?, etc.), and make educated guesses on what the missing words might be.

Audioscript 6

- *Bonjour, Camille. Quelle est ta ville préférée?*
- *Annecy... là où j'habite.*
- *C'est quel genre de ville?*
- *La vieille ville est **historique** et pittoresque. C'est aussi le centre régional administratif et **culturel**.*
- *C'est une destination touristique?*
- *Oui, l'**ancienne** ville se trouve au bord d'un grand lac entouré par de **hautes montagnes**. Le paysage est magnifique!*
- *C'est joli, alors?*
- *Oui, c'est très joli. Il y a de beaux et **anciens** bâtiments et des **commerces** modernes, des grandes surfaces hors de la ville et des espaces verts dans la ville. La plupart des parkings sont **souterrains**.*
- *Où se trouve-t-elle?*
- *Elle se situe dans le sud-est de la France près de la frontière **suisse**. On est à vingt minutes de Genève par l'autoroute.*
- *Comment est le temps?*
- *En été, il fait chaud, mais pas trop. On peut toujours aller au bord du lac ou en montagne. En hiver, par contre, il fait froid, il **neige** et on peut faire du ski. De temps en temps il arrive que le lac gèle, alors, on peut faire du patin à glace. C'est un climat très **agréable**.*
- *Qu'est-ce qu'un touriste peut y faire?*
- *On peut faire des sports aquatiques; comme de la planche, de la voile, du canoë-kayak, des sports d'aventures comme de la plongée, du canyoning, du **rafting**, du parapente et de l'**escalade**, et **en hiver**, des sports de glisse, du ski, du snowboard et de la luge.*
- *Et pour ceux qui n'aiment pas le sport? Qu'est-ce qu'ils pourraient faire?*
- *Ils pourraient visiter des musées, des vieux **châteaux** et des centres historiques et culturels et pour ceux qui aiment les sites touristiques naturels, il y a le lac, des grottes et des chutes d'eau. Il y en a pour tout le monde. Il y a même une fête du **cinéma**!*
- *Est-ce qu'il y a quelque chose que tu n'aimes pas?*
- *Oui, il y a trop de circulation dans la vieille ville, mais on est en train d'agrandir la zone piétonne.*

Answers

See also bold in the audioscript.
1 historique **2** culturel **3** ancienne **4** hautes montagnes **5** anciens **6** commerces **7** souterrains **8** suisse **9** neige **10** agréable **11** rafting **12** escalade **13** en hiver **14** châteaux **15** cinéma

Expo-langue: *pouvoir* + infinitive

Use this grammar box to review the modal verb **pouvoir** in the forms **on peut/on pourrait** + infinitive. There is more information on p. 216 of the Student Book.

2 À deux. Posez et répondez aux questions en rouge dans l'exercice 1. Adaptez des phrases dans le dialogue pour vous aider.

Speaking. In pairs: students take it in turn to ask and answer the questions shown in red in the text in exercise 1. They should also use that text to help them with their answers, adapting the language as necessary. A grid of useful language is supplied for support.

Starter 2

Aim
To learn more connectives.

Write up the following lists of connectives (jumbling the order of the second column) and give students working in pairs three minutes to match the French with the correct English versions.

par exemple	for example
car	for, because
donc	so
comme	as
puisque	since
pendant que	while
y compris	including
c'est-à-dire	that is (to say)
en général	in general
pourtant	yet
aussi	also
par contre	on the other hand

After checking answers, suggest students note down any new connectives here in their vocabulary lists.

3 Projet de ville. C'est quel problème? Trouvez la bonne phrase pour chaque image.

Reading. Students match each of the four pictures to the appropriate description (six sentences (**a–f**) are supplied).

Answers
1 d **2** e **3** b **4** c

4 Écoutez. Quelle est la bonne solution pour chaque problème? (1–4)

Listening. Students listen to four people being interviewed about problems in their area and identify the solution for each from the five pictures (**a–e**).

Audioscript 7

1

– *Bonjour. On fait un sondage au sujet des problèmes de la vie en ville. Est-ce que je peux vous poser des questions, monsieur?*
– *Oui, bien sûr.*
– *Selon vous, quel est le plus grand problème dans votre ville?*
– *Le parking, on ne peut jamais trouver un endroit pour garer la voiture.*
– *Est-ce que vous avez une solution à proposer?*
– *Ah oui, on pourrait construire des parcs-relais. Comme ça, les voitures ne viennent pas jusque dans la ville. On gare la voiture et on entre en ville en navette.*
– *Merci, monsieur.*

2

– *Bonjour. On fait un sondage au sujet des problèmes de la vie en ville. Est-ce que je peux vous poser des questions, madame?*
– *Oui, bien sûr.*
– *Selon vous, quel est le plus grand problème?*
– *Ben, la circulation. Il y a trop de véhicules qui traversent la ville, sans s'arrêter.*
– *Et qu'est-ce que vous proposez comme solution?*
– *On pourrait construire une route périphérique, comme autour d'autres grandes villes. Comme ça, les poids lourds n'auraient plus besoin de passer par la ville.*
– *C'est une bonne idée, madame. Merci.*

3

– *Bonjour, monsieur. On fait un sondage au sujet des problèmes de la vie en ville. Est-ce que je peux vous poser des questions?*
– *Oui, bien sûr.*
– *Selon vous, quel est le plus grand problème?*
– *Mais c'est de garer sa voiture, bien sûr ... Il n'y a pas assez de places de stationnement en ville.*
– *Avez-vous une solution à proposer?*
– *On pourrait construire un nouveau grand parking souterrain.*
– *Merci, monsieur.*

4

– *Bonjour. On fait un sondage au sujet des problèmes de la vie en ville. Est-ce que je peux vous poser des questions, madame?*
– *Oui, bien sûr.*
– *Selon vous, quel est le plus grand problème?*
– *Il y a toujours des embouteillages aux heures de pointe.*
– *Avez-vous une solution à proposer?*
– *On pourrait créer des couloirs réservés aux bus et aux taxis. Comme ça, les bus et les taxis pourraient circuler plus vite. Voilà! Et moi, ... je pourrais prendre le bus pour venir en ville, mais je déteste attendre à l'arrêt de bus surtout quand le bus n'arrive pas.*
– *Merci, madame.*

Answers
1 a **2** e **3** b **4** d

5 À deux. Discutez des problèmes et trouvez des solutions.

Speaking. In pairs: students discuss problems in a town (from those covered earlier in the spread) and possible solutions. Sample sentence openings are supplied for support.

6 Là où j'habite. Décrivez votre ville.

Writing. Students write a paragraph describing their town. A list of points to include is supplied. Encourage students to use this to structure their text and to identify four connectives to use in their paragraph.

Plenary

Put the class into teams. Read out the following sentences in English using language taken from the whole module (answers supplied in brackets for reference only). The teams write down the French version, conferring as necessary. At the end, the teams swap and check another team's answers. The team with the fewest errors is the winner.

1 In my room, there's a wardrobe, a bed and a laptop.
(**Dans ma chambre, il y a une armoire, un lit et un portable.**)
2 I live in an old house.
(**J'habite une vieille maison.**)
3 When I was young, I used to live in the country.
(**Quand j'étais jeune, j'habitais à la campagne.**)
4 Seville is the most beautiful city in Spain.
(**Seville est la plus belle ville d'Espagne.**)
5 You could go to the swimming pool or the park.
(**On pourrait aller à la piscine ou au parc.**)

Cahier d'exercices, page 26

1

Answers

Robert Legris is talking about his town: Montréal. He says what there is to do there, what there is for young people and what he likes to do.

2

Answers

1 prendre un verre	**2** une ville bruyante
3 les rues piétonnes	**4** un paradis pour les jeunes
5 centres commerciaux	**6** une grande variété de magasins
7 un moment de calme	**8** une province francophone

3

Answers

1 Robert parle de sa ville.
2 La plupart des gens parlent français.
3 Les touristes peuvent visiter les restaurants et les rues piétonnes.
4 On peut voir le base-ball au stade Olympique.
5 On pourrait aller à la ville souterraine avec les centres commerciaux.
6 Les jeunes peuvent faire du patinage sur glace, du ski, du toboggan ou l'hockey sur glace ou aller au parc d'attractions, la Ronde.
7 Un avantage, c'est un paradis pour les jeunes et un inconvénient, c'est une ville bruyante avec trop de circulation.
8 On pourrait aggrandir la zone piétonne.

Cahier d'exercices, Grammaire, page 27

1

Answers

Example
J'habite un vieux appartement au deuxième étage dans un grand immeuble en ville. Nous avons une longue entrée, une cuisine moderne, un salon confortable, trois chambres, une salle de bains pratique, une douche nouvelle et des toilettes.
Mes parents ont une jolie chambre et les deux autres chambres sont à moi et à ma sœur. Dans ma belle chambre, j'ai un lit, une chaise, une étagère démodée, une armoire haute, une petite table, un vieux ordinateur et un placard.

2

Answers

Alex (possible answers)
1 *Sa chaise est plus confortable que la chaise de Vincent.*
2 *Son lit* est plus confortable que le lit de Vincent.
3 Son étagère est plus grande que l'étagère de Vincent.
4 Son ordinateur est moins moderne que l'ordinateur de Vincent.
5 Sa télévision est plus grande que la télévision de Vincent.

Vincent (possible answers)
1 *Son étagère* est moins grande que l'étagère d'Alex.
2 Sa commode est plus grande que la commode d'Alex.
3 Son ordinateur est plus moderne que l'ordinateur d'Alex.
4 Son lit est moins confortable que le lit d'Alex.

Contrôle continu: Lyon

(Student Book pages 52–53)

Topics revised

- Advertising the local area

1 Copiez les phrases en bleu dans le texte et trouvez l'équivalent de l'anglais ci-dessous.

Students copy out the blue phrases from the text and find the equivalent English phrase from those listed.

Answers

se trouve
  4 is situated
la vieille ville a été construite
  6 the old town was built
pour s'y rendre
  8 to get there …
Vous préférez l'avion?
  2 Do you prefer to fly?
Que peut-on faire?
  9 What can you do?
Vous intéressez-vous à l'histoire?
  1 Are you interested in history?
La ville ne manque pas de …
  7 There is no shortage of ... in the town
c'est pour son shopping que …
  5 it is for its shopping that ...
en train de construire
  3 in the course of constructing

2 Relisez le texte et répondez aux questions.

Students reread the text and answer the 10 comprehension questions in English.

Answers

1 half-way between Paris (in the north) and Marseille (on the Mediterranean in the south)
2 the Romans
3 43BC
4 it's at the crossroads of Europe/it's at the confluence of two rivers (the Rhone and the Saone)
5 by train/TGV, plane or car
6 exhibitions, concerts, shows, events
7 museums and gallo-Roman sites
8 public parks and (for children) an adventure playground in the forest
9 its shopping
10 the building of the Musée des Confluences, which will include a leisure area with a cinema and activities such as rollerblading and bowling

3 Faites une pub pour votre région.

Using the text and the **Boîte à outils** section to help them, students write an advert for their own region.

☑ The **Boîte à outils** section gives some suggestions on things students need to check when reading through written work. Encourage them to build up their own detailed checklist that they can use for every text they write. Using this regularly will make their writing more accurate and more interesting, and this will gain them a higher grade in the written coursework. Following this process is also good training for tackling activities in other parts of the exam.

À l'oral (AQA edition)

(Student Book page 178)

Topics revised
- talking about your house
- talking about the area you live in

1 Your penfriend is coming to see you and is ringing up to find out about the house you live in. Your partner will play the part of your friend and will speak first.

Roleplay. Students practise talking about their house and how they get into town, taking it in turn to play themselves/a visiting French penfriend.

2 Your penfriend wants to know something about the town you live in (or the nearest large town). Your partner will play the part of your friend and will speak first.

Roleplay. Students practise talking about the town they live in/a nearby large town, taking it in turn to play themselves/a visiting French penfriend.

3 Prepare a ninety-second presentation called *Ma maison*. Make yourself a cue card to help you remember what to say. Use pictures and/or key words on your cue card (see the example).

Presentation. Students prepare a ninety-second presentation on their home.

☑ Draw their attention to the sample cue card before they begin, pointing out that quick sketches can be a useful way of noting what they want to say.

☑ Listen to one or two talks and/or have students record them for reference. Ask questions to elicit more information, highlighting areas that students might have overlooked. Suggest they look at their presentation again bearing these in mind. Stress the importance of redrafting and improving work at this level.

4 Prepare a ninety-second presentation called *Ma ville*. Make yourself a cue card to help you remember what to say.

Presentation. Students prepare a ninety-second presentation on their town, again creating a cue card along the lines of the one supplied.

5 Possible conversation questions

Conversation. These are key questions to practise for the speaking exam, taken from the module as a whole. Students can practise asking and answering the questions in pairs.

Draw students' attention to the **Tu parles!** box on **pas mal de** before they begin.

☑ If students find they are struggling with any of these topics, encourage them to review material in the relevant unit.

À l'oral (Edexcel edition)

(Student Book page 178)

Topics revised

- talking about your house
- talking about the area you live in

1 Your penfriend is going to show you around Lille and asks you about your town. Your partner will play the part of your penfriend and will start the conversation.

Roleplay Type B. Students practise talking about their town, taking it in turn to play themselves/a French penfriend.

☑ Remind them what the **!** symbol signifies: they will have to give a response which they have not prepared. How can they get themselves ready for this?

2 Presentation

Presentation. Students prepare a one-minute presentation on their home.

Remind them to think about how they are going to split what they want to say between the presentation and the conversation.

☑ Draw their attention to the sample cue card before they begin, pointing out that quick sketches can be a useful way of noting what they want to say.

☑ Listen to one or two talks and/or have students record them for reference. Ask questions to elicit more information, highlighting areas that students might have overlooked. Suggest they look at their presentation again bearing these in mind. Stress the importance of redrafting and improving work at this level.

3 Presentation and general conversation

Presentation. Students prepare a one-minute presentation on their town.

Possible conversation questions. These are key questions to practise for the speaking exam, taken from the module as a whole. Students can practise asking and answering the questions in pairs.

☑ If students find they are struggling with any of these topics, encourage them to review material in the relevant unit.

Là où j'habite

3 À l'oral (OCR edition)

(Student Book page 178)

Topics revised

- talking about your house
- talking about the area you live in

1 Your penfriend is coming to see you and is ringing up to find out about the house you live in. Your partner will play the part of your friend and will speak first.

Roleplay Type 2. Students practise talking about where they live, taking it in turn to play themselves/a visiting French penfriend.

2 Your penfriend wants to know something about the town you live in (or the nearest large town). Your partner will play the part of your friend and will speak first.

Roleplay Type 2. Students practise talking about the town they live in/a nearby large town, taking it in turn to play themselves/a visiting French penfriend.

3 Prepare a one-minute presentation called *Ma maison.*

Presentation. Students prepare a one-minute presentation on their home.

☑ Draw their attention to the sample cue card before they begin, pointing out that quick sketches can be a useful way of noting what they want to say.

☑ Listen to one or two talks and/or have students record them for reference. Ask questions to elicit more information, highlighting areas that students might have overlooked. Suggest they look at their presentation again bearing these in mind. Stress the importance of redrafting and improving work at this level.

4 Prepare a one-minute presentation called *Ma ville.*

Presentation. Students prepare a one-minute presentation on their town, again creating a cue card along the lines of the one supplied.

5 *Chez moi*: possible conversation questions

Conversation. These are key questions to practise for the speaking exam, taken from the module as a whole. Students can practise asking and answering the questions in pairs.

☑ If students find they are struggling with any of these topics, encourage them to review material in the relevant unit.

À toi

(Student Book pages 190–191)

- Self-access reading and writing

1 Trouvez les mots dans le texte.

Reading. Students read the text advertising a house for sale and find the French for the 12 English expressions listed.

Answers

1 cadre **2** vue **3** propriété **4** à proximité **5** commerces **6** rez-de-chaussée **7** cuisine amenagée **8** cheminée **9** buanderie **10** salle d'eau attenante **11** salle de douche **12** WC indépendants

2 Écrivez une annonce: *Maison à vendre ...*

Writing. Students use the picture prompts supplied to write an advertisement for a house. They can use the text in exercise 1 to help them.

3 Faites une annonce pour votre maison.

Writing. Students write an advertisement for their own house.

4 Lisez le texte. Écrivez V (Vrai), F (faux) ou PM (Pas Mentionné).

Reading. Students read the text on Normandy. They then read the eight statements on the text and decide whether each is true or false or not mentioned in the text.

Answers

1 V **2** F **3** PM **4** V **5** F **6** V **7** F **8** PM

5 Écrivez un texte sur une région que vous connaissez.

Writing. Using the text in exercise 4 for reference, students write a text about a region they know. Some sample sentence openings are supplied for support.

6 Lisez le texte et répondez aux questions.

Reading. Students read the text and respond to the four comprehension questions in French.

Answers

1 Normandie, la famille, l'année dernière, deux semaines
2 la Tapisserie de Bayeux et les Plages du Débarquement
3 Quand il faisait beau, ils ont passé des journées entières sur la plage et on a fait des pique-niques et des balades en vélo.
Quand il a plu, ils ont fait un tour de la région: ils sont allés à Rouen (pour voir la Grosse Horloge et la cathédrale) et à Giverney (pour admirer les jardins et les peintures de Claude Monet).
4 (Their own answer)

Module 4 Allons-y! (Student Book pages 56–73)

Unit	Main topics and objectives	Grammar
Déjà vu 1 **C'est où?** (pp. 56–57)	Finding the way Using the preposition **à**	**à** (**au**, **à la**, **à l'**, **aux**) **tu**/**vous** usage
Déjà vu 2 **On fait les magasins!** (pp. 58–59)	Shopping for food and clothes Using the partitive article	**de** (**du**, **de la**, **de l'**, **des**); **de** with quantities Adjective agreement (colours, singular and plural)
1 Tout près d'ici (pp. 60–61)	Describing the location of a place Using prepositions and imperatives	Prepositions The imperative (**tu**, **vous**)
2 On prépare une fête (pp. 62–63)	Organising a beach party Using **il faut** and **en**	**il faut** + noun/the infinitive The pronoun **en**
3 Bon voyage! (pp. 64–65)	Making travel arrangements Learning more about the perfect tense	The perfect tense – irregular past participles (**eu**, **dû**, **mis**) – verbs which take **être**
4 *Ça me va?* (pp. 66–67)	Talking about buying clothes Using **ce**, **lequel**, **celui**, etc.	Adjectives – **ce (cet)**, **cette**, **ces** Pronouns – **lequel/laquelle/lesquels/lesquelles** – **celui-ci/-là**, **celle-ci/-là**, **ceux-ci/-là**, **celles-ci/-là** The conditional (**j'aimerais**, **je préférerais**, **je voudrais** + the infinitive)
5 Malheureusement … (pp. 68–69)	Describing what went wrong More on the imperfect tense	The perfect and imperfect: when to use
Contrôle continu **Une journée désastreuse!** (pp. 70–71)	*Coursework* Describing a day that went wrong	*All main grammar points of the module*
À l'oral (p. 179)	*Exam speaking practice* Hiring equipment Getting travel information Returning something to a shop Talking about shopping	*All main grammar points of the module*
À toi (pp. 192–193)	Self-access reading and writing	

Déjà vu 1: C'est où?

(Student Book pages 56–57)

Main topics and objectives

- Finding the way
- Using the preposition à

Grammar

- à (au, à la, à l', aux)
- **tu/vous** usage

Key language

Places in town

Resources

CD2, tracks 8–9
Cahier d'exercices, page 30
Grammaire 4.1

Starter 1

Aim
To practise using **tu** or **vous** as appropriate.
To revise the 'you' forms of key verbs.

Ask students which forms of the verbs **être**, **avoir** and **aller** they would use when addressing the following people:

- their best friend
- an elderly neighbour
- an adult they ask for directions on the street
- a teenager they are giving directions to
- a group of students in their class

1 Écoutez et regardez les images. Qui parle? (1–8)

Listening. Students listen to eight conversations and match each to the appropriate picture (from a–h).

Audioscript 8

1 – *Où vas-tu ce soir?*
– *Je vais au bowling avec ma sœur. Tu viens?*
– *Ah, oui, chouette! J'adore faire ça! On se retrouve où et à quelle heure?*

2 – *Salut! Où allez-vous?*
– *On va au parc. On va jouer au foot. Ça t'intéresse?*
– *Désolé, je voudrais bien y aller, mais je ne peux pas. Je dois faire mes devoirs pour demain.*

3 – *Où es-tu en ce moment?*
– *Je suis au centre commercial. Je fais des courses pour maman. Pourquoi?*
– *Parce que je vais aussi en ville. Si tu veux, on peut se retrouver vers dix heures.*

4 – *Salut, c'est moi! Qu'est-ce que tu fais?*
– *Je suis avec mon frère. On est à la piscine. On a fait de la natation.*
– *C'est bien, ça. Moi aussi, j'aime nager. La prochaine fois, je peux venir avec vous?*
– *Ah, oui, bien sûr.*

5 – *Alors, on se retrouve où demain?*
– *On se retrouve à la patinoire à dix heures et demie. D'accord?*
– *D'accord. Mais attention! Je ne sais pas très bien faire de patin.*
– *Pas de problème. Je vais t'aider.*

6 – *Où est-ce qu'on va, alors?*
– *D'abord, on va à la bibliothèque. Je dois chercher un livre sur l'Afrique pour mes devoirs.*
– *D'accord, d'accord. Mais ça va être tout à fait ennuyeux!*

7 – *Tu es où, alors?*
– *Je suis à l'hôpital parce que ma sœur est tombée de son vélo.*
– *C'est pas vrai! Elle s'est fait mal?*
– *Ah oui, elle s'est cassé le bras gauche.*
– *Oh, là là! Quelle horreur!*

8 – *On va regarder un DVD chez moi. Ça te dit?*
– *Désolé. Je ne peux pas. Je vais au stade. Je vais regarder le match de rugby.*
– *Oh! Je voudrais bien regarder le match aussi. C'est combien, l'entrée?*
– *Euh … je crois que c'est complet.*
– *Quel dommage! Alors, amuse-toi bien!*

Answers

1 f **2** h **3** a **4** g **5** e **6** b **7** c **8** d

Expo-langue: *à (au, à la, à l', aux)*

Use this grammar box to cover the different forms of **à** + the definite article before students do exercise 2. There is more information on p. 216 of the Student Book.

2 Complétez les phrases avec *au*, *à* + *la*, *à* + *l'* ou *aux*. Utilisez le glossaire ou un dictionnaire, si nécessaire.

Reading. Students complete the six gap-fill sentences with the correct form of à + the definite article. They can use the Vocabulaire section or a dictionary to check genders as necessary. Ask how they will locate this information in reference resources, drawing their attention to the tip box if they are unsure about the labels used to show gender.

Answers

1 Où vas-tu? Je vais **au** parc.
2 Où allez-vous? On va **à l'**église.
3 Où es-tu? Je suis **à la** bibliothèque.
4 Où êtes-vous? On est **au** centre commercial.
5 On se retrouve où? On se retrouve **à la** piscine.
6 On va où? Moi, je vais **aux** toilettes!

Expo-langue: *tu/vous* usage

Use this grammar box to review when **tu** and **vous** are used before students do exercise 3.

3 À deux. Posez des questions aux personnes de l'exercice 1. Utilisez *aller* ou *être*, comme précisé ci-dessous.

Speaking. In pairs: students pretend to be a character/a pair of characters in exercise 1. They take it in turn to ask and answer questions on where they are/where they are going. The verbs to use are listed and a sample exchange is given.

4 Écrivez des textos.

Writing. Students use the structures in exercise 3 and the sample answer given here to write three or four text messages saying where they are and what they need to do there.

Starter 2

Aim
To practise the forms of **à** + the definite article.
To revise the gender of nouns.

Write up:
au ...
à la ...
à l'...
aux

Ask students to complete each of the phrases with three appropriate nouns.

After checking answers, ask students to summarise when each form is used (**au** with masculine nouns, etc.).

5 Écoutez les directions et regardez le plan. C'est vrai ou faux? (1–4)

Listening. Using the map in the book, students listen to the four conversations and decide whether the directions given in each are correct or not. Give students time to familiarise themselves with the directions as shown in the book (**tout droit/ à droite/à gauche**) before playing the recording.

Audioscript 9

1 – *Pardon, madame. Où est le musée, s'il vous plaît?*
– *Vous allez tout droit et vous tournez à droite, monsieur.*
– *Merci, madame. Au revoir.*

2 – *Excusez-moi. Où est la poste, s'il vous plaît?*
– *Vous allez tout droit, vous tournez à gauche, puis vous tournez à droite.*
– *Tout droit, à gauche, puis à droite. Merci beaucoup.*

3 – *Pardon. Où est l'hôtel, s'il te plaît?*
– *Tu vas tout droit, tu tournes à droite et puis à gauche.*
– *Tout droit, à droite, puis ...*
– *À gauche.*
– *Puis à gauche. Merci. Au revoir.*

4 – *Excuse-moi. Où sont les magasins, s'il te plaît?*
– *C'est très facile, madame. Vous allez tout droit.*
– *Merci beaucoup, jeune homme.*

Answers
1 vrai **2** vrai **3** faux **4** vrai

6 À deux. Regardez encore le plan. Demandez la direction pour aller au camping, au collège et à la gare. Imaginez que vous parlez à un adulte.

Speaking. In pairs: students take it in turn to ask for directions to the campsite, the school and the station and, using the map, to respond with the appropriate information. They should address each other as though both were adults. A sample exchange is given, along with a box listing useful structures (showing both **vous** and **tu** forms).

7 À deux. Refaites les dialogues en imaginant que vous parlez à un enfant.

Speaking. In pairs: students redo the dialogues in exercise 6 as though the speakers were younger (and so using the **tu** form). You might want to point out **s'il te plaît** before they begin.

8 Lisez le texte et faites une liste en anglais des neuf magasins qui sont mentionnés.

Reading. Students read the text and list in English the nine shops mentioned in it.

Answers
supermarket, baker's, butcher's, post office, chemist, clothes shop, shoe shop, bookshop, music shop

9 Écrivez une réponse à Ahmed. Adaptez le texte ci-dessus, si vous voulez.

Writing. Students write a reply to Ahmed's e-mail in exercise 8, giving details of the shops in their own town. Encourage them to use Ahmed's text as a source of information.

Plenary

Ask two confident students to come to the front of the class. Tell them they are going to do a dialogue asking for directions. Write up the following prompts:
1 × adult, 1 × child; **patinoire** + ↑ + ←

When the students have done their dialogue, ask for feedback from the class.

Did they use the correct 'you' forms? Were the directions correct? Did they remember to include the expressions **pardon/excusez-moi** and **merci**? Was the French accurate?

If you have time, ask another two students to do a dialogue, giving them different prompts.

Cahier d'exercices, page 30

1

Answers

J'aime bien habiter à Perpignan! Il y a tant de choses à faire ici. Le samedi, je vais souvent au centre commercial avec mes copains, puis après, on va au cinéma ou au café ou quelquefois, au stade pour voir un match de foot.
Le dimanche, c'est souvent une journée sportive pour moi. Mon frère et moi, nous allons à la piscine ou au centre sportif ou même à la plage où on peut jouer au beach-volley. Le dimanche, ma mère va à l'église où elle chante dans la chorale. Quelquefois, elle doit aller à l'hôpital où elle travaille comme infirmière. On ne va pas dans les magasins le dimanche; ils sont fermés.
Pour les jeunes, c'est super; le week-end, on peut aller à la patinoire ou au bowling ou même au parc. On pourrait aller dans les skates-parcs et il ne faut pas oublier la mer et les sports nautiques!

2

Answers

Pupil's own answers

Déjà vu 2: On fait les magasins!

(Student Book pages 58–59)

Main topics and objectives

- Shopping for food and clothes
- Using the partitive article

Grammar

- **de (du, de la, de l', des);** de with quantities
- Adjective agreement (colours, singular and plural)

Key language

Food and drink
Clothes

Resources

CD2, tracks 10–13
Cahier d'exercices, page 31
Grammaire 1.5, 2.2

Starter 1

Aim
To revise food vocabulary.

Give students working in pairs two minutes to come up with as many items of vocabulary for food and drinks in French as they can. Each correct item wins a point. Any item not identified by another pair wins a bonus point. The team with most points wins.

1 Écoutez et notez les lettres des 16 choses qui sont mentionnées.

Listening. Students listen and note in order the letters of the 16 food items mentioned.

Before playing the recording, ask students to read through the grid which contains all the vocabulary for the food items, organised by gender.

Audioscript 10

- *Bon, je vais faire les courses pour ce soir. On est combien pour le dîner?*
- *On est six, dont deux qui sont végétariens.*
- *Ouf! D'accord, je vais faire une liste. Qu'est-ce qu'il faut acheter?*
- *Il faut acheter du pain parce qu'on n'en a pas et du fromage, bien sûr.*
- *Alors, du pain, du fromage … Mais qu'est-ce qu'on va manger comme plat principal? On va faire une omelette pour les végétariens?*
- *C'est une bonne idée, ça. Oui, alors, achète des œufs, et pour les autres … du poulet peut-être.*
- *D'accord, j'achète des œufs et du poulet.*
- *Il faut acheter des légumes aussi.*
- *Des pommes de terre, par exemple?*
- *Oui, tu peux acheter un kilo de pommes de terre et de la salade, s'il te plaît. Et comme entrée, on va manger une salade de tomates, alors il faut acheter cinq cents grammes de tomates.*
- *Bon, alors, des pommes de terre, de la salade, des tomates … Et pour le dessert?*
- *Bof, des fruits. Des fraises, par exemple, ou des raisins.*
- *Si j'achète d'autres fruits aussi, on peut faire une salade de fruits. Ça va?*
- *D'accord, alors achète aussi des pommes et des bananes. Et du yaourt, pour manger avec ça.*
- *OK, des fraises, des raisins, des pommes, des bananes, du yaourt. Et comme boisson, j'achète de l'eau minérale?*
- *Oui, de l'eau minérale et du jus d'orange, s'il te plaît.*
- *Et est-ce qu'il faut acheter quelque chose pour le petit déjeuner?*
- *Ah, oui! Tu peux acheter du beurre et de la confiture, s'il te plaît?*
- *D'accord. C'est tout?*
- *Oui, je crois que c'est tout.*
- *Bon, j'y vais! À tout à l'heure!*
- *À tout à l'heure!*

Answers

a, m, c, e, l, n, g, j, p, q, s, o, t, r, f, d

Expo-langue: *de (du, de la, de l', des)*

Use this grammar box to cover the partitive (the different forms of **de** + the definite article) before students do exercise 2. There is more information on p. 207 of the Student Book.

2 À deux. Jeu de mémoire. Une personne ferme le livre. Combien des choses de l'exercice 1 pouvez-vous nommer?

Speaking. In pairs: students play a memory game. One person closes his/her book and tries to remember as many food items in French (with the correct form of the partitive) from exercise 1 as possible. Then the second person has a go. Who can remember most?

3 Lisez et complétez le dialogue au marché. Il a plusieurs possibilités!

Reading. Students read the gap-fill dialogue set in the market. They identify the missing words from the list supplied. They should be aware that there is more than one possible answer for some of the gaps.

Answers

1 poires/pêches/petits pois
2 poires/pêches/petits pois
3 fromage
4 jambon
5 confiture à la fraise
6 café/petit pois
7 petit pois
8 lait

4 Écoutez et notez en français ce qu'on achète, les quantités et le prix. (1–3)

Listening. Students listen to the three conversations and note in French what each person buys, including the quantity, and the total price.

Audioscript 11

1 – *Bonjour, monsieur. Je peux vous aider?*
– *Un kilo de pêches et cinq cents grammes de raisins, s'il vous plaît.*
– *Voilà, monsieur. Et avec ça?*
– *Euh, je prends aussi deux cents grammes de fraises.*
– *C'est tout, monsieur?*
– *Oui, c'est tout, merci. C'est combien?*
– *Ça fait 8,60€, s'il vous plaît.*

2 – *Madame?*
– *Je voudrais cinq tranches de jambon, s'il vous plaît.*
– *Voilà. C'est tout, madame?*
– *Je voudrais aussi quatre pots de yaourt nature et un paquet de beurre, s'il vous plaît.*
– *Et avec ça, madame?*
– *Je crois que c'est tout, merci. Ça fait combien?*
– *7,80€, s'il vous plaît, madame.*
– *Voilà. Merci. Au revoir.*
– *Au revoir et bonne journée, madame!*

3 – *Bonjour. Je peux vous aider?*
– *Bonjour. Oui, une bouteille d'eau minérale, s'il vous plaît.*
– *Un litre, monsieur?*
– *Oui, un litre, s'il vous plaît. Et une boîte de petits pois et de carottes.*
– *Voilà, monsieur. C'est tout?*
– *Oui, euh, non, je prends aussi un pot de confiture aux abricots, s'il vous plaît.*
– *Et avec ça, monsieur?*
– *C'est tout, merci.*
– *Ça fait 5,70€, s'il vous plaît.*

Answers

1 un kilo de pêches, cinq cents grammes de raisins, deux cents grammes de fraises; 8.60€/huit euros soixante
2 cinq tranches de jambon, quatre pots de yaourt, un paquet de beurre; 7,80€/sept euros quatre-vingts
3 une bouteille/un litre d'eau minérale, une boîte de petits pois et de carottes, un pot de confiture aux abricots; 5,70€/cinq euros soixante-dix

5 À deux. Faites un dialogue comme celui de l'exercice 3. Changez les détails.

Speaking. In pairs: students use different details and make up a dialogue like the one in exercise 3.

Starter 2

Aim
To revise vocabulary for items of clothing.

Write up the following and ask students working in pairs to write a sentence on each of the four people saying what they usually wear.

un footballeur, une chanteuse rock, la reine d'Angleterre, un(e) professeur

If students need support, they can use the vocabulary grid in exercise 9 on p. 59 and/or the Vocabulaire section/a dictionary.

6 Dans le magasin de vêtements. Mettez le dialogue dans le bon ordre.

Reading. Students read the jumbled dialogue set in a clothes shop and put the statements in the correct order.

Answers

See audioscript for ex. 7.

7 Écoutez et vérifiez.

Listening. Students listen to the dialogue set in a clothes shop to check their answers to exercise 6.

Audioscript 12

– *Bonjour, mademoiselle. Je peux vous aider?*
– *Je voudrais un tee-shirt, s'il vous plaît.*
– *Un tee-shirt de quelle couleur, mademoiselle?*
– *Bleu ou noir, s'il vous plaît.*
– *Et de quelle taille, mademoiselle?*
– *Taille deux, s'il vous plaît.*
– *Attendez un instant. … Voilà.*
– *C'est combien, s'il vous plaît?*
– *C'est 5 euros 60, mademoiselle.*
– *D'accord. Ça va, merci.*
– *De rien, mademoiselle. Vous devez payer à la caisse.*

8 Écoutez et reliez les images et les prix. (1–3)

Listening. Students listen to the three conversations and for each find the appropriate item of clothing (from the labelled pictures **a–f**) and the appropriate price tag.

Audioscript 13

1 – *Bonjour, monsieur. Je peux vous aider?*
– *Je voudrais un pantalon noir, s'il vous plaît.*
– *De quelle taille, monsieur?*
– *Taille 40, s'il vous plaît.*
– *Voilà, monsieur.*
– *C'est combien, s'il vous plaît?*
– *C'est 53 euros, monsieur.*
– *D'accord. Et la chemise blanche, elle coûte combien?*
– *Elle coûte 38 euros, monsieur.*
– *D'accord, je les prends, s'il vous plaît.*

2 – *Excusez-moi. Je voudrais une jupe, s'il vous plaît.*
– *De quelle couleur, mademoiselle?*
– *Rouge ou jaune, s'il vous plaît.*
– *Nous avons ces jupes rouges, à 62 euros.*
– *Avez-vous quelque chose de moins cher?*
– *Ah, non. Je suis désolé.*
– *J'aime bien cette robe jaune. C'est combien?*
– *C'est 44 euros, mademoiselle.*
– *Je peux l'essayer?*

3 – *Bonjour, mademoiselle. Je peux vous aider?*
– *Bonjour. Est-ce que vous avez des chaussures ou des baskets marron?*
– *Vous faites quelle pointure, mademoiselle?*
– *39, s'il vous plaît.*
– *On a ces chaussures en 39, mademoiselle. Ça va?*
– *Oui, mais elles coûtent combien?*
– *Elles coûtent 75 euros.*
– *C'est trop cher pour moi. Vous avez ces baskets marron en 39?*
– *Non, je suis désolé, mademoiselle, mais nous avons ces baskets noires et blanches, à 35 euros.*
– *Ah, non, merci. C'est des baskets marron que je cherche.*

Answers

1 e 53€, c 38€
2 f 62€, a 44€
3 b 75€, d 35€

Expo-langue: adjective agreement (colours)

Use this grammar box to review adjectives of colour before students do exercise 9. There is more information on p. 210 of the Student Book.

9 À deux. Adaptez le dialogue de l'exercice 6 et présentez-le (de mémoire, si possible).

Speaking. In pairs: students do their own version of the dialogue in exercise 6, changing the details. Once they feel confident, they should aim to do the dialogue together without looking at the book or at notes. A grid showing different items of clothing is supplied for support.

10 Écrivez un paragraphe sur ce que vous portez le soir et le week-end.

Writing. Students write a paragraph on what they wear in the evening and at the weekend. Some sample sentence openings are supplied for support. Encourage them to look up words not covered on the spread in the Vocabulaire or a dictionary and to use adjectives and intensifiers to add interest to their texts.

Plenary

Write up the following:

orange, rouge, bleu, blanc, jaune, vert, noir, gris, marron, rose

Ask students to use these words to make lists as follows:

- adjectives which don't have a different plural form (**orange, gris, marron**)
- adjectives which change pronunciation in the feminine form (**blanc/blanche, vert/verte, gris/grise**)
- adjectives which have four different written forms (**bleu, blanc, vert, noir**)
- adjectives which come before the noun (*none of them*)

Cahier d'exercices, page 31

Answers

des tomates
du pain
des raisins
des pommes
du jambon
du fromage
de l'eau minérale
des œufs
des bananes
des fraises
de la salade
des pêches
des tomates
du jus d'orange

1 Tout près d'ici

(Student Book pages 60–61)

Main topics and objectives

- Describing the location of a place
- Using prepositions and imperatives

Grammar

- Prepositions
- The imperative (**tu, vous**)

Key language

Où est/se trouve ... ?/Où sont/se trouvent ... ?
le commissariat de police
le syndicat d'initiative
l'arrêt d'autobus
l'hôtel de ville (m)
la librairie
le centre commercial
Pour aller au/à la/à l'/aux ... ?
Est-ce qu'il y a un(e) ... près d'ici?
Tourne/Tournez aux feux rouges.
Va/Allez tout droit.
Prends/Prenez ...
la première/deuxième rue (à gauche/droite)
Traverse/Traversez le pont.
Continue/Continuez jusqu'au carrefour.
C'est sur ta/votre gauche/droite.
C'est loin d'ici?
C'est à quelle distance?
C'est à cinq minutes/200m.
C'est tout près d'ici/assez loin.

après/dans/devant/derrière/entre/sous/sur
jusqu'à
à côté de/au bout de/au coin (de)/au fond (de)/de l'autre côté de/en face de

Resources

CD2, tracks 14–16
Cahier d'exercices, page 32
Grammaire 3.11, 4.1

Starter 1

Aim
To revise the vocabulary for places in town.

Tell students that they will be working in pairs and the aim of the exercise is to produce a written English translation of a list of 20 French words. The pair to finish in the shortest time is the winner, but 5 penalty seconds will be added to their time if they are found to have made any errors when you confirm the answers.

Then tell students the items to be translated are **A–T** in the grid on the map, p. 61 of the Student Book, exercise 4.

1 Écoutez et lisez le texte.

Listening. Students listen to the recorded version of Sébastien's note to his friend and read the text at the same time.

Audioscript 14

Salut, Liam
Désolé de devoir aller au collège ce matin, mais on se retrouve vers 14h30 au Café Coupole, OK? Pour aller en ville, prends le bus numéro 14. L'arrêt d'autobus se trouve en face de l'appartement, de l'autre côté de la rue. Descends devant l'hôtel de ville, à la place du Marché. Tourne à gauche et traverse aux feux rouges. Continue tout droit et prends la première rue à droite. (Il y a une pâtisserie au coin qui s'appelle Le Petit Pain Doré.) Va tout droit jusqu'au carrefour et prends la deuxième rue à droite – c'est la rue principale. Le café est sur ta gauche à côté du syndicat d'initiative. Si tu as le temps, il y a une bonne confiserie au bout de la rue, entre la parfumerie et la charcuterie, où tu peux acheter des bonbons délicieux!
À tout à l'heure!
Sébastien

2 Mettez les directions en anglais dans l'ordre du texte ci-dessus.

Reading. Students reread the text and put the nine directions in English in the order these are mentioned in the text. Draw their attention to the tip box before they begin: this gives advice on how they can use what they know to do this.

Answers
f, c, a, e, i, h, b, d, g

Expo-langue: prepositions

Use this grammar box to review prepositions, particularly those which take **de** (and its variant forms). Students go on to list all the prepositions in the text in exercise 1 in two columns: those which take **de** and those which don't.

There is more information on p. 216 of the Student Book.

3 Écrivez les directions en français.

Writing. Students use prepositions to describe where the small figure is in each of the eight pictures.

Answers
1. *devant la confiserie*
2. en face du syndicat d'initiative
3. à côté de la pâtisserie
4. entre l'hôtel de ville et la librairie
5. de l'autre côté de la place
6. prends la première rue à droite, puis prends la deuxième rue à gauche
7. va tout droit jusqu'à la place
8. traverse aux feux rouges, tourne à gauche au carrefour

Starter 2

Aim
To revise giving directions.

Write up a list of four to six places in the centre of your/a nearby town, e.g. gym, cafeteria, etc., and identify a central well-known point. Ask students to take it in turn giving directions from this point to one of the places. Their partner confirms whether the directions given are correct or not.

4 Écoutez et regardez le plan. Où va-t-on? (1–6)

Listening. Students listen to the six conversations and follow the directions on the map in the book to identify the place where each of the people is going. The starting point is at the bottom middle, below the Place du Marché.

Audioscript 15

Scored-through text shows the answers; these words are omitted/obscured on the recording.

1 – *Pardon, madame. Où est le [~~**syndicat d'initiative**~~], s'il vous plaît?*
– *Voyons … Euh, oui. Allez tout droit jusqu'à la place du Marché, puis tournez à droite. C'est en face du commissariat de police, sur votre gauche.*
– *Bon, tout droit jusqu'à la place du marché, puis à droite et c'est en face du …*
– *En face du commissariat de police, sur votre gauche.*
– *C'est loin, madame?*
– *Ah non, c'est pas loin. C'est à trois cents mètres d'ici environ.*
– *Merci, madame.*
– *De rien, monsieur.*

2 – *Excuse-moi. Est-ce qu'il y a une [~~**charcuterie**~~] près d'ici?*
– *Il y en a une dans la rue principale. C'est à cinq minutes à pied.*
– *Euh, je ne connais pas la ville. Où se trouve la rue principale, s'il te plaît?*
– *Ben, va tout droit, traverse la place et prends la deuxième rue à gauche. C'est sur ta droite, après la boulangerie.*
– *Alors, tout droit, je traverse la place, puis …*
– *Puis prends la deuxième rue à gauche et c'est sur ta droite, après la boulangerie.*
– *Merci, au revoir.*
– *Au revoir.*

3 – *Excusez-moi. Où se trouve [~~**la pharmacie**~~] la plus proche, s'il vous plaît?*
– *Prenez la première rue à gauche, traversez aux feux et c'est sur votre droite. C'est en face de la gare routière.*
– *Bon, la première à gauche, je traverse aux feux et c'est en face de la gare routière.*
– *Oui, c'est ça.*
– *C'est à quelle distance, s'il vous plaît?*
– *Oh, c'est tout près.*
– *Merci beaucoup.*

4 – *Pardon. Pour aller à l'hôtel de ville, s'il te plaît?*
– *Oh, c'est assez loin d'ici, de l'autre côté de la ville. Il faut prendre le bus.*
– *Et où est [~~**l'arrêt d'autobus**~~], s'il te plaît?*
– *Tournez à droite à la place du Marché, passez devant le commissariat de police et le syndicat d'initiative et c'est sur votre droite.*
– *Peux-tu répéter, s'il te plaît?*
– *Tournez à droite à la place du Marché, passez devant le commissariat de police et le syndicat d'initiative et c'est sur votre droite.*
– *Bon, merci beaucoup.*
– *De rien.*

5 – *Excusez-moi, monsieur. Est-ce qu'il y a une [~~**pâtisserie**~~] près d'ici, s'il vous plaît?*
– *Continue tout droit, puis prends la troisième rue à droite. Il y a une boîte aux lettres au coin. C'est dans cette rue, sur la droite.*
– *D'accord. Je prends la troisième rue à droite au coin, où il y a une boîte aux lettres. C'est loin d'ici?*
– *Oh, non, pas trop loin. C'est à cinq minutes à pied, à peu près.*
– *Merci, monsieur.*
– *De rien. Bonne journée!*

6 – *Pardon. Pour aller à la [~~**bibliothèque**~~], s'il te plaît?*
– *C'est un peu loin, madame. C'est à un kilomètre environ.*
– *Oh, ça va. J'ai le temps.*
– *Bon, prenez la deuxième rue à droite, allez tout droit, puis tournez à gauche aux feux …*
– *Attends …. La deuxième rue à droite, tout droit, puis à gauche aux feux. C'est ça?*
– *Oui, c'est ça, madame. Puis traversez le pont et c'est sur votre droite.*
– *Je traverse le pont et c'est sur la droite. Bon, merci. Au revoir.*
– *Au revoir, madame.*

Answers

1 le syndicat d'initiative **2** la charcuterie **3** la pharmacie **4** l'arrêt d'autobus **5** la pâtisserie **6** la bibliothèque

5 Écoutez encore. C'est à quelle distance? Notez en français. (1–6)

Listening. Students listen to the recording for exercise 4 again and note the distance mentioned in each of the six conversations.

Audioscript 16

As for exercise 4.

Answers

1 C'est à trois cents mètres d'ici environ.
2 C'est à cinq minutes à pied.
3 C'est tout près.
4 C'est assez loin d'ici.
5 C'est à cinq minutes à pied, à peu près.
6 C'est à un kilomètre environ.

Expo-langue: the imperative (*tu, vous*)

Use this grammar box to review both forms of the imperative before students do exercise 6. Ask them to quickly recap on when they would use each form. There is more information on p. 214 of the Student Book.

R Students note down all the imperatives in the text in exercise 1. They then list the **vous** forms of these.

6 À deux. Faites un dialogue en utilisant le plan ci-dessus. Utilisez *vous*.

Speaking. In pairs: students use the map in exercise 4 and the box of useful structures supplied to make up their own dialogue. They should address each other as **vous**.

7 Écrivez pour un copain/une copine la direction pour aller à ces endroits. Utilisez le plan ci-dessus.

Writing. Using the map in exercise 4, students write out directions to each of the five places listed for a friend. (The tip box reminds them to use the **tu** form imperative in this context.)

Plenary

Hold a soft toy or other item of similar size in various locations (e.g. **dans, devant, entre, sous, sur, à côté de, au fond de, en face de,** etc.) around the classroom. Students need to come up with a phrase in French using the appropriate preposition (**dans la poubelle, devant le livre,** etc.).

Cahier d'exercices, page 32

1

Answers

1 l'office de tourisme
2 la poste
3 les toilettes

2

Answers

Possible answers

1 Du théâtre, tournez à droite, puis prenez la première rue à gauche après la place. Après les toilettes, tournez à droite. Allez tout droit sur l'Avenue de l'Europe. Passez la poste et la cabine téléphonique et après encore 200m, c'est à droite.

2 De la Place de la Liberté, tourne à gauche sur la Rue Montgolfier dans la direction de l'office de tourisme. Traverse le pont et au rond-point, tourne à gauche sur la Rue Sadi Carnot. Après le théâtre, prends la première rue à droite puis prends la première rue à gauche et c'est là devant toi!

2 On prépare une fête

(Student Book pages 62–63)

Main topics and objectives

- Organising a beach party
- Using **il faut** and **en**

Grammar

- **il faut** + noun/the infinitive
- The pronoun **en**

Key language

Il faut acheter ...
du bifteck/cidre/citron/pâté/riz/saucisson
de la bière/moutarde
de l'huile d'olive (f)
des abricots (m)/cerises (f)/champignons (m)/framboises (f)/haricots verts (m)/pâtes (f)/saucisses (f)
Il faut de la musique.
Il faut organiser les activités.
Je voudrais ...
envoyer un paquet à l'étranger
louer une planche de surf
des timbres

Resources

CD2, tracks 17–18
Cahier d'exercices, page 33
Grammaire 1.13, 4.6

Starter 1

Aim
To revise the near future tense.

Write up the following text, using your students' names to replace P1, P2, etc. (answers supplied in brackets for reference only). Tell the class you are organising a (fictional) party. Ask them to use the text to write out what everyone is going to do to help. They can work in pairs. What tense will they need to use?

To do	
me – going to choose some presents	**(Je vais choisir des cadeaux.)**
P1 – going to send the invitations	**(P1 va envoyer les invitations.)**
P2 – going to go shopping	**(P2 va faire les courses.)**
P3 + P4 – going to organise the CDs	**(P3 + P4 vont organiser les CD.)**
all of us – going to enjoy ourselves	**(Nous allons nous amuser.)**

1 Écoutez et lisez le texte. Puis regardez les huit mots. Qu'est-ce que c'est en anglais?

Listening. Students listen to the conversation in which four teenagers are planning a party and read the text at the same time. They then need to work out the meaning of the eight French expressions listed. The tip box reminds them to use the context to work these out.

Audioscript 17

- *Salut, les gars! J'ai bien acheté deux cartes et deux CD pour l'anniversaire de Claire et Vincent.*
- *Il faut les envoyer aujourd'hui, hein, parce que leur anniversaire c'est demain. Il faut faire des paquets, non?*
- *Oui, puis je vais aller à la poste pour acheter des timbres pour envoyer les cartes et les paquets.*
- *Et pour leur fête d'anniversaire? On est d'accord pour faire la fête sur la plage, samedi prochain? Afram, tu vas t'occuper du barbecue?*
- *D'accord, mais qui va faire les courses avec moi? Il faut de la viande – du bifteck et des saucisses, par exemple. Il faut préparer des salades aussi et comme dessert, je vais peut-être faire des tartes aux fruits, comme une tarte aux abricots ou une tarte au citron.*
- *Pas de problème. Je viens avec toi. Il faut de la musique aussi. Pour ça, je vais téléphoner à mon cousin. Il est DJ et il a toutes sortes de musique.*
- *Génial! Et moi, je vais organiser les activités sportives! On peut jouer au volley et puisqu'on est sur la plage, il faut faire du surf, non?*
- *Bonne idée, mais est-ce qu'on a assez de planches de surf?*
- *Non, il faut en louer. Ça ne coûte pas très cher. Ne t'inquiète pas. Je vais m'occuper de tout ça.*
- *Bon, alors. Au boulot, les gars!*

Answers

1 a stamp **2** a package **3** to send **4** (some) steak **5** (some) apricots **6** a lemon **7** a surfboard **8** to hire

Expo-langue: *il faut*

Use this grammar box to introduce **il faut** + a noun/an infinitive before students do exercise 2. There is more information on p. 217 of the Student Book.

2 Relisez le texte et complétez les phrases avec *il faut* et l'infinitif d'un verbe.

Reading. Students read the text in exercise 1 again and use it to complete the six gap-fill sentences with the correct **il faut** expression.

Answers

1 Il faut envoyer
2 il faut aller
3 Il faut acheter
4 il faut faire les courses
5 il faut téléphoner
6 il faut louer

➕ Ask students to summarise in French what each of the friends in exercise 1 has agreed to do.

Starter 2

Aim
To consolidate the structures **il faut** + noun/ **il faut** + infinitive.

Tell students they are planning a party of their own. Ask them (working in pairs) to write a list of five things they need to have and five things they need to do.

3 À deux. Imaginez que vous êtes Camille et Nicolas. Complétez les dialogues.

Speaking. In pairs: students take it in turn to play the part of Camille and then Nicolas, in dialogues set in the post office and the surf equipment hire shop. The lines for the employees are supplied and picture prompts given for Camille's/Nicolas's role.

4 Copiez le bon mot pour chaque nombre. Utilisez le glossaire, si nécessaire.

Writing. Students find the correct label for each food item pictured, copying it out from the list supplied. They should be able to remember much of this vocabulary from earlier years, but they can use the Vocabulaire section if they are stuck.

Answers

1 du cidre
2 des pâtes
3 du riz
4 des champignons
5 des saucisses
6 une baguette
7 des haricots verts
8 du pâté
9 des framboises
10 du saucisson
11 de la moutarde
12 de la bière

5 Écoutez Afram et Farida. Qu'est-ce qu'ils ont acheté pour le barbecue? Copiez et complétez la grille en français.

Listening. Students copy out the grid. They listen to Afram and Farida discussing what they have bought for the barbecue and fill in the details in the grid.

☑ Before students begin, draw their attention to the tip box on distinguishing similar-sounding words in French. You could suggest that they keep a list of the words they find confusing as they go along as a useful revision tool.

Audioscript 18

– *Bon, alors, est-ce qu'on a acheté tout ce qu'il faut pour le barbecue?*
– *Oui, je crois. J'ai acheté un kilo de saucisses pour faire des hot-dogs. Tu as acheté de la moutarde pour aller avec ça?*
– *Oui, j'en ai acheté un grand pot au supermarché.*
– *On a beaucoup de pain aussi – j'ai acheté quatre baguettes à la boulangerie. Est-ce qu'on a quelque chose pour faire des sandwichs? Du pâté ou du fromage, par exemple?*
– *On n'a pas de pâté, mais on peut faire des sandwichs au saucisson, si tu veux. J'ai acheté douze tranches de saucisson à la charcuterie.*
– *D'accord. Et pour les salades? Il n'y avait pas de haricots verts, mais j'ai acheté deux cents grammes de champignons. Je vais préparer une salade de riz et une salade de pâtes. Tu as acheté du riz et des pâtes, j'espère?*
– *Oh, excuse-moi, j'ai acheté un grand paquet de pâtes et une bouteille d'huile d'olive pour la sauce vinaigrette, mais j'ai oublié le riz. Tu en as à la maison?*
– *Non, je n'en ai plus. Mais on peut acheter ça demain.*
– *D'accord. Et qu'est-ce que tu as acheté pour les tartes aux fruits? Des abricots?*
– *Il n'y en avait plus, mais j'ai acheté cinq cents grammes de cerises et cinq cents grammes de framboises. Je vais faire une tarte aux cerises et une tarte aux framboises.*
– *Miam, miam! Délicieux!*
– *Et finalement, qu'est-ce que tu as acheté à boire? De la bière?*
– *J'ai décidé d'acheter six bouteilles de bière et un litre de cidre. Ça va aller comme ça?*
– *Oui, je crois que ça va aller. Ouf! C'est fatigant, les courses! Tu veux boire un pot au café?*
– *Oui, je veux bien!*

Answers

choses achetées	quantité
saucisses	*1 kilo*
moutarde	un grand pot
baguettes	quatre
saucisson	douze tranches
champignons	deux cents grammes
pâtes	un grand paquet
huile d'olive	une bouteille
cerises	cinq cents grammes
framboises	cinq cents grammes
bière	six bouteilles
cidre	un litre

Expo-langue: *en*

Use this grammar box to introduce the pronoun **en**, which replaces **de** + a noun, before students do exercise 6. There is more information on p. 210 of the Student Book.

6 Imaginez que vous préparez une fête. Écrivez un e-mail à votre copine Laure.

Writing. Students imagine they are planning a party and write an e-mail to their friend Laure about the arrangements and what each of their friends is going to do to help. A list of questions is supplied to help students structure their text. Students should also think up a question to ask Laure.

+ Students write another e-mail after the party to a friend who didn't come, describing what they did to prepare for the party, what happened at the party and how it went.

Plenary

Ask students to tell you about the pronoun **en**: what does it mean and how is it used?

Then consolidate usage by prompting, e.g., **j'ai cinq bananes** for students to reply **j'en ai cinq**. Start with the present tense, using a range of persons, and then move on to the perfect with **j'ai acheté, il a acheté**, etc.

Cahier d'exercices, page 33

1

Answers

1e **2**f **3**a **4**g **5**c **6**i **7**h **8**d **9**b

2

Answers

Pupil's own answers

3 Bon voyage!

(Student Book pages 64–65)

Main topics and objectives

- Making travel arrangements
- Learning more about the perfect tense

Grammar

- The perfect tense
  - irregular past participles (**eu, dû, mis**)
  - verbs which take **être**

Key language

un aller simple/aller-retour
première/deuxième classe
fumeurs/non-fumeurs
Le train arrive à quelle heure?
Est-ce qu'il faut changer de train?
Le train part de quel quai?
J'ai raté (l'avion).
l'aéroport
le vol
le retard
les bagages (m)
le pneu (crevé)
la grève
les objets trouvés (m)
J'ai perdu ...
On a volé ...
mon portefeuille
ma carte de crédit

Resources

CD2, track 19
Cahier d'exercices, page 34
Grammaire 3.3

Starter 1

Aim
To revise the vocabulary for transport.

Write up the following places and ask students to write a sentence saying how you could go to each place using **on pourrait** and the appropriate means of transport.

1 à Bruges pour le week-end (**On pourrait aller en train/en avion/par le Tunnel**)
2 à Melbourne pour les vacances (**... en avion**)
3 au centre-ville pour faire des lèches-vitrines (**... en voiture/en bus/en tram**)
4 à Barcelona pour un concert (**... en avion/en car**)
5 chez mon copain/ma copine (**... à pied/en vélo/en bus/en train/en voiture**)
6 dans le peloton du Tour de France (**en vélo**)

1 Léna et Karim vont à Bordeaux pour la fête sur la plage. Écoutez et notez les phrases dans l'ordre du dialogue.

Listening. Students listen to the conversation between Léna and Karim, who are talking about their trip to Bordeaux. They note the phrases listed in the order they are heard on the recording.

Audioscript 19

- *Alors, pour la fête sur la plage ... On va à Bordeaux en train?*
- *Oui, on y va en train.*
- *As-tu regardé l'horaire des trains?*
- *Oui, j'ai cherché sur Internet et j'ai trouvé les heures et les prix. Il y a un train toutes les heures le samedi ... Il y en a un qui arrive à Bordeaux juste après 13 heures.*
- *Le train part à quelle heure, alors?*
- *Euh ... Il part à 11 heures 25.*
- *Et il arrive à Bordeaux à quelle heure?*
- *Il arrive à 13 heures 05.*
- *Ça va. Si la fête commence à 14h, on a plein de temps. Mais est-ce qu'il faut changer de train?*
- *Non, c'est un train direct.*
- *C'est parfait, alors. Le train part de quel quai?*
- *D'habitude, c'est le quai numéro huit pour Bordeaux, mais on peut vérifier en arrivant à la gare.*
- *Et ça coûte combien, les billets?*
- *Un aller-retour, c'est 17 euros.*
- *Ouf! C'est un peu cher, ça.*
- *Oui, mais c'est moins cher avec la carte d'étudiant.*
- *D'accord, ça va. Tu crois qu'il faut acheter les billets à l'avance?*
- *Ah oui, je crois qu'il faut.*
- *OK, je vais aller à la gare demain. Je vais acheter deux allers-retours pour Bordeaux, deuxième classe, dans le train de 11 heures 25.*
- *Et non-fumeurs, s'il te plaît! N'oublie pas de demander un compartiment non-fumeurs!*
- *D'accord, alors, deux allers-retours, deuxième classe, non-fumeurs. C'est ça?*
- *Oui, c'est ça. Merci.*

Answers
g, e, c, d, i, j, a, h, f, b,

2 Trouvez l'équivalent en français de l'exercice 1.

Reading. Students match the 10 English expressions listed (**1–10**) with the appropriate French phrase in exercise 1 (from **a–j**).

Answers
1 f **2** b **3** h **4** d **5** i **6** a **7** e **8** j **9** g **10** c

3 À deux. Complétez la conversation au guichet en utilisant des phrases de l'exercice 1.

Speaking. In pairs: students complete the gap-fill dialogue set at the ticket desk in the station, using the phrases in exercise 1. (Not all of the phrases are used.)

4 Refaites le dialogue en utilisant les détails ci-dessous.

Speaking. In pairs: students make up three dialogues of their own using the prompts supplied.

R Students write out their own version of a dialogue at the ticket desk.

Starter 2

Aim
To consolidate how the perfect tense is formed.
To encourage students to use reference resources to check their work.

Write up the following verbs:
aller, finir, attendre, venir, faire, se lever, lire, écrire, essayer

Give students two minutes to write out the **je** form of each verb in the perfect tense, using the correct auxiliary. When they have finished, they swap and check their partner's answers using the verb tables in the Grammar section of the book.

5 Lisez et faites une liste des nouveaux mots de vocabulaire. Pouvez-vous deviner leur équivalent en anglais?

Reading. Students read the three texts and list all the new vocabulary they find. They then work out the meaning of as many of these as they can, using the usual strategies. (There is a tip box to remind them of some of these. What others can they add?)

Expo-langue: irregular past participles (*eu, dû, mis*); verbs taking *être* in the perfect tense

Use this grammar box before students do exercise 6. It covers the irregular past participles of **avoir, devoir** and **mettre** and lists the most useful verbs which take **être** in the perfect tense.

6 Relisez les textes de l'exercice 5 et écrivez le nom de la personne.

Reading. Students reread the texts in exercise 5 and answer the seven questions on them by identifying the correct person in each case.

Answers

1 Farid **2** Clément **3** Yasmina **4** Clément **5** Farid **6** Yasmina **7** Farid

7 Décrivez un voyage désastreux que vous avez fait.

Writing. Students write about a disastrous trip of their own (real or imaginary). They should use the list of points supplied to structure their texts.

Students could write their texts on computer. Encourage them then to get a partner to read over their texts and to identify (but not correct) any errors they see. Students then produce a second, corrected version.

Plenary

Ask students to tell you how the perfect tense is formed, covering details of the auxiliaries and the past participle.

Then give a range of verbs in the infinitive as prompts, mixing up **avoir** and **être** verbs, including reflexives. Students respond **avoir** or **être** according to which auxiliary each verb takes in the perfect tense.

Cahier d'exercices, page 34

2

Answers

bénéficier – to benefit
petits prix – cheap prices
disponible – available
trajets – journeys
échangeable – exchangeable
remboursable – refundable
en ligne – online
gratuitement – free
imprimer – to print
souhaitez-vous – Do you want
au meilleur prix – at the best price

3

Answers

1. The 'Tarif Prem' is a discounted ticket when you book in advance.
2. The earlier you book, the less you pay.
3. It's also available for travel abroad.
4. The ticket is non-exchangeable and non-refundable.
5. You buy the tickets online.
6. You can print them or receive them free by post.

4 Ça me va?

(Student Book pages 66–67)

Main topics and objectives
- Talking about buying clothes
- Using ce, lequel, celui, etc.

Grammar
- Adjectives
  - **ce (cet), cette, ces**
- Pronouns
  - **lequel/laquelle/lesquels/lesquelles**
  - **celui-ci/-là, celle-ci/-là, ceux-ci/-là, celles-ci/-là**
- The conditional (**j'aimerais, je préférerais, je voudrais** + the infinitive)

Key language
Le blouson est trop large.
Le manteau est trop court.
La ceinture est trop longue.
La cravate est démodée.
Les gants sont un peu serrés.
un chapeau
un imper(méable)
un maillot de bain
une casquette
des chaussettes (f)
en coton/cuir/laine
Je peux l'/les essayer?

Resources
CD2, tracks 20–22
Cahier d'exercices, page 35
Grammaire 1.10, 2.5, 3.10

Starter 1

Aim
To revise/introduce adjectives for describing clothes. To practise using context to work out new vocabulary.

Write up the following and tell students the list consists of ten pairs of opposites. Say also that these are all the same type of word grammatically and all used in the same context. Ask students to match the pairs and to translate them into English.

court, démodé, large, grand, bon marché, serré, long, cher, dernier cri, petit

(**court/long** – short/long; **démodé/dernier cri** – old-fashioned/trendy; **large/serré** – baggy/tight; **grand/petit** – big/small; **bon marché/cher** – cheap/expensive)

When checking answers, ask students to tell you how they worked the words out.

1 Écoutez. Qu'est-ce qu'on veut acheter et quel est le problème? Notez les *deux* bonnes lettres et les *deux* problèmes pour chaque dialogue. (1–5)

Listening. Students listen to the five conversations to find out what each person wants to buy and what the problem is with the item. For each they need to note two pictures (from **a–j**) and two phrases from those listed.

Audioscript 20

1 – *Alors, tu l'as achetée, la cravate?*
– *Non, parce qu'elle est beaucoup trop chère. Trente euros pour une cravate! C'est ridicule, non?*
– *Oui, un peu. Alors, tu vas acheter quelque chose pour les vacances au Portugal?*
– *Quoi, par exemple?*
– *Il te faut une casquette pour porter à la plage. Regarde. Tu aimes celle-là?*
– *Laquelle?*
– *Celle-là, la casquette bleue.*
– *Hm. J'aime bien la couleur, mais elle est un peu trop petite pour moi.*
– *D'accord, viens. On va chercher ailleurs.*

2 – *Je peux vous aider, monsieur?*
– *Je voudrais un blouson en cuir, s'il vous plaît. Noir ou marron.*
– *Nous avons celui-ci, monsieur. Vous voulez l'essayer?*
– *Il est de quelle taille?*
– *Euh… taille 46, monsieur. Ça vous va?*
– *Non, il est trop serré. Avez-vous quelque chose de plus grand?*
– *Ah, non, monsieur. Je regrette c'est tout ce qu'on a comme blousons en cuir.*
– *C'est dommage. … Mais j'aime bien cet imperméable.*
– *Lequel, monsieur? Celui-ci?*
– *Oui, celui-là. Je peux l'essayer, s'il vous plaît?*
– *Bien sûr, monsieur. Les cabines d'essayage sont au fond à droite.*
– *Ça va, je peux l'essayer ici.*
– *Il vous va très bien, monsieur.*
– *Oui, mais il est un peu trop court. Je préférerais un imper plus long.*

3 – *Bon, il me faut un nouveau maillot de bain pour aller en Espagne. Que penses-tu de ceux-là?*
– *Lesquels? Ceux-ci?*
– *Oui. Tu les aimes?*
– *Non, pas beaucoup. Je les trouve un peu démodés.*
– *Tu as peut-être raison. Je vais regarder les maillots au Printemps. Et ce chapeau? Comment tu le trouves?*
– *Il est joli, le chapeau. Tu veux l'essayer?*
– *Oui, … Ah, non, il est trop grand. Je vais demander s'ils ont quelque chose de plus petit.*
– *D'accord. Je t'attends ici.*

4 – *Tu as vu les belles chaussettes là-bas?*
– *Lesquelles? Les rouges ou les jaunes?*
– *Celles-là, les rouges. Tu en veux une paire?*

– *Ah, non, elles sont un peu trop courtes. Je voudrais de longues chaussettes pour l'hiver, tu sais?*
– *D'accord. Tu veux regarder autre chose?*
– *Hm. J'aimerais bien m'acheter un nouveau manteau. Les manteaux là-bas sont bien. Je vais en essayer un.*
– *OK, mais dépêche-toi. Je suis fatigué.*
– *Hmm, celui-ci est un peu trop large pour moi. Je préférerais quelque chose d'un peu plus serré.*
– *OK. C'est fini avec les courses maintenant? On peut aller boire un café?*

5 – *Bonjour, j'aimerais une paire de gants, s'il vous plaît.*
– *Oui, madame, Nous avons ceux-ci en laine, si vous voulez.*
– *J'aime bien les noirs. Je peux les essayer, s'il vous plaît?*
– *Bien sûr, madame. Les voilà.*
– *Ah, ils sont un peu petits. Vous avez quelque chose de plus grand?*
– *Oui, voici une paire un peu plus grande. Ça vous va?*
– *Ah, oui, c'est parfait. Je les prends.*
– *Vous prenez cette ceinture aussi, madame?*
– *Non, merci, elle est un peu trop chère pour moi. En tout cas, je préférerais une couleur différente. Avez-vous des ceintures blanches ou grises, s'il vous plaît?*
– *Attendez un moment, s'il vous plaît. Je vais regarder.*

Answers

1 e – trop chère **b** – un peu trop petite
2 a – trop serré **h** – trop court
3 i – un peu démodé **d** – trop grand
4 f – trop courtes **j** – trop large
5 g – un peu petit **c** – un peu trop chère

Expo-langue: *ce, lequel?, celui-ci,* etc.

Use this grammar box to introduce all the forms of the demonstrative adjective **ce**, the interrogative pronoun **lequel** and the demonstrative pronoun **celui-ci** before students do exercise 2. There is more information on p. 209 and p. 211 of the Student Book.

R Students take it in turn to prompt and to respond. The first student prompts with the correct form of **ce** plus an item of clothing (e.g. **ce manteau**). The second responds with one of the corresponding forms of the demonstrative pronoun (e.g. **celui-ci/celui-là**).

2 À deux. Complétez le dialogue dans le magasin de vêtements. Utilisez les idées ci-dessous ou vos propres idées.

Speaking. In pairs: students use the dialogue framework supplied to create their own dialogue set in a clothes shop. They can use the ideas given or their own.

 The sound **-ui**, practised in exercise 3.

3 Écoutez et répétez aussi vite que possible!

Listening. Students listen to the recording and, imitating the recorded model as closely as they can, say the phrase **Oui, celui en cuir gris est pour lui** over and over as quickly as possible.

Audioscript 21

Oui, celui en cuir gris est pour lui.

Starter 2

Aim
To consolidate using **ce** (etc.), **lequel?** (etc.), **celui-ci** (etc.) and **celui-là** (etc.).

Write up the following grid and ask students working in pairs to complete it.

	singular		**plural**	
	masculine	**feminine**	**masculine**	**feminine**
this/ those		cette	ces	
	lequel?			lesquelles?
this/ these one(s)			ceux-ci	
that/ those one(s)	celui-là			

Expo-langue: the conditional

Use this grammar box to focus on the conditional before students do exercise 4. It covers the key forms **je voudrais, j'aimerais** and **je préférerais.** You might also want to point out **vous voudriez** in the rubric to exercise 4. There is more information on p. 214 of the Student Book.

4 Imaginez que vous êtes très riche et que vous avez un shopper personnel. Laissez un mot pour lui dire quels vêtements vous voudriez.

Writing. Students imagine they are very rich and have a personal shopper. They write a note to tell him/her what clothes they would like purchased. A sample answer is supplied. Encourage students to use their imagination.

Students could research other vocabulary to do with shopping on the internet, by looking at the website for a large French department store, such as Galeries Lafayette or Printemps. Go to www.heinemann.co.uk/hotlinks and enter the express code 7898T. Ask them to identify and note down 10 new words or phrases and to look these up in a dictionary.

5 Lisez le guide du grand magasin et le texte dans les bulles. C'est à quel étage?

Reading. Students read the store guide and the 10 speech bubbles and identify the floor that each person needs to go to.

Answers

1 2ème étage **2** rez-de-chaussée **3** 4ème étage **4** sous-sol **5** 4ème étage **6** sous-sol **7** 1er étage **8** 3ème étage **9** 2ème étage **10** sous-sol

6 Écoutez. C'est la bonne direction? Répondez par oui ou non. (1–7)

Listening. Students listen to the seven conversations. Using the store guide, they decide whether each person is given the correct information or not, using **oui** or **non**.

Audioscript 22

1 – *Excusez-moi. Je cherche une bouteille de parfum pour ma femme. Ça se vend ici?*
– *Oui, monsieur. La parfumerie est au sous-sol. Prenez l'escalier là-bas.*
– *Merci, madame.*

2 – *Je peux vous aider, madame?*
– *J'aimerais acheter* Les Choristes *en DVD. Où faut-il aller pour ça?*
– *Il faut aller au rayon audio-visuel, madame. Ça se trouve au deuxième étage.*
– *Merci beaucoup.*
– *De rien.*

3 – *Pardon. On aimerait voir des canapés et des fauteuils. C'est à quel étage?*
– *Les meubles sont au troisième étage, monsieur. Vous pouvez prendre l'ascenseur là-bas, si vous voulez.*

4 – *Vous cherchez quelque chose, madame?*
– *Où se trouve le rayon des fruits et légumes, s'il vous plaît?*
– *Tous nos rayons alimentation sont au rez-de-chaussée, madame.*
– *Ah, bon? Merci bien.*

5 – *Excusez-moi. Il me faut acheter un nouveau frigo. Ça se trouve où dans le magasin, s'il vous plaît?*
– *Ça se trouve au rayon électroménager, monsieur.*
– *C'est à quel étage, s'il vous plaît?*
– *Il faut prendre l'ascenseur jusqu'au quatrième étage.*
– *Au quatrième étage? Bon, merci.*

6 – *Pardon. Je voudrais acheter des chaussures pour mon petit garçon. C'est au deuxième étage?*
– *Non, madame. Les vêtements pour enfants sont au premier étage, à côté du rayon hommes.*
– *D'accord. Merci beaucoup.*
– *De rien, madame.*

7 – *Je peux vous aider, madame?*
– *Je voudrais acheter des boucles d'oreilles pour aller avec cette robe. On vend des bijoux ici?*
– *Oui, bien sûr, madame. Notre bijouterie est au premier étage, tout près des vêtements pour femmes.*
– *Très bien. Merci de votre aide.*
– *De rien, madame.*

Answers

1 oui **2** non **3** non **4** oui **5** oui **6** non **7** oui

Plenary

Ask students to summarise the three ways of referring to items covered in this unit (the forms of **ce** + noun, the question form **lequel?** (etc.) and the forms of the pronouns **celui-ci/-là**).

Put the class into teams. Then prompt each team in turn (e.g. this skirt *or* that jacket) for them to respond with the appropriate demonstrative pronoun (e.g. **celle-ci** *or* **celui-là**).

Cahier d'exercices, page 35

1

Answers

1 Je voudrais acheter un manteau en laine, pas trop serré.
2 Il me faut un nouvel ordinateur. C'est à quel étage ?
3 J'aimerais voir un ceinture en cuir, mais pas trop large.
4 Je voudrais une nouvelle casquette. Comme marque, je préférerais Roxy.
5 J'aimerais acheter un blouson noir pas trop cher.
6 Ma mère m'a demandé d'acheter une petite bouteille de parfum.
7 Mon mari veut acheter des gants en cuir.
8 J'ai besoin d'un nouveau maillot de bain pour mes vacances d'été.

2

Answers

Pupil's own answers

5 Malheureusement ...

(Student Book pages 68–69)

Main topics and objectives

- Describing what went wrong
- More on the imperfect tense
-

Grammar

- The perfect and imperfect: when to use

Key language

Revision of language from earlier modules

Resources

CD2, tracks 23–24
Cahier d'exercices, pages 36–37
Grammaire 3.5

Starter 1

Aim
To revise the imperfect.

Write up the following and give students three minutes to complete each line with a different verb in the imperfect tense.

je	
tu	
il/elle/on	
nous	
vous	
ils/elles	

When checking answers, ask students to summarise how the imperfect tense is formed.

1 Écoutez et trouvez les deux bonnes images pour chaque personne qui parle. (1–4)

Listening. Students listen to the four conversations and identify for each speaker the two appropriate pictures (from **a–h**).

Audioscript 23

1. *J'ai acheté un beau sweat-shirt comme cadeau d'anniversaire pour mon petit copain. Mais il n'aimait pas la couleur et de plus, on a trouvé qu'il y avait un trou dedans. J'ai dû retourner au magasin et demander un remboursement. J'étais très fâchée!*
2. *J'allais au cinéma avec une fille que j'aimais bien, mais quand on est arrivés, on n'a pas pu voir le film qu'on voulait voir parce que c'était complet. On était tout à fait déçus.*
3. *Mes parents m'ont acheté une belle montre comme cadeau de Noël. Un soir, j'étais en boîte avec des copains et je portais ma montre. On s'amusait bien, mais pendant que je dansais, un garçon stupide m'a fait tomber et après, j'ai découvert que ma montre ne marchait plus. Il était désolé, mais quel idiot!*
4. *Ma petite copine et moi sommes allés à un concert en plein air. Quand on a quitté la maison, il faisait beau et très chaud, donc on portait un tee-shirt et un short. Mais quand on est arrivés au concert, il pleuvait à verse! On était trempés jusqu'aux os, mais on s'est bien amusés quand même.*

Answers
1 d, f **2** c, g **3** b, e **4** a, h

+ In pairs: students choose and talk about two of the pictures each, using the perfect to say what happened and the imperfect for descriptions.

2 Reliez et copiez les deux parties de chaque phrase.

Reading. Students read the text in exercise 1 again and copy out the sentences matching the sentence halves.

Answers
1. Mon petit copain n'aimait pas la couleur et en plus on a trouvé qu'il y avait un trou dedans.
2. J'ai dû retourner au magasin et demander un remboursement.
3. J'allais au cinéma avec une fille que j'aimais bien.
4. Mais on n'a pas pu voir le film qu'on voulait voir parce que c'était complet.
5. Pendant que je dansais, un garçon stupide m'a fait tomber.
6. Après, j'ai découvert que ma montre ne marchait pas.
7. Quand on a quitté la maison, il faisait beau et très chaud, donc on portait un tee-shirt et un short.
8. Mais quand on est arrivés au concert, il pleuvait à verse.

3 Écoutez et lisez le dialogue.

Listening. Students listen to Ahmed talking to a friend about his date with Claire and read the text at the same time.

Audioscript 24

– *Salut, Ahmed! Ça s'est bien passé avec Claire samedi?*
– *Non, pas du tout!*
– *Ah, bon, pourquoi?*
– *On est allés en boîte. On s'amusait bien, mais je suis allé aux toilettes et quand je suis revenu, elle parlait avec un autre garçon! Puis, quand on est sortis, il pleuvait et le bus avait 20 minutes de retard. C'était nul.*
– *Je suis désolé.*

4 À deux. Inventez un autre dialogue. Changez les détails en bleu. Utilisez les mots dans la grille ou vos propres idées.

Speaking. In pairs: students make up another dialogue, adapting Ahmed's by changing the text in blue. A grid of useful language is supplied for support.

Starter 2

Aim
To practise using the perfect tense and the imperfect tense appropriately.

Ask students which tense they would use in French in each of the following situations in the past:

1 to say where you used to live
2 to say what you did last night
3 to say what you usually did every weekend in the summer
4 to say you were going to the cinema when you met your friend (2 tenses)
5 to say that your birthday party last year was great
6 to talk about something you wanted to do

Ask students to summarise when the perfect and imperfect are used.

5 Lisez le texte. Trouvez tous les verbes à l'imparfait et au passé composé.

Reading. Students read the text. They then identify all the verbs in the imperfect tense and all those in the perfect.

Answers

bold = imperfect *italic = perfect*

je *suis sortie*	on **avait**
c'**était** un désastre	c'**était** complet
Il y **avait**	ce n'**était** pas
on **voulait** voir	Sébastien *a vu*
on *a quitté*	j'**étais** toute rouge
tout **allait** bien	je **portais**
On **attendait**	elle **avait** les cheveux blonds
il **faisait** beau	elle **portait** une nouvelle robe
on **parlait** ensemble	Ils **parlaient** ensemble
c'**était** sympa	ils **flirtaient**
on *a attendu*	J'**étais** si furieuse
n'*est* pas *arrivé*	je *suis partie*
On ne **pouvait** pas	il **pleuvait**
on n'**avait** pas	je *suis arrivée*
on *est partis*	Sébastien *s'est excusé*
on *est arrivés*	
on **avait**	

6 Relisez le texte et choisissez les bonnes réponses.

Reading. Students read the text again. They then read the eight sentences and choose the correct ending for each from the two options given (**a** or **b**).

Answers

1 b **2** a **3** a **4** b **5** b **6** a **7** b **8** a

7 Décrivez une sortie désastreuse. Adaptez le texte de l'exercice 5, si vous voulez.

Writing. Students write a description of a disastrous outing of their own (real or imaginary). They can use Chloé's text in exercise 5 as a model, adapting it as necessary. Some sample sentence openings are supplied for support. Ask them to read the tip box before they begin, to remind them of what types of language they need to think about including in writing activities.

Plenary

As a class, read through the text in exercise 5. Students identify the tense of each verb used and explain why it is used. Ask students to summarise when the perfect is used and when the imperfect is used.

Cahier d'exercices, page 36

1

Answers (Correct order)

1 *G* **2** B **3** D **4** H **5** F **6** E **7** A **8** C

2

Answers

underlined in blue:
était; il y avait; avaient; prenais; c'était; disait; était; pouvait; c'était; voulait; allait; il y avait; était; pleuvait; avait; j'allais; devait; avais
underlined in red:
nous sommes arrivés; on a annulé; a sonné; on a ri; j'ai trouvé; on a décidé; est arrivé; j'ai vu; on est descendus; on a dû; j'ai dû; j'ai couru; je suis entré; on a dû; a été; on a dû; on a marché; on est arrivés; je me suis rendu compte

3

Answers

Pupil's own answer

Cahier d'exercices, Grammaire, page 37

1

Answers

1 *Pour faire un sandwich, il faut* du pain et, par exemple, du fromage ou de la salade.
2 *Pour faire un gâteau, il faut* du beurre, de la farine, des œufs, du sucre et du lait.
3 *Pour faire du ski,* il faut acheter des lunettes du soleil, des salopettes, un blouson et des gants.
4 *Pour écouter de la musique,* il faut des CDs ou un Ipod.
5 *Pour aller en France,* il faut acheter un billet.
6 *Pour faire un cocktail de fruits,* il faut acheter beaucoup de fruits différents.
7 *Pour avoir assez de vitamines C,* il faut manger beaucoup d'oranges.
8 *Pour jouer au tennis,* il faut une raquette et des ballons de tennis.

2

Answers

1

Avez-vous ces gants en rouge?
Non, mais nous avons ceux-ci en rouge et ceux-là en bleu.
J'aime bien ceux-là en rouge.
Lesquels, monsieur?
Ceux-là. Je peux les essayer?
Oui, je les prends.

2

J'ai besoin d'une ceinture.
Alors, regardez, nous avons celle-ci en cuir ou celle-là en métal.
Mmm ... je préfère celle-ci. J'aime cette ceinture aussi.
Laquelle?
Celle-ci. Oui, je la prends.

Contrôle continu: Une journée désastreuse! (Student Book pages 70–71)

Topics revised

- Describing a day that went wrong

1 Copiez les phrases en bleu dans le texte et trouvez l'équivalent en anglais ci-dessous.

Students copy out all the phrases shown in blue in the text and find the English phrase from those listed (**1–18**).

Answers

on a rendez-vous
14 we meet/we have a meeting
tout s'est mal passé
1 everything went wrong
au lieu de me réveiller
3 instead of waking up
j'ai fait la grasse matinée
15 I had a lie-in/slept in late
j'ai dû me dépêcher
18 I had to hurry
j'ai raté le bus
6 I missed the bus
au début
7 at the beginning
peu après
8 a little bit later
je ne portais qu'un tee-shirt
12 I was only wearing a t-shirt
j'étais bientôt trempée jusqu'aux os
17 I was soon soaked to the skin
dans un tel état
11 in such a state
pour remplacer mes vêtements mouillés
4 to replace my wet clothes
pendant que j'étais en train d'essayer la robe
13 while I was trying on the dress
mon porte-monnaie
9 my purse
la voleuse
5 the thief (female)
fâchée
16 angry
j'ai pleuré
2 I cried
non seulement ... mais aussi
10 not only ... but also

2 Écrivez V (Vrai), F (Faux) ou PM (Pas Mentionné).

Students reread the text. They then read the ten statements and decide whether each is true or false or not mentioned in the text.

Answers

1 V **2** F **3** V **4** F **5** V **6** F **7** PM **8** V **9** V **10** PM

3 Décrivez une journée désastreuse, réelle ou imaginaire.

Using the text and the **Boîte à outils** section to help them, students write a description of a day that went wrong (real or imaginary).

☑ Encourage students to develop and use their own checklist when they are reading through materials they have written.

À l'oral (AQA edition)

(Student Book page 179)

Topics revised

- hiring equipment
- getting travel information
- returning something to a shop
- talking about shopping

1 You are on holiday in France and want to hire bikes for you and your family. Your partner will play the part of the shop assistant and will speak first.

Roleplay. Students practise hiring equipment in a shop, taking it in turn to play themselves/the shop assistant.

2 You are at a railway station in France and want to find out about trains to Paris. Your partner will play the part of the railway employee and will speak first.

Roleplay. Students practise asking for information and buying tickets in a railway station, taking it in turn to play themselves/the railway employee.

3 You are in a department store and need to return a jumper. Your partner will play the part of the shop assistant and will speak first.

Roleplay. Students practise returning something unsuitable to a shop, taking it in turn to play themselves/the shop assistant.

4 Possible conversation questions

Conversation. These are key questions to practise for the speaking exam, taken from the module as a whole. Students can practise asking and answering the questions in pairs.

☑ Draw students' attention to the tip box, which lists ways students can enhance their performance in this section of the exam.

À l'oral (Edexcel edition)

(Student Book page 179)

Topics revised

- getting travel information
- returning something to a shop

1 You are at a railway station in France and want to find out about trains to Paris. Your partner will play the part of the railway employee and will begin the conversation.

Roleplay Type B. Students practise asking for information and buying tickets in a railway station, taking it in turn to play themselves/the railway employee.

2 You have been shopping. You discover a problem with an item of clothing you have bought and you return to the shop. Your partner will play the part of the shop assistant and will begin the conversation.

Roleplay Type C. Students practise returning something unsuitable to a shop, taking it in turn to play themselves/the shop assistant.

☑ Draw students' attention to the box on *Roleplay Type C*, which gives suggestions on how students might expand their answers when preparing this kind of roleplay. Being able to do this will gain them extra marks in the exam.

Also point out the tip box, which suggests ways in which students might respond to a question prompt.

Allons-y! 4

À l'oral (OCR edition)

(Student Book page 179)

Topics revised
- hiring equipment
- getting travel information
- returning something to a shop
- talking about shopping

1 You are on holiday in France and want to hire bikes for you and your family. Your partner will play the part of the shop assistant and will speak first.

Roleplay Type 2. Students practise hiring equipment in a shop, taking it in turn to play themselves/the shop assistant.

2 You are at a railway station in France and want to find out about trains to Paris. Your partner will play the part of the railway employee and will speak first.

Roleplay Type 2. Students practise asking for information and buying tickets in a railway station, taking it in turn to play themselves/the railway employee.

3 You are in a department store and need to return a jumper. Your partner will play the part of the shop assistant and will speak first.

Roleplay Type 2. Students practise returning something unsuitable to a shop, taking it in turn to play themselves/the shop assistant.

4 *Les courses:* possible conversation questions

Conversation. These are key questions to practise for the speaking exam, taken from the module as a whole. Students can practise asking and answering the questions in pairs.

À toi

(Student Book pages 192–193)

- Self-access reading and writing

1 Reliez les phrases et les panneaux à la gare SNCF. Utilisez un dictionnaire, si nécessaire.

Reading. Students match each speech bubble with the relevant railway station sign. They can use a dictionary.

Answers

1 f **2** c **3** b **4** h **5** a **6** e **7** d **8** g

2 Lisez la publicité du magasin, puis trouvez l'équivalent en français des phrases anglaises.

Reading. Students read the shop advertisement about a sale and find the French for the eight English expressions listed.

Answers

1 soldes d'été **2** prix de plancher **3** rabais de 15%
4 ouvert **5** sauf dimanche **6** heures d'ouverture **7** fermé
8 congé annuel

3 Imaginez que vous voulez aller chez Monachat Aimé pour acheter des vêtements pour vos vacances en Espagne. Écrivez un e-mail à un copain/une copine français(e). Mentionnez:

Writing. Students imagine that they want to go to the shop advertised in exercise 2 to buy some clothes for a holiday in Spain. They write an e-mail to a friend covering the points listed (what they are going to do, when they want to go and why, what they are going to buy and how much it will cost). First get them to read the tip box, which summarises useful structures to use.

4 Regardez l'horaire des trains. Pour chaque phrase ci-dessous, écrivez V (Vrai), F (Faux) ou PM (Pas Mentionné).

Reading. Students look at the train timetable. They then read the eight statements about it and decide whether each is true or false or not mentioned in the text.

Answers

1 V **2** F **3** V **4** PM **5** V **6** F **7** F **8** V

5 Imaginez que vous avez pris le train de Paris à Rouen avec un groupe d'ami(e)s. Écrivez un paragraphe sur le voyage. Mentionnez:

Writing. Students imagine they took a train from Paris to Rouen with a group of friends. They write a paragraph describing the trip covering the points listed (when they left and arrived, why they chose that train, what they did on the train and how the journey was).

Before they start, students should read the tip box, which reminds them that many useful verbs in this context take **être** in the perfect tense.

6 Lisez la publicité. Imaginez que vous allez faire un pique-nique avec quatre ami(e)s. Écrivez une liste de ce que vous allez acheter. Vous avez un budget de 20€!

Reading. Students read the supermarket advert. They then write a list of what they're going to buy, imagining that they are going to have a picnic with four friends and have a budget of 20€.

7 Faites une liste des nouveaux mots utiles dans la publicité ci-dessus et traduisez-les en anglais.

Writing. Students read through the supermarket advertisement in exercise 6 again, this time to make a list of new words. They translate these into English, resorting to a dictionary only if necessary.

Module 5 Le collège (Student Book pages 74–91)

Unit	Main topics and objectives	Grammar
Déjà vu 1 **L'emploi du temps** (pp. 74–75)	Expressions of time Referring to the past, the present and the future	
Déjà vu 2 **Un uniforme** (pp. 76–77)	Talking about what you wear for school Adjectives of colour	Adjective agreement (colours, singular and plural)
1 La formation (pp. 78–79)	Talking about schools Irregular forms of the third person plural	Present tense (**ils/elles** forms)
2 Ma journée – aujourd'hui et hier (pp. 80–81)	Your school day Reflexive verbs in the present and perfect	Reflexive verbs – present tense – perfect tense
3 Qu'est-ce que j'ai oublié? (pp. 82–83)	Talking about things you have lost Participle agreement with **avoir**	Agreement in the perfect tense with **avoir** (direct object pronouns)
4 Vive la différence! (pp. 84–85)	Comparing school in Britain and France Negative expressions	Negative expressions
5 Que feras-tu? (pp. 86–87)	Talking about your plans Using the future tense	Future tense (formation)
Contrôle continu **Le collège Louis Pasteur** (pp. 88–89)	*Coursework* Advertising your school/college	*All main grammar points of the module*
À l'oral (p. 180)	*Exam speaking practice* Reporting a loss Talking about your school Talking about your subjects Talking about future plans	*All main grammar points of the module*
À toi (pp. 194–195)	Self-access reading and writing	

Déjà vu 1: L'emploi du temps

(Student Book pages 74–75)

Main topics and objectives

- Expressions of time
- Referring to the past, the present and the future

Key language

School subjects
Opinions

Resources

CD2, tracks 25–27
Cahier d'exercices, page 40

Starter 1

Aim
To review the vocabulary for school subjects.

Give students working in pairs three minutes to write down all the school subjects they can remember. They need to include the correct form of the article with each one. Each correct subject wins a point; a subject which no other pair has thought of wins two points. Which pair has the highest score?

1 Écoutez. Copiez et complétez l'emploi du temps.

Listening. Students copy out the grid. They listen to someone talking about his school timetable and note the details in the grid.

Audioscript 25

*Lundi, je commence à huit heures. J'ai un cours d'espagnol et puis une heure de **maths**. Après la récré, c'est l'anglais et une heure d'étude où je fais mes devoirs. L'après-midi, je commence avec une heure d'histoire-géo, puis continue avec deux heures de **dessin**.*

*Mardi, c'est l'**anglais**, l'histoire-géo, les maths, le français, les sciences nat, l'**espagnol** et les maths.*

*Mercredi, je commence avec les sciences physiques. Je continue avec la techno et puis une heure de **musique** (je déteste ça) et une heure d'EPS.*

*Jeudi, c'est le français, suivi par l'**histoire-géo**, l'anglais, les maths, l'espagnol, le **français** et le latin … Pfui!*

*Vendredi, la techno et le latin, suivis par l'anglais et le français et l'après-midi, l'**EPS**, les sciences physiques et les **maths**.*

Answers

Also highlighted in bold in the audioscript.

	lun	**mar**	**mer**	**jeu**	**ven**
8h00	espagnol	**d anglais**	sciences phys	français	technologie
9h00	**a maths**	histoire-géo	technologie	**g histoire-géo**	latin
10h00	recré				
10h15	anglais	maths	**f musique**	anglais	anglais
11h15	étude	français	EPS	maths	français
12h15	déjeuner				
13h30	histoire-géo	SVT		espagnol	**i EPS**
14h30	**b dessin**	**e espagnol**		**h français**	sciences phys
15h30	**c dessin**	maths		latin	**j maths**

2 Quel jour sommes-nous?

Reading. Students read the four speech bubbles and use their completed timetable from exercise 1 to identify which day each speaker is referring to.

Answers

1 jeudi **2** lundi **3** vendredi **4** mercredi

R Students discuss their own timetables using the following model: **Lundi, j'ai un cours de … Mardi, …**

3 Que pensent-ils des différentes matières? Pour chaque personne, mettez le symbole et le numéro de la bonne raison dans la grille. (1–4)

Listening. Students copy out the grid. They listen to four conversations in which people discuss which school subjects they like/dislike and note the details in the grid for each subject mentioned: the opinion expressed (using the symbols in the *Opinions* box) and the reason (from the list of phrases **1–10**).

Audioscript 26

1 – *Bonjour. Nous faisons un sondage. Je vais te poser quelques questions?*
– *Volontiers.*
– *Que penses-tu des maths?*
– *Euh, moi ... ben, c'est difficile. Je n'aime pas ça.*
– *Et le français?*
– *C'est intéressant ... ce qu'on fait en ce moment ... c'est bien.*
– *Et l'anglais?*
– *J'aime pas ... J'ai trop de contrôles à preparer.*
– *Les sciences?*
– *Ben, j'aime bien. Je suis fort en sciences.*
– *Et le sport?*
– *Alors ça, c'est ma matière préférée. Il n'y a pas de devoirs!*
– *Merci!*
– *De rien.*

2 – *Quelle est ta matière préférée?*
– *Les maths.*
– *Les maths?*
– *Oui, j'aime les maths, c'est intéressant.*
– *Et le français?*
– *C'est nul ... Ben, ... ça dépend du prof et on a toujours trop de devoirs.*
– *Et l'anglais?*
– *C'est génial! On lit beaucoup et il y a moins de devoirs!*
– *Et le sport?*
– *Ben, non, ben ... tu sais, le sport, ce n'est pas mon truc.*
– *Les sciences?*
– *Je suis accro à la science-fiction et aux sciences. C'est vraiment intéressant!*

3 – *Qu'est-ce que tu n'aimes pas comme matières?*
– *Moi? Ben, ... le français.*
– *Pourquoi?*
– *Ben, ... c'est ennuyeux et le prof est trop sévère.*
– *Euh ... quelle est ta matière préférée?*
– *L'anglais.*
– *L'anglais? Pourquoi?*
– *Ben, il n'y a pas trop de devoirs.*
– *Bon ... et les maths?*
– *Nul! ... Je suis faible en maths. Je n'y comprends rien.*
– *Les sciences?*
– *Non, beurk! Le prof est trop sévère.*
– *Le sport?*
– *Ben ... j'aime le sport, mais pas au collège. Je fais du cyclisme, mais le sport au collège, ce n'est pas mon truc.*
– *Qu'est-ce que je mets alors? Tu aimes ou tu n'aimes pas?*
– *Bof, je n'aime pas.*

4 – *Maintenant, c'est à toi de répondre. Quelle est ta matière préférée?*
– *La SVT parce que c'est intéressant.*
– *Et comment trouves-tu les maths?*
– *Bof. Ça dépend du prof et cette année, on a trop de devoirs.*
– *Et le sport?*
– *Ah non, le prof est trop sévère.*
– *Et l'anglais?*
– *Non plus. Je suis faible en langues. Et je ne comprends pas ce que dit le prof.*
– *Et finalement, le français?*
– *Ben, c'est nul. Je déteste le français parce que je suis ni forte en grammaire ni en orthographe. J'aime lire, mais je n'aime pas discuter!*
– *Merci ...*

Answers

	maths	français	anglais	sciences	sport
1	✗ 5	✓ 6	✗ 1	✓ 8	✓✓ 2
2	✓✓ 6	✗ 3	✓ 2	✓✓ 6	✗ 7
3	✗ 9	✗ 10, 4	✓✓ 2	✗ 4	✗ 7
4	– 3	✗ 9	✗ 9	✓✓ 6	✗ 4

Starter 2

Aim

To practise giving and justifying opinions.

Go round the class. Each student makes a statement about a subject he/she studies, giving and justifying an opinion (e.g. **Je n'aime pas le dessin. C'est trop difficile.**). The class signifies if it agrees/disagrees with the statement by using a thumbs up/thumbs down gesture. Encourage students to use as wide a range of expressions in giving and justifying their opinions as possible.

4 À deux. Posez et répondez aux questions.

Speaking. In pairs: students take it in turn to ask the questions supplied and to respond to them. Before they start, draw student's attention to the tip box, which reminds them to use the definite article with school subjects and also to include intensifiers when expressing and justifying opinions.

5 Utilisez ce que vous avez fait dans l'exercice 4 pour écrire un petit discours sur vos matières.

Writing. Students use their responses from exercise 4 to write a short text about their school subjects.

6 Quelle heure est-il? Choisissez la bonne horloge. (1–8)

Listening. Students listen to the eight conversations and note the time mentioned in each using the clocks pictured (**a–h**).

Audioscript 27

1 – *Pardon, monsieur, avez-vous l'heure, s'il vous plaît?*
– *Oui, il est onze heures moins le quart.*

2 – *Excusez-moi, quelle heure est-il, s'il vous plaît?*

– *Il est dix heures vingt-cinq.*

3 – *Bonjour. Excusez-moi, avez-vous l'heure, s'il vous plaît?*

– *Oui, euh … il est onze heures cinquante-cinq.*

4 – *Salut … Quelle heure est-il?*

– *Ben … il est midi et quart, on va déjeuner.*

5 – *Bon … euh … je dois m'en aller. Il est quelle heure?*

– *Il est quatorze heures dix.*

6 – *Vite! Il faut aller en classe … Il est déjà dix heures quinze.*

7 – *On se revoit à quelle heure?*

– *Ben, vers dix-huit heures … disons, six heures moins cinq.*

8 – *À quelle heure sortons-nous ce soir?*
– *Le film commence à vingt heures dix.*

Answers

1 c **2** e **3** a **4** f **5** d **6** b **7** h **8** g

7 On est quel jour aujourd'hui? Regardez l'emploi du temps dans l'exercice 1.

Reading. Students read the five speech bubbles and use their completed timetable from exercise 1 to identify which day each speaker is referring to. This time the texts include a range of tenses (plus the appropriate time phrases) and it is more than a question of simply identifying the subjects mentioned.

Answers

1 mardi **2** lundi **3** mercredi **4** jeudi **5** mardi

8 Qu'as-tu fait hier, que fais-tu aujourd'hui et qu'est-ce que tu vas faire demain?

Writing. Students write a short text about their school timetable, saying what they did yesterday, are doing today and are going to do tomorrow. Sentence openings are supplied for support.

Plenary

Ask students to recap on the language points covered in this unit, giving you examples.

Which of these were easy? Which areas did they find more difficult? Ask students how they might help themselves to improve in areas of difficulty. Get each student to identify two areas for improvement and to target these over the next week. Note the most common ones to come back to in a later lesson.

Cahier d'exercices, page 40

1

Answers

1 F **2** C **3** A **4** D **5** B **6** E

2

Answers

Alexis:
Passé: Dad told me to do my homework in my bedroom; was not happy
Présent: Favourite subject is history/geography. Prefer to do my homework in the living room
Futur: Tomorrow have history/geography after lunch

Anaïs:
Passé: Yesterday, got German homework
Présent: Like German but too many tests to work for.
Futur: Tomorrow have a German test

3

Answers

Pupil's own answers

Déjà vu 2: Un uniforme

(Student Book pages 76–77)

Main topics and objectives

- Talking about what you wear for school
- Adjectives of colour

Grammar

- Adjective agreement (colours, singular and plural)

Key language

Clothes
Colours

Resources

CD2, track 28
Cahier d'exercices, page 41
Grammaire 2.2

Starter 1

Aim
To revise the vocabulary for clothes.

Bring in and/or ask students to bring in some photographs of celebrities or themselves and get them to discuss in pairs what the people pictured are wearing. Alternatively, you could use the pictures in exercise 1 on p. 70 as the prompts. Encourage students to include as much detail in their descriptions as possible.

1 Que portent-ils? (1–4)

Listening. Students listen to four people describing what they wear to school and note the appropriate pictures (from **a–n**).

Audioscript 28

1 *J'habite en Grande-Bretagne parce que mes parents travaillent ici. Pour aller au collège ici je porte un pantalon noir, une chemise blanche, une cravate à rayures rouges et noires, un pull noir et une veste noire. J'aurais préféré porter un jean et un sweat.*

2 *Pour aller au collège je porte un jean bleu, un tee-shirt ou un polo blanc et un sweat bleu marine.*

3 *Moi, aujourd'hui, pour aller au collège, je porte un pantalon ou un jean, un polo bleu et un grand pull que ma grand-mère m'a tricoté. Je le déteste, mais pour aller au collège, ça peut aller!*

4 *Mon père travaille en Grande-Bretagne et pour aller au collège ici, je porte un pantalon noir, une chemise grise, un pull bordeaux et une veste bordeaux. Ma cravate est à rayures bordeaux et jaunes. Je déteste la couleur bordeaux!*

Answers

1 a, c, e, g, n
2 b, j, k, i
3 a, b, l, h
4 a, d, h, m, f

2 Lisez et trouvez qui écrit.

Reading. Students read the two speech bubbles and identify the correct picture for each.

Answers

1 a **2** c

Starter 2

Aim
To revise adjective agreement.

In pairs: give students three minutes to come up with as many different sentences about wearing clothes in particular situations as they can. Write up a couple as models. Encourage them to be imaginative and to use the Vocabulaire section/a dictionary as necessary.

Quand on va au collège, on porte une jupe, une chemise et une cravate.

Quand il fait chaud, on porte un short et un tee-shirt.

Which pair came up with the most inventive situation/clothes?

Expo-langue: Adjective agreement (colours, singular and plural)

Use this grammar box to review agreement of colours (in the singular and plural) and to cover invariable colours. Ask students to think carefully about pronunciation of feminine and plural forms when doing exercise 3. There is more information on p. 210 of the Student Book.

3 À deux. Décrivez: (a) ce que vous portez au collège, (b) ce que vous portez d'habitude le week-end, (c) ce que vous portez pour le sport.

Speaking. In pairs: students take it in turn to describe (**a**) what they wear to school, (**b**) what they usually wear at the weekend and (**c**) what they wear when doing sports. Encourage them to include colours.

4 Décrivez votre uniforme.

Writing. Students write a description of the uniform for boys and for girls at their school. Sentence openings are supplied for support.

Ask students to research on the Internet in which countries students wear school uniform and to describe the uniforms in two countries other than Britain.

5 À deux. Regardez les images et décrivez ce qu'ils portent.

Speaking. In pairs: students look at the picture of the four French teenagers and take it in turn to describe what they are wearing. Encourage them to give as much detail as possible: a box listing useful phrases they can use in addition to colours is supplied for support.

6 Décrivez un nouvel uniforme pour votre collège.

Writing. Students write a description of an alternative uniform for boys and girls at their school. Sample sentence openings are supplied for support. Draw students' attention to the fact that they will need to give reasons for their choices.

Plenary

Remind students that when they completed the first *Déjà vu* section in this module, they identified areas they felt they could improve in. Ask them to remind you of what these were. What have they done to address weaknesses?

Suggest students keep an ongoing list of problem areas and set themselves targets for improving by each one (ideas on how to do it and a schedule).

Cahier d'exercices, page 41

1

Answers

1 Amandine, Florian
2 Kévin

2

Answers

1 Choice of clothes reflect a part of this personality …
2 students become aware of their individuality …
3 When all pupils dress in the same way …
4 … manage to learn better.
5 everyone is equal; …
6 it avoids people making fun or people provoking each other …
7 it creates divisions …
8 more money is spent on more important things

3

Answers

Pupil's own answers

1 La formation

(Student Book pages 78–79)

Main topics and objectives

- Talking about schools
- Irregular forms of the third person plural

Grammar

- Present tense (**ils/elles** forms)

Key language

Ils vont à l'école primaire.
Ils vont au lycée à l'âge de ...
Notre collège s'appelle ...
C'est un collège mixte.
Il y a environs ... élèves.
Les cours débutent à ...
Les collèges prennent le nom ...
l'instituteur/institutrice
le/la professeur
le directeur/la directrice
le comportement
la discipline
les devoirs
la récré

Resources

CD2, track 29
Cahier d'exercices, page 42
Grammaire 3.2

Starter 1

Aim
To review the third person form in the present tense.

Give students three minutes to write down as many verbs in the third person form (**ils/elles**) of the present tense as they can. When the time is up, they swap with a partner and check each other's answers. Who came up with the most (correctly spelled) forms?

1 La formation à la française. Lisez le texte et répondez aux questions en français.

Reading. Students read the text on the education system in France and reply to the seven comprehension questions in French.

Answers

1 3 ans **2** 10 ans **3** 15 ou 16 ans **4** 16 ans **5** entre 17 et 19 ans **6** le lycée technique ou le lycée général **7** Ils lisent et ils fonts des exercices de compréhension et des calculs.

Expo-langue: the present tense (*ils/elles* forms)

Use this grammar box to focus on the third person plural in the present tense before students do exercise 2.

Encourage students to look for patterns like the ones listed here as ways of helping them to remember vocabulary/verb forms.

2 Écoutez et remplissez les blancs.

Listening. Students listen to the recording and note the words missing in the gap-fill version of the text.

Audioscript 29

Mes frères jumeaux ***ont*** *cinq ans. Ils* ***vont*** *en maternelle. Quand ils* ***arrivent****, ils* ***disent*** *bonjour à l'institutrice, ils* ***posent*** *leur sac par terre et* ***mettent*** *leurs pantoufles.*

En classe, ils ***écoutent*** *l'institutrice,* ***regardent*** *des livres et* ***lisent*** *des mots simples. Ils* ***font*** *des puzzles,* ***chantent*** *des chansons et* ***apprennent*** *des poésies par cœur.*

À midi, ils ***mangent*** *à la cantine où ils* ***choisissent*** *un plat et un dessert et* ***boivent*** *de l'eau.*

Answers

Also in bold in the transcript
1 ont **2** vont **3** arrivent **4** disent **5** posent **6** mettent **7** écoutent **8** regardent **9** lisent **10** font **11** chantent **12** apprennent **13** mangent **14** choisissent **15** boivent

Starter 2

Aim
To review question words.

Write up the following. Give students two minutes to translate them into English.

où?
quel?
qu'est-ce que ... ?
combien?
qui?
quand?
comment?
pourquoi?

After checking answers, ask students to give you some examples of questions using these words.

3 À deux. Posez des questions sur le texte de l'exercice 2 et répondez-y.

Speaking. In pairs: students take it in turn to ask questions about the text in exercise 2 and to respond. Some useful question words are supplied for support.

4 Faites la comparaison.

Writing. Students write a paragraph outlining the differences between the French education system (as detailed in exercises 1 and 2) and the education system in their own country.

5 Le collège Louis Pasteur. Lisez et répondez aux questions.

Reading. Students read the text about a French school. They then read the six sentences and choose the correct ending for each from the three options given (**a**, **b** or **c**).

Answers

1 c **2** a **3** c **4** c **5** a **6** b

6 À deux. Discutez.

Speaking. In pairs: students discuss the differences between schools in France and those in their own country, using the information in exercise 5 to make comparisons. Some sentence openings are supplied for support.

7 Faites un exposé: *Mon collège.*

Writing. Students write a description of their school. Some support is given in the form of sentence openings. Remind students that they should look back over all the exercises in this unit to find useful material for this activity.

8 Vidéoconférence. Préparez une présentation de votre collège.

Speaking. Students imagine that they are going to have a videoconference with students at a French school. They prepare a presentation on their own school. They should use their work in exercise 7 to create a cue card.

If possible, allow students to record their presentations. Get them to swap recordings and comment on a partner's work.

☑ Encourage students to keep recorded versions of their work. Point out that it is helpful to listen to these later on to revise a topic. Students can also use them as a starting point in putting together improved versions in preparation for the speaking part of the exam.

Plenary

Write up the following. Remind students that all these verbs have irregular 3rd person plural forms in the present tense.

vouloir, prendre, finir, connaître, tenir, boire, pouvoir, écrire

Ask students to group the infinitives in pairs by identifying the 3rd person plural forms which have the same pattern.

Check answers and ask students to summarise the pattern in each case (e.g. **boire** (**boi<u>v</u>ent**) + **écrire** (**écri<u>v</u>ent**): **-v-** added).

Cahier d'exercices, page 42

1

Answers

a *3 The number of years of study in a lycée.*
b 45% of pupils under 15 think that school is there for you to learn things.
c At secondary school pupils have at least 30 hours of lessons per week.
d School is compulsory from the age of 6.
e 38% think that school helps you get a job.
f 63% of pupils get A levels (the Bac).
g There are about 26 pupils in each class at nursery school.
h There are about 23 pupils in each class in primary school.
i 12% think school is a place to make friends.
j At secondary school, there are 4 years of study.
k 24% of pupils go to a private school.

2

Answers

Pupil's own answers

2 Ma journée – aujourd'hui et hier

(Student Book pages 80–81)

Main topics and objectives

- Your school day
- Reflexive verbs in the present and perfect

Grammar

- Reflexive verbs
  - present tense
  - perfect tense

Key language

Je me réveille à 7 heures.
Je me lève tout de suite.
Je me douche et je m'habille.
Je me couche vers 10 heures.
Hier, je me suis réveillé(e) …
je me suis levé(e)
je me suis douché(e)
je me suis habillé(e)
je me suis couché(e)
Au petit déjeuner, j'ai mangé du pain.
J'ai bu du chocolat chaud.
Je suis sorti(e) à 8h15.
Je suis allé(e) au collège en car.
Je suis rentré(e) à 4h30.

Resources

CD3, tracks 2–3
Cahier d'exercices, page 43
Grammaire 3.15

Starter 1

Aim
To review the vocabulary for daily routines. To revise times.

Ask students in pairs to choose five specific times of the day (e.g. **7h30**) and to write five sentences saying what they usually do at each time (e.g. **Je me lève à 7h30.**).

Get students to read their sentences aloud, with the rest of the class giving feedback as necessary on their accuracy.

1 Une journée scolaire. Lisez et écrivez V (Vrai), F (Faux) ou PM (Pas Mentionné) à côté de chaque phrase.

Reading. Students read Amélie's text about her typical school day. They then read the eight statements on the text and decide whether each is true or false or not mentioned in the text.

Answers
1 V **2** V **3** F **4** V **5** F **6** V **7** V **8** PM

Expo-langue: reflexive verbs (present tense)

Use this grammar box to review the present tense of reflexive verbs before students do exercise 2. There is more information on p. 215 of the Student Book.

R Ask students to choose another reflexive verb and to write out all the parts.

2 La journée scolaire. Écoutez et notez les réponses de Mélinda et Romain.

Listening. Students listen to Mélinda and then Romain being interviewed about their typical school day and answer for each of them the eight comprehension questions in French.

Audioscript 2

– *Bonjour, Mélinda. Je peux te poser quelques questions?*
– *Volontiers.*
– *À quelle heure te réveilles-tu?*
– *Ben, vers six heures et demie.*
– *Et tu te lèves à quelle heure?*
– *Je me lève tout de suite … à six heures et demie.*
– *Que manges-tu au petit déj?*
– *Euh … des céréales et un yaourt.*
– *Que bois-tu?*
– *Du chocolat chaud.*
– *À quelle heure sors-tu de la maison?*
– *À sept heures vingt.*
– *Comment vas-tu au collège?*
– *En car.*
– *À quelle heure rentres-tu?*
– *Vers 16h30 d'habitude.*
– *À quelle heure te couches-tu?*
– *Ben, disons 22h00.*
– *Merci.*
– *C'est tout?*
– *Oui, merci.*

– *Bonjour, Romain. Je peux te poser quelques questions?*
– *Ben … pourquoi pas?*
– *À quelle heure te réveilles-tu?*
– *Euh … ça dépend de mes parents, mais normalement à sept heures moins le quart.*
– *Et tu te lèves tout de suite?*
– *Non, je reste encore cinq minutes au lit.*
– *Que manges-tu au petit déj?*
– *Ben, des céréales, du pain, des toasts, … un yaourt, … un fruit.*
– *Que bois-tu?*
– *Du lait.*
– *À quelle heure sors-tu de la maison?*

- *Sept heures et demie.*
- *Comment vas-tu au collège?*
- *J'y vais à pied.*
- *À quelle heure rentres-tu à la maison?*
- *16h20.*
- *Tu te couches à quelle heure?*
- *Ça dépend de mes parents, mais disons que s'il faut aller au collège le lendemain, je dois me coucher avant neuf heures et demie.*

Answers

Mélinda
1 vers 6h30 **2** à 6h30 **3** des céréales et un yaourt **4** du chocolat chaud **5** à 7h20 **6** en car de ramassage **7** vers 16h30 **8** vers 22h00

Romain
1 à 6h45 **2** à 6h50 **3** des céréales, du pain, des toasts, un yaourt, un fruit **4** du lait **5** à 7h30 **6** à pied **7** à 16h20 **8** avant 9h30

3 À deux. Comparez la journée de Mélinda et Romain.

Speaking. In pairs: using their answers to exercise 2, students take it in turn to compare an aspect of Mélinda's day and Romain's day. A sample opening is given.

4 Ma journée. Que faites-vous d'habitude quand vous avez cours? Décrivez une journée scolaire typique.

Writing. Students write an account of their own typical school day.

Starter 2

Aim
To revise reflexive verbs in the perfect tense.

Write up:

Je me réveille à sept heures. Je me lève tout de suite, je me douche et je m'habille.

Ask students to adapt this text in pairs, writing it out in the perfect tense as though they were describing the actions of (1) Mathilde (**elle ...**) and (2) themselves and a sister/brother (**nous ...**).

Each pair swaps with another and checks the text for accuracy.

5 Lisez et remplissez les blancs.

Reading. Students read the text. They then copy and complete the six gap-fill sentences using information from the text.

Answers

1 Hier **2** a **3** fait **4** petit déjeuner **5** pull **6** moqués

Expo-langue: reflexive verbs (perfect tense)

Use this grammar box to cover reflexive verbs in the perfect tense, reminding students that these take **être**. Ask students to give you examples from the text in exercise 5.

There is more information on p. 211 of the Student Book.

6 Écoutez et choisissez les bonnes images pour Vincent et puis pour Pascaline. (1–2)

Listening. Students listen to Vincent and Pascaline talking about what they did yesterday. For each of them they choose the correct five pictures, choosing from the three options given in each case (**a**, **b** or **c**).

Audioscript 3

- *Qu'est-ce que tu as fait hier, Vincent?*
- *Hier, je me suis réveillé en retard à six heures trente. Je n'avais pas le temps de prendre une douche. J'ai mangé des céréales et j'ai bu un jus d'orange. Et comme j'avais raté le bus, j'ai dû aller au collège en vélo.*
- *Et toi, Pascaline? Qu'est-ce que tu as fait hier?*
- *Moi, je me suis réveillée à sept heures moins le quart. Ben ... j'ai dû me dépêcher ... Je n'avais pas le temps de sécher mes cheveux. J'ai mangé un toast et j'ai pris un yaourt liquide pour boire dans le bus, mais j'ai raté le car de ramassage et j'ai dû aller au collège à pied. Heureusement ce n'est pas loin.*

Answers

Vincent: **1** b **2** b **3** a **4** a **5** b
Pascaline: **1** c **2** c **3** b **4** c **5** c

7 Choisissez Vincent ou Pascaline et comparez ce que vous avez fait hier.

Writing. Using the details they worked out in exercise 6 for either Vincent or Pascaline, students write a comparison of Vincent's or Pascaline's day and their own day yesterday. Sample sentence openings are supplied for support.

8 À deux. Posez et répondez aux questions.

Speaking. In pairs: students take it in turn to ask and to respond on what they did yesterday. The questions are supplied.

Students could keep a journal for a week, listing three different things they have done each day in French. Encourage them to aim to use the language they already know for two of the things and to look up the French for one new thing each day.

9 Vidéoconférence. Hier. Préparez cinq questions à poser et vos réponses par écrit.

Writing. Students imagine that they are going to have a videoconference with students at a French school. This will take the form of a discussion about what they did yesterday. They prepare five questions to ask and their own responses to those questions. A sample question and response opening is supplied for support.

Plenary

Ask students to summarise how the perfect tense of reflexive verbs is formed, giving you some examples.

Then go round the class with each person telling you something they/someone else did yesterday using a reflexive verb. Encourage them to try and use the full range of subject pronouns.

Cahier d'exercices, page 43

1

Answers

Pascal: D'habitude, en semaine, je me réveille à six heures et demie, mais hier, je me suis réveillé à sept heures et quart! Je ne me suis pas douché; je me suis vite habillé et je suis parti en courant. Il n'y avait pas d'autres élèves à l'arrêt d'autobus et je me suis dit:
'Zut! J'ai raté le bus!' Alors, j'ai pris mon vélo et je suis reparti à toute vitesse. Mais, quand je suis arrivé au collège, il n'y avait personne dans la cour. C'était à ce moment que je me suis rendu compte que on était dimanche!

Freddy: Normalement, le dimanche, je me lève tard, vers huit heures et demie. Je prends mon petit déjeuner puis je m'habille. Un jour, j'étais dans la cuisine, en pyjama, une tartine à la main, quand ma mère est entrée. Elle m'a dit: 'Mais, pourquoi n'es-tu pas au collège? Il est déjà neuf heures!' On n'était pas dimanche, on était lundi! Alors, j'ai vite mis mes baskets et je suis parti. Je suis arrivé une heure en retard et quand je suis entré dans le cours de sciences physiques, tout le monde s'est moqué de moi: j'étais toujours en pyjama!

2

Answers

Pupil's own answers

3

Answers

Example:
Normalement, je me lève à sept heures moins le quart puis je me douche et je prends mon petit déjeuner. Généralement, je bois du chocolat chaud et je mange des tartines avec de la confiture.
Hier, je me suis levée à sept heures et demie. Je ne me suis pas douchée et je n'avais pas le temps de prendre mon petit déjeuner. Je suis allée au collège en vélo très vite! Mais quand je suis arrivée au collège, je me suis rendu compte que c'était les vacances! Zut!!

3 Qu'est-ce que j'ai oublié?

(Student Book pages 82–83)

Main topics and objectives

- Talking about things you have lost
- Participle agreement with **avoir**

Grammar

- Agreement in the perfect tense with **avoir** (direct object pronouns)

Key language

J'ai oublié ...
J'ai perdu ...
mes affaires
mon sac
mon cartable
ma trousse
mes clés
mon porte-monnaie
mon forfait
mon portable
Je l'ai laissé(e) ...
Je les ai laissé(e)s ...
à la maison
à l'arrêt de bus
dans le bus
le bureau des objets trouvés

Resources

CD3, track 4
Cahier d'exercices, page 44
Grammaire 1.7

Starter 1

Aim
To revise the vocabulary for items you might lose.

Write up: **J'ai perdu ...**

Give students in pairs three minutes to come up with four examples of things they have lost and where. The rule is both items need to begin with the same letter, e.g. **J'ai perdu mes affaires de gym à l'arrêt d'autobus.**

1 Lisez l'histoire de Denis Distrait. Regardez bien. Où a-t-il perdu ses affaires?

Reading. Students read the story of Denis Distrait. They note for each of the six things he lost where he lost it (from the list **a–f**).

Answers
1 f **2** f **3** c **4** e **5** a **6** a

✚ Students could write their own description of a disastrous start to the day, along the same lines as Denis's. Encourage them to be as imaginative as possible.

Expo-langue: agreement in the perfect tense with *avoir* (direct object pronouns)

Use this grammar box to introduce agreement of past participles in perfect tense verbs with **avoir** (when a direct object pronoun is used). Point out to students that this often doesn't affect the pronunciation of the participle, but they do need to be careful to show the agreement in writing. There is more information on p. 208 of the Student Book.

Starter 2

Aim
To consolidate agreement in the perfect tense with **avoir** (direct object pronouns).

Write up the following. Ask students to write sentences for each of the items listed, following the example you have given for the first one. Remind them they can check the gender of any words they are unsure of in the Vocabulaire section.

Mon sac à dos? **Je l'ai perdu.**
Mes clés?
Mon portable?
Mes stylos?
Mes affaires de gym?
Ma règle?
Ma trousse?

When checking answers, ask students to spell out the participles.

2 Écoutez. Qu'est-ce qu'ils ont perdu? Ils sont comment? Où est-ce qu'ils les ont perdus? Copiez et remplissez la grille. (1–3)

Listening. Students copy the grid. They listen to three people talking about things they have lost and note the details in the grid.

Audioscript 4

1 *J'ai perdu mon sac ce matin. C'est un sac à dos rouge. Je l'avais à la main quand je suis sorti de la maison, mais quand je suis monté dans le bus, je ne l'avais plus. Je crois que je l'ai laissé à l'arrêt de bus.*

2 *Hier, j'ai laissé mon sac dans le bus. C'est un cartable noir, assez grand. ... Je suis descendue du bus et, quand je suis arrivée au collège, je n'avais plus de sac.*

3 *Jeudi matin, je suis allé dans un magasin pour acheter des bonbons et quand je suis arrivé au collège, je n'avais plus mon porte-monnaie. Il est en cuir marron. Je crois que je l'ai laissé dans le magasin, sur le comptoir.*

Answers

	quoi?	description	où?
1	sac à dos	rouge	l'arrêt de bus
2	cartable	noir, assez grand	dans le bus
3	porte-monnaie	en cuir marron	dans le magasin

3 À deux. Imaginez que vous avez perdu votre sac. Décrivez-le.

Speaking. In pairs: students imagine they have lost their bag, which contained various items such as their pencil case, books, purse, etc. They take it in turn to report the loss and provide a description of the bag and the items. A tip box listing all the possessive adjectives is given for support.

4 Imaginez. Vous avez perdu vos affaires. Écrivez des petites annonces.

Writing. Students imagine they have lost various items. Using the pictures supplied, they write adverts describing them and where they lost them. Sample openings are supplied for support.

5 À deux. Vous avez laissé votre sac dans le bus. Téléphonez au bureau des objets trouvés.

Speaking. In pairs: students imagine they have lost their bag on the bus and are phoning the lost property office. Using the questions and text/picture prompts supplied, they take it in turn to be the person reporting the loss and to be the office employee.

Go to www.heinemann.co.uk/hotlinks and enter the express code 7898T for a link to an interesting Belgian Lost and Found website.

Plenary

Write up:

J'ai écrit ...

Ask students to tell you the French for 'I wrote it/them', using the following as prompts: **une lettre, des e-mails, des cartes, un poème.** In each case, get them to spell out the past participle.

Ask students to summarise when there is agreement in the perfect tense, both for verbs taking **avoir** and those taking **être**.

Cahier d'exercices, page 44

Answers

1 oublié
2 déjeuner
3 arrivée
4 réveillée
5 affaires
6 chocolat
7 cours
8 basket
9 laissés
10 partie
11 est
12 journée
13 copains
14 devoirs

4 Vive la différence!

(Student Book pages 84–85)

Main topics and objectives

- Comparing school in Britain and France
- Negative expressions

Grammar

- Negative expressions

Key language

ne ... pas
ne ... plus
ne ... que
ne ... jamais
ne ... rien
personne ne ...
ni ... ni ...
La journée n'est pas si ...
Les cours ne commencent/finissent qu'à ...
La récré ne dure que ...
On ne porte que ...

Resources

CD3, tracks 5–6
Cahier d'exercices, page 45
Grammaire 3.13

Starter 1

Aim
To revise the comparative.

Write up:

Le français est _____ que l'anglais.
Ma sœur est _____ que moi.
Un chien est _____ qu'un chat.
Des frites sont _____ que des pommes.
Les sciences physiques sont _____ les maths.

Ask students working in pairs to complete the sentences using an appropriate comparative. Remind them (as necessary) that in the comparative form, adjectives also need to agree.

1 Écoutez et lisez. Choisissez la bonne réponse: a ou b.

Listening. Students listen to a French boy now at school in England talking about his experience. They then read the six sentences and choose the correct ending for each from the two options given (**a** or **b**).

Audioscript 5

Mes parents ont déménagé en Grande-Bretagne il y a un an et maintenant, je fréquente un collège britannique. Au début, ce n'était pas facile. Je pouvais à peine comprendre ce qu'on me disait parce qu'ils avaient un fort accent. Maintenant, ça va, mais je dois me concentrer tout le temps.

Le collège est moins grand que mon ancien collège en France. Il n'y a que 800 élèves. En France, il y avait 1200 élèves. Ici, il y a 30 élèves au maximum dans chaque classe. Je trouve ça mieux.

Heureusement, ce qu'on fait dans les cours est plus facile que chez nous. Par exemple, en sciences naturelles, ce que je fais en ce moment, je l'ai déjà fait en France l'année dernière. Il n'y a rien de vraiment nouveau. Ni les maths ni les sciences physiques ne sont difficiles. En plus, on peut faire de la musique pop ou du théâtre en cours facultatif. Je n'ai jamais fait de théâtre au collège en France et pourtant, j'aime bien ça.

En France, les cours commencent à huit heures. Ici, les cours ne commencent qu'à neuf heures, il ne faut pas se lever aussi tôt qu'en France. Super! Les cours sont moins longs et les journées aussi sont moins longues. Il n'y a jamais de cours le samedi. C'est un jour de congé.

Je ne mange pas à la cantine. Je trouve la nourriture moins bonne qu'en France. Je préfère apporter des sandwichs.

J'ai eu de la chance. Dans ma classe, personne ne se moque de moi, de mon accent. Il y en a qui m'appellent Frog, mais si on ne fait pas attention, ils s'ennuient rapidement et ne le font plus. Ils me demandent si j'ai déjà mangé des escargots ou des cuisses de grenouilles, et quand je dis «oui», ils disent «beurk», mais c'est tout. Je m'entends bien avec la plupart des élèves de ma classe et on n'a jamais essayé de me racketter.

Answers

1 b **2** a **3** b **4** b **5** b **6** b

Expo-langue: negatives

Use this grammar box to cover negatives before students do exercise 2. You could also take the opportunity to review the position of negatives (around the verb/the first verb in verb + infinitive constructions/the auxiliary in the perfect tense) and the fact that **du/de la/de l'/des** all become **de** after a negative. There is more information on p. 214 of the Student Book.

R In pairs: students take it in turn to come up with sentences featuring the negatives listed in the **Expo-langue** box.

2 Trouvez les phrases dans le texte de l'exercice 1.

Reading. Students reread the text in exercise 1 and find the French for the seven expressions listed.

Answers

1 ni les maths ni les sciences physiques
2 il n'y a rien de vraiment nouveau
3 personne ne se moque de moi de mon accent
4 ce n'était pas facile
5 il n'y a que ... élèves
6 je n'ai jamais
7 les cours ne commencent qu'à

Starter 2

Aim
To practise using negative expressions.

Write up the following and ask students working in pairs to translate them into French:

1 He doesn't like going shopping. **Il n'aime pas faire des courses.**
2 There are only 20 students in my class. **Il n'y a que vingt étudiants dans ma classe.**
3 I don't drink lemonade any more. **Je ne bois plus de limonade.**
4 Nobody wants to go swimming. **Personne ne veut faire de la natation.**
5 There's nothing to do. **Il n'y a rien à faire.**

3 Écoutez et complétez les réponses de Patrick.

Listening. Students listen to Patrick and complete his responses to the seven questions in French.

Audioscript 6

– *Patrick, tu passes une année scolaire dans un collège en Grande-Bretagne. Ça se passe bien?*
– *Oui, c'est très intéressant ... Au début, c'était très fatigant parce que ... il fallait que je me concentre tout le temps pour comprendre. ... Ils ont un accent un peu fort ici, ... et puis le plus difficile, c'est de parler toujours anglais.*
– *Qu'est-ce que tu aimes le plus?*
– *Ce que j'aime? Euh ... ben, ... c'est de ne pas me lever trop tôt. Ici, je prends le car de ramassage à huit heures vingt. En France, il fallait être à l'arrêt de bus à sept heures et quart.*
– *Et la plus grande différence?*
– *Porter un uniforme, bien sûr ...*
– *Pourquoi?*
– *Parce que ce n'est ni confortable ni chic, et en plus, ça coûte très cher.*
– *Comment trouves-tu les cours?*
– *Il y a une grande variété. Par exemple, j'ai fait du théâtre en cours facultatif, ce qui m'a beaucoup plu d'ailleurs.*
– *Fais-tu beaucoup de sport?*
– *Ah oui, il y a un grand centre sportif à côté du collège où l'on peut jouer au foot ou au basket pendant la récré, à midi ou en fin de journée. Il y a aussi une piscine et ma classe fait de la natation le vendredi, à midi. Je fais aussi partie d'un club de foot. Nous jouons le soir après le collège.*
– *Est-ce qu'il y a d'autres avantages?*
– *Oui, on n'a pas beaucoup de devoirs!*
– *Et d'autres inconvénients?*
– *Ben, ... il y a un peu trop de discipline. On ne doit pas courir, il faut marcher en file et on ne doit pas crier. Il y a moins de bruit que chez nous.*
– *Merci.*

Answers

1 *Le plus difficile, c'est* de parler toujours anglais.
2 *Je ne dois pas* me lever trop tôt.
3 *Il faut* porter un uniforme.
4 *J'aime beaucoup* le théâtre.
5 *Je* joue au foot et au basket et je nage/fais de la natation.
6 *On n'a pas* beaucoup de devoirs.
7 *Il y a un peu* trop de discipline.

4 L'uniforme. Pour chaque déclaration écrivez P (Positive), N (Négative) ou P/N (Positive/Négative).

Reading. Students read the 10 statements on uniforms and decide whether each one is positive (P), negative (N) or both (P/N).

Answers

1 P **2** P **3** N **4** N **5** N **6** P/N **7** P/N **8** N **9** N **10** P

5 L'uniforme. Discutez!

Speaking. Students discuss the advantages and disadvantages of school uniform. A box of useful phrases is supplied for support.

✚ Students write a text on school uniform, outlining the arguments for and against and presenting their own conclusion.

6 À deux. Discutez. Quelles différences y a-t-il entre la scolarité en Grande-Bretagne et en France. Utilisez le plus d'expressions négatives possibles de l'exercice 1!

Speaking. In pairs: students discuss the differences between going to school in Britain and in France. They should try to incorporate as many as possible of the negative expressions used in exercise 1 (and summarised in the **Expo-langue** box on p. 84).

7 Faites un exposé: *Les différences entre la scolarité en Grande-Bretagne et en France.*

Writing. Students write a description of the differences between going to school in Britain and in France.

Before they begin, ask students for ideas on how they will structure their texts and what information they will include.

Plenary

Ask the class to list the negative expressions covered in this unit and to summarise how they are used (position). Write these up and then get students to give you an example of each one used in a sentence.

Cahier d'exercices, page 45

1

Answers

1 George
2 Camille
3 George
4 George
5 Camille
6 Camille
7 Camille
8 George

2

Answers

Camille
ne se sent plus; n'est pas; il n'y a que; n'ont pas de limites; ne s'intéressent pas à eux; personne ne sait

George
n'a ni de règles strictes ni; ne les voient jamais; Personne ne semble se préoccuper; ne voulait pas; on n'a rien

(possible answers)

1 Leurs parents ne s'intéressent pas à eux. Their parents aren't interested in them.
2 On ne sent plus au sécurité au collège. We no longer feel safe at school.
3 Personne ne sait où ils sont ou ce qu'ils font. No-one knows where they are or what they're doing.
4 Les profs ne les voient jamais. The teachers never see them.
5 On n'a ni les règles strictes ni la punition efficace. We have neither strict rules nor punishments which work.
6 On n'a rien vu. They didn't see anything.
7 Il n'y a que notre école ... There is only our school ...

5 Que feras-tu?

(Student Book pages 86–87)

Main topics and objectives

- Talking about your plans
- Using the future tense

Grammar

- Future tense (formation)

Key language

Si j'ai de bonnes notes ...
J'irai au lycée/à l'université.
Je ferai une licence de commerce.
Je ferai un apprentissage chez Citroën.
Je travaillerai à l'étranger.
Je ferai du bénévolat.
J'aurai ma propre entreprise.
Je serai très riche.
J'habiterai aux États-Unis.
Je continuerai mes études.
Je rencontrerai le/la partenaire de mes rêves.
Je ne sais pas exactement ce que je ferai quand je quitterai le collège.
Je m'intéresse beaucoup à ...

Resources

CD3, tracks 7–8
Cahier d'exercices, pages 46–47
Grammaire 3.9

Starter 1

Aim
To use strategies and context to work out new vocabulary.

Write up the following and give students three minutes to translate the sentences into English.

1 **Si j'ai de bonnes notes, j'irai à l'université où je ferai une licence de commerce.**
2 **Quand je quitterai le collège, je ferai un apprentissage chez Microsoft.**
3 **Si c'est possible, je ferai du bénévolat en Afrique.**
4 **J'espère que je rencontrerai la femme de mes rêves.**

When checking answers, ask students how they worked out words they didn't know and how they knew which tense the verbs were in.

1 Écoutez et lisez le texte. Trouvez les 22 verbes au futur.

Listening. Students listen to Raoul and Marine talking about what they intend to do when they leave school, following the text in the book at the same time. They then find in the texts 22 verbs in the future tense.

Audioscript 7

– *Que **feras**-tu quand tu **quitteras** le collège, Raoul?*
– *Si j'ai de bonnes notes, j'**irai** au lycée où je **continuerai** mes études. Puis quand je **quitterai** le lycée, j'**irai** à l'université où je **ferai** une licence de commerce.*
– *Et toi, Marine?*
– *Moi, je **quitterai** le collège à seize ans et je **ferai** un apprentissage chez Macintosh. J'**apprendrai** à réparer les ordinateurs parce que je m'intéresse beaucoup à l'informatique.*
– *Raoul, que **feras**-tu plus tard dans la vie?*
– *Je ne sais pas exactement ce que je **ferai** quand je **quitterai** la fac, mais si c'est possible, je **travaillerai** à l'étranger – aux États-Unis, par exemple – ou bien je **ferai** du bénévolat en Afrique.*
– *Et toi, Marine?*
– *Si mes rêves se réalisent, j'**aurai** ma propre entreprise à trente ans! Ce **sera** un magasin d'informatique ou un service de réparation d'ordinateurs, par exemple.*
– *Comment **sera** ta vie personnelle, Raoul?*
– *J'espère que je **rencontrerai** la femme de mes rêves et qu'on **aura** deux ou trois enfants!*
– *Et Marine?*
– *Je **serai** très riche et très heureuse, bien sûr! Et j'**habiterai** à la campagne ou au bord de la mer, je crois.*

Answers

Also shown in bold in the script.
feras, quitteras
irai, continuerai, quitterai, irai, ferai
quitterai, ferai, apprendrai
feras
ferai, quitterai, travaillerai, ferai
aurai, sera
sera
rencontrerai, aura
serai, habiterai

R Looking just at their answers to exercise 1 (not the text in the Student Book), ask students to translate each of the verbs into English, including the correct subject pronoun.

Expo-langue: the future tense

Use this grammar box to cover the future tense in detail before students do exercise 2. There is more information on p. 214 of the Student Book.

2 Relisez le texte et écrivez V (Vrai), F (Faux) ou PM (Pas Mentionné) à côté de chaque phrase.

Reading. Students reread the text in exercise 1. They then read the ten statements on the text and decide whether each is true or false or not mentioned in the text.

Answers
1 V **2** F **3** V **4** PM **5** F **6** F **7** PM **8** V **9** V **10** F

Starter 2

Aim
To practise forming the future tense.

Write up the following and ask students to supply the correct form of the future tense using the pronouns supplied (e.g. **il travaillera**, etc.).

travailler – il
aller – nous
finir – tu
quitter – elles
être – elle
écrire – je
avoir – vous
faire – on
apprendre – ils

3 Copiez et complétez le texte.

Writing. Students copy out and complete the gap-fill text with verbs in the future tense.

Answers
Quand je (**1**) **quitterai** le collège à seize ans, j'(**2**) **irai** au lycée, où je (**3**) **continuerai** mes études. Après, j'(**4**) **irai** en faculté, où je (**5**) **ferai** une licence de marketing. Mais mon copain, Thomas, n'(**6**) **ira** pas au lycée. Il (**7**) **fera** un apprentissage chez Citroën, où il (**8**) **apprendra** à réparer les voitures. Plus tard dans la vie, je (**9**) **travaillerai** dans le marketing et j'(**10**) **habiterai** à la campagne, mais Thomas espère qu'il (**11**) **aura** son propre garage. J'espère qu'on (**12**) **sera** tous les deux riches et heureux!

➕ Using the future tense, students come up with six statements about what they will do in the future.

This covers liaison with **s**, **t** and **x** (although normally silent at the end of a word, they are pronounced if the next word begins with a vowel sound). Read through this before students do exercise 4.

4 Prononcez les paires de phrases. Attention aux lettres en gras!

Speaking. Students practise saying the pairs of phrases, paying particular attention to the letters in bold: pronounced or silent?

5 Écoutez et vérifiez.

Listening. Students listen to the recorded version of the phrases in exercise 4 to check their pronunciation.

Audioscript 8

– J'irai aux magasins.
*– J'irai au**x** États-Unis.*
*– Un adolescen**t** heureux.*
– Un adolescent content.
*– Je continuerai me**s** études.*
– Je continuerai mes devoirs.

6 À deux. Répondez aux trois questions de l'exercice 1. Parlez de vous-même ou utilisez les détails ci-dessous.

Speaking. In pairs: students take it in turn to ask and answer the three questions asked in exercise 1. They can either respond for themselves or use the details supplied.

7 Imaginez que vous êtes Bart ou Lisa Simpson, ou un(e) autre enfant célèbre. Écrivez un paragraphe sur votre avenir (utilisez votre imagination!).

Writing. Students imagine they are Bart or Lisa Simpson or another famous child/teenager and write a paragraph on their future. Encourage them to use their imagination. They should use the list of points supplied to structure their text.

Plenary

Ask students to summarise how the future tense is formed and used. Test them quickly on useful verbs which have irregular stems in the future (**j'aurai, je ferai, j'irai, je serai**).

Then go round the class, with each student giving a sentence about what they will be/do/have, etc., in the future. Encourage them to be as imaginative as possible.

Cahier d'exercices, page 46

1

Answers
1 quitterai le college en juin
2 je continuerai avec mes études
3 Je ferai
4 si j'ai de bons résultats, j'irai à l'université
5 j'irai en Angleterre
6 j'aiderai les élèves avec leur français
7 je ne travaillerai pas en France tout de suite
8 je travaillerai à l'étranger
9 je serai prof d'anglais dans un lycée
10 je rencontrerai un homme qui sera beau et très riche
11 je serai riche, j'habiterai une grande maison et j'aurai trois enfants parfaits et deux chiens

2

Answers
Pupil's own answers

Cahier d'exercices, Grammaire, page 47

1

Answers

1 (ils viennent) *The last one as the first two come from the –ir family and double the 's'.*
2 elles connaissent as the other two are modal verbs
3 ils doivent as the other two double the 'n'
4 elles disent as the other two are regular –er verbs
5 ils écrivent as the other two take an 's' in the 3rd person plural

2

Answers

Le matin, je me réveille à six heures et demie. Je me lève dix minutes plus tard, puis je me douche tout de suite et je m'habille dans ma chambre. Ma sœur se douche après moi parce qu'elle reste longtemps dans la salle de bains!

Je partage la chambre avec elle et on se dispute tout le temps. Cependant, je m'entends bien avec mon petit frère.

Généralement, je me dépêche parce que je dois prendre le bus à sept heures et quart.

Le soir, je me couche vers dix heures et ma sœur et mon frère se couchent vers huit heures et demie. Super!

3

Answers

Ce matin, je me suis réveillée à six heures et demie. Je me suis levée dix minutes plus tard, puis je me suis douchée tout de suite et je me suis habillée dans ma chambre. Ma sœur s'est douchée après moi parce qu'elle reste longtemps dans la salle de bains!

Je partage la chambre avec elle et hier on s'est disputées.

Ce matin, je me suis dépêchée parce que j'ai dû prendre le bus à sept heures et quart.

Le soir, je me suis couchée vers dix heures et ma sœur et mon frère se sont couchés vers huit heures et demie.

5 Contrôle continu: Le collège Louis Pasteur (Student Book pages 88–89)

Topic revised
- Writing about school

1 Copiez les phrases en bleu dans le texte et trouvez l'équivalent en anglais ci-dessous.

Students copy out the blue phrases from the text and find the equivalent English phrase from those listed.

Answers

a été fondé
3 was founded in
les locaux
9 the premises
ont besoin d'être modernisés
5 need to be modernised
environ
8 about
les personnes les plus importantes
4 the most important people
la propreté
10 the cleanliness
nous avons cours
6 we have lessons
elle ne dure plus qu'
12 it lasts only
pour moi, ce qu'il y a de mieux, c'est
2 for me the best thing is
très populaires auprès des élèves
7 very popular with the pupils
un grand nombre d'activités musicales et sportives
1 a large number of musical and sporting activities
ce sera trop tard
11 it will be too late

2 Choisissez a ou b.

Students reread the text. They then read the five sentences and choose the correct ending for each from the two options given (**a** or **b**).

Answers

1 b **2** a **3** a **4** b **5** b

3 Décrivez votre collège.

Using the text and the **Boîte à outils** section to help them, students write a description of their own school.

À l'oral (AQA edition)

(Student Book page 180)

Topics revised

- reporting a loss
- talking about your school
- talking about your subjects
- talking about future plans

1 You are reporting the loss of your bag at the lost property office. Your partner will play the part of the person at the office and will speak first.

Roleplay. Students practise reporting a loss at the lost property office, taking it in turn to play themselves/the lost property office employee.

2 Your penfriend wants to know about your school. Your partner will play the part of your penfriend and will speak first.

Roleplay. Students practise talking about their school, taking it in turn to play themselves/a visiting French penfriend.

3 Prepare a ninety second presentation called *Mon collège.*

Presentation. Students prepare a ninety-second presentation on their school. A sample cue card is supplied.

☑ Before starting, students should read through the tip box on how to work a range of tenses into their presentation.

4 Possible conversation questions

Conversation. These are key questions to practise for the speaking exam, taken from the module as a whole. Students can practise asking and answering the questions in pairs.

☑ Draw students' attention to the tip box, which reminds them to listen carefully for the tense the examiner uses in each question: they will then know which tense they need to use when replying.

À l'oral (Edexcel edition)

(Student Book page 180)

Topics revised

- reporting a loss
- talking about your plans on an exchange visit
- talking about your school
- talking about future plans

1 You are in the lost property office of a French town. Your partner will play the part of the clerk and will begin the conversation.

Roleplay Type B. Students practise reporting a loss at the lost property office, taking it in turn to play themselves/the lost property office employee.

2 You are on an exchange visit to your penfriend and are discussing plans for the weekend. Your partner will play the part of your penfriend and will begin the conversation.

Roleplay Type C. Students practise talking about their plans on an exchange visit, taking it in turn to play themselves/a French penfriend.

☑ Before starting, students should read through the tip box, which offers suggestions on how to tackle the question prompt and how to expand their answers.

3 Presentation and general conversation

Presentation. Students prepare a one-minute presentation on their school. A sample cue card is supplied.

☑ Before starting, students should read through the tip box on using tenses in the presentation and conversation.

Possible conversation questions. These are key questions to practise for the speaking exam, taken from the module as a whole. Students can practise asking and answering the questions in pairs.

À l'oral (OCR edition)

(Student Book page 180)

Topics revised

- reporting a loss
- talking about your school
- talking about your subjects
- talking about future plans

1 You are reporting the loss of your bag at the lost property office. Your partner will play the part of the person at the office and will speak first.

Roleplay Type 2. Students practise reporting a loss at the lost property office, taking it in turn to play themselves/the lost property office employee.

2 Your penfriend wants to know about your school. Your partner will play the part of your penfriend and will speak first.

Roleplay Type 2. Students practise talking about their school, taking it in turn to play themselves/a visiting French penfriend.

3 Prepare a one-minute presentation called *Mon collège.*

Presentation. Students prepare a one-minute presentation on their school. A sample cue card is supplied.

☑ Before starting, students should read through the tip box on how to work plenty of opinions and justifications into their presentations in order to gain maximum marks.

4 *Au collège:* possible conversation questions

Conversation. These are key questions to practise for the speaking exam, taken from the module as a whole. Students can practise asking and answering the questions in pairs.

☑ Draw students' attention to the tip box, which reminds them to listen carefully for the tense the examiner uses in each question so they can work out which tense they need to use when replying.

À toi

(Student Book pages 194–195)

- Self-access reading and writing

1 Lisez le texte et complétez les phrases.

Reading. Students read Louis's text and then use the picture prompts to complete the sentences summarising a typical school day.

Answers

1 *Lors d'une journée scolaire, il se* réveille à sept heures.
2 *Il se* douche et il s'habille.
3 *Il* prends une tartine de pain grillé et un café.
4 *Il* court à l'arrêt d'autobus.
5 *Le soir, il* fait ses devoirs, il dîne, il envoie des textos et il se couche.

2 Que fait-il le samedi?

Writing. Students write a short paragraph saying what Louis does on a Saturday.

3 Hier, il y avait cours. Qu'est-ce que Louis a fait?

Writing. Adapting the text in exercise 1, students write about what Louis did yesterday, a school day.

4 Trouvez la bonne définition.

Reading. Students read Alizée's text about what she does at school and match the seven French words to the appropriate French definition (from **a–g**).

Answers

1 g **2** f **3** d **4** e **5** b **6** c **7** a

5 Relisez et répondez en anglais.

Reading. Students reread the text in exercise 4 and answer the six comprehension questions in English.

Answers

1 15 or 16
2 painting/sculpture
3 Monday
4 she lives in (so can sleep later), everyone in her class likes the course
5 Apart from painting/sculpture, she doesn't find them very interesting.
6 chatty (j'ai de la chance, mais déjà midi sonne, Le pire menu? Les épinards!, tout le monde aime les frites!, n'est-ce pas?, etc.)

6 Relisez et trouvez les mots.

Reading. Students reread the text and make a list of the opening words/phrases in each sentence. They then translate these into English, using the Vocabulaire section or a dictionary as necessary.

7 Écrivez un paragraphe.

Writing. Using the text in exercise 4, students write a short paragraph about their own school. They should try to incorporate at least four of the opening words/phrases used by Alizée.

Module 6 Il faut bosser! (Student Book pages 92–107)

Unit	Main topics and objectives	Grammar
Déjà vu **L'argent, l'argent** (pp. 92–93)	Discussing jobs and money Indirect object pronouns	Indirect object pronouns **du/de la/de l'/des**
1 Avez-vous un job? (pp. 94–95)	Talking about part-time jobs Looking for detailed meaning in a text	–
2 Au boulot! (pp. 96–97)	Discussing different jobs Forming questions	Questions
3 C'est de la part de qui? (pp. 98–99)	Applying for jobs Using formal language	Formal language
4 Ce n'est pas juste! (pp. 100–101)	Discussing problems at work Using **qui** and **que**	Relative pronouns **qui** and **que**
5 Les stages – pour ou contre? (pp. 102–103)	Talking about work experience Contrasting the perfect and imperfect tenses	The perfect and imperfect: when to use
Contrôle continu **Mon stage en entreprise** (pp. 104–105)	*Coursework* Talking about work experience	*All main grammar points of the module*
À l'oral (p. 181)	*Exam speaking practice* Talking about household chores Talking about pocket money	*All main grammar points of the module*
À toi (pp. 196–197)	Self-access reading and writing	

Déjà vu: L'argent, l'argent

(Student Book pages 92–93)

Main topics and objectives

- Discussing jobs and money
- Indirect object pronouns

Grammar

- Indirect object pronouns
- **du/de la/de l'/des**

Key language

Household chores
Pocket money

Resources

CD3, tracks 9–10
Cahier d'exercices, page 50
Grammaire 1.5, 1.8

Starter 1

Aim
To revise indirect object pronouns.

Write up the following and ask students working in pairs to translate the sentences:

1 **Je te téléphonerai ce soir.**
2 **Ils ne me donnent rien.**
3 **Ses parents lui disent qu'il est encore trop jeune.**
4 **Est-ce qu'on te donne de l'argent de poche?**
5 **Je lui a envoyé un texto.**

When checking the answers, ask students to explain the function of **te**, **me**, **lui** in each example. Can they come up with a rule on where indirect object pronouns go in a sentence?

1 Reliez les images et les phrases.

Reading. Students find the correct phrase for each picture.

Answers

a garder ma petite sœur
b mettre la table
c passer l'aspirateur
d promener le chien
e faire la vaisselle
f vider le lave-vaisselle
g ranger ma chambre
h laver la voiture
i sortir la poubelle

2 On parle de l'argent de poche et du travail à la maison. Écoutez et complétez la grille. Utilisez les lettres des images de l'exercice 1. (1–5)

Listening. Students copy out the grid. They listen to five people talking about their pocket money and the household chores they do and complete the grid with the details. For the chores, they should use the letters of the pictures in exercise 1.

There is a lot of detail to note in this activity. You may want to suggest students concentrate on identifying specific details on the first listening and the rest of the information on a second listening.

Audioscript 9

1 *Mes parents me donnent dix euros par semaine comme argent de poche. Pour ça, je dois aider beaucoup à la maison. Je dois ranger ma chambre deux fois par semaine et faire la vaisselle tous les soirs, après le dîner. C'est affreux. Je trouve ça un peu dur parce que j'ai beaucoup de devoirs à faire aussi.*

2 *Mes parents sont divorcés et j'habite chez ma mère. Elle n'a pas beaucoup d'argent, donc elle ne me donne pas d'argent de poche, mais mon père me donne cinq euros si je lave sa voiture le week-end et mes grands-parents me donnent quinze euros par mois, donc ça va.*

3 *Chez moi, je ne dois pas aider mes parents parce que j'ai des examens cette année, donc j'ai beaucoup de travail scolaire à faire. Mais mon frère cadet doit passer l'aspirateur une fois par semaine et sortir la poubelle. Pour ça, ma mère lui donne huit euros par semaine comme argent de poche. C'est un peu injuste parce qu'on ne m'en donne pas. J'ai quand même besoin d'argent!*

4 *Mes parents me disent tout le temps «Si tu fais ça, on te donnera de l'argent de poche.» Par exemple, quelquefois je dois promener le chien ou garder ma petite sœur quand mes parents veulent sortir. Mais ils sont assez généreux quand même. Ils me donnent vingt-cinq euros par mois, donc c'est bien.*

5 *Moi, je dois mettre la table tous les soirs avant le dîner et vider le lave-vaisselle le matin. C'est dur, hein? Et mes parents refusent de me donner de l'argent de poche! Ils paient mes affaires scolaires et mes vêtements, donc ils disent que je n'ai pas besoin d'argent de poche. Ce n'est pas juste!*

Answers

	argent de poche	travail à la maison	content(e) ☺ ou pas content(e)? ☹
1	*10€ par semaine*	*g (2 x par sem.) …* e (tous les soirs)	☹
2	35€ par mois	h (le week-end)	☺
3	–	–	☹
4	25€ par mois	d (quelquefois) a (quelquefois)	☺
5	–	b (tous les soirs) f (tous les matins)	☹

Expo-langue: indirect object pronouns

Use this grammar box to cover the indirect object pronouns **me, te** and **lui** before students do exercise 3. There is more information on p. 208 of the Student Book.

3 À deux. Choisissez deux personnes de l'exercice 2 et faites un dialogue en utilisant les questions ci-dessous.

Speaking. In pairs: students each choose a person from exercise 2 and take part in a dialogue about what household chores they do, their pocket money and whether they're happy with the situation. The questions are supplied. They could repeat the dialogue with two different characters if there is time.

4 Écrivez un paragraphe sur deux des personnes de l'exercice 2.

Writing. Students write a paragraph on two of the people in exercise 2. Sentence openings are supplied for support.

Starter 2

Aim

To revise the partitive.

Write up the following and ask students to fill in the gaps with the appropriate form of **de**:

1 ____ bonbons
2 ____ bière
3 une tranche ____ jambon
4 ____ baskets
5 beaucoup ____ magazines
6 ____ matériel scolaire
7 un litre ____ eau minérale
8 ____ DVD
9 100g ____ raisins
10 ____ confiture

5 Écoutez ce qu'ils achètent avec leur argent de poche. Combien de fois est-ce qu'on mentionne chaque chose?

Listening. Students listen to an interview with three teenagers, Mélanie, Luc and Nabila about what they spend their pocket money on and note how many times the items pictured (**a–h**) are mentioned.

Audioscript 10

- *Ce soir, on demande aux jeunes ce qu'ils achètent avec leur argent de poche. J'ai avec moi Mélanie, Luc et Nabila. Commençons avec toi, Nabila. Est-ce que tu reçois de l'argent de poche?*
- *Oui, mes parents me donnent environ douze euros par semaine.*
- *Et tu le dépenses comment?*
- *Bof … D'abord, je dois acheter tout mon matériel scolaire – des stylos, des cahiers, des classeurs, etc. Puis avec l'argent qui me reste, j'achète des magazines de musique pop, des bonbons … et parfois du maquillage.*
- *Tu fais des économies aussi?*
- *C'est pas évident d'économiser avec douze euros par semaine, mais si je peux, je mets un peu d'argent de côté pour m'acheter des DVD ou des CD.*
- *Bon, merci. Et toi, Luc, qu'est-ce que tu fais de ton argent?*
- *Ben, je reçois un peu moins que Nabila – j'ai dix euros par semaine de la part de ma mère, mais j'achète un peu les mêmes choses que Nabila, c'est-à-dire des bonbons ou des chocolats, des magazines de jeux d'ordinateur – et du matériel scolaire. Mais j'économise toujours trois ou quatre euros par semaine pour acheter des jeux de console parce que jouer à l'ordinateur, c'est une de mes distractions préférées. Mais les jeux coûtent assez cher, alors je n'en achète qu'un tous les deux ou trois mois.*
- *D'accord, merci, Luc. Et finalement, Mélanie. Tu peux nous parler un peu de tout ça, toi aussi?*
- *Euh, je dois dire que j'ai de la chance, moi, parce que mes parents paient tout mon matériel scolaire, donc avec les vingt euros par mois qu'ils me donnent, je peux acheter les choses qui sont importantes pour moi. Par exemple, moi aussi, je suis fan des jeux de console, donc j'en achète pas mal. À part ça, j'achète des CD et des DVD, bien sûr, des magazines… et quelquefois je dois acheter des cadeaux d'anniversaire aussi. La chose que je trouve très chère, c'est les baskets, surtout parce que je préfère les marques comme Nike ou Fila. Donc, j'essaie de mettre de côté un peu d'argent tous les mois pour une nouvelle paire.*
- *Merci, Mélanie, et au revoir à tout le monde.*

Answers

***a** 2 fois* **b** 2 fois **c** 1 fois **d** 1 fois **e** 3 fois **f** 2 fois **g** 2 fois **h** 1 fois

Expo-langue: *du/de la/de l'/des*

Use this grammar box to remind students that the partitive (**du/de la/de l'/des**) is always used when talking about what you buy, even when you might omit 'some' in the English translation. There is more information on p. 207 of the Student Book.

R In pairs: students take it in turn to prompt with an item in English (from this unit or earlier Modules) (e.g. sweets) and to respond in French using the partitive (e.g. **des bonbons**).

6 Vidéoconférence. Répondez aux questions en utilisant les phrases ci-dessous. Utilisez un dictionnaire si nécessaire.

Speaking. Students imagine that they are going to have a videoconference with students at a French school. They are going to talk about what they buy with their pocket money and what they save for. The questions are supplied, along with a box of useful language to use.

Encourage them to use a dictionary for any items not covered in the book. Before they start, draw their attention to the tip box, which gives advice on how to use a dictionary effectively.

If possible, allow students to record their presentations. Ask them to take a partner's recording home to listen to it and to come up with two suggestions for improvement.

7 Écrivez un paragraphe sur ce que vous achetez avec votre argent. Mentionnez aussi si vous mettez de l'argent de côté et si oui, pourquoi. Essayez d'utiliser ces mots et expressions:

Writing. Students write a paragraph on what they buy with their pocket money. They should include details of any money they save and what they are saving for. Encourage them to use the list of expressions supplied.

Plenary

Write up:

Ses parents *lui* donnent de l'argent de poche.

Ask students to translate the sentence and then to explain what kind of word **lui** is, what it replaces and where it goes in a sentence.

Then write up:

Je *la* donne à mon frère.

Ask students what **la** is doing in this sentence. Get them to summarise the difference between direct and indirect object pronouns.

Cahier d'exercices, page 50

1a

Answers

1 Amandine
2 Rachid
3 Nicolas

1b

Answers

1 Rachid
2 Amandine
3 Nicolas
4 Nicolas
5 Amandine
6 Rachid
7 Rachid
8 Rachid

2

Answers

Example:
Ma mère me donne 40€ par mois comme argent de poche. Pour ça, je dois sortir la poubelle et faire la vaisselle chaque soir. Je trouve ça un peu dûr. Avec mes 40€, je dois acheter du matériel scolaire et des vêtements de mode. Je mets de côté l'argent qui me reste pour acheter des cadeaux pour mes copains. J'aimerais un peu plus!

1 Avez-vous un job?

(Student Book pages 94–95)

Main topics and objectives

- Talking about part-time jobs
- Looking for detailed meaning in a text

Key language

Je travaille dans …
un centre de loisirs
un fast-food
un salon de coiffure
un supermarché
Je fais du baby-sitting.
Je livre des journaux.
Je travaille de (9h00) à (17h30).
Je gagne (5€) par heure.
Je fais le café pour les clients.
Je travaille à la caisse.
Je fais des livraisons.
Je sers les clients.
Je range l'équipement sportif.
Je remplis les rayons.

Resources

CD3, tracks 11–12
Cahier d'exercices, page 51

Starter 1

Aim
To introduce some vocabulary for part-time jobs.
To revise **devoir** + the infinitive.

Write up:

1 Je ____ _____ l'aspirateur.
2 Il ____ ______ le café pour les clients.
3 Nous _____ _____ des journaux.
4 On _____ _____ à manger aux animaux.
5 Ils _____ ______ l'équipement sportif.

devoir +
donner, livrer, faire, ranger, passer

Ask students to complete the sentences with the correct form of **devoir** plus one of the verbs listed and then to translate the sentences.

1 Qui fait quel job? Écoutez et trouvez les bonnes images. (1–8)

Listening. Students listen to eight people talking about the job they do and identify the correct picture for each (from **a–h**).

Audioscript 11

1 *J'ai un petit job dans un fast-food. Je fais ça tous les samedis de treize heures à dix-huit heures et je gagne trente-deux euros cinquante.*

2 *Je travaille quatre soirs par semaine dans un centre de loisirs. Je gagne sept euros par heure et je fais douze heures par semaine.*

3 *Mon petit boulot, c'est dans un supermarché. Je commence à neuf heures et demie le dimanche et je finis à midi. Pour ça, je gagne dix-huit euros.*

4 *Je fais du baby-sitting deux fois par semaine pour mes voisins. D'habitude, je fais ça entre vingt heures et vingt-trois heures et je reçois vingt euros par semaine.*

5 *J'ai un job tous les week-ends dans une ferme. On me paie vingt-cinq euros et je travaille quatre heures en tout.*

6 *Moi, je livre des journaux aux maisons près de chez moi. Je fais ça tous les jours sauf le dimanche de sept heures à huit heures. Le salaire, c'est vingt-quatre euros par semaine.*

7 *J'ai un petit boulot dans un salon de coiffure le samedi matin. Je fais trois heures de travail et je gagne treize euros cinquante.*

8 *Mon travail, c'est le lundi et le mercredi soir dans l'épicerie de mon oncle. Je commence à seize heures et je finis à dix-huit heures trente. Il me paie vingt-sept euros cinquante par semaine.*

Answers
1 d **2** g **3** b **4** a **5** h **6** c **7** f **8** e

2 Écoutez encore une fois. Copiez et complétez la grille en français. (1–8)

Listening. Students copy out the grid. They listen to the recording again and complete the grid with the details in French. Warn students that some people give details of the pay as an hourly rate, so they will need to work out the total pay for the answer.

Audioscript 12

As for exercise 1.

Answers

	jour(s)/fréquence	horaires	salaire
1	*tous les samedis*	*de 13h à 18h*	*32,50€*
2	quatre jours par semaine	douze heures par semaine	84€
3	le dimanche	de 9h30 à 12h	18€
4	deux fois par semaine	de 20h à 23h	20€
5	tous les week-ends	quatre heures	25€
6	tous les jours sauf le dimanche	de 7h à 8h	24€
7	le samedi matin	trois heures	13,50€
8	le lundi et le mercredi	de 16h à 18h30	27,50€

3 Trouvez les paires de phrases pour les images de l'exercice 1.

Reading. Students read the 16 sentences. For each of the pictures in exercise 1 (**a–h**), they identify the two correct sentences.

Answers

a *13,* 16 **b** 1, 5 **c** 6, 8 **d** 3, 10 **e** 7, 15 **f** 2, 11 **g** 12, 14 **h** 4, 9

4 À deux. Imaginez que vous êtes une des personnes de l'exercice 1. Faites un dialogue en utilisant ces questions:

Speaking. In pairs: students use the questions supplied to have a dialogue. They take it in turn to imagine that they are one of the people in exercise 1 and to respond accordingly.

Starter 2

Aim
To recognise key words and phrases which affect meaning in a text.

Write up the following in two columns, jumbling the order of the second column. Ask students to match the French and English versions.

trop	too
sauf	except
parfois	sometimes
mais d'habitude	but usually
ne … que	only
par contre	on the other hand
même si	even if
malgré cela	in spite of that

5 Lisez les textes. Puis regardez les phrases en dessous. Pour chaque personne, écrivez P (Positive), N (Négative) ou P/N (Positive/Négative).

Reading. Students read the four texts. They then read the question on each text and decide whether the writer's opinion on each of the points listed is positive (**P**), negative (**N**) or a mixture of the two (**P/N**).

☑ Before starting, students should read through the tip box, which highlights a key pitfall when tackling reading texts in an exam. It advises students on looking out for small but important words that can easily be overlooked but which can completely change the meaning of a sentence.

Answers

1 a N **b** P/N **c** P   **3 a** P **b** N
2 a N **b** N **c** P   **4 a** P **b** P/N

6 Préparez une présentation d'une minute sur votre job. Si vous n'avez pas de job, utilisez les détails ci-dessous. Mentionnez:

Speaking. Students prepare a one-minute presentation on their job, using details of a job they actually do or the prompts supplied. They should use the list of points to be covered to structure their presentation.

7 Écrivez un paragraphe sur votre job, réel ou imaginaire. Adaptez les textes de l'exercice 5, si vous voulez.

Writing. Students write a paragraph on a real or imaginary job that they do. Remind them they can adapt the texts in exercise 5 or simply use them for ideas.

Plenary

☑ Ask students to identify the vocabulary in this unit that they are intending to note down to learn. What vocabulary is important? How will they approach this?

Emphasise how important it is that students learn and revise vocabulary as they go along, especially at this level where such a broad range of vocabulary is used. Discuss ways in which students note vocabulary down and how they learn it. Remind students as necessary of the 'look, say, cover, write, check' approach for learning words. Point out that regularly reviewing vocabulary (spending at least ten minutes on it every day) will really help them when it comes to revising for the exam.

Cahier d'exercices, page 51

1

Answers

A Je donne des cours à des enfants plus petits que moi.
B Quelquefois les clients sont un peu impolis.
C Je dois me lever tôt le samedi.
D Le week-end quelquefois, c'est difficile.

2

Answers

1 Oui, les parents des enfants lui donne de l'argent.
2 Oui, elle aime bien son travail.
3 Elle travaille dans un café ou dans un restaurant.
4 Quelquefois, les clients sont un peu impolis.
5 Oui, ses collègues sont sympas.
6 Parce qu'elle doit choisir entre le baby-sitting et sortir avec ses copains.

3

Answers

Pupil's own answers

2 Au boulot!

(Student Book pages 96–97)

Main topics and objectives

- Discussing different jobs
- Forming questions

Grammar

- Questions

Key language

l'agent de police
le/la boulanger/ère
le/la caissier/ère
le/la chauffeur/euse de poids lourds
le/la chef de cuisine
le facteur/la factrice
le/la médecin
le serveur/garçon de café
la serveuse
le steward/l'hôtesse de l'air
Ce que j'aime surtout, ...
c'est la variété du travail
le/la patron(ne)
mes collègues
le salaire
les horaires de travail
les (autres) gens
sauf
même (si)
C'est/Ce n'est pas bien payé.
monotone
satisfait(e)
sévère
enfermé(e) dans un bureau
fatigant(e)
gratifiant(e)
sale
stressant(e)
On (n')a (pas) ...
beaucoup de/pas mal de
contact avec les gens
responsabilité
temps libre
On doit se lever tôt.
On reçoit un pourboire.
On travaille en équipe.
On voyage beaucoup.
les heures sont longues

Resources

CD3, tracks 13–14
Cahier d'exercices, page 52
Grammaire 4.2

Starter 1

Aim
To practise listening for gist.

Tell students they are going to hear a recording: explain that their aim is to get a general idea of what is going on, not to note the details. They should listen for the answers to the following questions:

1 Where might you hear this kind of recording? (on the radio)
2 What is the man's job? (he's a TV cameraman)
3 Does he like it? (yes, it's a fascinating job)

Play the recording for exercise 1.

1 Écoutez cette interview avec un reporter cameraman. Notez les questions dans le bon ordre.

Listening. Students listen to the interview with a TV cameraman who travels the world shooting news films. They put the nine questions asked in the interview in the same order as on the recording.

Audioscript 13

– *Comment vous appelez-vous?*
– *Je m'appelle Guillaume Marchant.*
– *Et qu'est-ce que vous faites comme travail?*
– *Je suis reporter cameraman.*
– *Depuis quand faites-vous ce travail?*
– *Depuis quinze ans à peu près.*
– *Comment vous êtes devenu reporter cameraman?*
– *Après avoir quitté le lycée, j'ai fait des études de journalisme dans une école spécialisée à Bordeaux.*
– *Où travaillez-vous en ce moment?*
– *En ce moment, je travaille beaucoup en Afrique. Je suis en train de tourner un reportage sur le sida, pour une chaîne de télévision française.*
– *Vous travaillez combien d'heures par semaine?*
– *Ça peut varier énormément. Mais en général, je travaille entre trente-cinq et quarante heures par semaine.*
– *Vous aimez votre travail?*
– *Ah, oui, c'est un travail fascinant.*
– *Pourquoi l'aimez-vous?*
– *Ce que j'aime surtout, c'est la variété du travail. D'ailleurs, j'aime beaucoup voyager; je n'aimerais pas être enfermé dans un bureau. Et c'est assez bien payé aussi!*
– *Quels sont les inconvénients de votre travail?*
– *Les inconvénients sont qu'on n'est pas souvent à la maison et que quelquefois, on doit travailler le week-end.*
– *Guillaume Marchant, merci beaucoup.*
– *Il n'y a pas de quoi.*

Answers

5, 8, 3, 6, 7, 2, 9, 1, 4

Expo-langue: questions

Use this grammar box to cover the different ways questions can be formed and to revise question words (including the various forms of **quel?**). There is more information on p. 217 of the Student Book.

R Ask students to identify what kind of question each question in exercise 1 is.

2 Complétez le texte en utilisant les mots ci-dessous.

Reading. Students read the gap-fill text and identify the ten missing words. The words are supplied for reference.

➕ Before students look at the list of words, ask them to identify what kind of word they are looking for in each case (noun, verb, etc.).

Answers

1 depuis **2** études **3** Afrique **4** entre **5** semaine **6** variété **7** voyager **8** payé **9** inconvénients **10** doit

3 À deux. Faites une interview avec Nathalie Lafontaine ou Jean-Luc Blier en utilisant les détails à droite.

Speaking. In pairs: students carry out an interview, taking it in turn to ask the questions and to play the part of Nathalie Lafontaine or Jean-Luc Blier, whose details are supplied.

4 Écrivez un paragraphe pour Nathalie ou Jean-Luc. Adaptez le texte de l'exercice 2.

Writing. Students write a paragraph about Nathalie or Jean-Luc, adapting the completed texts from exercise 2.

Starter 2

Aim

To revise forming questions.

Ask students to come up with three questions, each one using a different kind of question structure.

Listen to some answers. Ask students to summarise the various ways questions are formed.

5 Trouvez la bonne image pour chaque texte.

Reading. Students read the five texts about various jobs and match each one to the correct picture.

Answers

1 b **2** c **3** d **4** a **5** e

6 Trouvez dans le glossaire ou dans un dictionnaire l'équivalent en anglais des mots en bleu dans l'exercice 5.

Reading. Students translate into English the words in blue in the texts in exercise 5, using either the Vocabulaire section at the back of the Student Book or a dictionary. Encourage an able class to see how much they can manage to work out for themselves before using these references.

7 Écoutez. Donnez au moins un avantage et un inconvénient de chaque métier. Complétez la grille en français. (1–5)

Listening. Students copy out the grid. They listen to five conversations in which people talk about their job and note in the grid an advantage and a disadvantage for each job mentioned.

Audioscript 14

1 *– Je voudrais bien travailler comme caissier. On a beaucoup de contact avec les gens et les heures sont flexibles.*
– Oui, mais tu sais, c'est assez monotone comme travail et le salaire n'est pas toujours très bon.

2 *– L'avantage d'être chauffeur de poids lourds, c'est qu'on n'a pas beaucoup de responsabilités et on voyage beaucoup.*
– D'accord, tu as raison, mais il ne faut pas oublier que les horaires sont longues et on doit souvent travailler la nuit aussi.

3 *– Je n'aimerais pas être boulangère. On doit se lever très tôt le matin pour faire le pain et il fait très chaud aussi.*
– Oui, seulement c'est bien comme métier si on s'intéresse à l'alimentation. Et on a beaucoup d'indépendance si on est propriétaire de la boulangerie.

4 *– Si on travaille comme coiffeuse, on a beaucoup de contacts avec ses clients et c'est parfait si on s'intéresse à la mode ou à la beauté.*
– Oui, mais quelquefois, ce n'est pas très bien payé et n'oublie pas qu'on doit travailler le samedi aussi!

5 *– Travailler comme garçon de café, je crois que c'est dur. Ça doit être fatigant de servir les clients toute la journée et on doit souvent travailler le soir.*
– Oui, mais c'est agréable de travailler avec les gens comme ça. Et un autre avantage, c'est qu'on reçoit souvent un pourboire des clients.

Answers

	avantages	inconvénients
1 *caissier/caissière de supermarché*	*contact avec les gens* horaires flexibles	*monotone* salaire pas très bon
2 *chauffeur/chauffeuse de poids lourds*	pas beaucoup de responsabilité voyage beaucoup	heures longues travaille la nuit
3 *boulanger/boulangère*	intéressant beaucoup d'indépendence	se lève très tôt très chaud
4 *coiffeur/coiffeuse*	beaucoup de contact intéressant	pas très bien payé travaille le samedi
5 *garçon de café (serveur)/serveuse*	travaille en équipe pourboires	fatigant travaille le soir

8 À deux. Quels métiers voudriez-vous ou ne voudriez-vous pas faire?

Speaking. In pairs: students discuss which jobs they would like to do and which they wouldn't like to do. A sample exchange is given.

Plenary

Explain that the class is going to play a game to revise the advantages and disadvantages of particular jobs. Start it off by prompting a student with a job (e.g. **caissier de supermarché – inconvénient?**). The student responds with an example of an advantage or disadvantage of the job, as specified (e.g. **c'est monotone**). That student then prompts another student, and so on round the class.

Cahier d'exercices, page 52

1

Answers

Comment vous appelez-vous?
Qu'est-ce que vous faites comme travail?
Depuis quand faites-vous ce travail?
Comment êtes-vous devenu propriétaire?
Vous aimez votre travail?
Vous travaillez combien d'heures par semaine?
Quels sont les inconvénients de votre travail?
Qu'est-ce qu'il faut faire pour réussir?
Votre restaurant a reçu des étoiles?

2

Answers

1 Il a quitté le collège à quinze ans.
2 Il a réussi son Brevet professionnel.
3 Il a commencé à travailler comme cuisinier à vingt et un ans.
4 Il a commencé son travail comme propriétaire à trente ans.
5 Il aime bien créer les repas.
6 Il travaille entre cinquante-cinq et soixante-dix heures par semaine.
7 Un inconvénient, c'est que les heures sont longues et il aime être avec sa famille.
8 Pour avoir du succès, il pense qu'il faut être curieux et vouloir faire plaisir.

3 C'est de la part de qui?

(Student Book pages 98–99)

Main topics and objectives

- Applying for jobs
- Using formal language

Grammar

- Formal language

Key language

l'aptitude sportive (f)
la maîtrise de l'anglais
les langues étrangères (f)
J'ai vu votre annonce ...
Je voudrais poser ma candidature pour le poste de ...
Comme vous verrez dans mon CV, ...
Veuillez trouver ci-joint ...
Dans l'attente de votre réponse
Je vous prie d'agréer l'expression de mes salutations sincères
Ici (Pierre Dupont).
Je voudrais parler ...
Je regrette. Il/Elle n'est pas là en ce moment.
Vous voulez laisser un message?
C'est de la part de qui?
Ça s'écrit comment?
Ne quittez pas.
Je vais vous passer (Mademoiselle Mériel).
Quel est votre numéro de téléphone/portable/fax?
Je rappellerai demain.

Resources

CD3, tracks 15–16
Cahier d'exercices, page 53

Starter 1

Aim
To practise reading for gist.

Give students one minute to read the texts in exercise 1 on p. 98 of the Student Book. Explain that their aim is to get a general idea of what is going on, not to note the details. They are looking for the answers to the following questions:

1 Where would you find texts like these?
2 What is the job described in each one?
3 Where is each job based?

1 Lisez les offres d'emploi et répondez aux questions en anglais.

Reading. Students read the three job adverts. They answer the ten questions in English by identifying the job referred to in each case.

☑ Draw students' attention to the tip box before they start. This covers the very important technique of focusing on what you need to understand in a more complex text and not being distracted by the fact the texts contain language you don't know. Stress that developing an ability to identify the appropriate 'clue' words will greatly help them in the exam.

Answers
1 A, C **2** B **3** B **4** A **5** C **6** A **7** B **8** C **9** A **10** C

2 Écrivez l'équivalent en anglais de ces mots et expressions tirés des annonces de l'exercice 1. Devinez d'abord, puis vérifiez dans un dictionnaire.

Reading. Students translate the 10 expressions from the adverts in exercise 1. They should try to do this using the reading strategies they have learned and then use a dictionary to check their answers.

Answers
1 your aptitude for sports/your sporting ability
2 interest in/liking for sport
3 mastery of English
4 two months' training
5 available in the evenings until 2am and at the weekend
6 the Caribbean
7 welcoming visitors
8 a foreign language would be appreciated
9 your application
10 your availability

3 On téléphone pour avoir des renseignements sur quel emploi ci-dessus? A, B ou C? (1–3)

Listening. Students listen to three people phoning for further information on jobs they have seen advertised. They identify which of the jobs in exercise 1 each person is interested in.

⊞ You could replay the recordings and ask students to note down what each person wants to know and what response they receive.

Audioscript 15

1 *– Allô. Ici Robert Lavigne. Je peux vous aider?*
– Bonjour, monsieur. C'est Chantal Gautier à l'appareil. J'ai bien vu votre annonce dans le journal et je voudrais vous poser une petite question, s'il vous plaît.
– Pas de problème, Mademoiselle Gautier. C'était pour quel poste?
– C'est pour le poste d'opérateur ou opératrice d'attractions.
– Ah oui, et quelle est votre question?
– J'ai bien lu dans l'annonce qu'il faut être disponible le soir et le week-end, mais je voudrais connaître les horaires de travail exacts, si possible.

– *Les horaires sont flexibles, mademoiselle, mais en général on demande aux opérateurs de travailler sept heures par jour, cinq jours par semaine. Ça vous ira?*
– *Oui, ça ira, merci, monsieur. C'est que je m'entraîne pour une compétition de natation, mais je peux m'entraîner avant ou après le travail, selon vos besoins.*
– *Ah, je vois que vous avez un goût prononcé pour le sport, comme on a précisé dans notre annonce. C'est bien ça. Vous avez d'autres questions?*
– *Non, merci, monsieur, c'est tout.*

2 – *Allô, LMCB, je vous écoute.*
– *Bonjour, madame. Je voudrais parler à Isabelle Lepage, s'il vous plaît.*
– *Ah, je regrette, monsieur, elle n'est pas là en ce moment. Vous voulez laisser un message?*
– *Oui, je veux bien, s'il vous plaît. C'est de la part de Sélim Nadour.*
– *Ça s'écrit comment, monsieur, s'il vous plaît?*
– *S-É-L-I-M N-A-D-O-U-R.*
– *Merci. Et quel est votre message?*
– *C'est pour avoir plus de renseignements sur votre annonce, qui a paru dans le journal d'hier.*
– *C'est pour les postes d'hôtes et hôtesses d'accueil, monsieur?*
– *Oui, madame, c'est ça. Je voudrais travailler à temps partiel, mais je ne peux pas travailler les mercredis, à cause de mes études, donc …*
– *Si vous voulez, monsieur, je peux vous passer Mademoiselle Mériel, qui travaille avec Madame Lepage. Elle pourra vous renseigner sur ce poste.*
– *Ce serait très gentil, merci, madame.*
– *De rien, monsieur. Ne quittez pas …*

3 – *Allô, oui?*
– *Je voudrais parler à Monsieur Perrault, s'il vous plaît.*
– *C'est lui-même.*
– *Bonjour, monsieur. J'aimerais poser ma candidature pour le poste paru dans le journal de la semaine dernière, si ce n'est pas trop tard.*
– *C'est pour quel poste, monsieur?*
– *C'est pour le poste d'animateur en club.*
– *Ah, oui. Ce n'est pas encore trop tard, mais il faudrait envoyer votre dossier le plus tôt possible. Pourriez-vous nous envoyer votre CV et votre lettre de motivation par fax, s'il vous plaît?*
– *Oui, monsieur. Quel est votre numéro de fax, s'il vous plaît?*
– *C'est le 01 41 26 88 02.*
– *Pourriez-vous répéter, s'il vous plaît, monsieur?*
– *Oui, c'est le 01 41 26 88 02, monsieur.*
– *Merci, monsieur. Je vous l'envoie tout de suite.*
– *De rien, monsieur. Au revoir.*

Answers
1 C **2** B **3** A

Starter 2

Aim
To practise using grammar and logic to work out language.

Write up the following in two columns, jumbling the order of the second column. Ask students working in pairs to match the halves to make complete sentences/questions and then to translate them.

1 Je peux	**vous aider?**
2 Quel est	**votre message?**
3 Elle vous	**rappellera plus tard.**
4 Ça s'écrit	**comment?**
5 Quel est votre	**numéro de téléphone?**
6 Je lui	**passerai votre message.**
7 C'est	**de la part de qui?**

When checking answers, ask students how they worked out the pairings.

4 Écoutez et complétez le dialogue.

Listening. Students listen to the recording and note the words missing in the gap-fill version of the text. The words are supplied for support.

Audioscript 16

– *Allô,* ***ici*** *Cécile Moreau. Je peux vous aider?*
– *Bonjour, madame. Je voudrais* ***parler*** *à Mademoiselle Chagny, s'il vous plaît.*
– *Ah, je* ***regrette****, monsieur, mais elle n'est pas là en ce moment. Vous voulez* ***laisser*** *un message?*
– *Oui, je veux bien, s'il vous plaît.*
– *C'est de la* ***part*** *de qui, monsieur?*
– *C'est de la part de Mathieu Gesbert.*
– *Gesbert, ça* ***s'écrit*** *comment, s'il vous plaît?*
– *G-E-S-B-E-R-T.*
– ***Quel*** *est votre numéro de téléphone, s'il vous plaît, monsieur?*
– *C'est le 06 10 77 34 30.*
– *Et quel est votre message?*
– *C'est que je* ***serai*** *un peu en retard pour notre réunion cet après-midi parce que mon train a une demi-heure de* ***retard****.*
– *Bon, merci. Je lui passerai* ***votre*** *message. Elle vous rappellera plus tard.*
– *Merci, madame. Au revoir.*
– *De rien, monsieur. Au revoir.*

Answers
Also in bold in the audioscript.
1 ici **2** parler **3** regrette **4** laisser **5** part **6** s'écrit **7** quel **8** serai **9** retard **10** votre

R In pairs: students translate the dialogue into English.

Expo-langue: formal language

Use this grammar box to focus on formal language before students do exercise 5. Remind students of the use of **vous** and the possessive adjectives **votre/vos** in a formal/work context.

Also draw attention to the fact that it is considered polite to address people directly using **monsieur, madame** and **mademoiselle**. Students should look at how this is done in the dialogue in exercise 4 and try to copy this in their own speech to sound authentic.

5 À deux. Pratiquez le dialogue de l'exercice 4.

Speaking. In pairs: students practise the dialogue in exercise 4, taking it in turn to play the role of Mathieu and the person who answers the phone.

6 Adaptez le dialogue de l'exercice 4 en changeant les mots en bleu. Utilisez les détails ci-dessous.

Speaking. Students make up a different dialogue, adapting the dialogue in exercise 4 by changing the words in blue and using the details supplied instead.

7 Posez votre candidature! Adaptez la lettre à droite en utilisant l'annonce A ou B de l'exercice 1. Inventez certains détails, si vous voulez.

Writing. Students write a letter of application for a job, using the details from advert A or B in exercise 1. A model letter is supplied for them to adapt. They can also include further details of their own, if they want to.

Before they start, remind students to check their use of the terms **madame** and **monsieur** in letters, as detailed in the **Expo-langue** box on this page. Also emphasise the importance of reading the advert they choose very carefully so that they can make their application as clear and as focused as possible.

Students could do this activity on computer using a word-processing package like Word.

They could also use the Internet to research job opportunities in France, for example by keying in a company name and the word **emploi** in Google or another search engine. Ask them to see how much they can understand, using all the reading skills techniques they have been practising. They should be encouraged by how much the context helps them.

Plenary

Ask students to summarise when they would use the **tu** form and when the **vous** form, giving you examples of situations. (You could remind them that if in doubt, **vous** is a safe bet.)

Ask them what other words apart from verbs are affected by the formality of the situation, getting them to list the forms of the **tu** and **vous** possessive adjective **(ton, ta, tes; votre, vos)**.

Cahier d'exercices, page 53

1

Answers

Possible answers:

A: Shop assistant between 17–23 with some experience. Working in a team of 5–6 people. Energetic and excellent presentation. Available immediately.

B: Restaurant looking for barman/barmaid. Experience, good presentation and motivation required. Start at the beginning of August; fixed salary.

C: Improve your German: go to Germany for 6 months. Be an au pair or get a job in the hotel industry. Food, accommodation provided + salary.

2

Answers

Pupil's own answers

4 Ce n'est pas juste!

(Student Book pages 100–101)

Main topics and objectives

- Discussing problems at work
- Using **qui** and **que**

Grammar

- Relative pronouns **qui** and **que**

Key language

Le plus grand problème, c'est ...
le racisme
le sexisme
les blagues racistes
la discrimination contre
l'handicapé(e)
l'immigré(e)
le/la musulman(e)
il ne faut pas tolérer
tout à fait inacceptable
le préjugé

Resources

CD3, tracks 17–18
Cahier d'exercices, page 54
Grammaire 1.9

Starter 1

Aim
To practise identifying the subject and object of a sentence.

Write up the following:

1 Le chien a mordu l'homme.
2 On me donne un cadeau.
3 Je lui téléphonera demain.
4 Loulou a vu Matthieu.
5 Je connais ta sœur.
6 Elle ne l'aimait pas.

Ask students to list in two columns
(1) the subjects of the verbs and
(2) the objects of the verbs.

After checking answers, ask students to define subject and object.

1 Trouvez les paires de phrases.

Reading. Students read the eight speech bubbles and identify the pairs which go together.

Answers
a h **b** g **c** f **d** e

Expo-langue: *qui/que*

Use this grammar box on the relative pronouns **qui** and **que** before students do exercise 2. There is more information on p. 209 of the Student Book.

R Ask students to identify all the examples of **qui** and **que** and what they refer to in the texts in exercise 1.

2 Traduisez en français en adaptant les phrases de l'exercice 1.

Writing. Students translate the five sentences into French, adapting similar phrases in exercise 1 to help them.

Answers
1 Le racisme est quelque chose qu'on ne doit pas tolérer.
2 On ne doit jamais accepter de blagues sexistes d'un patron.
3 Un collègue qui permet la discrimination est quelqu'un qu'on ne peut pas respecter.
4 Une chose que je trouve inacceptable est la discrimination contre les handicapés.
5 J'ai un copain/une copine pour qui le chômage pose des difficultés.

3 Écoutez et notez la bonne lettre. Pour chaque personne, le problème, c'est ... (1–5)

Listening. Students listen to five people talking about problems relating to work. They identify the problem for each from the list supplied (a–e)

Audioscript 17

1 Le problème que j'ai au bureau, c'est mon patron. Il ne croit pas que les femmes sont capables de faire du travail difficile. Alors, il donne les postes à responsabilités à mes collègues masculins, tandis qu'il demande aux femmes de faire des photocopies et préparer le café.

2 Il est très difficile de trouver un emploi dans ma ville. Il y a pas mal de gens qui sont sans emploi et mon père, qui est ingénieur de profession, ne travaille pas depuis huit mois. Il est déprimé d'être chômeur et on a pas mal de problèmes financiers aussi.

3 Je travaille dans une épicerie et j'ai une collègue qui fait souvent des blagues sur les noirs et les musulmans. Je n'aime pas ça parce que mes parents viennent d'Algérie. Je me suis plaint au propriétaire. Il a dit que c'était juste son sens de l'humour, mais je crois que c'est parce qu'elle a des préjugés.

4 Je travaille dans une usine et il y a deux semaines, un de mes collègues est parti parce qu'il a trouvé un nouvel emploi. Le directeur de l'usine a dit que je devais faire le travail de mon collègue aussi. Je suis complètement stressé et j'ai tant de travail que je n'arrive pas chez moi avant neuf heures du soir.

5 *J'ai un copain en fauteuil roulant, qui voudrait aller à la même faculté que moi, l'année prochaine, mais on a refusé de l'accepter à cette université. Ils disent qu'il aura trop de difficulté, à cause des escaliers et des portes qui sont trop étroites. Je trouve que c'est scandaleux que les bâtiments ne soient pas adaptés à l'accès en fauteuil roulant.*

Answers
1 c **2** a **3** b **4** e **5** d

Starter 2

Aim
To practise using **qui** and **que**.

Write up the following and ask students to complete the sentences with **qui** or **que** as appropriate and to translate them.

1 J'ai vu le garçon ____ habite à Carcassonne.
2 Une chose ____ je n'aime pas, c'est le salsa.
3 Il aime le gâteau ____ ta mère a fait.
4 Elle a une copine ____ s'appelle Amandine.

When checking answers, ask students to summarise when **qui** and **que** are used.

Covering the pronunciation of cognates in French and English. Read through this together before students do exercise 4.

4 Prononcez les paires de mots français et anglais.

Speaking. Students read aloud the pairs of French and English cognates, taking care to follow the guidelines given in the pronunciation box.

5 Écoutez et vérifiez. Répétez les mots si vous avez fait des erreurs de prononciation.

Listening. Students listen to a recorded version of the text in exercise 4 to check their pronunciation. After listening, give them time to do exercise 4 again in pairs, to correct any errors and/or consolidate the pronunciation.

Audioscript 18

1 *sexisme – sexism*

2 *raciste – racist*

3 *discrimination – discrimination*

4 *problème – problem*

5 *inacceptable – unacceptable*

6 Vidéoconférence. Préparez et mémorisez votre réponse aux questions ci-dessous.

Speaking. Students imagine that they are going to have a videoconference with students at a French school. They prepare and memorise their responses to the two questions supplied. A framework is supplied for support.

Students should then practise their dialogues in pairs, taking it in turn to ask and answer the questions.

7 Écrivez un paragraphe sur le(s) problème(s) dont vous avez parlé dans l'exercice 6.

Writing. Students write a paragraph on the problem(s) they talked about in exercise 6.

8 Lisez et complétez ces lettres.

Reading. Students read the four gap-fill letters and note the ten missing words. The words are supplied for support.

Answers
1 patron **2** blagues **3** quelque chose **4** faut **5** l'usine **6** fauteuil **7** difficultés **8** handicapés **9** sera **10** respecter

Plenary

✓ As a follow up to the discussion about vocabulary in Unit 1, ask students which vocabulary they are planning to learn from this unit. Which approaches have they used to list and learn vocabulary and which have they found most effective? Point out different approaches work for different people.

If your students have regular access to a computer, they could create their own vocabulary notebook on computer using Word or Excel. Again, encourage them to think about different ways of organising vocabulary (topic, gender, type of word, etc.) to help them remember it. They could also save and print out edited lists of vocabulary, with either the English or French missing, to test themselves/ each other.

Cahier d'exercices, page 54

1

Answers

Pupil's own answers

2

Answers

Possible answers

1 White people
2 He has probably experienced some sort of racist comment from others and he is black.
3 He feels a bit upset that people call him 'coloured'.
4 That everyone is really the same, no matter what colour their skin is. We all have the same emotions.
5 Pupil's own answers

3

Answers

Pupil's own answers

5 Les stages – pour ou contre?

(Student Book pages 102–103)

Main topics and objectives

- Talking about work experience
- Contrasting the perfect and imperfect tenses

Grammar

- The perfect and imperfect: when to use

Key language

J'ai fait mon stage dans …
J'ai fait ça pendant une semaine.
J'ai passé deux semaines dans …
un garage
une agence de voyages
une banque
une école primaire/maternelle
une usine
J'ai appris beaucoup de choses.
Je n'ai pas appris grand-chose.
Je n'ai rien appris.
C'était …
une perte de temps totale
une expérience positive
Ce n'était pas complètement positive.
J'aidais les mécaniciens.
Je rangeais les outils.
Je faisais des photocopies.
Je classais des fiches.
Je prenais des commandes.
Je prenais les rendez-vous.
Je servais les clients.
Je travaillais à l'ordinateur.
Je répondais au téléphone.
J'envoyais des brochures.
Je faisais le café.
Je surveillais les enfants.
J'aidais pendant leurs leçons.
Je n'avais pas grand-chose à faire.
Je (ne) m'entendais (pas) bien avec …
Je m'amusais bien.
Je me suis ennuyé(e).
Je me sentais un peu exploité(e).

Resources

CD3, tracks 19–20
Cahier d'exercices, pages 55–56
Grammaire 3.5

Starter 1

Aim
To practise using the perfect and the imperfect tenses.

Write up the following and ask students to supply the correct form of each verb given in the infinitive, in either the perfect or imperfect tense as appropriate. Remind them to think about agreement where necessary, reading the text closely to find out what is required.

Vendredi dernier, ma copine Élodie me (**téléphoner**) et me (**dire**) «Mes parents vont partir pour le week-end. Donc, je t'invite à une fête chez moi ce soir!» Je (**être**) très contente!

Donc, à sept heures, je (**se doucher**) et je (**s'habiller**). Quand je (**partir**) à huit heures, il (**faire**) beau, mais … Je (**marcher**) très vite quand … je (**tomber**)! Mon nouveau jean – tout sale! Je (**être**) furieuse!

Et la fête? C'(**être**) nul!

1 Écoutez, et lisez les phrases dans les bulles. Qui parle? (1–6)

Listening. Students listen to six people talking about the work experience they have done. They read the six speech bubbles and use these to identify each of the speakers.

Audioscript 19

1. *J'aidais les mécaniciens à réparer les véhicules, je rangeais les outils et parfois, je changeais les pneus des voitures.*
2. *Je faisais des photocopies, je classais des fiches et je prenais les commandes des clients au téléphone qui voulaient acheter un lave-vaisselle ou une machine à laver.*
3. *Je m'occupais des animaux qui arrivaient pour des opérations, je prenais les rendez-vous au téléphone et quelquefois, j'accompagnais la vétérinaire dans ses visites à des fermes.*
4. *Je servais des clients avec des employés permanents, je travaillais à l'ordinateur et de temps en temps, je devais compter l'argent.*
5. *Je répondais au téléphone, j'envoyais des brochures de vacances aux clients et je faisais le café pour les autres employés.*
6. *Je jouais avec les enfants, je les surveillais pendant l'heure du déjeuner et je les aidais pendant leurs leçons.*

Answers
1 Ryan **2** Lydie **3** Hakim **4** Amélie **5** Yann **6** Shazia

Expo-langue: the perfect and imperfect – when to use

Use this grammar box to remind students when to use the perfect (single events) and when to use the imperfect (regular/repeated events). Point out that using both accurately is key in this topic. There is more information on p. 213 of the Student Book.

2 Trouvez la seconde partie des phrases pour les personnes de l'exercice 1.

Reading. Students match the sentence halves to produce six sentences describing the people in exercise 1.

Answers

1 e 2 d 3 f 4 c 5 a 6 b

3 Écrivez d'autres phrases à l'imparfait pour les personnes de l'exercice 1 en utilisant les verbes ci-dessous.

Writing. Students use the prompts supplied to write a sentence on each of the people in exercise 1. They need to use the first person and the imperfect tense.

Before they start, ask students to look at the example given in question 1. Can they work out why it is **rangeais** and not **rangais**?

Answers

1 *Je rangeais les outils et je* changeais les pneus des voitures.
2 Je prenais des commandes au téléphone.
3 Je prenais les rendez-vous au téléphone et j'accompagnais la vétérinaire dans ses visites à des fermes.
4 Je travaillais à l'ordinateur et je devais compter l'argent.
5 Je répondais au téléphone et je faisais le café pour les autres employés.
6 Je jouais avec les enfants et je les aidais pendant leurs leçons.

Starter 2

Aim

To review some of the language to describe a work experience.

In pairs: students take it in turn to prompt with a work experience (e.g. **J'ai fait mon stage dans une boulangerie.**) and to respond by saying what they did there, using the imperfect tense (e.g. **Je servais des clients.**).

4 Écoutez et notez si leur stage en entreprise était une expérience positive (P), négative (N) ou positive-négative (P/N), et pourquoi. Complétez la grille. (1–5)

Listening. Students copy out the grid. They listen to five people talking about their work experience and note in the grid whether the people found the experience positive (**P**), negative (**N**) or a mixture of both (**P/N**) and the reasons why.

☑ Before students start, draw their attention to the tip box: this reminds them to use non-verbal clues such as tone of voice to help them when trying to understand spoken French. This is an important strategy for listening tasks in the exam.

Audioscript 20

1 *J'ai travaillé pendant deux semaines dans un bureau. Mes collègues étaient tous sympa, donc on s'amusait bien ensemble et je m'entendais bien avec ma patronne, Madame Auger. De plus, le travail était assez varié et j'ai beaucoup appris.*

2 *Mon expérience au restaurant n'a pas été complètement positive. D'une part, les chefs de cuisine et les serveuses étaient aimables. D'autre part, je me sentais un peu exploité. Je ne gagnais rien, mais j'avais beaucoup de travail à faire et c'était fatigant.*

3 *Moi, j'étais très déçue de mon stage dans un salon de coiffure. Je n'avais pas le droit de couper les cheveux des clients et il n'y avait pas grand-chose à faire pour moi, donc c'était assez monotone.*

4 *En général, j'ai beaucoup apprécié mon stage au centre de loisirs. On me traitait bien et on me donnait des choses intéressantes à faire. Les seuls inconvénients étaient que je devais me lever très tôt le matin pour y arriver avant neuf heures, et puis j'avais pas mal de travail à faire et j'étais souvent très fatiguée le soir.*

5 *Mon stage en entreprise était une perte de temps totale. D'abord, le propriétaire du magasin était toujours de mauvaise humeur et tout à fait désagréable. Il n'était jamais content de mon travail et il me critiquait tout le temps. De plus, il n'y avait pas beaucoup de clients et je me suis souvent ennuyé.*

Answers

	Expérience P, N ou P/N?	Pourquoi?
1	*P*	collègues étaient sympa; s'entendait bien avec la patronne; travail assez varié; a beaucoup appris
2	P/N	collègues étaient sympa/aimables se sentait un peu exploité (gagnait rien, mais avait beaucoup de travail à faire et c'était fatigant)
3	N	pas grand-chose à faire – monotone
4	P/N	on le traitait bien; des choses intéressantes à faire devait se lever très tôt; pas mal de travail à faire, donc était fatiguée
5	N	le propriétaire était toujours de mauvaise humeur/ désagréable – il le critiquait tout le temps; pas beaucoup de clients – s'est souvent ennuyé

5 À deux. Pratiquez le dialogue ci-dessous.

Speaking. In pairs: students practise the dialogue on work experience supplied, taking it in turn to ask questions and to respond with details.

6 Interviewez votre partenaire sur son stage en entreprise en changeant les détails en bleu dans le dialogue ci-dessus. Si vous n'avez pas fait de stage, inventez les détails.

Speaking. In pairs: students adapt the dialogue in exercise 5 (changing the text in blue). They can use the facts of their own work experience or make up the details. A box of useful language is supplied for support.

7 Vous avez lu un article dans un magazine *«Les stages en entreprise: une bonne chose ou une perte de temps?»*. Écrivez une réponse au magazine en français en donnant vos idées et vos opinions sur les stages. Mentionnez:

Writing. Students imagine they have read a French magazine article on work experience (*Work experience: a good thing or a waste of time?*) They now write a response to the article to send to the magazine, expressing their own ideas and opinions on work experience placements. A list of points to cover is supplied: they should use this to structure their text.

Students could do this activity on computer using a word-processing package like Word.

Plenary

Ask students for examples of sentences using (1) the perfect tense and (2) the imperfect tense. Get the rest of the class to feed back on whether the correct tense has been used in each case and to say why the particular tense is the appropriate one in the context.

Cahier d'exercices, page 55

1

Answers

J'ai fait mon stage dans un hôpital. J'ai travaillé pendant deux semaines en mai avec un physiothérapeute. J'ai choisi de faire un stage dans ce domaine car ça m'intéresse fortement.
Tous les jours, j'aidais la physiothérapeute à faire des exercices aux patients. Je téléphonais pour faire les rendez-vous ou pour les changer. Je préparais les boissons et je jouais avec les enfants handicapés.
C'était une expérience très positive. J'ai appris beaucoup de choses et le travail était très varié. Les patients étaient tous différents; j'ai travaillé avec des personnes paralysées et des enfants handicapés.
La physiothérapeute avec qui je travaillais était très gentille. Elle avait un bon sens de l'humeur, ce qui est important dans ce travail. Pour être physiothérapeute, il faut savoir bien communiquer, bien écouter, il faut être patient(e), diplomate et plein de dynamisme!
Pour le moment, c'est ce que je veux faire plus tard!

2

Answers

Domaine de travail: *Physiothérapie*
Opinion générale: Très positive
Patients: des personnes paralysées; des enfants handicapés
Tâches principales: téléphoner pour faire des rendez-vous; préparer des boissons; jouer avec les enfants
Qualités nécessaires pour être physiothérapeute: il faut savoir bien communiquer, bien écouter, il faut être patient(e), diplomate et plein de dynamisme!
Avantages: le travail était très varié.

3

Answers

Pupil' s own answers

Cahier d'exercices, Grammaire, page 56

1

Answers

1 Il me téléphone tous les jours.
2 Combien d'argent te donnent tes parents?
3 Il lui demande de sortir ce week-end.
4 Elle lui parle chaque soir.
5 Ils ne me donnent pas beaucoup.
6 Tu ne lui parles pas souvent.

2

Answers

La discrimination des handicapés est quelque chose **qu**'il ne faut pas tolérer. J'ai un frère en fauteuil roulant **qui** a des problèmes au collège. Par exemple, les bâtiments ne sont pas adaptés aux gens **qui** sont en fauteuil roulant; il y a des élèves **qui** font des blagues et un prof a dit que mon frère ne pouvait pas faire de sport à cause de ses problèmes. Mais le sport, c'est la chose **qu**'il aime le plus!
Même en ville, il y a des problèmes. Il y a beaucoup de magasins **qui** sont difficiles d'accès. Par exemple, dans la librairie dans notre ville, pour aller au rayon d'enfants **qui** est au premier étage, il n'y a pas d'ascenseur. Le patron a dit: «Je trouve qu'il n'y a pas beaucoup de personnes **qui** ont besoin d'ascenseur.»
Moi, je trouve **que** c'est une chose **qui** est tout à fait inacceptable!

Il faut bosser!

6 Contrôle continu: Mon stage en entreprise (Student Book pages 104–105)

Topic revised

- Talking about work experience

1 Copiez les phrases en bleu dans le texte et trouvez l'équivalent en anglais ci-dessous.

Students copy out all the phrases shown in blue in the text and find the English phrases from those listed (**1–14**).

Answers

tous les élèves de troisième
5 all Year 10 pupils
le stage a duré quinze jours
8 the work experience lasted for a fortnight
j'ai eu de la chance de trouver
3 I was lucky enough to find
je pensais que ce serait une bonne expérience pour moi
10 I thought it would be a good experience for me
dans l'ensemble
11 on the whole
je n'avais pas le droit de réparer les véhicules tout seul
6 I wasn't allowed to repair vehicles alone
on me laissait changer les pneus
13 they let me change tyres
pour aider les clients dont la voiture était en panne
2 to help customers whose cars had broken down
des petits boulots moins intéressants
12 some less interesting chores
ça ne me dérangeait pas
14 it didn't bother me/I didn't mind
Je m'entendais bien avec
1 I got on well with
il a dit qu'il était très content de mon travail
9 he said he was very pleased with my work
il m'a proposé de faire un apprentissage
4 he offered me an apprenticeship
Je ne sais pas encore
15 I don't know yet
je voudrais bien retourner y travailler
7 I'd like to go back and work there

2 Écrivez V (Vrai), F (Faux) ou PM (Pas Mentionné) pour chaque phrase ci-dessous.

Students reread the text. They then read the ten statements and decide whether each is true or false or not mentioned in the text.

Answers

1 F **2** F **3** F **4** PM **5** V **6** PM **7** V **8** V **9** F **10** V

3 Décrivez votre stage en entreprise en donnant votre opinion.

Using the text and the **Boîte à outils** section to help them, students describe a work placement (real or imaginary), including their opinions of the experience.

À l'oral (AQA edition)

(Student Book page 181)

Topics revised

- talking about household chores
- talking about pocket money

1 You are talking to your French friend about what you do to help at home. Your partner will play the part of your friend and will speak first.

Roleplay. Students practise talking about what household chores they do and their pocket money, taking it in turn to play themselves/a French friend.

2 You are talking to your French friend about your part-time job in a supermarket. Your partner will play the part of your friend and will speak first.

Roleplay. Students practise talking about a part-time job they have, taking it in turn to play themselves/a French friend.

Encourage students to try to include the colloquial word **bosser** in their roleplay, as featured in the **Tu parles!** box at the top of the page.

3 Prepare a ninety-second presentation called *Mon stage en entreprise*.

Presentation. Students prepare a ninety-second presentation on their work experience. A sample cue card is supplied for students to refer to when preparing their own prompts.

☑ Students should read through the two tip boxes, which are particularly useful for this activity and the conversation.

The first concerns verb tenses: how important it is to use a variety of tenses; how they must listen in the conversation part of the exam to the tense used by the examiner in each question and respond accordingly.

The second tip box encourages students to work extra information into their answers. This will help them be in control of the conversation and will gain them extra marks. Stress how important it is to prepare for this by studying the questions carefully and working out how and where they could offer additional information.

4 Possible conversation questions

These are key questions to practise for the speaking exam, taken from the module as a whole. Students can practise asking and answering the questions in pairs.

☑ If students find they are struggling with any of these topics, remind them they can review material in the relevant unit.

À l'oral (Edexcel edition)

(Student Book page 181)

Topics revised

- talking about a part-time job
- telephoning for details of a job
- talking about a work placement

1 You are talking to a French penfriend. Your partner will play the part of your penfriend and will begin the conversation.

Roleplay B. Students practise talking about their Saturday job, taking it in turn to play themselves/a French penfriend.

2 You have seen an advertisement for work placements in Paris and telephone for details. Your partner will play the part of the personnel manager and will begin the conversation.

Roleplay C. Students practise telephoning for details of a work placement in Paris, taking it in turn to play themselves/the personnel manager.

☑ Before starting, students should read through the tip box, which offers suggestions on how to expand their answers and how to tackle the question prompt.

3 Presentation and general conversation

Presentation. Students prepare a one-minute presentation on their work experience. A sample cue card is supplied for students to refer to when preparing their own prompts.

☑ Students should read through the two tip boxes, which are particularly useful for this activity and the conversation.

The first concerns verb tenses: how important it is to use a variety of tenses; how they must listen in the conversation part of the exam to the tense used by the examiner in each question and respond accordingly. The second reminds them of the need to think about what material to use in the presentation and what to hold in reserve for the conversation.

Possible conversation questions. These are key questions to practise for the speaking exam, taken from the module as a whole. Students can practise asking and answering the questions in pairs.

☑ If students find they are struggling with any of these topics, remind them they can review material in the relevant unit.

À l'oral (OCR edition)

(Student Book page 181)

Topics revised

- talking about work experience
- talking about household chores
- talking about part-time/future jobs

1 Use the notes and pictures below to describe a day during your work experience last summer on a campsite in France.

Roleplay Type 3. Students practise talking about a day of work experience in the past, using the text and picture prompts supplied.

☑ Remind pupils that they can improve their exam marks by developing the story and by expressing and justifying opinions.

2 *Ma vie:* possible conversation questions

These are key questions to practise for the speaking exam, taken from the module as a whole. Students can practise asking and answering the questions in pairs.

☑ If students find they are struggling with any of these topics, remind them they can review material in the relevant unit.

À toi

(Student Book pages 196–197)

- Self-access reading and writing

1 Lisez les deux textes et répondez aux questions en anglais.

Reading. Students read the two texts and answer the ten comprehension questions in English by identifying who is described in each.

Answers

1 Cécile **2** Pascal **3** Cécile **4** Cécile **6** Cécile **7** Pascal **8** Pascal **9** Cécile **10** Pascal

2 Répondez aux questions pour Pascal et Cécile.

Reading. Students respond to the six questions, pretending they are Pascal/Cécile as appropriate.

Answers

1. Je travaille de 2h à 10h et de 17h à 20h (cinq jours par semaine).
2. J'ai six employés.
3. Je dois/On doit faire 600 baguettes par jour.
4. Ma mère est infirmière.
5. Je ne travaille pas le mercredi parce que je m'occupe de mon fils.
6. Je gagne 1400€ mensuels.

3 Vous lisez cette annonce dans un journal français. Écrivez une lettre en posant votre candidature, comme à la page 99. Utilisez les détails ci-dessous.

Writing. Students read the French newspaper advert. They write a letter of application for the job advertised, using the text on page 99 as a model and the personal details supplied.

4 Lisez les textes et répondez aux questions en français.

Reading. Students read the two texts and answer the 10 comprehension questions in French.

Before students start, read through the tip box, which outlines how students can use the questions supplied in a comprehension activity in their answers.

Answers

1. Ben doit se lever à six heures parce que il livre des journaux avant d'aller au collège.
2. Avant de livrer les journaux, il doit aller chercher les journaux à la papeterie.
3. Il trouve son petit boulot très fatigant, mais assez bien payé.
4. Il gagne 30 livres par semaine.
5. Abdul ne voudrait pas faire cela en hiver ou quand il pleut. Il n'aimerait pas se lever de si bonne heure.
6. Kirsty travaille dans un supermarché.
7. Elle doit ranger les produits et remplir les rayons.
8. Elle trouve les gens avec qui elle travaille assez sympa.
9. C'est un peu ennuyeux et elle n'aime pas travailler dans les rayons de viande parce qu'elle est végétarienne.
10. Laure aimerait avoir un tel travail parce que elle s'ennuie toujours le samedi et elle aimerait gagner un peu d'argent pour partir en vacances.

5 Imaginez. Votre copain ou copine a un des petits boulots ci-dessous. Écrivez un paragraphe sur son job. Adaptez les textes de l'exercice 4, si vous voulez.

Writing. Students imagine that their friend has one of the part-time jobs shown and write a paragraph about the job. They can adapt one of the texts in exercise 4, if they find this useful.

Module 7 Tourisme (Student Book pages 108–127)

Unit	Main topics and objectives	Grammar
Déjà vu 1 **Destinations touristiques** (pp. 108–109)	Talking about holiday venues Using the verb **aller**	**aller** (present, perfect, near future)
Déjà vu 2 **La météo** (pp. 110–111)	Talking about the weather Past, present and future tenses	Weather expressions in the imperfect, present and future tenses
1 L'hôtel (pp. 112–113)	Choosing and booking into a hotel The uses of **si**: if, so, yes	**si**
2 Une auberge de jeunesse (pp. 114–115)	Booking into a youth hostel The imperative	The imperative (formal)
3 Camping la Forêt (pp. 116–117)	Talking about a holiday Using the **nous** form in different tenses	The **nous** form (present, perfect, imperfect, future, conditional)
4 La nourriture (pp. 118–119)	Eating out Using the conditional	The conditional
5 Plage, mer et soleil (pp. 120–121)	More about holidays Using the present, imperfect and conditional	Using a range of tenses (present, imperfect) + the conditional
6 L'année dernière (pp. 122–123)	Talking about past holidays Using the perfect tense	The perfect and imperfect: when to use
Contrôle continu **Mes vacances** (pp. 124–125)	*Coursework* Writing about a holiday in the past	*All main grammar points of the module*
À l'oral (p. 182)	*Exam speaking practice* Asking for hotel information Booking a youth hostel Talking about holidays	*All main grammar points of the module*
À toi (pp. 198–199)	Self-access reading and writing	

Déjà vu 1: Destinations touristiques

(Student Book pages 108–109)

Main topics and objectives

- Talking about holiday venues
- Using the verb **aller**

Grammar

- **aller** (present, perfect, near future)

Key language

Holiday venues

Resources

CD3, track 21
Cahier d'exercices, page 59

Starter 1

Aim
To practise understanding tourist information.

Ask students working in pairs to identify the places in the following descriptions:

1 **la plus haute montagne d'Europe** (Mont Blanc)
2 **le plus long fleuve d'Angleterre** (Thames)
3 **un grand parc d'attractions près de Paris** (Disneyland Paris/Parc Astérix)
4 **la plus grande ville d'Espagne** (Madrid)
5 **une région de vacances dans le sud-ouest d'Angleterre** (Devon/Cornwall)

1 C'est quel site touristique?

Reading. Students read the eight descriptions and identify the tourist landmark for each (from **a–h**).

Answers
1 c **2** b **3** d **4** a **5** e **6** f **7** h **8** g

Expo-langue: *aller* (present, perfect and near future tense)

Use this grammar box to review the verb **aller** before students do exercise 2.

2 Où sont-ils allés l'année dernière et où vont-ils cette année?

Speaking. Using the information in the box supplied, students talk about where the people featured went last year and are going to go this year.

R Students write a few sentences on where they themselves went last year and what they are going to do this year.

Starter 2

Aim
To revise country names. To practise using the verb **aller** in the present tense.

Write up:
the Coliseum
the Grand Canyon
the Real Maestranza Bullring
the Great Barrier Reef
the Louvre
Edinburgh Castle

Ask students working in pairs to write out a sentence for each of the prompts. Each sentence must contain a different part of the verb **aller** and the appropriate country, e.g. (for the first one) **Il va en Italie.**

3 Où passe-t-on la nuit? Faites correspondre les images, les titres et les textes.

Reading. For each picture (**1–5**), students choose the appropriate title and the appropriate text (from **a–e**).

Answers
1 auberge de jeunesse, e
2 hôtel, a
3 camping, d
4 gîte, c
5 chambre d'hôte, b

4 Écoutez et notez. Où vont-ils, avec qui et où vont-ils loger? Écrivez les bonnes lettres pour chaque personne. (1–5)

Listening. Students listen to five people being interviewed about their forthcoming holidays. They note the details of where they are going, who they are going with (from **1–5**) and where they are going to stay (from **a–e**).

Audioscript 21

1 *– Où vas-tu, Mélanie?*
– Nous allons à Paris. J'y vais avec ma classe. On va passer deux nuits dans une auberge de jeunesse. On y va en car.

2 *– Et toi, Nicolas?*
– Je pars avec ma mère. On prend l'avion jusqu'à Paris, puis il y a un train direct jusqu'au Parc, à Disneyland Paris. On va loger dans un hôtel sur le site.

3 *– Et toi, Jérôme? Pars-tu avec ta famille?*
– Oui, on va au bord de la mer, comme toujours. On part en voiture. On loue une caravane dans le même camping chaque année.

4 *– Et toi, Sébastien?*
– Ben … On part en vélo!!! Papa est accro au sport. Je pars avec lui. On porte tout ce qu'on peut mettre dans un sac à dos: tente, sacs de couchage … Direction la Dordogne … et c'est parti!!

5 *– Et toi, Delphine?*
– Je pars avec mes grands-parents en voiture. Nous avons loué un gîte parce que nous allons faire le tour des châteaux de la Loire.

Answers

Mélanie *à Paris, 2, b*
Nicolas Disneyland Paris, 5, a
Jérôme au bord de la mer, 1, d
Sébastien en Dordogne, 4, e
Delphine les châteaux de la Loire, 3, c

5 Imaginez que vous êtes Mélanie, Jérôme, etc. Écrivez un paragraphe sur les projets de vacances pour chaque personne.

Writing. Students imagine they are the people in exercise 4 and write a short paragraph for each saying what their holiday plans are. Sentence openings are supplied for support.

Before they start, point out the tip box on the false friend **visiter**.

Plenary

Ask students to quickly recap on how the near future tense is formed.

Then go round the class asking students to say where they are going on holiday this year (**Je vais/On va/Nous allons ...**) and where they are going to stay (**Je vais loger ...**).

Cahier d'exercices, page 59

1

Answers

a 12 million people visit Disneyland each year.
b 34% of French people book their holidays on the Internet.
c Almost 90% of French people take their holidays in France.
d 1 out of 2 French people have a winter holiday.
e 1/3 of all holidays are in the countryside.
f 22% of French people go abroad for their holidays.
g 4 out of 10 holidays are by the sea.
h 44% of French people book their holidays at a travel agent's.
i 24% prefer walking as the most popular holiday activity.
j 14% prefer swimming or the beach as the most popular holiday activity.

2

Answers

Pupil's own answers

Déjà vu 2: La météo

(Student Book pages 110–111)

Main topics and objectives

- Talking about the weather
- Past, present and future tenses

Grammar

- Weather expressions in the imperfect, present and future tenses

Key language

Weather expressions
The seasons

Resources

CD3, tracks 22–24
Cahier d'exercices, page 60

Starter 1

Aim
To revise language to describe the weather.

Write up the following in two columns, jumbling the order of the second column. Ask students in pairs to match the weather phrase with the appropriate activity:

Il fait beau.	go for a picnic
Il pleut.	splash in puddles
Il neige.	build a snowman
Il y a des nuages.	wait for the sun to reappear
Il y a des orages.	watch the lightning
Il fait du brouillard.	switch on extra lights in your car
Il fait du vent.	fly a kite

1 À deux. Discutez. Mettez les phrases dans la grille.

Speaking. In pairs: students copy out the grid and complete it by putting all the weather phrases in the correct boxes, discussing their choices as they go.

Expo-langue: weather expressions

Use this to summarise the verb tenses used to describe the weather in the past, present and future.

2 Écoutez et vérifiez.

Listening. Students listen to the recording to check their answers to exercise 1.

Audioscript 22

Hier
Il faisait beau.
Il pleuvait.
Il neigeait.
Il y avait des nuages.
Il y avait des orages.
Il faisait du brouillard.
Il faisait du vent.

Aujourd'hui
Il fait beau.
Il pleut.
Il neige.
Il y a des nuages.
Il y a des orages.
Il fait du brouillard.
Il fait du vent.

Demain
Il fera beau.
Il pleuvra.
Il neigera.
Il y aura des nuages.
Il fera du brouillard.
Il fera du vent.

3 À deux. Quel temps faisait-il, fait-il et fera-t-il?

Speaking. In pairs: students take it in turn to describe the weather in the three pictures supplied, using the appropriate tenses.

4 Trouvez la bonne définition.

Reading. Students find the correct French definition for the five French weather words listed.

Answers

1 d **2** a **3** b **4** e **5** c

Starter 2

Aim
To revise language for describing the weather.

In pairs: students take it in turn to prompt and respond. The first student prompts with a kind of weather (e.g. **beau**) and a time from past, present or future (e.g. past); the second responds with a complete sentence (e.g. **il faisait beau**).

5 Écoutez la météo et choisissez les bons symboles pour chaque région.

Listening. Students listen to the weather forecast and choose the correct symbols for each region.

Audioscript 23

La météo par région
Aujourd'hui, dans le nord et sur les côtes bretonnes, c'est une journée nuageuse … Il y a un fort risque de pluie et de vent.
Sur l'Île-de-France, il y aura du brouillard et les températures seront en baisse.
À l'est et au nord-est, le ciel sera couvert et il y a un fort risque d'averses, surtout dans le Jura.
Ce matin sur le Massif Central, il y aura du brouillard.
Dans les Hautes-Alpes, il y a un risque d'orage dans l'après-midi.
Dans le Midi-Pyrénées, il y aura de la pluie et du vent, mais plus tard il y aura des éclaircies.
Dans le Midi, ce sera une journée ensoleillée …

Answers
1 *b, c, h* **2** g **3** b, d **4** g **5** e **6** c, h, f **7** a

6 Le temps chez nous. Écoutez et lisez. C'est vrai (V), faux (F) ou pas mentionné (PM)?

Listening. Students listen to Alizée describing the weather where she lives and read the text at the same time. They then read the six statements on the text and decide whether each is true or false or not mentioned in the text.

Audioscript 24

J'habite en montagne. D'habitude en été, il fait beau et il y a du soleil. De temps en temps, il y a un vent désagréable qui arrive du sud et qui s'appelle le foehn. Quelquefois, il y a de grands orages le soir, mais normalement, le mauvais temps passe vite.

En automne, il y a souvent des nuages et il pleut beaucoup. C'est un moment un peu triste. Les feuilles tombent des arbres et il commence à faire froid.

Un jour, en hiver, on se réveille et le monde est couvert d'une neige qui brille au soleil. Quelquefois, nous avons plus d'un mètre de neige en une nuit. Les jours d'hiver sont souvent ensoleillés et même chauds: il faut mettre de la crème solaire. En altitude, le soleil est dangereux!

Le printemps arrive souvent en retard chez nous. La neige fond, les rivières débordent et nous avons beaucoup de brume et de précipitations, mais finalement, les fleurs apparaissent à nouveau sur les alpages et on peut de nouveau ranger ses pulls!

Answers
1 F **2** F **3** PM **4** PM **5** V **6** F

+ Students write a summary of the weather where Alizée lives in all four seasons of the year.

7 Écrivez la météo pour la Grande-Bretagne.

Writing. Students use the two maps of Great Britain to write two weather forecasts, using the appropriate tenses.

Plenary

Ask students to summarise which verb tenses are used to talk about the weather yesterday, today and tomorrow.

Then ask them to give you a weather report for the following places, talking about yesterday, today and tomorrow for all three:

1 Málaga
2 Moscow
3 Manchester

Cahier d'exercices, page 60

1

Answers

1 faire du vent: *Il fait du vent.*
faire beau: Il fait beau.
pleuvoir: Il pleut.
neiger: Il neige.
2 nuages: *Il y aura des nuages.*
orages: Il y aura des orages.
vent: Il fera du vent.
brouillard: Il fera du brouillard.
3 il neige: *Il neigeait.*
il fait beau: Il faisait beau.
il y a des nuages: Il y avait des nuages.
il pleut: Il pleuvait.
4 beau: *Il fera beau.*
neige: Il neigera.
pleut: Il pleuvra.
mauvais: Il fera mauvais.
5 averses: *Il y avait des averses.*
éclaircies: Il y avait des éclaircies.
la pluie: Il pleuvait.
du brouillard: Il avait du brouillard.
6 il neigera: *la neige*
le ciel sera nuageux: les nuages
le temps sera orageux: les orages
il pleuvra: la pluie

2

Answers
Example
À Pau, il fera beau
À Valloire il fera du brouillard
À Montreux, il sera nuageux
À Coutras, il neigera.
À Nancy, il aura des éclaircies
À Caen, il fera du vent
À Soulages, il y aura des orages
À Arras, il pleuvra

7 Tourisme

1 L'hôtel

(Student Book pages 112–113)

Main topics and objectives

- Choosing and booking into a hotel
- The uses of **si**: if, so, yes

Grammar

- si

Key language

Avez-vous ... ?
un restaurant
le parking
une piscine (chauffée)
un aire de jeux

Avez-vous ... ?
des chambres libres
des chambres non-fumeurs
une chambre à deux lits
avec douche
avec des WCs en suite
avec salle de bains
avec une connexion pour Internet

Est-ce qu'il y a ... ?
un sèche-cheveux
un poste de télévision
L'hôtel est près de la gare?
Est-ce qu'il y a des commerces à proximité?
Ça coûte combien?

Resources

CD3, tracks 25–26
Cahier d'exercices, page 61
Grammaire 4.3

Starter 1

Aim
To revise the language for talking about hotels.

Give students three minutes to come up with as many examples of French words and phrases to do with hotels as they can. Which pair can make the longest list?

When listening to answers, ask the rest of the class to translate each item.

1 Lisez et trouvez. C'est quel hôtel?

Reading. Students read the two hotel brochures. They then read the list of eight amenities in French and identify for each amenity which hotel it is in.

Answers
1 Hôtel Les 3 Ours **2** Hôtel Belle-vue **3** Hôtel Les 3 Ours **4** Hôtel Belle-vue **5** Hôtel Les 3 Ours **6** Hôtel Les 3 Ours **7** Hôtel Les 3 Ours **8** Hôtel Belle-vue

2 Ils choisissent quel hôtel? Pourquoi? Notez les raisons en anglais.

Listening. Students listen to two people discussing the hotels in exercise 1 and trying to decide which hotel they're going to stay in. Students note which hotel they finally choose and say why in English.

Audioscript 25

- *Il faut choisir un hôtel.*
- *Lequel?*
- *Ben ... moi, je préfère l'hôtel Belle-vue.*
- *Pourquoi?*
- *Parce que c'est plus grand.*
- *Mais il n'y a pas de piscine.*
- *Si, il y en a une, regarde: salle fitness et jacuzzi.*
- *Le jacuzzi n'est pas une piscine, et en plus, c'est trop cher.*
- *Non, ce n'est pas si cher.*
- *Je préfère Les 3 Ours.*
- *Pourquoi?*
- *Parce qu'il y a une aire de jeux.*
- *C'est pour les petits.*
- *Non, il y a aussi une aire de jeux pour les enfants de 8 à 14 ans avec passerelle dans les bois. Regarde. Et en plus, on peut louer des vélos et il y a une piscine extérieure chauffée.*
- *Bon, si tu préfères.*
- *Oui, moi, je préfère celui-là.*
- *D'accord.*

Answers
Les 3 Ours – there's an adventure playground for children aged 8–14; you can hire bikes; there's a heated outdoor pool

Expo-langue: *si* (if, so, yes)

Use this grammar box to focus on the different meanings of **si** before students do exercise 3. There is more information on p. 217 of the Student Book.

3 C'est quel *si*? Choisissez (a) *if*, (b) *so* ou (c) *yes!*

Reading. Students read the eight sentences and decide what **si** means in each of them – (a) *if*, (b) *so* or (c) *yes!*

Answers
1 (b) so **2** (a) if **3** (c) yes! **4** (a) if **5** (c) yes! **6** (a) if **7** (b) so **8** (a) if

Starter 2

Aim

To revise language for talking about hotels.

Write up the following in two columns, jumbling the order of the second column. Ask students working in pairs to match the halves to make complete sentences/questions and then to translate them.

1 Est-ce qu'il y a une	**connexion pour Internet?**
2 Avez-vous	**des chambres libres?**
3 On peut	**louer des vélos?**
4 Avez-vous des chambres	**non-fumeurs?**
5 Est-ce qu'il y a des	**commerces à proximité?**
6 Ça coûte	**combien?**
7 Est-ce que les chambres	**sont avec douche et WC?**

When checking answers, ask students how they worked out the pairings.

4 L'hôtel. Écoutez et mettez les questions dans le bon ordre.

Listening. Students listen to someone phoning a hotel for some information and put the questions she asks in the correct order.

Audioscript 26

- *Hôtel du lac, bonjour.*
- *Bonjour, monsieur. Avez-vous des chambres libres du 15 au 22 juillet?*
- *Du 15 au 22 juillet … Attendez que je regarde … Oui … pour combien de personnes?*
- *Pour huit personnes. Avez-vous quatre chambres de deux lits?*
- *Euh … oui.*
- *Avez-vous des chambres non-fumeurs?*
- *Oui …*
- *Est-ce que les chambres sont avec douche et WC?*
- *Oui.*
- *Est-ce qu'il y a une piscine?*
- *Oui, il y a une piscine extérieure chauffée et une pataugeoire pour les jeunes enfants.*
- *Est-ce qu'il y a une aire de jeux?*
- *Oui, il y a une aire de jeux pour les petits et une aire de jeux pour les enfants jusqu'à quinze ans.*
- *Est-ce qu'on peut louer des vélos?*
- *Oui, on peut louer des vélos dans le village, à deux minutes d'ici.*
- *Est-ce qu'il y a une connexion pour Internet?*
- *Bien sûr.*
- *Et ça coûte combien?*
- *Une chambre pour deux personnes coûte 40€ par nuit.*
- *Est-ce qu'il y a des commerces à proximité?*
- *Non, il y a uniquement un petit magasin dans le village.*
- *Bien, merci. Je vais m'informer auprès des autres et vous rappeler.*

Answers

3, 8, 5, 10, 2, 7, 4, 1, 9, 6

5 À deux. Posez des questions.

Speaking. In pairs: using the picture prompts, students take it in turn to ask questions about a hotel. Question openings are supplied for support.

6 Faites une pub pour un hôtel près de chez vous.

Writing. Students write an advertisement for an imaginary hotel near where they live.

Students could put this together using a word-processing or DTP package, incorporating photographs or clip-art.

Plenary

Ask students to summarise the three uses of the word **si**, giving examples.

Then give prompts for them to practise saying **si** in response to a negative question/statement (suggestions below). Encourage them to answer in full sentences (e.g. **Si, j'ai fait mes devoirs!** or even, **Si, je les ai faits./Si, j'y peux venir.**, etc.).

Tu n'as pas fait tes devoirs?
Tu ne peux pas venir à la fête. C'est dommage!
Tu n'as pas d'argent?
Tu n'aimes pas le rap?, etc.

Cahier d'exercices, page 61

1

Answers

Hotel location: 4km from La Rochelle, 10km from Rochefort and 2km from the beach
Rooms: 14 rooms and suites
Children's facilities: Children's room, games room, baby equipment, games and swimming pool toys
Other facilities: Tea room with tea and cakes
Restaurant: no restaurant at the hotel
Breakfast: delicious; large breakfast so you won't need a lunch
Afternoon tea: fruit cocktails, sorbets and cakes
Evening meal: hotel will recommend a selection of restaurants and will help make a reservation

2

Answers

Pupil's own answers

2 Une auberge de jeunesse

(Student Book pages 114–115)

Main topics and objectives

- Booking into a youth hostel
- The imperative

Grammar

- The imperative (formal)

Key language

Nous sommes cinq.
J'aimerais réserver 18 places …
pour 8 filles, 8 garçons et 2 accompagnateurs
pour les nuits de 23 au 29 juin
Nous voudrions quatre chambres avec/sans sanitaires.
J'aimerais savoir s'il est possible de …
Est-ce que le petit déjeuner est inclus?
Est-ce qu'il faut apporter un sac de couchage?
Est-ce que le linge est fourni?
Est-ce qu'on peut louer des vélos?
Y a-t-il une piscine à proximité?
Je vous serais reconnaissant(e) … si vous pouviez m'envoyer un dépliant

Resources

CD3, tracks 27–28
Cahier d'exercices, page 62
Grammaire 3.11

Starter 1

Aim
To revise the imperative.

Write up the following and ask students to complete the grid. They can do this in pairs if they need support.

infinitive	**tu** imperative	**vous** imperative	English
aller	va		*go!*
venir		venez	
écouter	écoute		
finir		finissez	
attendre			*wait!*
envoyer			

1 Faites correspondre le français et l'anglais.

Reading. Students match the eight French expressions listed with the correct English translations.

Answers
1 home page **2** choose **3** book online **4** contact us
5 type in your details **6** rates

Expo-langue: the imperative (formal/ *vous* form)

Use this grammar box to review the formal imperative. Students then identify all the imperative forms used on the web page in exercise 1. There is more information on p. 214 of the Student Book.

2 La réservation. Écoutez. Copiez et complétez la grille. (1–2)

Listening. Students copy out the grid. They listen to two people making bookings at two different youth hostels and complete the grid with the details.

Audioscript 27

- *Allô? Auberge de jeunesse Les Pins, j'écoute.*
- *Avez-vous des places libres du 20 au 25 juillet?*
- *Allô? Je ne vous entends pas … Ah! Bonjour.*
- *Avez-vous des places libres du 20 au 25 juillet?*
- *Du 20 au 25 juillet? Un moment …. Combien êtes-vous?*
- *Nous sommes treize filles, douze garçons et quatre accompagnateurs.*
- *Treize filles, douze garçons et quatre accompagnateurs … Combien de temps resterez-vous?*
- *5 nuits du 20 au 25 juillet.*
- *5 nuits du 20 au 25 juillet …*
- *Quel est le nom de votre groupe?*
- *Le collège Victor Hugo.*
- *Le collège Victor Hugo …*
- *Et le nom du responsable?*
- *M. Charvet.*
- *À quelle heure arriverez-vous?*
- *Vers 16h00.*
- *Très bien.*
- *Est-ce qu'il y a une piscine près de l'auberge?*
- *Non, je regrette, mais il y a un lac … on peut s'y baigner, s'il fait chaud. Vous voulez d'autres renseignements?*
- *Est-ce qu'on peut dîner à l'auberge?*
- *Oui, mais il faut réserver à l'avance. Voulez-vous réserver?*
- *Oui, s'il vous-plaît.*
- *Bien, c'est noté.*
- *Merci. Au revoir.*
- *Au revoir.*

- *Bonjour! Auberge de jeunesse les Vagues, je vous écoute.*
- *Avez-vous des places libres du 29 juillet au 4 août?*
- *Du 29 juillet au 4 août … Combien êtes-vous?*
- *Nous sommes cinq filles et huit garçons …*
- *Entendu … Cinq filles et huit garçons … Et combien d'accompagnateurs?*

- *Deux.*
- *Voulez-vous des chambres avec ou sans sanitaires?*
- *Avec sanitaires si possible.*
- *Pour combien de nuits?*
- *6.*
- *À quelle heure arriverez-vous?*
- *Vers 18h00.*
- *Bon, je note … 18h00 … Vous souhaitez savoir autre chose?*
- *Est-ce que vous servez le petit déjeuner?*
- *Oui, bien sûr.*
- *Et est-ce qu'on peut louer des vélos?*
- *Il n'y a pas de problème, c'est fait.*
- *Merci. Au revoir.*
- *Au revoir.*

Answers

	les Pins	**les Vagues**
dates	20–25 juillet	29 juillet–4 août
filles	13	5
garçons	12	8
accompagnateurs	4	2
nuits	5	6
heure d'arrivée	vers 16h00	vers 18h00
autre détails	il y a un lac; on peut dîner à l'auberge	chambres avec sanitaires; on sert le petit déj; on peut louer des vélos

3 Faites les réservations.

Speaking. In pairs: students use the framework and prompts supplied to make up a dialogue about reserving accommodation at a youth hostel. They take it in turn to play the person making the booking and the youth hostel employee.

Before they start, draw their attention to the tip box on telephone numbers.

R Each pair performs their dialogue to another pair, who note down the key details.

Starter 2

Aim
To revise structures which are followed by the infinitive.

Write up the following and ask students to identify which of them are usually followed by the infinitive:

1 j'ai
2 on peut
3 c'est possible de
4 il faut
5 nous sommes été
6 ils voudraient
7 je dois
8 il y a
9 c'est
10 elle travaillait

4 Lisez et complétez la lettre en utilisant les mots en dessous.

Reading. Students copy out and complete the gap-fill letter using the words supplied.

Answers

1 accompagnateurs **2** possible **3** prendre **4** louer **5** faut **6** fourni **7** piscine **8** envoyer **9** d'agréer **10** distingués

5 L'auberge a répondu à la lettre de Sally. Notez les détails.

Listening. Students listen to a conversation between Sally and her friend, who are discussing the youth hostel's response to Sally's letter in exercise 4. Students note the details.

Audioscript 28

- *Voilà la réponse de l'auberge de jeunesse … pour les 30 places, il n'y a pas de problème.*
- *Et les dates?*
- *C'est bon … ah, non. Ils les ont changées du 22 au 28 juin…*
- *Mais ce n'est pas grave pour nous?*
- *Oui … Ah, super! Le petit déjeuner est inclus.*
- *Et le dîner?*
- *Non ….*
- *On peut louer des vélos?*
- *Non, on ne peut pas en louer … Désolée.*
- *Ce n'est pas grave … Dans ce cas-là, on va emporter les nôtres. On aura besoin d'un sac de couchage?*
- *Non, le linge de maison est fourni …*
- *Est-ce qu'il y a une piscine?*
- *Oui, mais pas de cinéma … Voici une brochure, regarde!*
- *Ça va être sensass!!!*

Answers

dates: 22–28 juin
places: 30
le petit déjeuner est inclus
on ne peut pas dîner
on ne peut pas louer des vélos
le linge de maison est fourni
il y a une piscine; il n'y a pas de cinéma

6 Écrivez une lettre.

Writing. Using the prompts supplied, students write a letter to a youth hostel enquiring about accommodation.

Students could word-process this on computer, which would make it easier to create a second draft (see Plenary below).

Go to www.heinemann.co.uk/hotlinks and enter the express code 7898T for a link to the French Youth Hostel Association website.

Plenary

☑ Ask students to make a list of the criteria they would use to assess the letter in exercise 6. What do they think an examiner would be looking for? Make sure you cover:

- a clear structure, e.g.
  (1) the details of the booking,
  (2) some questions,
  (3) a request for further information to be sent
- accurate French (correct use of vocabulary, tenses, agreements, etc.)
- inclusion of set phrases for starting and ending a letter

Ask students to look at their texts for exercise 6 in the light of this and to work out how they could improve them.

Cahier d'exercices, page 62

1

Answers

Possible answers:
Youth hostel at Albertville; €16.50 per night; meals available; 10 minutes from the centre of Albertville on foot; Gives details of sporting and cultural activities.

2

Answers

Example:
Mademoiselle,
Merci pour votre lettre. J'espère que je pourrai répondre à toutes vos questions. Tout d'abord, l'auberge de jeunesse est située à 10 minutes à pied du centre d'Albertville. En tout, ça fait 66€ pour deux personnes pour deux nuits. Le petit déjeuner est inclus et le repas du soir coûte 9,50€ par personne. Les draps sont inclus aussi. Il y a une gare SNCF et une gare d'autobus à Albertville. Dans la région, on peut visiter la cité médiévale de Conflans, le château de Manuel de Locatel, l'église baroque de St Grat et beaucoup d'autres sites historiques. Il y a beaucoup à faire ici! Pour les sportifs, il y a une ville olympique avec de nombreux équipements sportifs; stades et gymnases omnisports; mur d'escalade; patinoire et on peut aussi faire des randonnées, du VTT et des sports d'eau vives.
J'espère que vous viendrez dans notre région!
Mme Leclerc

3 Camping la Forêt

(Student Book pages 116–117)

Main topics and objectives

- Talking about a holiday
- Using the **nous** form in different tenses

Grammar

- The **nous** form (present, perfect, imperfect, future, conditional)
- The **nous** form of possessive adjectives

Key language

la pataugeoire
l'épicerie (f)
la salle de jeux
le terrain de pétanque
les randonnées (f)
Je vous écris pour me plaindre de mon séjour.
complet
... fonctionnait/fonctionnaient à peine
Il n'y avait pas d'emplacements.
Les sanitaires n'étaient pas propres.
Il y avait trop de bruit.
vu que les conditions n'étaient pas acceptables
J'attends donc un remboursement.

Resources

CD3, tracks 29–30
Cahier d'exercices, page 63
Grammaire 2.3

Starter 1

Aim
To revise language for talking about holidays.

Give students working in pairs three minutes to come up with six sentences in French about what they did on holiday last year. These must all use the **nous** form and the perfect tense. To get them started, write up:

L'année dernière, nous sommes allés ... Nous avons logé ...

1 Trouvez les mots/les phrases dans le dépliant.

Reading. Students read the flyer about the campsite in the Ardèche. They then find in the text the French for the eight English words/phrases listed.

Answers
1 pétanque **2** ateliers pour les enfants **3** aire de jeux **4** salle de jeux **5** épicerie **6** randonnées **7** pataugeoire **8** commerces

Expo-langue: the *nous* form

Use this grammar box to review the **nous** form in different tenses (present, perfect, imperfect, and future), plus the conditional.

Expo-langue: *notre/nos*

Use this grammar box to cover the possessive adjectives **notre/nos**. There is more information on p. 211 of the Student Book.

2 À deux. Décrivez ce que vous avez fait hier au camping.

Speaking. In pairs: using the picture prompts, students take it in turn to describe what they did yesterday at the campsite. Draw students' attention to the tip box on which verb forms to use before they start.

3 Écrivez un e-mail à votre copain/copine. Dites-lui ce que vous avez l'intention de faire demain.

Writing. Students write an e-mail to a friend, saying what they intend to do at the campsite tomorrow.

Starter 2

Aim
To revise the **nous** form in various tenses.

Write up the following grid and ask students working in pairs to complete it with the appropriate **nous** form of the verbs.

nous ...	*présent*	*passé composé*	*imparfait*	*futur*	*conditionnel*
être					
s'amuser					
prendre					
choisir					
aller					

4 Camping des Sapins. Écoutez les informations sur le camping et choisissez (a), (b) et/ou (c).

Listening. Students listen to the description of the Camping des Sapins. Students read the six sentences and choose the correct ending for each from the three options given (**a**, **b** or **c**).

Audioscript 29

Le camping des Sapins se situe au milieu d'une forêt et près d'un petit lac. On peut louer une des cinq caravanes ou installer sa tente. Il y a une dizaine d'emplacements. Il y a aussi six chalets. On trouve une boulangerie-épicerie à cinq minutes. La piscine fait 150m^2 et la pataugeoire 25m^2. Il y a un atelier pour les enfants chaque matin.

Answers

1 Situation: b
2 Hébergement: a, b, c
3 Distances des commerces: b
4 Piscine: b
5 Pataugeoire: b
6 Animations enfants: b

5 Lisez la lettre et choisissez la bonne réponse.

Reading. Students read the letter. They then read the five sentences and choose the correct ending for each from the three options given (**a**, **b** or **c**). The tip box reminds students that the imperfect is used to describe things in the past, including things not working.

Answers

1 a **2** b **3** a **4** b **5** a

6 Ils se plaignent de quoi? (1–5)

Listening. Students listen to five conversations in which people talk about their holidays. Using the pictures supplied, they note for each what the person is complaining about (from **a–e**).

Audioscript 30

1 – *Alors, les vacances? Tous s'est bien passé?*
– *Oui … mais la piscine était vraiment dégueulasse … C'était sale.*
– *Qu'est-ce que vous avez fait alors?*
– *On s'est plaints.*

2 – *Et c'était comment au camping?*
– *Ben, c'était très bien. Seulement les sanitaires n'étaient pas propres. Beurk!*

3 – *Eh bien, les vacances se sont bien passées?*
– *Oui, pour moi, c'était bien, mais pas pour ma petite sœur parce que la pataugeoire était fermée. Comme elle ne sait pas encore nager, elle ne peut pas aller dans la piscine.*

4 – *C'était comment alors, les vacances?*
– *Super …*
– *Tout s'est bien passé?*
– *Ah oui, sauf les commerces! Ils étaient à cinq kilomètres et il n'y avait pas de bus.*

5 – *C'était comment les vacances?*
– *Bien, sauf que nous étions dans un hôtel et la nourriture n'était pas bonne. Il n'y en avait pas assez d'après mon père et mon frère. En revanche, il y avait trop de frites et de hamburgers, et pas assez de salade.*

Answers

1 c **2** e **3** d **4** b **5** a

R In pairs: drawing on language from this spread and from earlier in the Module, students take it in turn to complain about something that was wrong on a holiday.

7 Imaginez. Vous avez passé de mauvaises vacances. Écrivez une lettre pour vous plaindre.

Writing. Students imagine they have had a bad holiday and write a letter of complaint. They should use the letter in exercise 5 as a model. Encourage them to be inventive about the things they wish to complain about.

Plenary

Ask students to look at the first **Expo-langue** box on p. 116 again, where the **nous** forms of **faire** in various tenses are listed.

Ask students when each of the tenses shown is used, giving examples using other verbs and other persons.

☑ Emphasise the importance of using a wide range of tenses in the speaking and writing parts of the exam. Encourage students to practise doing this in their classroom work and also to review tenses regularly using the Grammar section and verb tables at the back of the Student Book, so that their work is accurate.

Cahier d'exercices, page 63

1

Answers

1	propre	**6**	parfait
2	calme	**7**	bien
3	ne … jamais	**8**	superbe/excellent/super
4	à l'ombre	**9**	superbe/excellent/super
5	toujours	**10**	superbe/excellent/super

2

Answers

Possible answers
1 La machine à laver ne marchait pas.
2 Il y avait un emplacement au soleil. Il faisait trop chaud.
3 Les sanitaires étaient très sales.
4 L'électricité ne marchait jamais.
5 La piscine était nul; c'était fermée toute la journée.
6 Les douches étaient abominables. Il n'y avait jamais d'eau chaude.
7 Le camping était bruyant. C'était nul pour des vacances calmes!
8 On ne pouvait jamais acheter des croissants à la boulangerie.
9 On pouvait entendre toujours les voisins après minuit.
10 Les conditions étaient affreux. Je vous écris pour vous dire que les vacances étaient nuls!

4 La nourriture

(Student Book pages 118–119)

Main topics and objectives

- Eating out
- Using the conditional

Grammar

- The conditional

Key language

au restaurant
au fast-food
à la pizzeria
à la crêperie
Que voudrais-tu?
Je voudrais ...
Qu'est-ce que tu prends?
Je prends ... (comme entrée).
le plat
la crêpe
le dessert
le plat du jour
le plateau de fromages
la salade (de tomates)
la soupe du jour
l'agneau (m)
l'omelette (f)
les frites (f)
les lasagnes (f)
les boissons (f)
l'eau minérale (f)
le vin rouge/blanc
la tarte au citron/aux pommes
la glace
l'addition (f)

Il/Elle était trop ...
cuit(e)
salé(e)
sec/sèche
sucré(e)
Il n'y avait pas assez de sauce.

Resources

CD3, tracks 31–33
Cahier d'exercices, pages 64–65
Grammaire 3.10

Starter 1

Aim
To revise vocabulary for items on a menu. To use given language as a pattern for new forms.

Give students three minutes in pairs to read through the menu at the top of page 119 of the Student Book and to come up with an English translation for each item listed, including the section headings.

1 Où vont-ils? Qu'est-ce qu'ils mangent? (1–4)

Listening. Students listen to four conversations in which people are discussing what they want to eat. They note for each where the speakers decide to go (from the restaurants pictured) and what kind of food they decide to eat (from the pictures **a–f**).

Audioscript 31

1 – *Où est-ce qu'on va dîner ce soir?*
– *On pourrait aller à la pizzeria.*
– *Ah non, je ne veux plus de pizza. J'en ai mangé une à midi.*
– *On peut y manger autre chose, tu sais. On pourrait manger des pâtes, par exemple.*
– *Ah oui, d'accord. On y va.*

2 – *Est-ce que tu as faim?*
– *Pas énormément.*
– *Moi non plus. Où est-ce qu'on dîne alors?*
– *Qu'est-ce que tu proposes?*
– *On pourrait aller au Quick, non?*
– *J'y suis allée hier. Je ne veux pas de hamburger.*
– *On pourrait manger une crêpe, alors?*
– *Ah oui, bonne idée.*

3 – *J'ai faim, mais je n'ai pas d'argent. Est-ce que tu en as?*
– *Ben ... j'ai ... vingt euros.*
– *Qu'est-ce qu'on pourrait s'acheter pour vingt euros?*
– *Des glaces?*
– *Non, j'ai faim, moi. Je préférerais un hamburger avec des frites.*
– *OK, c'est parti. On va au Quick.*

4 – *Bon, on va dîner.*
– *Où est-ce qu'on va?*
– *On pourrait aller au restaurant L'Estaminet.*
– *Ah non, nous y sommes déjà allés hier.*
– *Et alors ... on pourrait y aller encore une fois. On y mange bien.*
– *Non, je préférerais quelque chose de plus simple.*
– *Quoi?*
– *Un poulet frites avec une salade verte.*
– *Oui!*
– *Ben, on pourrait aller à la brasserie.*
– *OK, allons-y.*

Answers
1 pizzeria, e **2** Crêperie, c **3** Quick, d **4** Brasserie, a

2 Écoutez Nicolas et Sophie au restaurant. C'est Vrai (V), Faux (F) ou Pas Mentionné (PM)?

Listening. Students listen to two people in a restaurant talking about what they are going to eat. Students then answer the six questions on the text, saying whether they are true, false or not mentioned.

Audioscript 32

– *Voilà le menu. Tu as faim, Nicolas? Qu'est-ce que tu voudrais?*
– *Bon, j'ai faim. Je voudrais une entrée et un plat.*
– *Qu'est-ce que tu veux boire?*
– *Je voudrais un coca, mais comme je n'ai pas assez d'argent, je vais prendre de l'eau du robinet.*
– *Je préfère l'eau minérale, gazeuse. C'est mieux quand on a soif.*

- *Bon, on partage une bouteille?*
- *Oui, pourquoi pas?*
- *Est-ce que tu veux une salade comme d'habitude?*
- *Oui, je voudrais une salade niçoise, moi. Et toi?*
- *Tu ne manges que ça!*
- *Ce n'est pas vrai!*
- *Je préférerais un potage suivi d'un poulet frites.*
- *C'est quoi comme potage?*
- *Je ne sais pas, mais j'aime le potage.*
- *Regarde, c'est écrit sur le panneau. C'est potage aux champignons.*
- *Euh … non … j'ai changé d'avis. Pas de potage, pas de poulet. Je préférerais des pâtes. Je prends des lasagnes.*
- *J'en ai mangé ici la semaine dernière et elles n'étaient pas bonnes.*
- *Bon, je prends les tagliatelles carbonara, alors.*
- *Et pas de poulet frites?*
- *Non. C'est trop cher. Les pâtes sont moins chères.*
- *D'accord. C'est fait avec quoi, la carbonara?*
- *C'est avec du jambon, des œufs et de la crème.*
- *Uhm … bon …. j'en prends aussi … et puis il nous reste de l'argent pour choisir un dessert.*
- *Mousse au chocolat pour toi comme d'habitude?*
- *Non, je préférerais une crème brûlée et tu prends une glace comme toujours.*
- *Oui. Maintenant, il faut trouver quelqu'un pour nous servir … Monsieur!*

Answers

1 V **2** F **3** F **4** F **5** F **6** F

Expo-langue: the conditional

Use this grammar box to introduce how the conditional is formed. There is more information on p. 214 of the Student Book.

Starter 2

Aim
To consolidate forming the conditional.

Write up the following and ask students to complete the grid to give **aimer** and **vouloir** in the conditional.

		vouloir
je		voudrais
tu		
il/elle/on	aimerait	
nous	aimerions	
vous		voudriez
ils/elles		

3 À deux. Vous avez faim et soif et 35€ à vous partager! Regardez le menu et décidez ensemble ce que vous allez commander.

Speaking. In pairs: students read through the menu and discuss what they are going to order with a budget of 35€ between them.

4 Ils ont mangé où? Qu'est-ce qu'ils ont mangé? C'était comment? (1–3)

Listening. Students copy out the grid. They listen to three conversations in which people talk about where they ate earlier in the evening. Students note in the grid the details of where the people ate, what they ate and what it was like.

Before you give feedback on the answers, give students time to read through the vocabulary box and check agreements, etc.

Audioscript 33

1 *– Où as-tu dîné ce soir?*
– À la brasserie.
– Est-ce que tu as bien mangé?
– Non, ce n'était pas super.
– Qu'est-ce que tu as mangé?
– J'ai mangé un poulet frites.
– C'était comment?
– Le poulet était trop sec et les pâtes de ma copine étaient trop cuites.

2 *– Et toi? Où as-tu dîné?*
– Nous sommes allés au restaurant.
– C'était comment?
– C'était très bien.
– Qu'est-ce que vous avez mangé?
– Moi, j'ai pris un steak … qui était juste à point et délicieux et ma copine a mangé du poisson qui était aussi bon … mais cher!

3 *– Vous avez mangé au fast-food?*
– Non, pas du tout. Nous sommes allés à la pizzeria.
– Vous avez mangé une pizza?
– Non, pas du tout. J'ai mangé des lasagnes, qui n'étaient pas bonnes – trop sèches. Ma copine a mangé des côtelettes d'agneau, qui n'étaient pas bonnes non plus.
– Pourquoi?
– Elles étaient trop salées.
– Oh, dommage.

Answers

	Où?	**plat 1**	**opinion**	**plat 2**	**opinion**
1	Brasserie	poulet frites	trop sec	pâtes	trop cuites
2	Restaurant	steak	délicieux	poisson	bon (mais cher)
3	Pizzeria	lasagnes	pas bonnes/ trop sèches	côtelettes d'agneau	pas bonnes/ trop salées

5 À deux. Discutez: *En vacances.*

Speaking. In pairs: students discuss where and what they eat and drink on their holidays, taking it in turn to ask and answer questions. The questions and some sentence openings are supplied for support.

⊞ ✓ For homework, students could find out about three dishes which are French specialities (their names and what kind of dish they are) that they can include in speaking activities like exercise 5. Point out that being able to add this kind of personal detail to their answers will impress examiners.

6 Imaginez. Hier, c'était l'anniversaire de ta grand-mère. Vous êtes sortis dîner au restaurant. Où êtes-vous allés? Qu'est-ce que vous avez mangé? C'était comment? Écrivez un paragraphe.

Writing. Students imagine yesterday was their grandmother's birthday and there was a family outing to a restaurant to celebrate. They write a paragraph about it, including details of where they went, what they ate and how it was.

Plenary

Ask students to summarise when the conditional is used.

Then get them to pretend they are ordering for a very large group. You are the waiter, taking the orders. They need to give the orders using the conditional of **aimer** or **vouloir** (using as wide a range of different subject pronouns as they can) and referring to the items listed in the menu at the top of p. 119 as necessary.

Cahier d'exercices, pages 64–65

See Unit 5 for answers.

5 Plage, mer et soleil

(Student Book pages 120–121)

Main topics and objectives

- More about holidays
- Using the present, imperfect and conditional

Grammar

- Using a range of tenses (present, imperfect) + the conditional

Key language

Quand j'étais petit(e), …
on faisait des balades
ça allait
Maintenant, j'aimerais …
je préférerais
Je n'aimerais pas faire ce séjour parce que …
L'année dernière, nous avons pris le train à Paris.
Nous sommes partis à 6h.
Il y avait du monde à la gare.
Nous nous sommes arrêtés à …
L'année prochaine, j'irai aux États-Unis.
Je ferai un séjour d'escalade.

Resources

CD3, track 34
Cahier d'exercices, pages 64–65

Starter 1

Aim
To revise the time markers and other phrases associated with various tenses.

Write up the following in two columns, jumbling the order of the second column. Ask students working in pairs to match the halves to make complete sentences/questions and then to translate them.

1 D'habitude,	**il passe ses vacances au bord de la mer.**
2 Quand j'étais petit,	**j'aimais me reposer sur la plage.**
3 Maintenant,	**elle préférerait aller à l'étranger.**
4 La semaine prochaine,	**j'irai en Écosse.**
5 Le week-end dernier,	**il est parti en vacances.**
6 À Noël,	**elle voudrait faire du ski.**

1 Qu'est-ce qu'ils aiment faire et qu'est-ce qu'ils n'aiment pas faire? Copiez et complétez la grille.

Reading. Students copy out the grid. They read the texts by four different people and identify what each of them likes doing on holiday and what they don't like doing, using the pictures **a–l**.

Answers

nom	aime	n'aime pas
Vincent	*d*, b, k, e	*c*
Sophie	i, j, g	a
Christian	g	a, h
Coralie	b, e, k	f

2 Écoutez et notez. Relisez les textes de l'exercice 1 si nécessaire. (1–4)

Listening. Students listen to the four people in exercise 1 talking about what they usually do on holiday and what they would prefer to do. They then answer the three comprehension questions in English. Students may also find it helpful to refer back to the texts in exercise 1 for support.

Audioscript 34

1 *– Que fais-tu d'habitude pendant les vacances?*
– Je vais dans un camping à la campagne avec ma famille.
– Tu aimes ça?
– Pas tellement.
– Qu'est-ce que tu préférerais alors?
– Ben, je voudrais … faire un stage de sport ou d'aventures.
– Pourquoi?
– Parce que les vacances sans rien faire, c'est ennuyeux.
– Quelle sorte d'activités veux-tu faire par exemple?
– Apprendre un nouveau sport comme l'alpinisme ou le parapente. Je vais trouver quelque chose sur Internet.

2 *– Que fais-tu d'habitude pendant les vacances?*
– Cela dépend de mes parents. Mon père est au chômage pour le moment et nous ne pouvons pas partir en vacances.
– Mais si tu avais de l'argent, qu'est-ce que tu aimerais faire?
– Ce que j'aimerais faire? … Aller à l' étranger.
– Pourquoi?
– Je n'y suis jamais allée. Tous mes amis sont allés en Floride ou à la Martinique.
– Où voudrais-tu aller?
– Je voudrais aller à Disneyland en Floride. Tout le monde dit que c'est vraiment une expérience à ne pas manquer.
– Il y a des échanges scolaires entre des élèves français et des élèves américains.
– Bon, je vais chercher des renseignements, alors.
– Il faut chercher sur Internet.

3 – *Qu'est-ce que les vacances représentent pour toi?*
– *Pour moi? … Les vacances, c'est plage, mer, soleil et mes amis!*
– *Que fais-tu d'habitude?*
– *Jusqu'à présent je pars toujours avec ma famille, on va au bord de la mer, dans un camping et on s'amuse.*
– *Et qu'est-ce que tu préférerais faire?*
– *Je voudrais partir avec mes copains.*
– *Pourquoi?*
– *Parce que mes parents sont trop stricts. Avec eux, le soir, il faut se coucher à neuf heures. Imagine, se coucher à neuf heures en vacances!*
– *Et que feriez-vous avec tes copains?*
– *On installerait notre tente dans un petit camping au bord de la mer quelque part, … sans les parents … Et comme ça, on pourrait se lever et se coucher quand on veut.*
– *Ahhhh!*

4 – *Qu'est-ce que les vacances représentent pour toi?*
– *La campagne … la tranquillité …*
– *Que fais-tu pendant les vacances?*
– *D'habitude, je vais en vacances avec mon père. On fait du camping sauvage.*
– *Et qu'est-ce que vous voudriez faire?*
– *Nous aimerions faire le tour du Mont-Blanc.*
– *Dis-m'en plus …*
– *C'est une longue route qu'on fait à pied, dans les Alpes, autour du Mont-Blanc.*
– *Il faut combien de temps pour la faire?*
– *À peu près 9 jours.*
– *Il faut être en forme alors?*
– *Oui.*
– *Pourquoi voulez-vous faire cela?*
– *C'est un défi, comme courir un marathon, on veut savoir si on peut le faire … chercher ses limites. …*
– *Euh … Bonne chance, alors!*

Answers

1 **a** Sophie **b** goes camping with her family **c** do a sports or adventure course
2 **a** Coralie **b** stays at home **c** go abroad (to Disneyland in Florida)
3 **a** Vincent **b** goes on holiday to the seaside/camping with his family **c** go on holiday to the seaside/camping with his friends
4 **a** Christian **b** goes camping in the wild with his dad **c** do a walking tour on Mont Blanc

Expo-langue: using different tenses/the conditional

Use this grammar box to review the function of the present and imperfect tenses and the conditional before students do exercise 3.

3 À deux. Posez les questions et répondez-y.

Speaking. In pairs: students take it in turn to ask questions about the people in exercises 1 and 2 and to respond to the questions. The questions are supplied.

Starter 2

Aim
To revise language for holidays. To practise using the present, the imperfect and the conditional.

Write up the following. Ask students in pairs to write six sentences about holidays using the activities supplied – two in the present, two in the imperfect and two in the conditional.

faire …
la plongée sous-marine
le kayak
le cyclisme
le beach-volley
des baignades
des excursions

4 Lisez les textes et les phrases. C'est quel séjour?

Reading. Students read the three holiday websites. They then read the nine statements about them and identify which website each refers to.

Answers

a 3 **b** 1 **c** 3 **d** 2 **e** 3 **f** 2 **g** 1 **h** 1 **i** 2

5 À deux. Discutez. Donnez votre opinion sur chaque séjour.

Speaking. In pairs: students discuss the holidays in exercise 4, giving their opinion on each and justifying these opinions. Some structures are given for support.

6 Mes vacances. Faites un résumé.

Writing. Students write a short report about their holidays. As the sample structures supplied show, they need to include a range of tenses – here the present and the imperfect – plus the conditional. Ask them before they start how they could also work in the near future tense.

Ask students to choose and research two types of holidays on the internet, using key phrases from the Module in the search engine. They should summarise details in English. Go to www.heinemann.co.uk/hotlinks and enter the express code 3857HTG for a link to a website for backpackers in France.

➕ Using the information found on the internet, students write a short text saying which of two holidays they would choose and why. (Alternatively, they could select a holiday from the types covered in this Module in the Student Book.)

Plenary

Ask students to summarise when the present, the imperfect and the conditional are used in this topic.

Then go round the class. Presuming that money were no object, each student says what he/she would do or where he/she would go on holiday, using the conditional.

Cahier d'exercices, pages 64–65

1

Answers

1 e **2** a **3** f **4** h **5** g **6** c **7** b **8** d

2

Answers

1 Luc
2 Malika
3 Robert
4 Malika
5 Luc
6 Malika
7 Luc
8 Luc + Robert

3

Answers

1 Malika **2** Robert **3** Luc

4

Answers

Luc: prefers holidays abroad. Wants to visit different countries. Last year went to Italy but this year is going to England to spend one week in London and one week somewhere quieter. Wants to improve his English. Loves the sun.

Robert: Loves the sea and the sun. Has family in Biarritz so goes there in the summer holidays. Went twice a year when he was younger and learnt to swim there. Loves water sports and is going to do a water skiing course this year.

Malika: Most important thing for her is eating on holiday! Often lies in and then has brekafast around midday so no need to have lunch. Loves Italian food and likes going to resturants on holiday. The family have difficulty in choosing a restaurant because they all like different foods.

5

Answers

Pupil's own answers

6 L'année dernière

(Student Book pages 122–123)

Main topics and objectives

- Talking about past holidays
- Using the perfect tense

Grammar

- The perfect and imperfect: when to use

Key language

Language from throughout the module

Resources

CD3, tracks 35–37
Cahier d'exercices, pages 66–67
Grammaire 3.5

Starter 1

Aim
To revise time markers associated with past tenses.

Give students working in pairs three minutes to list as many time phrases as they can that could be used when talking about the past. Which pair can come up with the longest (accurate) list?

1 Les vacances de Jérôme. Écoutez et lisez le texte. Décidez: Vrai (V), Faux (F) ou Pas Mentionné (PM)?

Listening. Students listen to Jérôme talking about his holidays, reading the text at the same time. They then read the ten statements on the text and decide whether each is true or false or not mentioned in the text.

Audioscript 35

L'année dernière, nous sommes allés en Bretagne, chez mes grands-parents. Le voyage était affreux. La voiture était pleine à craquer. Nous étions cinq personnes, le chien, tous les bagages, les vélos et deux planches à voile. Chose curieuse, ma sœur a toujours une grande valise, mais un fois qu'on est là-bas, elle ne porte que des bikinis!

Nous sommes partis à six heures du matin. Mais il y avait tellement de monde qui partait au même moment qu'il y avait des embouteillages partout sur l'autoroute. On a dû faire la queue pour l'essence et aux toilettes. Heureusement, nous avions emporté des sandwichs. Quand nous sommes arrivés, mes grands-parents dormaient dans leurs fauteuils devant la télé.

Le lendemain, il a plu et nous sommes allés faire du shopping à l'hypermarché, mais après, il y a eu du soleil presque tout le temps. La mer était un peu froide pour nager, mais nous avons mis une combinaison de plongée et mon frère et moi, nous avons joué dans l'eau et fait de la planche. Mon grand-père a un bateau à voile et il nous a appris à faire de la voile. Nous avons aussi pêché avec lui, et nous avons fait des balades en vélo avec nos parents. J'ai trouvé une nouvelle petite amie. Un jour, je promenais mon chien et elle est venue me parler. Elle était super chouette. Elle voulait apprendre à faire de la planche. Nous nous entendions très bien. J'espère qu'elle viendra l'année prochaine. J'ai voulu lui envoyer des e-mails, mais j'ai perdu son adresse.

Answers

1 V **2** V **3** V **4** F **5** PM **6** F **7** F **8** PM **9** V **10** F

Expo-langue: tense usage in the past

Use this grammar box to review when to use the perfect/the imperfect. There is more information on p. 213 of the Student Book.

R Ask students to find examples of verbs in the past used in each of the ways listed in the **Expo-langue** box (single occasion, something done regularly, description, happening when something else happened).

2 Écoutez et choisissez les bonnes lettres. (1–3)

Listening. Students listen to the three conversations about holidays in the past. For each conversation, they answer the four questions given, using the phrases **a–p**.

Audioscript 36

1 *– Où es-tu allée, Céline?*
– Pendant les vacances?
– Oui, où est-ce que tu as passé tes dernières vacances ?
– Ben, j'ai fait un échange scolaire avec ma classe en Floride.
– Tu as de la chance!
– Oui, c'était super, on a passé une semaine en Floride, et puis une semaine à Saint-Louis.
– Le voyage était long?
– Oui, le vol a duré huit heures, et puis nous avons dû changer d'avion pour arriver à notre destination.
– Tu étais fatiguée?
– Au début, non, mais plus tard, oui.

2 *– Qu'as-tu fait pendant les grandes vacances?*
– Moi? Rien. Nous ne sommes pas partis en vacances parce que mes parents ont un café et qu'ils travaillent tout le temps, surtout les vacances.
– Tu n'es pas parti du tout?
– Si, ma sœur et moi, on a passé une semaine chez mes grands-parents, puis ils sont partis en vacances avec des amis.
– Ils habitent près de chez vous?
– À deux minutes. On peut y aller à pied.

3 – Et toi, Hakim … tu es parti en vacances?
– Oui, je suis allé en Espagne avec ma mère.
– Pour combien de temps?
– Trois semaines.
– Comment y êtes-vous allés?
– On voulait y aller en avion, mais on n'a pas pu trouver de vol. J'ai cherché sur Internet, mais pas de chance, je n'ai rien trouvé. Finalement, on y est allés en train.

Answers

1 a, e, j, n
2 d, h, l, o
3 b, f, k, p

Starter 2

Aim
To practise the perfect tense.

Write up the following and ask students working in pairs to put all of the verbs into the perfect tense.

1 **Je nage dans la mer.**
2 **Il joue au volley.**
3 **Ils viennent aujourd'hui.**
4 **Elle se repose sur la plage.**
5 **On fait du parapente.**
6 **Nous dormons à la belle étoile.**
7 **Vous allez à une station balnéaire?**
8 **Je regarde la télé.**
9 **Elles partent en vacances.**
10 **Tu fais des balades?**

3 Tour de France. À deux. Décrivez le voyage de Tom et Matthieu.

Speaking. In pairs: students interpret the map to describe the trip Tom and Matthieu made round France.

4 Imaginez. Vous êtes partis avec Tom et Matthieu. Décrivez vos vacances!

Writing. Students imagine they went on the trip with Tom and Matthieu and write a paragraph describing their holiday, using the **nous** form.

5 Qu'est-ce qu'ils ont fait, font et feront? Copiez et complétez la grille. (1–3)

Listening. Students copy the grid. They then listen to three people talking about their holidays and fill in the details of what they did last year, this year and next year in the grid.

Audioscript 37

1 Je m'appelle Adrien. L'année dernière, j'ai fait un stage de planche à voile en Bretagne. L'année prochaine, je rendrai visite à mon correspondant en Angleterre, mais cette année, je reste à la maison et je ne fais rien. C'est ennuyeux.

2 Je m'appelle Claude. L'année dernière, je suis allé en Italie. Il faisait très chaud et je me suis baigné tous les jours. L'année prochaine, je vais faire un stage d'escalade dans les Alpes et cette année, je fais du camping sur la côte d'Azur.

3 Je m'appelle Mélanie. L'année dernière, nous sommes allés en Espagne et nous avons fait de l'équitation. J'adore ça! Les chevaux, c'est ma passion. Cette année, je vais rendre visite à mon correspondant aux États-Unis, et l'année prochaine, je n'aurai plus d'argent et je chercherai un petit travail dans un bar ou quelque chose comme ça.

Answers

	l'année dernière	**cette année**	**l'année prochaine**
1	*un stage de planche à voile en Bretagne*	Il reste à la maison/ne fait rien.	Il va rendre visite à son correspondant en Angleterre.
2	Il est allé en Italie.	Il fait du camping sur la côte d'Azur.	Il va faire un stage d'escalade dans les Alpes.
3	Elle est allée en Espagne/a fait de l'équitation.	Elle va rendre visite à son correspondant aux États-Unis.	Elle cherchera un petit travail.

6 Écrivez. Qu'est-ce que vous avez fait l'année dernière, qu'est-ce que vous faites cette année et qu'est-ce que vous ferez l'année prochaine?

Writing. Students write a paragraph about their own holidays, detailing what they did last year, what they're doing this year and what they'll do next year. The tip box offers some suggestions to use if they don't have definite plans.

Plenary

Put the class into teams for a game to consolidate the work on tenses.

Read out a series of prompts, e.g. **aller – nous** – conditional, **partir – elle** – perfect, etc. (keeping a note of them). The students consult in teams and write down the answers. They then swap answers with another team and give each other a score (one point per correct verb). The team with the most points wins.

Cahier d'exercices, page 66

Answers

1 down suis parti
2 down faisait
3 down regardais
5 down faisais
6 down ai fait
11 down ai eu
12 down suis resté
14 down avais
15 down était
17 down ai adoré

4 across a eu
7 across ai nagé
9 across allait
10 across dormait
11 across assistait
13 across est allés
16 across avons fait
18 across sommes

Cahier d'exercices, Grammaire, page 67

1

Answers

1. Je vais; tu vas; nous allons
2. Tu es allé(e); elle est allée; nous sommes allé(e)s
3. Il allait; nous allions; ils allaient
4. On ira; j'irai; nous irons
5. Elle irait; nous irions; elles iraient
6. Je vais aller; on va aller; nous allons aller

2

Answers

L'année dernière, nous sommes allés en Espagne. Un jour, nous allions à Barcelone quand il y a eu un accident.
L'année prochaine, nous irons à Londres en Angleterre, mais si j'avais le choix, j'irais aux USA.
En ce moment, je suis dans le train; je vais à Paris pour le week-end. Demain, j'irai à la Tour Eiffel et le soir on va voir un spectacle.

3

Answers

Soyez organisé(e)!
Cherchez sur l'internet et regardez toutes les auberges de jeunesse dans votre région choisie.
Notez l'adresse et le numéro de téléphone ou imprimez la page sur Internet.
Écrivez un e-mail, contactez-les par téléphone ou envoyez une lettre.
Réservez vos places au moins deux mois à l'avance.
Une semaine avant votre départ confirmez vos réservations!

Tourisme 7

Contrôle continu: Mes vacances

(Student Book pages 124–125)

Topics revised

- Talking about a holiday in the past

1 Trouvez huit mots qui indiquent *quand* quelque chose a eu lieu. Essayez de les utiliser dans votre exposé.

Students read Vincent's text and find eight time markers. They should note these down and try to use them in their own piece of writing on this topic.

Answers

l'année dernière, le matin, l'après-midi, le soir, un jour, un autre jour, cette année, l'année prochaine

2 Trouvez les phrases françaises dans le texte.

Students reread the text and find the French for the six English phrases listed.

Answers

1 être à l'heure
2 nous avons dû attendre
3 (pour) récupérer nos bagages
4 il y avait une grève
5 tout le monde
6 était sensass

3 Imaginez que vous êtes Vincent. Répondez aux questions en français.

Students imagine they are Vincent and reply to the 10 questions in French from his perspective.

Answers

1 Je suis allé en Espagne.
2 avec ma famille
3 Nous y sommes allés en avion.
4 Le voyage était long.
5 Nous avons logé dans un appartement.
6 C'était grand et commode.
7 Le matin, nous nous sommes levés tard, nous avons déjeuné et fait les courses. L'après-midi, nous sommes restés autour de la piscine. Mon frère et moi, nous avons trouvé des amis. Le soir, nous nous sommes douchés, bien habillés et sortis dîner.
8 J'ai apprecié le plus aller dans un parc aquatique.
9 Je n'ai pas aimé faire du karting.
10 Je veux aller/retourner en Espagne.

4 Décrivez des vacances

Using the text and the **Boîte à outils** section to help them, students write their own description of their holidays, covering the past, the present and the future.

À l'oral (AQA edition)

(Student Book page 182)

Topics revised

- asking for hotel information
- booking a youth hostel
- talking about holidays

1 You are at the tourist information office, looking for a hotel. Your partner will play the part of the person at the office and will speak first.

Roleplay. Students practise asking for hotel information in a tourist information office, taking it in turn to play themselves/the tourist office employee.

2 You are making a reservation for a youth hostel. Your partner will play the hostel employee and will speak first.

Roleplay. Students practise booking a youth hostel, taking it in turn to play themselves/the youth hostel employee.

3 Prepare a ninety-second presentation called *Mes vacances*.

Presentation. Students prepare a ninety-second presentation on holidays. A sample cue card is supplied for students to refer to when preparing their own prompts.

☑ Draw attention to the structure used on the card (**L'année dernière, Cette année**, etc.), pointing out how the full range of tenses is covered and encourage students to copy this in their own presentation.

4 Possible conversation questions

These are key questions to practise for the speaking exam, taken from the module as a whole. Students can practise asking and answering the questions in pairs.

☑ Remind students to listen out for the tense used in each question and to respond using the same tense.

À l'oral (Edexcel edition)

(Student Book page 182)

Topics revised

- booking accommodation
- checking into a youth hostel
- talking about holidays

1 You are talking to the receptionist at a hotel in France. Your partner will play the part of the receptionist and will begin the conversation.

Roleplay Type B. Students practise booking accommodation in a hotel, taking it in turn to play themselves/the hotel employee.

2 You are on holiday with your family in France and arrive at a youth hostel. Your partner will play the part of the receptionist and will begin the conversation.

Roleplay Type C. Students practise checking into a youth hostel, taking it in turn to play themselves/ the youth hostel receptionist.

☑ Draw students' attention to the tip box, which suggests how they might expand one of the answers.

3 Presentation and general conversation

Presentation. Students prepare a one-minute presentation on holidays. A sample cue card is supplied for students to refer to when preparing their own prompts.

☑ Draw attention to the structure used on the card (**L'année dernière, Cette année,** etc.), pointing out how the full range of tenses is covered and encourage students to copy this in their own presentation.

Possible conversation questions. These are key questions to practise for the speaking exam, taken from the module as a whole. Students can practise asking and answering the questions in pairs.

☑ Remind students to listen out for the tense used in each question and to respond accordingly.

À l'oral (OCR edition)

(Student Book page 182)

Topics revised

- talking about holidays
- talking about a holiday in the past
- talking about future holidays

1 Use the notes and pictures below to describe a family holiday to Belgium last year.

Roleplay Type 3. Students practise talking about a holiday in the past, using the text and picture prompts supplied.

☑ Remind pupils that they can improve their exam marks by developing the story and by expressing and justifying opinions.

2 Prepare a one-minute presentation called *Mes vacances*.

Presentation. Students prepare a one-minute presentation on holidays. A sample cue card is supplied for students to refer to when preparing their own prompts.

☑ Draw attention to the tip box: it highlights how students can work the full range of tenses into this topic and reminds them to include a variety of opinions and justifications in order to gain maximum marks.

3 *Les vacances:* possible conversation questions

These are key questions to practise for the speaking exam, taken from the module as a whole. Students can practise asking and answering the questions in pairs.

☑ Remind students to listen out for the tense used in each question and to respond using the same tense.

Tourisme 7

À toi

(Student Book pages 198–199)

- Self-access reading and writing

1 Trouvez les mots ou les phrases dans le texte.

Reading. Students read the text and then find the French for the 12 English expressions listed.

Answers

1 douches chaudes gratuites
2 vaisselle
3 réchaud
4 meubles de jardin
5 couchage
6 draps
7 oreillers
8 serviettes
9 mitigeur
10 arrhes/caution
11 désistement
12 Dépôt de garantie

2 Vos parents veulent en savoir plus. Répondez en anglais aux questions qu'ils vous posent.

Reading. Students imagine their parents want to know more about the campsite in exercise 1 and answer the eight questions posed in English.

Answers

1 350€
2 200€
3 150€ a week
4 no
5 yes
6 yes
7 no
8 crockery is provided; you need to take bedding

3 Regardez le site web du Ze Bus. Choissisez la bonne réponse, a, b ou c.

Reading. Students read the Ze Bus website. They then read the seven sentences and choose the correct ending for each from the three options given (**a**, **b** or **c**).

Answers

1 b **2** a **3** c **4** b **5** c **6** b **7** c

4 Faites correspondre les verbes.

Reading. Referring back to the text in exercise 4 as necessary, students match the French and English verbs.

Answers

1 c **2** d **3** b **4** e **5** a **6** f

5 Faites correspondre pour compléter les phrases.

Reading. Students read the text. For the six sentence openings they find the appropriate ending (from **a–i**).

Answers

1 i **2** e **3** d **4** f **5** g **6** h

6 Imaginez que vous êtes parti(e)s en Ze Bus.

Writing. Students imagine they made a trip on Ze Bus and write a paragraph describing what happened. A list of questions is supplied to help them structure their piece.

Module 8 Mes copains et mes héros

(Student Book pages 128–143)

Unit	Main topics and objectives	Grammar
Déjà vu **Ils sont comment?** (pp. 128–129)	Describing people The comparative and superlative	The comparative The superlative
1 Les champions sportifs (pp. 130–131)	Describing famous sportspeople Using the perfect infinitive	**après** + the perfect infinitive
2 Je ferai un stage sportif (pp. 132–133)	Discussing sporting holidays More on the future tense	The future tense
3 J'étais comme ça (pp. 134–135)	Saying how things used to be More practice with the imperfect tense	The imperfect
4 Toujours le sport! (pp. 136–137)	Describing a sporting event Using the pluperfect tense	The pluperfect tense
5 Qui admirez-vous? (pp. 138–139)	Describing someone's qualities Using abstract nouns	
Contrôle continu **Thierry Henry: le roi des footballeurs!** (pp. 140–141)	*Coursework* Writing about a famous person	*All main grammar points of the module*
À l'oral (p. 183)	*Exam speaking practice* Talking about the sports/sportspeople you like	*All main grammar points of the module*
À toi (pp. 200–201)	Self-access reading and writing	

Déjà vu: Ils sont comment?

(Student Book pages 128–129)

Main topics and objectives
- Describing people
- The comparative and superlative

Grammar
- The comparative
- The superlative

Key language
Adjectives to describe appearance/personality

Resources
CD4, tracks 2–3
Cahier d'exercices, page 70
Grammaire 2.4

Starter 1

Aim
To revise language for describing someone's personal appearance.

Ask students to write a description of themselves, to include the following information:

- height
- hair – colour, length, type (e.g. curly)
- eyes – colour

They can look up any information they need reminding of in the Vocabulaire or a dictionary.

Listen to some answers, reminding the class as necessary of the meaning of any vocabulary items and highlighting agreements.

1 Écoutez et lisez. Identifiez chaque personne de l'image.

Listening. Students listen to Tariq's description of his basketball team, following the text in the book at the same time. They use the information given to name each of the five boys pictured (**a–e**).

Audioscript 2

Je t'envoie cette photo de notre équipe de basket, Les Casse-Filets. Tu veux savoir qui est qui? Bon, c'est moi le joueur de taille moyenne, aux cheveux bruns frisés. Tu me vois? Sélim, lui aussi, il est brun, mais il a les cheveux plus courts que moi. Je suis moins grand que Sélim et j'ai les yeux verts, tandis que lui, il a les yeux marron. David est facile à identifier. C'est le plus petit de l'équipe, mais il est l'un des meilleurs joueurs! Il est aussi le seul à avoir les cheveux blonds et les yeux bleus. Les deux autres sont Luc et Fabien. Luc a les plus longs cheveux de l'équipe. Il est aussi grand que Sélim, mais un peu plus petit que Fabien. Non seulement Fabien est le plus grand, mais il est le plus beau joueur aussi – les filles l'adorent! De plus, il joue mieux que moi. C'est pas juste!

Answers

a David **b** Sélim **c** Fabien **d** Tariq **e** Luc

Expo-langue: the comparative and superlative

Use this grammar box to review the comparative and superlative before students do exercise 2. There is more information on p. 211 of the Student Book.

2 Écrivez V (Vrai), F (Faux) ou PM (Pas Mentionné) pour chaque phrase.

Reading. Students reread the text in exercise 1. They then read the eight statements on the text and decide whether each is true or false or not mentioned in the text.

Answers

1 V **2** F **3** F **4** PM **5** V **6** V **7** F **8** PM

Starter 2

Aim
To practise using the comparative and superlative. To revise some adjectives used to describe people.

Write up:
plus grand que
moins court que
aussi intelligent que
le plus beau
le moins agréable

Ask students working in pairs to come up with a sentence using each expression. They can use celebrities or friends in their comparisons or fictional people.

Students can look back at the **Expo-langue** box on p. 128 for support if necessary.

3 Lisez les opinions. Écrivez P (Positive), N (Négative) ou P/N (Positive/Négative) pour chaque opinion.

Reading. Students read the six speech bubbles and decide whether the opinion expressed in each is positive (**P**), negative (**N**) or a mixture of both (**P/N**).

Answers

1 P **2** P/N **3** P/N **4** N **5** N **6** P

4 Copiez et complétez la grille des adjectifs.

Writing. Students copy out the grid of adjectives and complete it.

Answers

singular		plural		anglais
masculine	**feminine**	**masculine**	**feminine**	
beau	*belle*	*beaux*	belles	*good-looking/ beautiful*
laid	laide	*laids*	laides	*ugly*
riche	riche	riches	riches	*rich*
pauvre	*pauvre*	pauvres	pauvres	*poor*
gentil	*gentille*	gentils	gentilles	*kind*
pénible	pénible	pénibles	*pénibles*	*irritating/ a pain*
sérieux	sérieuse	sérieux	sérieuses	*serious*
travailleux	*travailleuse*	travailleux	travailleuses	*hard-working*
poli	polie	polis	polies	*polite*
rigolo	*rigolote*	rigolos	rigolotes	*funny/a laugh*

5 Écoutez et vérifiez.

Listening. Students use their knowledge of sound-spelling links to predict which endings in the grid in exercise 4 change the sound of the adjectives. They then listen and check.

Audioscript 3

beau, belle, beaux, belles
laid, laide, laids, laides
riche, riche, riches, riches
pauvre, pauvre, pauvres, pauvres
gentil, gentille, gentils, gentilles
pénible, pénible, pénibles, pénibles
sérieux, sérieuse, sérieux, sérieuses
travailleur, travailleuse, travailleurs, travailleuses
poli, polie, polis, polies
rigolo, rigolote, rigolos, rigolotes

6 À deux. Faites des comparaisons entre ces personnes célèbres en donnant votre opinion.

Speaking. In pairs: students make comparisons between famous people, voicing their own opinions. A sample exchange is given.

7 Imaginez que vous connaissez des gens célèbres. Écrivez des phrases, comme dans l'exercice 3.

Writing. Students imagine they know three or four famous people and write a few sentences on each of them, using the texts in exercise 3 as models. A sample opening is given.

Plenary

Ask students to summarise how the comparative and superlative are formed and to give examples of how they are used with the adjectives from the grid in exercise 4. Ask them to spell out adjectives to make sure agreement of feminine and plural forms is covered.

Cahier d'exercices, page 70

1

Answers

Prénom	Taille	Caractère	Cheveux
Anne	1m85	paresseuse	bruns
Sophie	1m60	bavarde	noirs
Sarah	1m70	bruyante	blonds
Audrey	1m80	sérieuse	courts
Amandine	1m65	marrante	longs

1 Les champions sportifs

(Student Book pages 130–131)

Main topics and objectives

- Describing famous sportspeople
- Using the perfect infinitive

Grammar

- après + the perfect infinitive

Key language

Il/Elle est né(e) le 2 février.
Il/Elle habite à Paris.
Il/Elle est …
marié(e)/divorcé(e)/célibataire
Il/Elle s'est inscrit(e) au club (de foot).
Il a marqué un but pendant la finale.
Elle a essayé trois fois pour l'équipe.

Resources

CD4, tracks 4–5
Cahier d'exercices, page 71
Grammaire 3.6

Starter 1

Aim
To review grammatical terms. To think about how words work in a sentence.

Write up the following:

Toujours célibataire, le très beau gosse aux cheveux noirs et aux yeux marron ne manque pas de fans!

Ask students working in pairs to put each of the words in the sentence into one of the following categories.

Verbs
Nouns
Adjectives
Adverbs
Prepositions
Words for 'a'/'some'/'the'
Connectives
Qualifiers
Other words

1 Écoutez et lisez. Complétez les détails sur ce joueur de tennis.

Listening. Students copy out the form. They listen to the profile of the French tennis player Richard Gasquet and complete the form with the relevant details.

Audioscript 4

Le jeune Français Richard Gasquet est déjà une étoile du tennis et un des meilleurs joueurs du monde. Né le 18 juin 1986 à Béziers, Richard habite actuellement à Paris, où il s'entraîne au Centre National de l'Entraînement. Toujours célibataire, ce beau gosse aux cheveux châtain clair et aux yeux marron, qui mesure 1,82 m, ne manque pas de fans et pas seulement à cause de ses talents au tennis! Positif, courageux et ambitieux, Richard vit pour le tennis, mais en dehors des courts, il aime être avec ses amis, passe pas mal de temps à sa PlayStation et joue un peu au foot.

Answers

Nom: Gasquet
Prénom: Richard
Nationalité: français
Âge: *work out from date of birth 18/6/1986*
Date de naissance: 18 juin 1986
Lieu de naissance: Béziers
Résidence: Paris
État civil (marié/divorcé/célibataire): célibataire
Taille: 1,82m
Cheveux: châtain clair
Yeux: marron
Passe-temps: être avec ses amis, jouer à sa PlayStation, jouer au football
Caractère: positif, courageux et ambitieux

2 Reliez les deux parties de ces questions.

Reading. Students read and match the texts to make 10 questions that you might use in an interview.

Answers

1 j **2** f **3** d **4** i **5** e **6** a **7** g **8** c **9** b **10** h

3 À deux. Vous faites une interview avec Richard Gasquet. Utilisez les questions de l'exercice 2.

Speaking. In pairs: students do an interview with Richard Gasquet, taking it in turn to be the interviewer. They should use the questions from exercise 2 and the information on Richard from exercise 1.

4 Écrivez un paragraphe sur cette joueuse de tennis française en utilisant les détails à droite.

Writing. Pupils use the details supplied for the French tennis player Amélie Mauresmo to write a paragraph about her.

Students could research a favourite sportsperson on the internet in French by choosing the French preferences option in Google or another search engine. Set them the challenge of listing six new French expressions they find and are able to work out from the context.

Starter 2

Aim
To revise infinitive forms.

Write up the following and ask students to list the infinitive form for each verb.

va, jouons, sont, attendraient, connaissez, eu, court, finis, voient, écrirai

When checking answers, ask students to summarise the contexts in which you need to use the infinitive (near future tense, with structures like **on peut, j'aime**, etc., to form the future tense and the conditional).

5 Lisez le texte et répondez aux questions en français.

Reading. Students read the text on the French footballer Zinédine Zidane and answer the 10 comprehension questions in French.

Answers

1 Zinédine Zidane est né à Marseille.
2 Il a deux frères.
3 Pendant son enfance, il jouait au football sur la place de La Castellane.
4 Il a passé six ans à Cannes.
5 Son surnom est Zizou.
6 Il a quitté la France en 1996 pour aller en Italie/jouer pour l'équipe de la Juventus.
7 Il a marqué deux buts pendant la finale de la Coupe du Monde contre le Brésil.
8 La France a gagné la Coupe du Monde de 1998.
9 Il est marié.
10 L'équipe espagnole s'appelle le Real Madrid.

Expo-langue: *après* + the perfect infinitive

Use this grammar box to introduce **après** + the perfect infinitive. There is more information on p. 213 of the Student Book. Encourage students to try to work this structure into their own writing.

R Ask students to find examples of this structure in the text in exercise 5 and to translate them.

Go to www.heinemann.co.uk/hotlinks and enter the express code 7898T for a link to the Zinédine Zidane website.

6 Écoutez l'interview avec une jeune footballeuse et mettez les événements dans le bon ordre.

Listening. Students listen to the interview with a young footballer and put the events described (**1–5**) in the order they hear them.

Audioscript 5

– *On parle aujourd'hui avec Leila ... une jeune lycéenne qui se passionne pour le football. Leila, vous jouez au football depuis quand?*
– *Euh ... depuis dix ans à peu près. Quand j'avais cinq ans, je jouais déjà au foot au parc avec mes deux frères, puis ... voilà.*
– *Vous jouiez au foot à l'école et au collège aussi?*
– *Bon, ... euh, pas tellement à l'école, mais au collège, on jouait au foot pendant les cours d'EPS, ... et puis le mercredi après-midi, il y avait un club de foot ...*
– *Vous vous êtes inscrite au club de foot ... ?*
– *Oui, c'est ça et après avoir joué au club pendant quelques mois, le prof – enfin, l'entraîneur – Monsieur Gérard – m'a proposé d'essayer pour l'équipe junior régionale.*
– *Et vous avez réussi?*
– *J'ai essayé trois fois, mais j'ai fini par réussir! J'ai joué pour l'équipe junior pendant trois ans.*
– *Et vous avez continué à jouer au lycée?*
– *C'est-à-dire ... Après avoir quitté le collège, j'ai décidé d'aller dans un lycée avec une section sportive.*
– *Et finalement, Leila, quel est le plus grand moment de votre vie sportive?*
– *Bof ... c'est difficile parce que ... enfin, je crois que c'est le but que j'ai marqué pendant la finale du tournoi régional l'été dernier. C'était contre une super bonne équipe, mais nous avons gagné le match 1–0 ... et c'est moi qui ai marqué le but!*
– *Bon, merci, Leila, et bonne chance pour l'avenir!*
– *Merci.*

Answers

3, 1, 5, 4, 2

7 Faites une présentation sur Leila (de mémoire, si possible) en adaptant les phrases de l'exercice 6. Ajoutez des détails si vous voulez.

Speaking. Students do a presentation about Leila, adapting sentences 1–6 and adding other details if they want to. They should aim to work in two examples of the perfect infinitive. Encourage them also to work towards doing the presentation from memory.

Plenary

Ask the class to summarise how the perfect infinitive is used in this unit. Then put them into teams and give them two minutes to come up with as many sentences featuring the perfect infinitive as possible. They then swap with another team and check answers. Which team came up with the most correct sentences?

Cahier d'exercices, page 71

1

Answers

Né le 14 décembre 1979 à Douala (Cameroun), Jean-Alain Boumsong est défenseur pour Newcastle United en Angleterre. Enfant, il jouait au football et au volley avec ses cinq frères. Ses parents jouaient aussi au volley à un très haut niveau. Son père jouait dans l'équipe nationale du Cameroun. C'est en regardant les stars du Cameroun à la télé qu'il a su qu'il voulait devenir footballeur. Ses idoles étaient Joseph-Antoine Bell et Thomas N'Kono. Ils avaient beaucoup de classe! À dix ans, il n'était pas très grand ni très fort, c'est pourquoi il n'était pas choisi par les recruteurs. Il était dégoûté. Alors, il s'est tourné vers le volley, mais il savait qu'un jour, il retournerait au foot. À l'âge de 14 ans, il est arrivé en France. Il a été au club du Havre entre 1997 et 2000. Après avoir quitté Le Havre, il a passé quatre années au club d'Auxerre. Avec Auxerre, il a remporté la Coupe de France en 2003. C'est lui qui a marqué le but pour gagner 2-1 contre Paris Saint Germain. De 2004 à 2005 il a joué en Écosse pour Glasgow Rangers, puis en janvier 2005, il est allé à Newcastle United.
Sa première sélection pour la France était en juin 2003 face au Japon (2-1). Il a joué 17 fois pour la France. Il veut prouver qu'il figure parmi les futures stars de la défense française.

2

Answers

Pupil's own answers

2 Je ferai un stage sportif

(Student Book pages 132–133)

Main topics and objectives

- Discussing sporting holidays
- More on the future tense

Grammar

- The future tense

Key language

J'irai dans les Alpes/
en Normandie/
à l'Auberge d'Aix-en-Savoie.
On fera un stage de ski.
Je suis débutant(e).
J'en ai fait deux fois.
Je veux perfectionner ma technique.
On logera dans un hôtel.
On prendra la demi-pension.
On y passera une semaine.
On aura deux heures de cours par jour.
le canoë-kayak
le cyclisme/le vélo
le parapente
le ski
le ski nautique
le snowboard
le surf
le VTT
le vol libre
la boxe
la pêche
la planche à voile
la plongée
la randonnée
la voile
l'alpinisme (m)
l'équitation (f)
l'escalade (f)

Resources

CD4, tracks 6–7
Cahier d'exercices, page 72
Grammaire 3.9

Starter 1

Aim
To revise language for sporting holidays. To use strategies to work out new vocabulary.

Write up the following in two columns, jumbling the order of the second column. Ask students to match the French and English versions.

faire ...	to go/do ...
des balades en quad	quad biking
du tir à l'arc	archery
de l'équitation	horseriding
du saut à l'élastique	bungee jumping
des randonnées avec des ânes	hiking by donkey
de la montgolfière	hot-air ballooning
du VTT	mountain biking
de la plongée extrême	high diving

When checking answers, ask students how they managed to work them out.

1 Écoutez et lisez cette publicité, puis trouvez l'équivalent en français des phrases en dessous.

Listening. Students listen to two advertisements for sporting holidays and read the text at the same time. Then they find in the texts the French for the 12 English expressions listed.

When students have done the exercise, read through the tip box on false friends and ask the students to do the activity there. You could suggest that students keep a note of any false friends they come across in a separate section of their vocabulary lists/notebooks.

Audioscript 6

– *Vous rêvez de connaître un jour cette sensation de liberté ou alors vous savez déjà surfer et vous voulez perfectionner votre «cut back»?*
Débutant(e) ou confirmé(e), nous vous proposons ce stage comprenant deux heures de cours de surf intenses par jour avec nos deux écoles de surf partenaires labellisées par la Fédération Française de Surf.
Louez une planche de surf, nous avons du matos sur place: shortboards, mini mailbus, longboards, combis rip curl à des tarifs préférentiels. Louez un vélo à l'AJ pour vous rendre sur les spots de surf.
Prix en demi-pension en camping à partir de 299€.

– *Vous vous réveillez chaque matin avec une folle envie d'ouvrir votre fenêtre et de battre frénétiquement des bras? Vous devez souffrir d'une grosse frustration au vol libre! Votre place est ici, à l'Auberge new-look d'Aix-en-Savoie. Amoureux de la nature, indiscutablement sportif, préparez-vous à passer 5 jours de rêve, entre 900m et 1500m au-dessus du grand lac naturel de France: le lac du Bourget. Désormais, il ne tient qu'à vous que votre rêve devienne réalité. Le directeur technique, 22 années de pédagogique du vol libre et pilote chevronné, a pour objectifs prioritaires: la sécurité, la rigueur dans la technique et la formation de pilote. Prix en pension complète à partir de 545€.*

Answers

1 sensation de liberté
2 vous savez déjà surfer
3 perfectionner
4 débutant(e) ou confirmé(e)
5 nous vous proposons
6 demi-pension
7 vol libre
8 lac
9 votre rêve
10 sécurité
11 la formation de pilote
12 pension complète

Expo-langue: the future tense

Use this grammar box to remind students that the future tense is used to talk about definite plans. You may want to take the opportunity also to review how the tense is formed in detail (it is also practised in Starter 2). There is more information on p. 214 of the Student Book.

2 Lisez. On parle du stage A ou B ou tous les deux?

Reading. Students read the 10 speech bubbles and decide whether each refers to holiday A or holiday B in exercise 1, or both.

Answers

1 A **2** A **3** A **4** B **5** B **6** tous les deux **7** A **8** tous les deux **9** B **10** B

+ In pairs: student choose one of the holidays (A or B) and come up with a list of reasons to recommend it to a friend.

Starter 2

Aim

To revise the future tense.

Ask students working in pairs to come up with five sentences, each featuring one of the following verbs in the future.

aller, faire, être, avoir, apprendre

3 Écoutez le dialogue et trouvez les mots qui manquent.

Listening. Students read the gap-fill dialogue and identify the 10 missing words. The words are supplied in random order.

Audioscript 7

- *Alors, qu'est-ce que tu feras pendant les grandes vacances?*
- *J'**irai** en Normandie avec une copine.*
- *Qu'est-ce que vous ferez là-bas?*
- *On fera un stage de **voile**.*
- *Ah, bon? Tu as déjà fait de la voile?*
- *Oui, j'en ai fait deux ou trois fois, mais je veux perfectionner ma technique.*
- *Et ta copine, elle en a **déjà** fait?*
- *Non, c'est sa **première** fois. Elle est débutante.*
- *Vous logerez où?*
- *On **logera** dans une auberge de jeunesse. On prendra la **demi-pension**.*
- *Vous y passerez combien de temps?*
- *On y **passera** une semaine et on aura deux heures de cours par jour.*
- *Et qu'est-ce que vous **ferez** le reste du temps?*
- *Bof, on **fera** des randonnées. Et moi, je ferai peut-être de l'**équitation** aussi.*
- *Ce sera chouette! Alors, amusez-vous bien, toutes les deux!*

Answers

Also in bold in the audioscript.

1 irai **2** voile **3** déjà **4** première **5** logera **6** demi-pension **7** passera **8** ferez **9** fera **10** équitation

4 À deux. Adaptez le dialogue de l'exercice 3 en changeant les phrases soulignées. Utilisez les détails ci-dessous ou vos propres idées.

Speaking. In pairs: students adapt the dialogue in exercise 3, changing the underlined phrases. They should take it in turn to play each role. They can either use the prompts supplied or their own ideas. A box of useful language is also supplied for support.

5 Écrivez un e-mail à votre copain Karim sur un stage sportif que vous ferez.

Writing. Students write an e-mail to a French friend, Karim, about a sporting holiday they are going to go on. They should use the list of points supplied as a structure.

Plenary

Put students into teams and get them to list as many of the sports which came up in this unit as they can. Ask for totals and get the team with the longest list to read it out, and then have the rest of the class give further suggestions.

Then ask the class to give you some sentences using these sports and the verb **faire** in the future tense, covering each subject pronoun in turn.

Cahier d'exercices, page 72

1

Answers

Underlined in blue: Chamonix
Underlined in black: Du 2 juillet au 19 août, 7 jours. À partir de 430€.
Underlined in red: badminton, volley-ball, basket, stretching, mini-foot, tennis de table; canyoning, l'escalade, les randonnées, descente en raft + piscine; VTT.
Underlined in green: Dimanche: Accueil de 9 à 12h. Fin de stage à 14h.

2

Answers

1. Je ferai un stage multi-montagne à Chamonix.
2. Ça s'est passé à Chamonix, dans un centre au pied du Mont-Blanc.
3. Ça coûtera à partir de 430€.
4. Je ferai du canyoning, de l'escalade, des randonnées, de la descente en raft, de la natation et du VTT.
5. Pupil's own answers
6. J'y passerai une semaine.
7. La première journée, il y aura une réunion d'information et puis je ferai une petit randonnée.
8. Pupil's own answers.
9. Le soir, je pourrai jouer au badminton, au volley, au mini-foot; au tennis de table, jouer aux grands jeux, surfer sur Internet ou danser!
10. Je partirai le samedi à 14h.

3 J'étais comme ça

(Student Book pages 134–135)

Main topics and objectives

- Saying how things used to be
- More practice with the imperfect tense

Grammar

- The imperfect

Key language

Il y a dix ans ...
j'allais à l'école primaire
j'avais les cheveux courts
j'étais mignon(ne)
je portais toujours un jean
je ne faisais pas d'exercice
je jouais de la guitare
j'achetais
je buvais
je fumais
j'habitais
je mangeais
je sortais
je travaillais
je voyageais

Resources

CD4, tracks 8–9
Cahier d'exercices, page 73
Grammaire 3.4

Starter 1

Aim
To use strategies to work out new language. To practise listening skills.

Write up the following.

J'étais ...
a réalisateur de films
b mannequin de mode
c chanteur punk
d comédien
e première danseuse

Tell students you are going to read out statements from each of these people: they need to identify the correct person for each statement.

1 J'étais très mince. Je portais des vêtements de haute couture.
2 Je m'appelais Johnny Plastique. J'avais les cheveux teints en rose.
3 J'étais riche. J'habitais à Hollywood.
4 J'étais très en forme parce que je pratiquais tous les jours.
5 Je jouais un des rôles principaux dans une série de télévision.

1 Écoutez et lisez. Mettez les personnages dans le bon ordre.

Listening. Students listen to the description of the reality TV show *Le bateau célébrités* and read the speech bubbles **a–e**. They use the information in the speech bubbles to put the five people in the order they are mentioned on the recording.

Audioscript 8

– *Bienvenue à bord du bateau célébrités, la nouvelle émission de télé-réalité! La formule, c'est très simple: un bateau de luxe et cinq célébrités. Chaque semaine, vous, les téléspectateurs, devez éliminer une personne. Rencontrons maintenant les participants!*

– *À la fin des années 70, je m'appelais Johnny Plastique. J'étais chanteur punk et j'avais les cheveux teints en rose. Je fumais et je buvais trop. J'étais un peu fou.*

– *Pendant les années 60, je travaillais comme mannequin de mode. J'étais très mince. Je portais des vêtements de haute couture et je voyageais partout dans le monde.*

– *Il y a dix ans, j'étais footballeur professionnel. J'étais très en forme parce que je faisais de la natation tous les jours et j'allais souvent à la gym.*

– *En 1995, j'étais actrice et je jouais un des rôles principaux dans une série de télévision. J'étais très mignonne. J'avais les cheveux longs et noirs. Et je sortais avec un acteur très connu.*

– *Quand j'avais trente ans, j'habitais à Hollywood. J'étais réalisateur de films. J'étais riche. Je mangeais dans les meilleurs restaurants et je buvais du champagne.*

Answers
e, d, a, b, c

Expo-langue: the imperfect tense

Use this grammar box to remind students that one of the uses of the imperfect tense is to say 'used to'. There is more information on p. 213 of the Student Book.

2 Relisez les textes et écrivez un résumé des cinq célébrités en anglais.

Reading. Students reread the texts in exercise 1 and write a summary of the five celebrities in English.

Answers

***Arnaud Dupré** used to be a professional footballer. He used to be very fit because* he used to swim every day and often went to the gym.

Juliette Perrault was an actress in 1995 and played one of the principal roles in a television series/soap opera. She used to be very cute. She had long black hair. And she used to go out with a very well-known actor.

Patrick DeLasalle used to live in Hollywood, when he was 30. He was a film director. He was rich. He used to eat in the best restaurants and drink champagne.

Minou used to work as a fashion model during the 60s. She was very thin. She used to wear designer clothes and travel throughout the world.

Johnny Girot was called Johnny Plastique at the end of the 70s. He was a punk singer and had dyed pink hair. He used to smoke and drink too much. He was a bit crazy.

Endings in the imperfect tense. Read through this together before students do exercise 3. Give students the opportunity to say some of the verbs in exercise 1 aloud to practise their pronunciation.

3 À deux. Interviewez une des célébrités ci-dessus. Utilisez ces questions.

Speaking. In pairs: students interview their partner, who pretends to be one of the celebrities in exercise 1. They then swap roles. The questions are supplied.

Starter 2

Aim

To practise using the imperfect tense.

Working in pairs, students take it in turn to prompt and to respond. The first student makes a statement about one of the characters from exercise 1 (on p. 134) (e.g. **J'étais très mignonne.**). The second student has to say who it is (e.g. **Juliette Perrault**).

4 Écoutez les interviews avec Marianne et Jean-Luc. Copiez et complétez la grille pour chaque personne. (1–2)

Listening. Students copy out the grid twice. They listen to Marianne and Jean-Luc being interviewed and fill in the details in the grid.

☑ Draw students' attention to the tip box on tackling complex texts before playing the recording: it emphasises the need to listen for key words and phrases. This is a key listening skill and one that will be tested in the exam.

Audioscript 9

1 *– Marianne, votre vie, comment est-elle différente de ce qu'elle était il y a 10 ans?*
– Eh bien, une grande différence, c'est le travail! Je suis actuellement professeur de langues dans un lycée, tandis qu'il y a dix ans, j'étais toujours étudiante à l'université.
– Et votre mode de vie a-t-il beaucoup changé?
– C'est-à-dire que je suis un peu plus riche qu'avant! Quand j'étais étudiante, je n'avais pas beaucoup d'argent, mais maintenant, ça va. Donc, il y a dix ans, je ne sortais pas souvent, mais maintenant, je vais au cinéma ou au restaurant une fois ou deux par semaine. Et je m'achète des vêtements aussi. À l'université, je portais toujours un jean et un tee-shirt parce que je n'avais pas beaucoup de vêtements.
– Et si ce n'est pas indiscret, avez-vous beaucoup changé physiquement?
– Malheureusement, oui! Il y a dix ans, j'étais assez mince, mais aujourd'hui, j'ai quelques kilos de trop. J'ai changé de coupe de cheveux aussi. Avant, j'avais les cheveux très longs et noirs. Maintenant, j'ai les cheveux assez courts parce que c'est plus pratique.
– Bon, merci beaucoup.

2 *– Et vous, Jean-Luc? Votre vie, est-elle différente d'il y a dix ans?*
– Ah, oui! Très différente! Il y a dix ans, je jouais de la guitare dans un groupe de rock. Mais .... euh, voilà .... on n'a pas eu beaucoup de succès, donc j'ai dû trouver un autre travail. Maintenant, je travaille dans une banque. C'est moins intéressant, mais c'est mieux payé.
– D'autres choses ont changé aussi?
– Oui. Je me suis marié! Il y a dix ans, j'étais célibataire. Je sortais avec beaucoup de filles. Maintenant, je suis marié et j'ai deux enfants, donc je dois être plus sérieux, plus responsable. Je fais plus d'exercice aussi. Il y a dix ans, je fumais et je ne mangeais pas bien. Aujourd'hui, je ne fume plus, je vais à la gym trois fois par semaine et je mange sain.
– Finalement, avez-vous changé physiquement?
– Le plus grand changement, c'est les cheveux! Quand j'étais guitariste, j'étais jeune, je voulais être cool, quoi. J'avais les cheveux teints en blond. Mais pas plus, comme vous le voyez. Et maintenant, je porte des vêtements un peu moins extravagants. Mais je suis assez content de ma vie.
– Merci beaucoup, Jean-Luc. Au revoir.

Answers

Marianne	actuellement	il y a 10 ans
profession	*professeur de langues*	*étudiante*
mode de vie (travail/argent/loisirs/vêtements/état civil)	– plus riche – va au cinéma et au restaurant/sort plus souvent – achète des vêtements	– pas beaucoup d'argent – ne sortait pas souvent – portait toujours les mêmes choses/n'avait pas beaucoup de vêtements
aspect physique (taille/cheveux/forme)	– est moins mince/a quelques kilos de trop – a les cheveux assez courts	– était mince – avait les cheveux très longues

Jean-Luc	actuellement	il y a 10 ans
profession	– travaille dans une banque	– jouait de la guitare dans un groupe de rock
mode de vie (travail/argent/loisirs/vêtements/état civil)	– travail mieux payé – marié, a deux enfants – ne fume plus et mange sain; va à la gym – porte des vêtements un peu moins extravagants	– travail pas bien payé – célibataire – fumait et ne mangeait pas bien
aspect physique (taille/cheveux/forme)	n'a plus les cheveux teints en blond	avait les cheveux teints en blond

5 Lisez et complétez le texte.

Reading. Students read the gap-fill text and identify the missing words. The words are supplied in random order.

Answers

1 étudiante **2** professeur de langues **3** argent **4** sortait **5** portait **6** riche **7** achète **8** mince **9** avait **10** courts

6 Écrivez un paragraphe sur Jean-Luc.

Writing. Students use the information in exercise 4 to write a text about Jean-Luc, along the lines of the one on Marianne in exercise 5.

7 Vidéoconférence. Interviewez votre partenaire.

Speaking. Students imagine that they are going to have a videoconference with students at a French school. They interview their partner about how his/her life used to be ten years ago. Some sample openings are supplied for support.

+ Get a few pairs to do their videoconference in front of the class. If possible, record it on video and play it back, inviting constructive comment from the class.

8 Votre vie, comment est-elle différente d'il y a dix ans? Écrivez un paragraphe.

Writing. Students write a paragraph on their own life, saying how it was different 10 years ago.

Plenary

Play a chain game round the class. Each student repeats the chain so far and adds an item of their own using the imperfect tense (**j'étais, je portais, je faisais**, etc.). If they make a mistake, miss something out or can't add an item, they are out. Start it off. **Quand j'étais petit(e), j'avais les cheveux blonds.**

Cahier d'exercices, page 73

1

Answers

1 20s **2** 60s **3** 20s **4** 60s **5** 20s **6** 90s **7** 60s **8** 20s **9** 90s **10** 90s

2

Answers

20s: women had few rights; most girls finished their education after primary school; most women stayed at home; men were paid twice the amount for the same job; men did hardly anything in the house

60s: girls could go to university; women for the first time did not have to choose between an interesting job or looking after their family; women could take the pill; things changed but men still managed the factories and offices

90s: first time France had woman prime minister and an astronaut in space; men looked after children and the house more and more; women had the right to do nearly all jobs, e.g. pilots, police commissioners, and firemen

3

Answers

Pupil's own answers

4 Toujours le sport!

(Student Book pages 136–137)

Main topics and objectives

- Describing a sporting event
- Using the pluperfect tense

Grammar

- The pluperfect tense

Key language

le but
le/la buteur/euse
le/la capitaine
le/la champion(ne)
le championnat
le concours
la Coupe du Monde
le/la coureur/euse
la course
l'équipe (f)
l'essai (m)
l'étape (f)
la finale
les Jeux Olympiques (m)
le/la joueur/euse
la ligue
la médaille (d'or)
le/la meilleur(e)
le/la perdant(e)
le/la pilote
le/la supporter/trice (de)
le terrain (de rugby)
le tournoi
le/la vainqueur
contre

Il/Elle a fini en (deuxième) place.
Il/Elle a marqué (un but).
Il/Elle a réussi (à) ...
On a gagné/perdu.
J'étais fier/fière de ...
C'était un match plein de suspense.
La course était passionnante.
J'étais très déçu du résultat.

Resources

CD4, tracks 10–11
Cahier d'exercices, page 74
Grammaire 3.7

Starter 1

Aim
To revise language for talking about sports. To use strategies to work out new language.

Write up the following. Give students three minutes working in pairs to translate the phrases in each group into English and to identify the three sports they refer to.

1 **mon équipe préférée – le dernier match – il a marqué un essai**
2 **l'étape final – un coureur américain – le maillot jaune**
3 **je suis fière d'être supportrice de Betis – on est sorti vainqueur – notre superbe buteur a marqué deux buts**

1 Lisez et trouvez les deux parties de chaque texte.

Reading. Students match each of the four texts from Jamel, Mélissa, Arthur and Danielle with its correct ending (**a–d**).

Answers

For reference only: students check their own answers using the recording in exercise 2.
Jamel d, **Mélissa** a, **Arthur** b, **Danielle** c

2 Écoutez et vérifiez.

Listening. Students listen and check their answers to exercise 1.

Audioscript 10

1 *Ma passion, c'est le rugby et je suis toulousain, donc il va sans dire que mon équipe préférée, c'est Toulouse! J'ai regardé notre dernier match, contre Narbonne, à la télé. On a gagné 64–22, malgré l'absence d'un de nos meilleurs joueurs, Frédéric Michalak, qui a dû quitter le terrain après trente minutes, à cause d'une cheville blessée. Mais il avait déjà marqué un essai fantastique. J'étais fier de lui.*

2 *Je suis fan de cyclisme et j'ai regardé l'étape finale du Tour de France sur mon portable. Malheureusement, le Français Christophe Moreau n'a terminé qu'à la onzième place. C'est dommage parce qu'il avait gagné l'étape du prologue à Dunkerque. C'est un coureur américain, Lance Armstrong, qui a gagné la course (pour la septième fois!) et qui portait le maillot jaune.*

3 *Je suis accro au skate et une fois, j'ai eu la chance d'assister à la Coupe du Monde de Skate à Marseille. J'étais allé en vacances à Marseille avec mes parents et ils m'avaient donné la permission d'aller voir le championnat de skate. Les meilleurs du monde y participaient, y compris les Français Alex Coccini et Alex Giraud. Coccini a terminé à la deuxième place, mais c'est Omar Hassan, des États-Unis, qui a gagné. C'est le roi des skateurs!*

4 *J'adore le foot et je suis fière d'être supportrice de PSG (c'est-à-dire Paris Saint-Germain). Je vais souvent les voir au stade du Parc des Princes à Paris parce que c'est pas loin de chez moi. Le dernier match que j'ai vu était contre Strasbourg. On avait perdu le match d'avant (contre Nice), donc il était important de gagner celui-ci. Heureusement, on est sortis vainqueurs, grâce à notre superbe buteur Bonaventure Kalou. On a gagné 1–0 et maintenant, on est deuxième en Ligue 1!*

Expo-langue: the pluperfect tense

Use this grammar box to introduce the pluperfect tense. Point out that using this tense is a good way of working in interesting additional detail in their own writing. There is more information on p. 213 of the Student Book.

R Ask students to identify and translate the pluperfect forms in the four texts in exercise 1.

3 Répondez aux questions en anglais.

Reading. Students reread the texts and answer the 12 comprehension questions in English.

Answers

1 because he's from Toulouse
2 Frédéric Michalak
3 he had to go off after 30 minutes
4 on her mobile
5 11th
6 Lance Armstrong
7 he was in Marseilles on holiday when it was on
8 Omar Hassan
9 the USA
10 Parc des Princes Stadium
11 they had lost the match before (against Nice)
12 Bonaventure Kalou

Students could go on to the French version of a website of a major sporting event in their favourite sport. Ask them either to summarise some of the information there, reporting back to the class with the details of the event, or to find 10 useful words/ expressions in French that they can incorporate into their own writing and speaking on this topic.

Encourage students to look up topics like this on French websites regularly. The familiar context will really help them get to grips with authentic materials. It is also a useful and interesting way to expand their vocabulary.

Starter 2

Aim
To practise forming the pluperfect tense.

Write up the following and ask students to write the verbs in the pluperfect tense.

1 on (perdre)
2 il (être)
3 je (aller)
4 vous (marquer)
5 ils (donner)
6 nous (finir)

4 Qu'est-ce que c'est en anglais?

Reading. Students translate the 10 French expressions from the text into English. Remind them to use the context of the text to work these out.

Answers

1 against
2 score a try
3 proud of
4 to win the race
5 the best in the world
6 the king of
7 to lose the match
8 the winner
9 our scorer
10 the premier league

5 Écoutez et choisissez la bonne phrase pour décrire les sentiments de chaque personne. (1–4)

Listening. Students listen to four people talking about a sporting event and choose the correct description for each one (from **a–d**).

Audioscript 11

1 *C'était un désastre! Nous, on n'a pas marqué de but, mais l'autre équipe en a marqué trois! On a joué très mal et on a perdu le match.*

2 *J'étais très nerveuse en regardant le match. Il était très important pour nous de gagner, mais l'autre équipe jouait bien. Le score était 1–1, mais à la dernière minute, notre buteur a marqué un deuxième but et on a gagné le match!*

3 *Le coureur français était à la deuxième place et l'Américain allait gagner, puis tout d'un coup, il est tombé de son vélo, donc c'est le Français qui a gagné!*

4 *C'est l'Américain qui a gagné le concours de skate, mais les Français ont fait de belles performances. Alex Giraud a fini en deuxième place et Alex Coccini en troisième. Ce sont nos meilleurs skateurs et je suis quand même contente du résultat.*

Answers

1 d **2** b **3** c **4** a

6 Préparez une présentation sur un match ou un autre événement sportif que vous avez vu ou regardé à la télé. Si vous préférez, utilisez les images ci-dessous. Utilisez les phrases de l'exercice 4 et adaptez les textes de l'exercice 1.

Speaking. Students prepare a presentation, either using their own experience of a match or other sporting event that they have been to or have watched on television or using the prompts supplied. They should use the phrases in exercise 4 and the texts in exercise 1 as models.

+ Bring in or print off the report of a few major sports events from the sports pages of a French newspaper such as *Le Figaro*. Ask students to discuss it in pairs, taking it in turn to ask and answer questions on who was competing, what happened, etc.

7 Écrivez un paragraphe sur un événement sportif, réel ou imaginaire.

Writing. Students write a paragraph about a sporting event (real or imaginary). They should use the points supplied to structure their texts. Encourage them to work the pluperfect tense into their account.

Plenary

Ask students to summarise how the pluperfect is formed. Construct paradigms for **faire** and **aller** on the board, with a different student contributing each person.

Then get the class to come up with some examples of sentences featuring the pluperfect and the language of the unit.

Cahier d'exercices, page 74

1

Answers

1 Safin a gagné en 4 sets.
2 Le match s'est passé à Melbourne en Australie.
3 Il y avait 15.000 spectateurs.
4 Hewitt a perdu le match.

2

Answers

1 après quatre ans et demi d'attente
2 il avait été battu deux fois en finale
3 il a commis beaucoup de fautes
4 grâce à … sa supériorité au service
5 tentait de devenir le premier Australien à remporter
6 Il mérite sa victoire

3

Answers

Pupil's own answers

5 Qui admirez-vous?

(Student Book pages 138–139)

Main topics and objectives

- Describing someone's qualities
- Using abstract nouns

Key language

Ce que j'aime/je n'aime pas, c'est ...
l'ambition (f)
l'arrogance (f)
la détermination
l'égoïsme (m)
l'entêtement (m)
la fierté
la générosité
la gentillesse
l'honnêteté (m)
l'intelligence (f)
la jalousie
la modestie
la paresse
le sens de l'humeur
la sincérité
le talent
doué(e)

Resources

CD4, track 12
Cahier d'exercices, pages 75–76

Starter 1

Aim
To revise adjective agreement. To predict feminine and plural forms of new adjectives.

Write up the following grid and ask students to fill it in. Tell them not to worry about the meanings of the words. They should concentrate on using what they know to predict the feminine and plural forms.

singular		plural	
masculine	feminine	masculine	feminine
ambitieux			
determiné			
égoïste			
gentil			
honnête			
jaloux			
rigolo			
têtu			

1 À votre avis, les adjectifs ci-dessous sont positifs (P), négatifs (N) ou positifs-négatifs (P/N)? Faites trois listes et notez l'anglais. Cherchez dans un dictionnaire, si nécessaire.

Reading. Students read through the 16 adjectives listed and sort them into three columns: positive, negative and those that could be used both positively and negatively. They can use a dictionary, if necessary.

Answers

P: déterminé(e) – *determined*, généreux/euse – *generous*, gentil(le) – *kind*, honnête – *honest*, intelligent(e) – *intelligent*, modeste – *modest*, rigolo(te) – *funny*, sincère – *sincere*, talentueux/euse – *talented*

N: arrogant(e) – *arrogant*, égoïste – *selfish*, jaloux/ouse – *jealous*, paresseux/euse – *lazy*, têtu(e) – *stubborn*

P/N: ambitieux/euse – *ambitious*, fier/fière – *proud*

2 On décrit son meilleur copain ou sa meilleure copine. Écoutez et notez la lettre des adjectifs de l'exercice 1. (1–4)

Listening. Students listen to four people describing their best friend and note for each the adjectives they use, from **a–p** in exercise 1.

Audioscript 12

1 *Ma meilleure copine s'appelle Natacha. Elle est toujours gentille et sincère. À mon avis, la gentillesse et la sincérité sont les qualités les plus importantes d'une bonne copine. Natacha est très intelligente aussi, mais elle n'est jamais arrogante. Son seul défaut, c'est qu'elle est parfois un peu têtue, mais ça va.*

2 *Mon meilleur copain, Raphaël, est très généreux. Par exemple, à Noël, il a acheté des cadeaux pour moi et pour toute ma famille. Au collège, il peut être un peu paresseux, mais c'est un joueur de rugby talentueux et déterminé. Il est ambitieux aussi – il veut être joueur de rugby professionnel. À mon avis, l'ambition, c'est une bonne chose, surtout quand on a du talent.*

3 *Pour moi, l'honnêteté est quelque chose de très important et ma meilleure copine, Lydie, est quelqu'un de très honnête. Elle ne cache rien et me dit toujours la vérité. Par contre, elle peut être un peu jalouse de moi et la jalousie, c'est quelque chose que je n'aime pas. Lydie est aussi une superbe joueuse de tennis, mais elle est modeste et elle dit toujours qu'elle ne joue pas très bien.*

4 *Je crois qu'il est important d'avoir un bon sens de l'humeur et mon meilleur copain, Afram, me fait beaucoup rire. Il est très rigolo. Son défaut, c'est qu'il est quelquefois un peu égoïste: il veut seulement faire ce qu'il veut faire, quoi. Mais ce que j'aime chez lui aussi, c'est sa fierté. Sa famille vient de Tunisie et il est très fier de ses origines tunisiennes.*

Answers

1 g, n, i, b, p
2 f, l, o, c, a
3 h, j, o, k
4 m, d, e

3 Trouvez le bon adjectif pour chaque nom en dessous et copiez les paires. Puis notez l'anglais pour chaque mot.

Reading. Students find the adjective (from **a–p** in exercise 1) which is related to each of the nouns listed, and copy out each pair with a translation.

Answers

la jalousie – *jealousy*; jaloux/ouse – *jealous*
la détermination – *determination*; déterminé(e) – *determined*
l'égoïsme – *selfishness*; égoïste – *selfish*
la sincérité – *sincerity*; sincère – *sincere*
la générosité – *generosity*; généreux/euse – *generous*
l'entêtement – *stubbornness*; têtu(e) – *stubborn*
la fierté – *pride*; fier/fière – *proud*
le talent – *talent*; talentueux/euse – *talented*
l'ambition – *ambition*; ambitieux/euse – *ambitious*
la gentillesse – *kindness*; gentil(le) – *kind*
l'honnêteté – *honesty*; honnête – *honest*
l'intelligence – *intelligence*; intelligent(e) – *intelligent*
la paresse – *laziness*; paresseux/euse – *lazy*
la modestie – *modesty*; modeste – *modest*
le sens de l'humeur – *sense of humour*; rigolo(te) – *funny*
l'arrogance – *arrogance*; arrogant(e) – *arrogant*

R Students take it in turn to prompt with a quality and to give the corresponding adjective.

4 À deux. Discutez des qualités d'un bon copain/une bonne copine.

Speaking. In pairs: students discuss what the qualities of a good friend are. A framework for the discussion is supplied.

This covers the pronunciation of words which are similar in French and English and the effect of accents.

Starter 2

Aim
To consolidate knowledge of abstract nouns. To practise justifying opinions.

Ask students working in pairs to choose four of the nouns listed in exercise 3. They choose a famous or fictional person to exemplify each of the words, giving a reason for their choice. Give them an example, e.g.

J.K. Rowling – l'intelligence: parce qu'elle écrit des livres très intéressants.

When they have finished, ask some students to read out answers and get the rest of the class to give feedback on whether they agree or not.

5 Écrivez un paragraphe sur les qualités d'un copain ou d'une copine idéale et sur ton meilleur copain/ta meilleure copine.

Writing. Students write a paragraph about the qualities of an ideal friend and about their best friend.

6 Lisez les textes et écrivez V (Vrai), F (Faux) ou PM (Pas Mentionné) à côté de chaque phrase en dessous.

Reading. Students read the three texts. They then read the 10 statements on the text and decide whether each is true or false or not mentioned in the text.

Answers

1 V **2** PM **3** F **4** V **5** V **6** PM **7** F **8** V **9** V **10** PM

7 Qui admirez-vous et pourquoi? Écrivez un paragraphe. Adaptez les textes ci-dessus.

Writing. Students write a paragraph on who they admire and why, using the texts in exercise 6 as models.

Plenary

Play a game to consolidate the abstract noun vocabulary covered in the unit. Prompt with an adjective (e.g. **arrogant**) for a student to respond with the relevant noun (e.g. **l'arrogance**). That student then prompts another student, and so on round the class.

Point out to students the usefulness of listing cognates like those given on this page together in their vocabulary lists and learning them as pairs (e.g. **jaloux/la jalousie**). It makes them easier to remember.

Cahier d'exercices, page 75

1

Answers

adjectif	nom	anglais
déterminé	détermination	*determination*
ambitieux	ambition	ambition
sincère	sincérité	sincerity
candide	candeur	candour
naïve	naïveté	naivety
mélancolique	mélancolie	melancholy
malheureux	malheur	misfortune
talentueux	talent	talent
sensible	sensibilité	sensitivity
émotionnel	émotion	emotion

2

Answers

1 Il a beaucoup de talent.
2 Sa musique est pleine de sincérité et d'émotion.
3 Sa voix est pleine de sensibilité.
4 Il s'est réfugié au Canada.
5 Il a crée un groupe./Il s'est lancé dans une carrière solo.
6 Sa voix est pleine de sincérité.

3

Answers

1 Underlined in blue, eight from: Il a fait; il s'est enfui; sa famille a été; il est arrivé; Il a dit: j'ai … découvert; qu'on m'a aimé; Il s'est réfugié; il s'est lancé; il a accepté
2 Underlined in red, eight from: j'admire; C'est; c'est; on reçoit; j'aime; je reste; se font sentir; on entend; sa voix est ; il chante; c'est
3 Underlined in black, one from: on pouvait; il y avait
4 Underlined in green: il partira

Cahier d'exercices, Grammaire, page 76

1

Answers

1 Après avoir quitté Manchester United, il est allé à Real Madrid.
2 Après avoir gagné, il est parti pour l'Australie.
3 Après être allée au match, elle est rentrée chez elle.
4 Après avoir vu le match de foot, j'ai rencontré les joueurs.
5 Après être parti de France, il est venu en Angleterre.

2

Answers

Ma passion, c'est le foot. Je vais au match tous les week-ends. Je suis supporteur d'Auxerre. Le week-end dernier, j'ai vu un match où Auxerre a gagné contre Monaco. C'était bien parce qu'on avait perdu le match d'avant. Pendant le match Luyindula, un attaquant a dû quitter le terrain à cause d'une jambe blessée, mais il avait déjà marqué un but.
Une fois, l'année dernière, j'étais allé avec mon père (je suis en fauteuil roulant) et une des personnes à la sécurité m'a demandé si je voulais rencontrer les joueurs. Une fois le match fini, je suis allé au bar et les joueurs ont signé dans mon album d'autographes. Supercool!

Contrôle continu: Thierry Henry: le roi des footballeurs! (Student Book pages 140–141)

Topic revised

- Writing about a famous person

1 Copiez les phrases en bleu dans le texte et trouvez l'équivalent en anglais ci-dessous.

Students copy out all the phrases shown in blue in the text and find the English phrase from those listed (**1–12**).

Answers

à part le foot **12** apart from football
de caractère **11** in terms of his character
il a grandi **9** he grew up
quand on a découvert **10** when they discovered
l'a poussé vers **4** pushed him towards
il a vite appris **8** he learned quickly
Il a aussi rapidement montré **3** he also soon showed
attaquant habile et puissant **6** a skilful and powerful striker
il a connu un des plus grands moments de sa carrière **5** he experienced one of the greatest moments of his career
ira-t-il ailleurs? **1** will he go somewhere else?
je lui souhaite de bonne chance **2** I wish him luck
quelqu'un qui mérite son succès **7** someone who deserves his success

2 Répondez aux questions en français.

Students reread the text and answer the 10 comprehension questions in French.

Answers

1 Il est né à Paris le 17 août 1977.
2 Il est français.
3 Il habite à Londres parce qu'il joue pour le club anglais Arsenal.
4 Il a les cheveux noirs et courts et les yeux marron et il mésure 1m88.
5 Ses passe-temps sont le cinéma et la musique./Il s'intéresse au cinéma et à la musique.
6 Il est gentil, modeste, patient et poli et il n'est jamais aggressif.
7 Il devait travailler dur au collège parce que ses parents étaient assez stricts.
8 Il a joué pour Monaco pendant quatre ans.
9 Il a joué pendant la finale de la Coupe du Monde en 1998.
10 Il a fait de la publicité à la télé pour la Renault Clio.

3 Faites le portrait d'une personne célèbre.

Using the text and the **Boîte à outils** section to help them, students write a detailed description of a famous person.

À l'oral (AQA edition)

(Student Book page 183)

Topic revised
- talking about the sports/ sportspeople you like

1 You are talking to your French friend about sport. Your partner will play the part of your French friend and will speak first.

Roleplay. Students practise talking about what sports they are interested in and what sportspeople they like, taking it in turn to ask and answer questions.

☑ The tip box emphasises the importance of reading the detail on the roleplay card very carefully and gives advice on the sort of detail to supply in response.

2 Prepare a ninety-second presentation called *Le sport et moi.*

Presentation. Students prepare a ninety-second presentation on their attitude to and involvement in sport. A sample cue card is supplied for students to refer to when preparing their own prompts.

☑ The tip box suggests a couple of colloquial expressions students could use in the exam.

3 Possible conversation questions

These are key questions to practise for the speaking exam, taken from the module as a whole. Students can practise asking and answering the questions in pairs.

☑ The tip box here focuses on tenses. Students are reminded to listen carefully to the examiner to note which tense he/she uses in each question and also any time markers. They should use these as a guide to the tense they need to use in replying.

À l'oral (Edexcel edition)

(Student Book page 183)

Topics revised

- talking about sport
- talking about a celebrity you like

1 You are planning a trip to a sports centre with your penfriend. Your partner will play the part of your penfriend and will begin the conversation.

Roleplay Type B. Students practise talking about a trip to a sports centre and what sports they like to do, taking it in turn to play themselves/a French penfriend.

2 Presentation and general conversation

Presentation. Students prepare a one-minute presentation on their attitude to and involvement in sport. A sample cue card is supplied for students to use for ideas and refer to when preparing their own prompts.

☑ The tip box suggests a few colloquial expressions students could use in the exam.

Possible conversation questions. These are key questions to practise for the speaking exam, taken from the module as a whole. Students can practise asking and answering the questions in pairs.

☑ The tip box reminds students of the need to think about what material to use in the presentation and what to hold in reserve for the conversation.

À l'oral (OCR edition)

(Student Book page 183)

Topics revised

- talking about sport
- talking about a celebrity you like

1 You are talking to your French friend about sport. Your partner will play the part of your French friend and will speak first.

Roleplay Type 2. Students practise talking about what sports they do and a sport they would like to do, taking it in turn to ask and answer questions.

2 Prepare a one-minute presentation called *Le sport et moi.*

Presentation. Students prepare a one-minute presentation on their attitude to and involvement in sport. A sample cue card is supplied for students to refer to when preparing their own prompts.

3 *Le sport:* possible conversation questions

These are key questions to practise for the speaking exam, taken from the module as a whole. Students can practise asking and answering the questions in pairs.

☑ The tip box here focuses on tenses. Students are reminded to listen carefully to the examiner to note which tense he/she uses in each question and also any time markers. They should use these as a guide to the tense they need to use in replying.

À toi

(Student Book pages 200–201)

- Self-access reading and writing

1 Lisez le texte, puis copiez et complétez les phrases en dessous.

Reading. Students read the text, then copy and complete the six sentences on it.

Answers

1 *À part le foot, Zinédine Zidane se passionne pour* le tennis.
2 *Pendant les vacances, il aime jouer* au tennis/à ce jeu individual.
3 *Quand il y a de grandes compétitions, il les regarde* à la télévision.
4 *Quand il arrêtera le football, il jouera* au tennis pour rester en forme.
5 *Un jour, s'il devient bon, il dit qu'il fera peut-être* quelques compétitions.
6 *Les gestes au tennis sont aussi techniques que les gestes au* foot.

2 Lisez le texte et choisissez les bonnes réponses, a, b ou c.

Reading. Students read the text. They then read the five sentences and choose the correct ending for each from the three options given (**a**, **b** or **c**).

Answers

1 c **2** a **3** a **4** c **5** b

3 Regardez ces articles de journaux. Pour chaque article, trouvez le gros bon titre.

Reading. Students read the five newspaper articles (**1–5**) and for each identify the correct headline (**a–e**).

Answers

1 c **2** a **3** e **4** d **5** b

4 Complétez ces phrases en choisissant les bons mots dans la case.

Reading. Students complete the five gap-fill sentences using the words supplied.

Answers

1 Amélie Mauresmo a **perdu** son match **contre** Ana Ivanovic.
2 Le pilote **espagnol** a gagné 36 points pour **l'équipe** Renault.
3 Michalak et Clerc ont **marqué** des essais et Toulouse a **gagné** le match.
4 Dans les **lycées** aux sections sportives, on doit **travailler** très dur.
5 **L'athlète** français Leslie Djhone **espère** participer aux Jeux Olympiques de 2012.

5 Regardez la publicité ci-dessous. Vous êtes allé(e) à ce festival. Écrivez un paragraphe.

Writing. Students imagine they went to the extreme sports festival which is advertised here, and write a paragraph about their experience. They should use the points listed to structure their text.

Module 9 Mode de vie (Student Book pages 144–159)

Unit	Main topics and objectives	Grammar
Déjà vu 1 **Ce qu'on mange et ce qu'on boit** (pp. 144–145)	Talking about food and drink **en** (of it/of them)	The pronoun **en**
Déjà vu 2 **Mon corps et moi** (pp. 146–147)	Parts of the body and saying where it hurts Expressions with **avoir**	Expressions with **avoir** **à** + the definite article
1 Ça ne va pas (pp. 148–149)	Talking about what is wrong with you Impersonal verbs	Impersonal constructions
2 Garder la forme (pp. 150–151)	Talking about a healthy lifestyle Adverbs	Adverbs
3 La dépendance (pp. 152–153)	Discussing addiction and other problems Giving your opinion	
4 Veux-tu te marier? (pp. 154–155)	Talking about family relationships More practice giving opinions	
Contrôle continu **La forme** (pp. 156–157)	*Coursework* Writing about your previous and current lifestyles	*All main grammar points of the module*
À l'oral (p. 184)	*Exam speaking practice* Talking about the healthiness of your lifestyle Visiting a chemist Talking about smoking Talking about marriage	*All main grammar points of the module*
À toi (pp. 202–203)	Self-access reading and writing	

Déjà vu 1: Ce qu'on mange et ce qu'on boit (Student Book pages 144–145)

Main topics and objectives
- Talking about food and drink
- **en** (of it/of them)

Grammar
- The pronoun **en**

Key language
Parts of the body

Resources
CD4, track 13
Cahier d'exercices, page 79
Grammaire 1.13

Starter 1

Aim
To revise the partitive. To revise vocabulary for food and drink.

Write up the following. Ask students to copy the grid and complete it by putting each of the items of food and drink in the correct column.

du	de la	de l'	des

céréales, chocolat chaud, eau, frites, fromage, jambon, jus d'orange, lait, légumes, pain, pain grillé, pâtes, pâté, pizza, poisson, poulet, soupe, salade

1 Écoutez Nicolas et Amélie. Que mangent-ils et que boivent-ils d'habitude? Copiez et remplissez la grille. (1–2)

Listening. Students copy out the grid. They listen to Nicolas and Amélie answering questions for a survey on what they usually eat and drink and fill in the details in the grid, choosing from the items listed.

Audioscript 13

- *On fait un sondage pour un magazine. Que manges-tu et que bois-tu pour le petit déjeuner, Nicolas?*
- *Pour le petit déjeuner, je mange des céréales avec du lait et puis, une tartine de pain avec du Nutella.*
- *Bois-tu du chocolat chaud?*
- *Non, je n'en bois pas. Je bois du jus d'orange.*
- *Où manges-tu à midi?*
- *Je mange à la cantine.*
- *Que manges-tu, par exemple?*
- *D'habitude, il y a de la salade verte, un steak haché et des pâtes et une mousse au chocolat comme dessert. Et je bois de l'eau.*
- *Manges-tu du poisson s'il y en a sur le menu?*
- *Non, je n'en mange pas.*
- *Et tu manges un goûter?*
- *Oui, pour le goûter, je mange un biscuit ou un gâteau.*
- *Et le soir, pour le dîner?*
- *Chez nous pour le dîner, il y a de la soupe, … , de la salade, du pain, … du jambon, … du fromage et un yaourt.*
- *Et qu'est-ce que tu bois?*
- *Je bois du chocolat chaud.*
- *Dis-moi, tu ne manges pas de pizza?*
- *Si j'en mange, mais pas d'habitude. C'est plutôt en vacances en Italie qu'on en mange.*

- *Amélie, manges-tu des céréales pour le petit déj?*
- *Non, je n'en mange pas. Je n'aime pas. Je préfère une tartine beurrée et un yaourt et je bois du chocolat chaud.*
- *Et à midi, tu manges à la cantine?*
- *Non, à midi, je rentre à la maison et je mange des pâtes et du fromage et je bois du jus d'orange.*
- *Tu ne prends pas de goûter?*
- *Si, j'en prends. Je mange une pomme et je bois du yaourt liquide.*
- *Et pour le dîner?*
- *Ça dépend, mais d'habitude, c'est de la salade, du jambon, des frites ou de la pizza et un fruit.*
- *Tu ne manges pas de poisson?*
- *Non, je n'en mange pas. Je n'aime pas.*
- *Merci.*

Answers

	petit déjeuner	à midi	goûter	dîner
Nicolas	des céréales avec du lait, une tartine avec du Nutella, du jus d'orange	de la salade verte, un steak haché et des pâtes, une mousse au chocolat, de l'eau	un biscuit ou un gâteau	de la soupe, de la salade, du pain, du jambon, du fromage, un yaourt, du chocolat chaud
Amélie	une tartine (beurrée), un yaourt, du chocolat chaud	des pâtes, du fromage, du jus d'orange	une pomme, du yaourt liquide	de la salade, du jambon, des frites, de la pizza, un fruit

2 Une journée scolaire. Choisissez ✓ ou ✗. Qu'est-ce qu'il mange et qu'est-ce qu'il ne mange pas?

Reading. Students read the text and then decide for each item of food pictured whether the person writing eats it (indicating by a tick) or doesn't eat it (indicating by a cross).

Answers
a ✓ b ✓ c ✗ d ✓ e ✗ f ✓ g ✗ h ✓ i ✓ j ✓ k ✗ l ✗

Expo-langue: the pronoun *en*

Use this grammar box to remind students of the pronoun **en**, which replaces a quantity with **de**, **du**, **de la**, **de l'** or **des**.

Also read through the tip box on **si**, the word you use for 'yes' when responding to a negative question.

Starter 2

Aim
To revise food and drink vocabulary. To practise using the pronoun **en**.

Working in pairs, students take it in turn to prompt and to respond. The first student prompts with a question beginning **Manges-tu ... ?** and an item of food or drink (e.g. **Manges-tu de la pizza?**) The second responds either **Oui, j'en mange.** or **Non, je n'en mange pas.**

3 À deux. Posez des questions et répondez.

Speaking. In pairs: students take it in turn to ask and answer questions on their eating habits. A framework is supplied for support.

4 Que mangez-vous et buvez-vous d'habitude, une journée scolaire? Écrivez. Trouvez des mots et des expressions dans les exercices ci-dessus pour vous aider.

Writing. Students write two paragraphs on what they usually eat and drink on a school day. Encourage them to use exercises 1–3 to help them. Sentence openings are supplied for support.

5 Lisez et puis faites correspondre les phrases.

Reading. Students read the text and then match the sentence halves (**1–6** and **a–f**).

Answers

1 e **2** d **3** c **4** f **5** b **6** a

6 Vidéoconférence. Préparez une présentation sur ce que vous mangez et buvez d'habitude pendant une journée scolaire.

Speaking. Students imagine that they are going to have a videoconference with students at a French school. They prepare a presentation on what they normally eat and drink on a school day.

Plenary

Ask students to summarise what the pronoun **en** does in a sentence, giving examples of some of the things it can stand for (**du fromage, des légumes,** etc.).

Then write up the following sentences and ask them to replace the nouns with **en**:

Nous boivons du chocolat chaud.
Ils n'achètent pas de gâteaux.
Je ne voudrais pas de salade.

Cahier d'exercices, page 79

1

Answers

Possible answers:

1 *D'habitude,* je mange du toast et je bois du thé pour mon petit déjeuner.
2 *Le matin,* je mange très peu et *le soir,* je prends mon dîner vers 8 heures; généralement, du poisson et de la salade et je bois du vin.
3 *Si je ne suis pas trop pressé(e),* je prends un sandwich pour mon déjeuner et je bois de l'eau.
4 *Quelquefois,* je prends un sandwich, *mais je préfère* une pizza ou une salade.
5 *On fait la grasse matinée* le dimanche alors, je prends le petit déjeuner vers midi; je mange un croissant et je bois un chocolat chaud.
6 *Alors, ça depend;* quelquefois je bois de l'eau ou un jus d'orange et quelquefois je bois du vin.
7 La bière *j'en bois quelquefois, mais en générale,* je bois du whisky!
8 *Mais hier, j'ai mangé* des frites et une pizza!
9 *Alors, demain,* je mangerai une salade et beaucoup de fruits.
10 *Je n'en mange pas, mais* je mange des légumes chaque jour.

2

Answers

Pupil's own answers

Déjà vu 2: Mon corps et moi

(Student Book pages 146–147)

Main topics and objectives
- Parts of the body and saying where it hurts
- Expressions with **avoir**

Grammar
- Expressions with **avoir**
- à + the definite article

Key language
Parts of the body
Ailments

Resources
CD4, tracks 14–15
Cahier d'exercices, page 80
Grammaire 4.1, 4.7

Starter 1

Aim
To revise vocabulary for parts of the body.

Give students three minutes in pairs to list as many parts of the body as they can. Which pair has the longest list?

1 À deux. Trouvez les parties du corps correspondantes.

Speaking. In pairs: students match the eight verbs with the corresponding parts of the body.

Answers
Students will check their own answers using the recording for exercise 2. Answers supplied here for reference only.
1 g **2** e **3** d **4** a **5** c **6** b **7** f **8** h

2 Écoutez et vérifiez vos réponses.

Listening. Students listen to the recording to check their responses to exercise 1.

Audioscript 14

- *Qu'est-ce qu'il faut faire?*
- *Choisir quelle partie du corps on utilise pour faire une action.*
- *Faire quoi?*
- *Marcher, par exemple.*
- *Les pieds?*
- *Non, les jambes.*
- *OK, les jambes.*
- *Et pour toucher?*
- *La main … ou le doigt?*
- *Oui, je dirais les doigts … Et pour regarder?*
- *Ça, c'est facile, les yeux.*
- *Pour sentir une odeur?*
- *Le nez.*
- *Pour digérer?*
- *L'estomac.*
- *Pour écouter?*
- *Les oreilles.*
- *Et pour goûter?*
- *La langue.*
- *Pour manger?*
- *La bouche ou les dents.*
- *La bouche, les dents, c'est pour croquer. C'est tout?*
- *Oui, c'est tout.*

Expo-langue: expressions with *avoir*

Use this grammar box to revise expressions with **avoir** (**avoir froid/chaud/faim/soif**). There is more information on p. 217 of the Student Book.

Expo-langue: *à* + the definite article

Use this grammar box to revise the forms of **à** + the definite article. There is more information on p. 216 of the Student Book.

✚ Ask students to find some other expressions which use **avoir** but are translated with 'to be' in English (e.g. **avoir honte/tort/raison/peur/quinze ans,** etc.).

3 Faites correspondre les phrases et les images.

Reading. Students read the eleven sentences in French and match each to the appropriate picture (**a–k**).

Answers
1 f **2** i **3** a **4** e **5** j **6** b **7** d **8** g **9** h **10** c **11** k

Starter 2

Aim
To practise using the different forms of **à** + the definite article.

Working in pairs, students take it in turn to prompt with a part of the body (e.g. **dos/le dos**) and to respond by saying that part hurts (e.g. **J'ai mal au dos.**).

4 Pourquoi sont-ils absents? Choisissez la bonne image de l'exercice 3 (8).

Listening. Students listen to a teacher taking the register and asking why certain students are absent. They note for each person the appropriate picture from exercise 3 (from **a–k**).

Audioscript 15

- Tout le monde a disparu ou quoi? Arthur est absent. Qu'est-ce qu'il a?
- Il avait mal aux dents hier et il est allé voir le dentiste.
- Et Louise?
- Elle est tombée et elle s'est fait mal à la jambe.
- Et Amélie?
- Elle a été piquée par une guêpe! Elle est allergique aux piqûres d'insectes.
- Jérôme?
- Lui? Il a de la fièvre. Le médecin dit que c'est une grippe.
- Et Hugo?
- Hugo s'est cassé le bras. Il se l'est coincé dans la portière de la voiture.
- Aïe!! Et Valentin? Qu'est-ce qu'il a?
- Il a mal à la tête.
- Il n'est pas tombé?
- Non.
- Et Charline?
- Charline est tombée, elle aussi, et elle s'est fait mal au dos. Elle est allé à l'hôpital.
- Et Boris?
- Il est enrhumé et il tousse tout le temps.
- Et toi alors, Camille?
- Moi? Ça va bien.
- Heureusement.

Answers

Arthur f
Louise h
Amélie c
Jérôme d
Hugo i
Valentin e
Charline a
Boris g, k

5 À deux. Vérifiez vos réponses de l'exercice 4.

Speaking. In pairs: students discuss their answers to exercise 4. A sample exchange is shown.

6 Copiez les articles sur la liste et trouvez les bonnes images.

Reading. Students copy out the list of items shown in the first-aid box and find the correct picture for each (from **a–f**).

Answers

de l'aspirine c
des pastilles antiseptiques b
de la crème antiseptique e
une paire de ciseaux a
des pansements adhésifs f
une solution antiseptique d

7 Imaginez: vous n'avez pas de la chance! Écrivez un paragraphe ...

Writing. Students imagine they are being very unlucky and write a paragraph on all the mishaps/illnesses that have befallen/are about to befall them, using the prompts supplied.

Plenary

Ask the class to summarise the forms of **à** + the definite article and when each is used.

Then play a miming game to consolidate this language. A student mimes an ailment for the class (e.g. touches his/her arm and groans). A second student responds by identifying the ailment (e.g. **Il/Elle a mal au bras.**). If correct, he/she now gets the chance to mime to the class.

You could set the class the challenge of correctly identifying 10 ailments within an allotted time.

Cahier d'exercices, page 80

See unit 1 for answers.

1 Ça ne va pas

(Student Book pages 148–149)

Main topics and objectives

- Talking about what is wrong with you
- Impersonal verbs

Grammar

- Impersonal constructions

Key language

Si vous avez (mal à la tête), ...
Il faut ...
prendre de l'aspirine/des comprimés
sucer un pastille antiseptique
mettre de la crème antiseptique
un pansement
des pansements adhésifs
un paire de ciseaux
une solution antiseptique
Je dois ...
rester à la maison/au lit
boire beaucoup d'eau
me reposer
Il m'a fait une ordonnance.
Il faut prendre le médicament toutes les deux heures.
Il faut/Il a fallu ...
aller à l'hôpital pour faire une radio/un examen
Il vaut mieux prendre ...
un rendez-vous chez le dentiste
un rendez-vous chez le médecin

Resources

CD4, tracks 16–17
Cahier d'exercices, page 80
Grammaire 4.6

Starter 1

Aim
To revise constructions with the infinitive.

Write up the following. Ask students to identify which of the expressions can be followed by an infinitive and to give examples of infinitives that could be used with these.

il aime
tu as
je déteste
il faut
on veut
tu vas
nous sommes
elles adorent
je voudrais
vous mangez

1 Les excuses. Lisez et trouvez l'image qui correspond à chaque texto.

Reading. Students read the five texts (**1–5**) and find the picture that corresponds to each one (**a–e**).

Answers
1 b **2** a **3** e **4** c **5** d

2 Julien et ses copains parlent au téléphone. Écoutez, et relisez les textos dans l'exercice 1. Qui parle? Quand est-ce qu'ils peuvent rentrer au collège? (1–5)

Listening. Students listen to the five people from exercise 1 talking on the phone and identify who is speaking in each case (they may need to reread the texts in exercise 1). They also note when the people are able to go back to school.

Audioscript 16

1 *Salut! La fête? Non ... Je n'y suis pas allé moi non plus parce que je suis malade. Ça va un peu mieux maintenant, mais je ne peux pas aller au collège demain, ça c'est sûr. J'ai eu de la fièvre et je prends des antibiotiques ... beurk ... dégoûtant ... Non ... le médecin a dit ... non ... je ne peux pas aller au collège avant la semaine prochaine.*

2 *Salut! La fête? Ah non, je n'y suis pas allée. J'avais une dent qui me faisait mal ... Je suis allée chez le dentiste hier ... Non ... il m'a fait un plombage ... Je déteste y aller. Le collège? Ah non ... tu ne peux pas??? ... Tu as de la chance ... Je viendrai te rendre visite vendredi après le collège.*

3 *Salut! La fête? Je n'ai pas pu aller à la fête hier moi non plus ... J'étais tellement enrhumée ... oui ... et j'ai toussé toute la nuit ... Mais ça va mieux maintenant et maman a décidé ... tu connais ma mère ... je peux retourner au collège jeudi. Et toi? Ah non!!!*

4 *La fête? Non, c'est stupide, mais je n'ai pas pu y aller. Hier matin, tu sais, j'étais dans le jardin, on jouait au foot et j'ai été piqué par une guêpe! C'est la première fois que cela m'arrivait et mon bras a gonflé comme un ballon. Ma mère a pris un rendez-vous chez le médecin, mais il m'a envoyé à l'hôpital pour un examen ... Je ne le savais pas, mais il semble que je suis allergique et il faut faire attention. Le collège? Non, il n'a rien dit. Je serai là après-demain.*

5 *Salut, Sophie! Tu es allée à la fête? Oui? Je n'ai pas pu y aller moi non plus parce que je suis tombé et je me suis cassé un os du pied. J'ai dû aller à l'hôpital et maintenant, j'ai le pied dans le plâtre... Oui? Ah non, le collège non, absolument pas, pas pendant deux semaines. Tu peux venir me voir? Maintenant, je dois rester à la maison avec mon pied sur une chaise.*

Answers
1 Raoul, next week **2** Sophie, Friday **3** Laurie, Thursday
4 Romain, the day after tomorrow **5** Julien, in two weeks

Expo-langue: impersonal constructions

Use this grammar box to cover impersonal constructions with **falloir** (**il faut** and **il a fallu**) + the infinitive) and **il vaut mieux** + the infinitive. There is more information on p. 217 of the Student Book.

Starter 2

Aim
To practise using impersonal verbs which are followed by the infinitive.

Write up the following. Ask students working in pairs to use the English prompts to come up with sentences in French: two using **il faut**, two using **il vaut mieux** and two using **il a fallu**.

- do your homework every night
- phone your friend tomorrow
- make an appointment
- stay at home
- go to hospital
- look after my brother

3 À deux. Discutez et complétez les instructions.

Speaking. In pairs: students discuss the possible remedies for the ailments listed, completing each sentence opening from the options supplied.

4 Qu'est-ce qu'il faut faire? Suggérez un remède pour chaque personne.

Writing. Students write suggestions for a remedy for each of the six people pictured.

Suggested answers

Eva – Il vaut mieux prendre un rendez-vous chez le médecin et il faut sucer des pastilles antiseptiques.
Clément – Il faut laver le genou et puis mettre un pansement adhésif. Il vaut mieux rester assis.
Julie – Il faut prendre des comprimés analgésiques et boire beaucoup d'eau.
Thibaud – Il vaut mieux prendre un rendez-vous chez le dentiste. Il faut prendre de l'aspirine.
Noélie – Il vaut mieux aller à l'hôpital pour faire une radio.
Bastien – Il faut laver la main et mettre de la crème antiseptique et un pansement adhésif.

5 Rendez-vous chez le médecin. Notez pour chaque personne le problème et le jour et l'heure du rendez-vous. (1–3)

Listening. Students listen to three people making a doctor's appointment and note for each their ailment and the day and time of the appointment.

Audioscript 17

1 *– Cabinet médical du docteur Leblanc, bonjour.*
– Bonjour, madame. Pourrais-je avoir un rendez-vous?
– Qu'est-ce qui ne va pas?
– Je ne me sens pas bien. J'ai de la fièvre et j'ai mal à la gorge. Je crois que j'ai une grippe.
– Bon, pouvez-vous venir demain?
– À quelle heure?
– À dix heures vingt. Avez-vous de l'aspirine à la maison?
– Oui, je crois.
– Bon, prenez-en deux toutes les quatre heures et venez voir le médecin demain.
– Oui …

2 *– Cabinet médical du docteur Leblanc, bonjour.*
– Bonjour, madame. Pourrais-je voir le médecin aujourd'hui?
– C'est urgent?
– Oui. Je me suis fait très mal au pied.
– Qu'est-ce qui s'est passé?
– Je suis tombé dans l'escalier et je me suis fait très mal. Je ne peux pas marcher.
– Comment est-ce que vous pouvez venir jusqu'au cabinet?
– Ma mère m'amènera.
– En voiture?
– Oui.
– À quelle heure pouvez-vous venir?
– Tout de suite.
– Non, le médecin est occupé … Mais dans une heure, à quinze heures quarante? Ça vous convient?
– Oui … merci.

3 *– Cabinet médical du docteur Leblanc, bonjour.*
– Bonjour, madame. Pourrais-je avoir un rendez-vous?
– Qu'est-ce qui ne va pas?
– J'ai mal au ventre et je vomis.
– Qu'est-ce que vous avez mangé?
– Pas grand-chose. Je n'ai envie de rien.
– Bon, vous pouvez venir à neuf heures demain matin.

Answers

	problème	jour du rendez-vous	heure du rendez-vous
1	*de la fièvre*, mal à la gorge	demain	10h20
2	mal au pied	aujourd'hui	15h40
3	mal au ventre, a vomis	demain	9h

6 À deux. Chez le médecin. Faites des dialogues.

Speaking. In pairs: students enact dialogues set at the doctor's surgery, taking it in turn to play the doctor and the patient. A framework is supplied for support.

Plenary

Ask students to tell you about the impersonal verbs in this unit. How are they used? What are they followed by?

Then prompt with ailments (e.g. **j'ai mal à la tête**) for students to respond with advice using either **il faut** or **il vaut mieux**.

Cahier d'exercices, page 80

1

Answers

1 Il faut mettre de la crème antiseptique.
2 Il vaut mieux prendre un rendez-vous chez le dentiste
3 Il faut prendre de l'aspirine immédiatement.
4 Il a fallu aller à l'hôpital faire une radio.
5 Il vaut mieux aller à l'hôpital pour vérifier que je n'ai rien de cassé.
6 Si vous toussez, il vaut mieux rester à la maison.
7 Il a fallu mettre un pansement adhésif sur la piqûre.

2

Answers

Possible answers:
1 Il faut rester au lit et il vaut mieux prendre de l'aspirine immédiatement.
2 Il faut rester à la maison et si ça vous fait mal, il vaut mieux prendre de l'aspirine.
3 Il vaut mieux prendre un rendez-vous chez le médecin. Si vous toussez, il vaut mieux rester à la maison.

3

Answers

Example:
1 Désolée, je ne peux pas aller au match de foot, mais je suis tombée en jouant et je me suis cassé le bras et j'ai aussi mal à la tête. J'ai dû aller à l'hôpital faire une radio et maintenant j'ai le bras dans le plâtre.
2 Désolé, mais je ne peux pas aller au concert samedi soir. J'ai mal à la gorge et mal à la tête, jai mal au ventre et j'ai de la fièvre. C'est affreux. Il faut rester au lit et je dois prendre de l'aspirine. Le médecin a dit que j'ai une grippe.

2 Garder la forme

(Student Book pages 150–151)

Main topics and objectives

- Talking about a healthy lifestyle
- Adverbs

Grammar

- Adverbs

Key language

Je suis en forme.
Pour garder la forme, ...
je mange sainement
je ne bois que d'eau
je ne mange pas des sucreries
je ne mange pas beaucoup de graisses
je fais beaucoup d'exercice
je fais de l'exercice regulièrement
Je mangeais/buvais/faisais ...
Je pourrais manger/boire/faire ...
Je pourrais faire un régime.
d'habitude
finalement
généralement
lentement
heureusement
malheureusement
personnellement
rapidement
régulièrement
sainement
seulement
tellement
uniquement
bien
mal
mieux
toujours

Resources

CD4, track 18
Cahier d'exercices, page 81
Grammaire 2.6

Starter 1

Aim
To revise language for talking about lifestyle in the present and the past.

Ask students working in pairs to complete the two texts by coming up with four facts to illustrate a healthy lifestyle in the present and four facts to illustrate an *un*healthy lifestyle in their youth.

D'habitude, je garde la forme. Je ...
Quand j'étais petit(e), je ne gardais pas la forme. Je ...

1 Lisez et trouvez qui parle.

Reading. Students read the three texts. They then read the eight questions and identify who each one refers to, Flavie, Antoine or Anaïs.

Answers
1 Anaïs **2** Flavie **3** Antoine **4** Anaïs **5** Antoine **6** Flavie **7** [Antoine/Anaïs – student's own answer] **8** Flavie

Expo-langue: adverbs

Use this grammar box to cover how adverbs are formed and a few key irregular adverbs. Point out that adverbs can add detail and interest to a text and so students should aim to include them in their speaking and writing. There is more information on p. 211 of the Student Book.

2 Écoutez Valentin et notez les bonnes réponses, a, b ou c.

Listening. Students listen to Valentin talking about his lifestyle and how it differs from when he was younger. They then read the five sentences and choose the correct ending for each from the three options given (**a**, **b** or **c**).

Audioscript 18

Je joue au basket et le sport, c'est ma vie. Pour le sport, il faut être en forme et je fais beaucoup d'entraînement. Je fais du fitness et je joue au squash, je fais du roller et du VTT, mais je déteste le jogging et la natation. Notre entraîneur demande que nous mangions sainement, mais c'est difficile parce que je suis un véritable gourmand!

Quand j'étais petit, je mangeais de tout, des bonbons, des gâteaux, des sucreries, et je buvais des boissons gazeuses. Maintenant, je fais plus d'efforts. Je n'aime pas la salade et les légumes, mais j'en mange quand même... pas assez, mais j'en mange un peu, ... et c'est déjà quelque chose!

J'ai essayé de manger un fruit à la récré au lieu d'un biscuit au chocolat, mais quelquefois, je prends un Twix. Je préférerais le biscuit tout le temps, mais il faut faire des sacrifices dans la vie! Quand j'étais petit, je regardais trop la télé et je passais des heures cloué devant l'ordinateur. Maintenant, je fais mes devoirs et puis, je sors faire du sport. C'est mieux.

Answers
1 a **2** c **3** c **4** b **5** b

Starter 2

Aim
To practise forming adverbs. To practise applying grammar knowledge to work out new forms.

Ask students to write out the adverbs that correspond to the following adjectives:

final, complet, lent, présent, heureux, sérieux, seul, suffisant

3 À deux. Posez et répondez aux questions.

Speaking. In pairs: students take it in turn to ask and answer questions about the healthiness of their current lifestyle, how they used to live when they were younger and how they could do better in the future. The questions are supplied for support.

4 Mettez les images dans l'ordre mentionné dans le texte.

Reading. Students read the text and put the pictures in the order they are mentioned in the text.

Answers
e, d, b, i, c, a, g, f, h

5 Que faisait-il et qu'est-ce qu'il fait maintenant? Lisez et complétez les phrases.

Reading. Students reread the text in exercise 4, then complete four sentences on what the writer used to do when he was young and four sentences on what he does now.

Answers
Quand il était jeune, …
1 il mangeait (presque uniquement) des pâtes ou des frites avec du ketchup et des bonbons et d'autres sucreries.
2 il buvait des boissons gazeuses.
3 il faisait du judo.
4 il n'était pas en forme.

Aujourd'hui, …
5 il mange sainement/du steak, des légumes, du riz, du pain aux céréales et des fruits.
6 il boit de l'eau.
7 il fait du judo et du jogging.
8 il est en forme/champion régional.

6 Que faisiez-vous et que faites-vous maintenant?

Writing. Students write a text comparing what they used to eat/drink/do in the past and their present situation and adding details of what they could do to have a healthier lifestyle. Paragraph openings are supplied to help them structure their text.

Plenary

Ask the class to summarise how adverbs are formed and to give you some examples. Then test them by prompting in English as follows:

happily, quickly, only, healthily, well, badly, regularly, better, slowly, generally

Cahier d'exercices, page 81

1

Answers
1 Je suis toujours fatigué. Qu'est-ce que je peux faire?
2 Après le collège j'ai toujours très faim, puis au dîner, je n'ai plus faim.
3 J'ai toujours froid en hiver!

2

Answers
Possible answer:
Varie tes repas!
Croque des fruits secs (noix, amandes) ou séchés (abricots secs, dattes).
Évite les barres chocolatées et les chips.
Pour produire la chaleur, mange du pain, des céréales, des pâtes.
Va te coucher au moment où t'endors le plus.
Évite aussi les ascenseurs.
Mange des oranges, pamplemousses et kiwis pour plus de vitamine C.

3

Answers
Possible answers
1 Mange un laitage ou des céréales quand tu rentres du collège.
2 Évite les barres chocolatées quand tu as faim.
3 Si tu habites à 1 km du collège, vas-y à pied.
4 Des pommes de terre, des céréales et des pâtes t'apportent des sucres lents.
5 Mange du poisson une fois par semaine.
6 C'est important d'aller au lit à heure fixe.
7 Ne mange pas de grand dîner avant d'aller au lit.

3 La dépendance

(Student Book pages 152–153)

Main topics and objectives

- Discussing addiction and other problems
- Giving your opinion

Key language

Il/Elle est dépendant(e).
Il voudrait renoncer à fumer.
Elle ne peut pas s'arrêter.
le fumeur
Les cigarettes coûtent cher.
Ses vêtements sentent la fumée.
C'est dégoûtant.
C'est déstressant.
Je déteste l'odeur.
Vous risquez de mourir.
Vous gaspillez de l'argent.
Le problème le plus grave, c'est …
le tabagisme
l'alcool (m)
le sida
la drogue
l'anorexie et la boulimie
Ils ne remarquent pas quand ils ont trop bu.
Ça va …
abîmer sa santé
compromettre son avenir
Il y a trop de pression sur …
C'est presque impossible de …
à mon avis
selon moi
je pense que …
je trouve que …
je suis pour/contre … parce que …

Resources

CD4, track 19
Cahier d'exercices, page 82

Starter 1

Aim
To work out new words using context and grammar.

Write up the following in two columns, jumbling the order of the second column. Ask students to match the French and English versions.

le tabagisme	smoking
la dépendance	addiction
le gaspillage	waste
la fumée	smoke
déstressant	relaxing
recommencer	to start again
renoncer	to give up
respirer	to breathe
un cancer des poumons	lung cancer
les restes	cigarette butts

1 Qui est pour (P) et qui est contre (C) le tabagisme?

Reading. Students read the eight speech bubbles and identify for each speaker (**a–h**) whether he/she is for (**P**) or against (**C**) smoking.

Answers
a C **b** C **c** P **d** C **e** P **f** P **g** C **h** C

R Ask students to identify a single word in each text which shows it is either positive or negative.

2 Écoutez et décidez. Sont-ils pour (P) ou contre (C) le tabagisme?

Listening. Students listen to eight people giving their opinion on smoking and identify whether each is for (**P**) or against (**C**) it.

Audioscript 19

1 *Mourir d'un cancer des poumons, c'est affreux. À la fin, ma tante ne pouvait plus respirer.*

2 *Les vêtements de mon grand-père sentent toujours la fumée. C'est dégoûtant!*

3 *Je me sens décontracté quand je fume dans un bar avec mes copains.*

4 *Je déteste l'odeur des cigarettes dans un bar ou restaurant. Je trouve ça dégoûtant qu'on fume à la table d'à côté quand vous êtes en train de manger. C'est impoli.*

5 *Les adultes fument, alors je ne vois pas pourquoi je ne devrais pas fumer.*

6 *Fumer, c'est cool entre amis. Ça me donne confiance! Je ne fume pas à la maison, mais quand je suis au café entre amis, je fume. J'aime l'ambiance.*

7 *Ça me dégoûte. Ce que je déteste, ce sont les restes d'une cigarette jetée par terre n'importe où.*

8 *C'est du gaspillage. Les cigarettes coûtent cher. On pourrait s'acheter quelque chose de vraiment meilleur avec l'argent qu'on dépense pour en acheter.*

Answers
1 C **2** C **3** P **4** C **5** P **6** P **7** C **8** C

3 Pour chaque phrase, écrivez V (Vrai), F (Faux) ou PM (Pas mentionné).

Reading. Students read Didier's text on why he smokes. They then read the eight statements on the text and decide whether each is true or false or not mentioned in the text.

Answers
1 F **2** V **3** PM **4** F **5** PM **6** V **7** V **8** F

Starter 2

Aim
To consolidate language for talking about addiction. To think about word order in sentences.

Write up the following jumbled sentences for students to put in the correct order. They can work in pairs.

1 **cigarette déstressant c'est de les copains fumer une avec**
(C'est déstressant de fumer une cigarette avec les copains.)
2 **où ne pas faut fumer il mangent d'autres**
(Il ne faut pas fumer où d'autres mangent.)
3 **renoncerai à fumer quand parents renoncent je aussi mes**
(Quand mes parents renoncent à fumer je renoncerai aussi.)
4 **l'argent pourrait s'acheter on meilleur avec de vraiment quelque chose de**
(On pourrait s'acheter quelque chose de vraiment meilleur avec de l'argent.)

4 À deux. Discutez. Qu'est-ce que vous pourriez dire à quelqu'un pour le convaincre de ...

Speaking. In pairs: students discuss what they would say to convince someone to stop smoking and to convince someone not to take up smoking. The questions and some openings for responses are given for support.

➕ Students write a text giving the arguments for and against smoking and presenting their own conclusion.

5 Quels sont les plus graves problèmes des jeunes? Lisez et identifiez le problème et la raison pour chaque personne.

Reading. Students read the four texts and identify in French for each of the writers what he/she thinks is the most serious problem facing young people and why.

Answers
Sébastien – l'alcool: beaucoup de jeunes boivent trop; ils deviennent agressifs et ils ne savent plus ce qu'ils font et disent
Patrick – le sida: c'est facile à attraper par les relations sexuelles sans protection, le sang contaminé ou le partage de séringues; des millions d'enfants meurent en Afrique parce que leurs parents ont le sida
Charlotte la drogue: après on prend de la drogue, on est de mauvaise humeur, on ne peut pas se concentrer en cours, ça va abîmer la santé et compromettre l'avenir.
Syanna – l'anorexie et la boulimie: il y a trop de pression sur les filles de ressembler à des stars de télé; quand on commence, c'est presque impossible de s'arrêter

6 Traduisez un des textes de l'exercice 5 en anglais.

Reading. Students choose one of the texts in exercise 5 and translate it into English.

7 Discutez. Selon vous, quels sont les problèmes les plus graves des jeunes? Pourquoi?

Speaking. In pairs: students discuss what they believe are the most serious problems for young people, justifying their opinions. A list of useful expressions is supplied for support.

8 Faites un exposé: *Les problèmes des jeunes.*

Writing. Students write a report on the problems facing young people.

9 Vidéoconférence. À deux. Choisissez un problème (le tabagisme/la drogue, etc.) et préparez une présentation.

Speaking. Students imagine that they are going to have a videoconference with students at a French school. Working in pairs, they choose a problem (from those introduced in the unit, or another they have been discussing) and prepare a presentation on it. A structure is outlined and some sentence openings are supplied for support.

➕ Get a few pairs to do their videoconference in front of the class. If possible, record it on video and play it back, inviting constructive comment from the class.

This would be an ideal topic for students to exchange e-mails on with students in a French school.

Plenary

Ask students to give you six phrases which can be used when introducing an opinion.

Then go round the class asking **Quels sont les problèmes les plus graves des jeunes?** Students should answer using one of the opinion phrases and include a justification for their choice.

Cahier d'exercices, page 82

1

Answers

1 comportement – behaviour
2 tentatives – attempts
3 proches – people close to me
4 un suivi – follow-up
5 régler – settle/sort out
6 le défi – challenge
7 réussir – to succeed
8 perçue (percevoir) – perceived
9 subissent (subir) – suffer
10 le sort – fate

2

Answers

Pupil's own answers

3

Answers

1 *Two years ago, Aurélie was overcome with problems including* drug abuse, behaviour problems, obsessive complusive tendencies and attempted suicides.
2 *She was sick of being* rejected, abandoned and left to her own devices by people close to her.
3 *Today she is in* a specialist hospital in rehabilitation.
4 *One thing she still has to sort out is* her reintegration with other young people.
5 *It's difficult because* people keep judging her and she is perceived as a monster.
6 *She would like* to be in contact with other young people who have suffered similar things.

4 Veux-tu te marier?

(Student Book pages 154–155)

Main topics and objectives

- Talking about family relationships
- More practice giving opinions

Key language

Je (ne) veux (pas) me marier.
On veut avoir des enfants.
Je ne veux pas avoir d'enfant.
Nous voulons vivre ensemble.
Les enfants coûtent cher.
Il faut s'occuper d'eux tout le temps.
Je veux ...
devenir médecin
tomber amoureux/euse
un grand mariage
un petit copain riche
Ils se disputent.
divorcé(e)
séparé(e)

Resources

CD4, track 20
Cahier d'exercices, pages 83–84

Starter 1

Aim
To revise vocabulary for family members.

Working in pairs, students take it in turn to prompt with a family member in English and to give the French. Get them to keep a score of all those they correctly guess. Which pair can guess most family members between them in three minutes?

1 Écoutez et notez. Qui veut se marier? (1–5)

Listening. Students listen to five people talking about whether or not they want to get married in the future, noting the numbers of those who say they do want to.

Audioscript 20

1 *Ben, je pense que ... oui ..., mais pas avant vingt-cinq ans, ... quand j'aurai un travail, quoi!*

2 *Euh ... Mon petit copain et moi, nous voulons nous marier ... Mais cela sera quand nous aurons terminé nos études ... tu sais ... Je veux être kinésitherapeute et lui, il veut être dentiste ... Mais on n'y pense pas pour le moment, on est trop jeunes.*

3 *Moi, personnellement, ... je ne vois pas pourquoi il faut se marier ... Si on s'aime, on n'a pas besoin de signer un papier devant le maire. Ça ne sert à rien.*

4 *Ça dépend. Si je trouve quelqu'un et nous décidons de fonder une famille, je crois qu'il faut se marier. Selon moi, les enfants ont besoin d'un père et d'une mère.*

5 *Je ne veux pas me marier. Je ne veux pas avoir d'enfants. Je veux voyager autour du monde et on ne peut pas voyager avec un bébé.*

Answers
1, 2, 4

2 Lisez et répondez aux questions.

Reading. Students read the three speech bubbles and answer the three comprehension questions in French.

Answers
1 Zoé. Elle veut un grand mariage parce qu'elle est romantique/veut porter une robe blanche, se faire belle et être la princesse d'une journée.
2 François. Il ne veut pas se marier parce qu'il veut devenir médecin et voyager.
3 Nathan. Il ne veut pas de grand mariage parce que ça coûte cher.

3 Qu'en pensez-vous? Discutez.

Speaking. In pairs: students discuss their own attitudes to marriage, weddings and children. The questions and some openings for the responses are supplied for support.

R Students write a short paragraph on their own attitudes to marriage, weddings and children and one on their partner's attitudes.

Starter 2

Aim
To revise language to talk about family relationships. To use grammar to work out connections.

Write up the following in two columns, jumbling the order of the second column. Ask students working in pairs to match the halves to make complete sentences/questions and then to translate them.

1 Les parents de mon copain	**se sont séparés.**
2 C'est mieux qu'	**ils restent ensemble.**
3 Il ne veut pas	**de demi-frère.**
4 Je crois qu'il	**ne nous aime plus.**
5 Je ne veux pas	**quitter ma maison.**
6 Mes parents se disputaient	**tout le temps.**
7 J'en ai marre	**de mon père.**

4 Lisez et trouvez les phrases dans les textes.

Reading. Students read the five texts and find the French for the six English expressions listed.

Answers
1 c'est normal **2** c'est mieux **3** ce n'est pas juste **4** ce n'est pas grave **5** c'est triste **6** c'est la honte

5 Que font-ils? C'est comment?

Speaking. Students use the pictures to talk about the experience of the couple pictured, from their falling in love to their post-divorce life. This can be done in pairs or as a class exercise. Encourage students to imagine and give as much detail as possible. Some sentence openings are supplied for support.

6 Lisez la lettre de Karima. Pour chaque phrase, écrivez V (Vrai), F (Faux) ou PM (Pas Mentionné).

Reading. Students read Karima's letter to an agony aunt. They then read the six statements on the text and decide whether each is true or false or not mentioned in the text.

Answers
1 F **2** PM **3** F **4** F **5** V **6** V

R Ask comprehension questions in French on the text, covering what is happening and how the people involved feel and why.

7 Écrivez une réponse à Karima.

Writing. Students pretend they are Loulou and write a response to Karima's letter in exercise 6. Some useful expressions are given for support.

Plenary

Ask students what kind of verb **vouloir** is and what they can tell you about it. Get them to tell you about other modals and to give you examples of how they are used.

Then ask students to come up with as many arguments as they can in support of getting married (or not).

Cahier d'exercices, page 83

1

Answers
Pupil's own answers

2

Answers
Pupil's own answers

Cahier d'exercices, Grammaire, page 84

1

Answers
Possible answers
1 *Oui, j'en mange tous les jours.*
2 Oui, j'en bois.
3 Non, je n'en mange pas.
4 Non, je n'en bois pas.
5 Si j'en bois.
6 Oui, j'en prends.
7 Si j'en mange.
8 Non, je n'en bois pas.

2

Answers
En général, je mange sainement mais le matin, généralement, je ne prends pas de petit déjeuner. Pendant la journée, je bois seulement de l'eau.
Le week-end, je fais toujours de l'exercice. Heureusement, j'aime le sport. Je joue régulièrement au tennis; je ne joue pas bien, en fait je joue mal mais j'adore ce sport! Pour faire plus d'exercice, je vais au travail à pied et je marche rapidement, pas lentement.

Contrôle continu: La forme

(Student Book pages 156–157)

Topic revised

- writing about your previous and current lifestyles

1 Qu'est-ce que Yves a fait pour rendre son texte plus intéressant? a, b ou tous les deux?

Students read the text and answer the seven questions, which focus attention on the style of Yves's writing (how he has conveyed his opinions, structured the material, etc.). After checking answers, ask students to summarise what useful strategies they could take from this and use in their own writing.

Answers

1 a **2** b **3** a **4** tous les deux **5** b **6** tous les deux **7** tous les deux

2 Trouvez ces mots utiles dans le texte. Essayez de les utiliser dans votre français.

Students reread the text and find the French for the 10 English words listed. Point out that these are useful words to incorporate in students' own writing (and speaking) and suggest students list and learn any they don't already know.

Answers

1 comme
2 puisque
3 entre
4 pour
5 tellement
6 Alors …
7 malheureusement
8 d'habitude
9 qui/que
10 avec

3 Copiez les phrases en bleu dans le texte et trouvez l'équivalent en anglais. Lesquelles pouvez-vous utiliser quand vous écrivez un texte?

Students copy out all the phrases shown in blue in the text and translate them into English. They then identify which of these they could use in their own texts.

Answers

comme je sais que – as I know that
c'est important pour la santé – it's important for your health
pour la plupart – for the most part, mostly
c'est tellement simple à cuisiner – it's so easy to cook
c'est-à-dire – that is
je trouve toujours une excuse – I always find an excuse
j'ai fait une nouvelle résolution – I've made a new resolution

4 Parlez de votre forme.

Using the text and the **Boîte à outils** section to help them, students write a detailed description of their own attitude to fitness, both now and in the past.

À l'oral (AQA edition)

(Student Book page 184)

Topics revised

- talking about the healthiness of your lifestyle
- visiting a chemist
- talking about smoking
- talking about marriage

1 You are being interviewed for a magazine article about young people and health. Your partner will play the part of the interviewer and will speak first.

Roleplay. Students practise talking about the healthiness of their lifestyle, taking it in turn to play themselves/the role of a magazine interviewer.

☑ Remind students that they should listen carefully to whether their partner addresses them as **tu** or **vous** and respond accordingly.

2 You are in a chemist's in France. You have a sore throat. Your partner will play the chemist and will speak first.

Roleplay. Students practise asking for advice in a chemist's. They take it in turn to play the roles of the customer and the chemist.

3 Prepare a ninety-second presentation called *Moi et la forme*. Say what you currently do, what you used to do and what you hope to do in the future to stay fit

Presentation. Students prepare a ninety-second presentation on what they currently do, what they used to do and what they hope to do in the future to stay fit.

A sample cue card is supplied for students to refer to when preparing their own prompts.

4 Possible conversation questions

These are key questions to practise for the speaking exam, taken from the module as a whole. Students can practise asking and answering the questions in pairs.

À l'oral (Edexcel edition)

(Student Book page 184)

Topics revised
- getting help from a chemist
- making a restaurant reservation
- talking about a healthy lifestyle
- talking about smoking
- talking about marriage

1 You are in a chemist's in France. Your partner will play the part of the chemist and will begin the conversation.

Roleplay Type B. Students practise talking to a chemist about an illness/injury, taking it in turn to play themselves/the role of a chemist.

2 You are on holiday in France and telephone a restaurant. Your partner will play the part of the restaurant owner and will begin the conversation.

Roleplay Type C. Students practise making a restaurant reservation, taking it in turn to play themselves/the role of the restaurant owner.

3 Presentation and general conversation

Presentation. Students prepare a one-minute presentation on what they currently do, what they used to do and what they hope to do in the future to stay fit.

A sample cue card is supplied for students to use for ideas and to refer to when preparing their own prompts.

Possible conversation questions. These are key questions to practise for the speaking exam, taken from the module as a whole. Students can practise asking and answering the questions in pairs.

À l'oral (OCR edition)

(Student Book page 184)

Topics revised
- getting help from a doctor/chemist
- talking about the healthiness of your lifestyle
- talking about smoking
- talking about marriage

1 While on holiday in France you don't feel well and have to see a doctor. Your partner will play the part of the doctor and will speak first.

Roleplay Type 2. Students practise talking to a doctor about an illness, taking it in turn to play themselves/the role of the doctor.

2 You are in a pharmacy in France. Your partner will play the part of the pharmacist and will speak first.

Roleplay Type 2. Students practise talking to a chemist about an injury, taking it in turn to play themselves/the role of the chemist.

3 Prepare a one-minute presentation called *Moi et la forme*.

Presentation. Students prepare a one-minute presentation on what they currently do and what they should do in the future to stay fit.

A sample cue card is supplied for students to refer to when preparing their own prompts.

4 *Moi et la forme:* possible conversation questions

These are key questions to practise for the speaking exam, taken from the module as a whole. Students can practise asking and answering the questions in pairs.

Mode de vie

9 À toi

(Student Book pages 202–203)

- Self-access reading and writing

1 Lisez le texte et répondez aux questions.

Reading. Students read Cyril's text and answer the five comprehension questions in French.

Answers

1 Il a trop mangé, il a trop bu et il a passé trop de temps collé devant son ordinateur pendant les vacances de Noël.
2 Entre les repas, il mange des confiseries et des chips.
3 Il boit du coca.
4 Il devrait manger plus/beaucoup de fruit et de légumes (et moins de graisses et de sucre).
5 Il n'aime pas jouer au tennis ou au badminton et il n'aime pas faire de sports d'équipe et de natation.

2 Ça veut dire quoi?

Reading. Students read the list of seven words from the text in exercise 1 and choose the correct translation from the three options given for each one (**a**, **b** or **c**).

Answers

Answers

1 c **2** b **3** a **4** c **5** c **6** b **7** c

3 Écrivez un conseil à Cyril.

Writing. Students write a paragraph giving Cyril advice on how he might live in a more healthy way.

4 Lisez le texte et trouvez les mots français.

Reading. Students read the text on cigarettes and smoking and find the French words for the five chemicals whose uses are described in English. The tip box reminds students of strategies to use in tackling new vocabulary.

Answers

1 acétone **2** méthanol **3** ammoniac **4** DDT **5** toluène

5 Pour chaque phrase, écrivez V (Vrai), F (Faux) ou PM (Pas Mentionné).

Reading. Students reread the text in exercise 4. They then read the five statements on the text and decide whether each is true or false or not mentioned in the text.

Answers

1 V **2** V **3** PM **4** F **5** PM

6 Écrivez une réponse au cri du cœur de Florence.

Writing. Students read the plea from Florence and write a response, suggesting advice she might give her friend to persuade him to give up smoking.

Module 10 Le monde en danger

[Student Book pages 160–175]

Unit	Main topics and objectives	Grammar
Déjà vu **On devrait faire ça!** (pp. 160–161)	Discussing world issues The conditional of modal verbs	Modal verbs in the conditional
1 Les problèmes locaux (pp. 162–163)	Talking about problems in your area Using more negatives	Negative expressions
2 Bonne route? (pp. 164–165)	Describing breakdowns and accidents Coping with unknown language in texts	
3 L'environnement va mal! (pp. 166–167)	Discussing the environment The present and future tenses	Irregular present tense verbs The future tense
4 Avant et après (pp. 168–169)	Talking about environmental projects Using direct object pronouns in the perfect tense	Agreement in the perfect tense with **avoir** (direct object pronouns)
5 À la une (pp. 170–171)	Understanding news stories The passive	The passive
Contrôle continu **Un problème environnemental** (pp. 172–173)	*Coursework* Writing about environmental problems	*All main grammar points of the module*
À l'oral (p. 185)	*Exam speaking practice* Getting help when your car breaks down Talking about the environment	*All main grammar points of the module*
À toi (pp. 204–205)	Self-access reading and writing	

Déjà vu: On devrait faire ça!

(Student Book pages 160–161)

Main topics and objectives
- Discussing world issues
- The conditional of modal verbs

Grammar
- Modal verbs in the conditional

Key language
World problems

Resources
CD4, track 21
Cahier d'exercices, page 87
Grammaire 3.10

Starter 1

Aim
To introduce vocabulary for discussing world issues. To use strategies to work out new vocabulary.

Write up the following in two columns, jumbling the order of the second column. Ask students to match the definitions in the first column with the correct labels in the second.

1 Il n'y a pas assez à manger.	**la faim**
2 Il y a beaucoup de pollution.	**le réchauffement de la planète**
3 Il manque des médicaments dans les pays en voie de développement.	**le sida**
4 Il n'y a pas assez d'argent.	**la pauvreté**
5 Les gens ne vivent pas en paix.	**la guerre**
6 Les gens sont tués partout dans le monde.	**le terrorisme**

1 Quel est le plus grand problème du monde, selon ces personnes? Trouvez la bonne photo pour chaque personne.

Listening. Students listen to the radio interview in which six people give their opinion on what is the most significant problem in the world. They need to note the picture corresponding to the issue he/she talks about (from **a–f**).

Audioscript 21

- *Bonsoir et bienvenue! J'ai avec moi six jeunes et je vais leur poser la question «Quel est le plus grand problème du monde?» Mathis, si je peux commencer avec toi. À ton avis, quel est le problème le plus grave du monde?*
- *Pour moi, c'est la faim. Il y a des milliers de gens qui meurent chaque jour de la faim. C'est un véritable scandale parce qu'il y a assez à manger dans le monde pour tout le monde. On devrait faire quelque chose.*
- *Merci, Mathis. Et toi, Éléa, tu es d'accord?*
- *Oui, mais je crois que le vrai problème, c'est la pauvreté. S'il n'y avait pas de pauvreté, si tout le monde avait du travail et de l'argent, il n'y aurait pas de faim. Donc, à mon avis, c'est la pauvreté qu'on devrait arrêter.*
- *D'accord. Écoutons maintenant Tariq. Tariq, quel est le plus grand problème, selon toi?*
- *Moi, je trouve qu'avant de sauver les gens, il faut sauver la planète! Le réchauffement de la planète, à cause de la pollution, c'est un grand problème qu'il faut résoudre parce que, sinon, la planète va mourir – et les gens aussi!*
- *Merci pour ton opinion. Blanche, que penses-tu? Faut-il sauver d'abord la planète?*
- *Bien sûr qu'il faut faire ça. Mais on devrait penser aussi aux gens qui souffrent et les aider. Par exemple, en Afrique, le sida tue plus de gens que la faim. Pour moi, le sida est le problème le plus grave et on pourrait faire quelque chose tout de suite, si on donnait des médicaments antisida aux pays en voie de développement.*
- *Merci, Blanche. Et Vincent, que penses-tu? Le plus grand problème, c'est la faim? La pauvreté? Le réchauffement de la planète? Le sida?*
- *Ce sont tous des problèmes importants. Mais ce qui m'inquiète, moi, c'est le terrorisme. Les terroristes ont déjà tué beaucoup de gens, partout dans le monde et il faut les arrêter. À mon avis, il faut combattre le terrorisme avant tout.*
- *D'accord. Merci, Vincent. Et finalement, Jade, quel est ton avis?*
- *Pour moi, le plus grand malheur du monde, c'est la guerre. Oui, le terrorisme tue les gens, mais la guerre tue encore plus! Je voudrais bien voir un monde où il n'y a plus de guerre et où tous les gens de la planète pourraient vivre en paix et en sécurité.*
- *Merci, Jade, et merci à tout le monde. Et vous, auditeurs et auditrices? Que pensez-vous? Envoyez-nous un e-mail ou un texto pour nous donner votre opinion! Au revoir et à bientôt!*

Answers
1 d **2** b **3** f **4** a **5** e **6** c

Expo-langue: the conditional of modal verbs

Use this grammar box to cover the conditional of modal verbs before students do exercise 2. There is more information on p. 214 of the Student Book.

R Ask students to summarise how the conditional is formed, listing all the forms of **aider**.

2 Trouvez la seconde partie de chaque phrase. Copiez la phrase complète et traduisez-la en anglais.

Reading. Students match the sentence halves, writing out each complete sentence and translating it into English.

Answers

1 Il y a assez à manger dans le monde, donc on pourrait arrêter la faim.
There is enough to eat in the world, so we should be able to stop hunger.
2 Pour combattre le sida, nous devrions donner des médicaments aux pays en voie de développement.
To combat AIDS, we should give medicine to developing countries.
3 Qu'est-ce que tu voudrais faire pour sauver la planète?
What would you like to do to save the planet?
4 Le gouvernement devrait donner plus d'argent à l'Afrique et à l'Inde.
The government should give more money to Africa and India.
5 Pour aider les gens pauvres, vous pourriez donner de l'argent aux bonnes causes.
To help poor people, you could give money to good causes.
6 Un jour, je voudrais voir un monde sans pauvreté.
One day I'd like to see a world without poverty.
7 Les pays riches du monde devraient arrêter le réchauffement de la planète.
The rich countries of the world should stop global warming.
8 Nous pourrions organiser des activités pour collecter de l'argent.
We could organise activities to collect money.

3 Écrivez une réponse aux questions. Utilisez ou adaptez les phrases de l'exercice 2.

Writing. Students write a response to the four questions listed, using or adapting the expressions from exercise 2.

Starter 2

Aim
To practise forming conditionals.

Write up the following and ask students to complete the grid. With a good class, you could consider leaving all parts of all verbs blank for students to fill in.

	devoir	pouvoir	vouloir
je			
tu	devrais		
il/elle/on			
nous		pourrions	
vous			
ils/elles			voudraient

4 À deux. Discutez avec votre partenaire. Changez les détails en bleu et complétez le dialogue ci-dessous.

Speaking. In pairs: students have a discussion on what they believe to be the most significant problems in the word. A framework, with the phrases to be changed highlighted, is supplied for support.

5 Qu'est-ce qu'il faut faire pour aider les gens des pays en voie de développement? Lisez les textes et les questions en dessous. Écrivez le bon prénom pour chaque question.

Reading. Students read the eight texts by young people, giving their opinions on what ought to be done to help people in developing countries. They then read the eight questions which follow and for each identify the correct writer.

Answers

1 Laure **2** Nadal **3** Omar **4** Yasmina **5** Nicolas **6** Sébastien **7** Élodie **8** Frédéric

Go to www.heinemann.co.uk/hotlinks and enter the express code 7898T for a link to the Médecins Sans Frontières website. Ask students to summarise in English six facts on the problems of one particular location or problem.

Plenary

✓ Ask students to identify in the texts in exercise 5 ten items of vocabulary to note down and learn for this topic. Which do they think are most useful to them and why?

Point out that it is always easier to learn and remember things you are interested in and that the speaking and writing parts of the exam give lots of opportunity to take advantage of this. Encourage students to develop a personal slant to their vocabulary lists – i.e. to think about which topics they are interested in writing and talking about and to use the Student Book and other resources to pull together information on these.

Remind students of the importance of noting, learning and reviewing vocabulary on an ongoing basis.

Cahier d'exercices, page 87

1

Answers

1 On pourrait organiser les activités au collège pour collecter de l'argent.
2 On pourrait donner de l'argent chaque mois aux bonnes causes comme Médecins sans Frontières.
3 Nous devrions réagir plus rapidement quand il y a un désastre ou une famine dans les pays pauvres.
4 On pourrait réduire le prix des médicaments essentiels aux pays en voie de développement.
5 On devrait acheter les produits issus du commerce équitable comme le chocolat et le café.
6 On devrait écrire au gouvernement pour le persuader de faire quelque chose.
7 Nous pourrions parrainer un enfant dans un pays pauvre comme en Afrique ou en Inde.
8 Nous devrions faire quelque chose pour arrêter le réchauffement de la planète.

2

Answers

Pupil's own answers

3

Answers

Pupil's own answers

1 Les problèmes locaux

(Student Book pages 162–163)

Main topics and objectives

- Talking about problems in your area
- Using more negatives

Grammar

- Negative expressions

Key language

Ce qui est bien/nul, c'est ...
On ne peut pas respirer à cause de la pollution.
Il n'y a qu'un bus par jour.
Il n'y a plus de cinéma.
Le club des jeunes est fermé.
Il n'y a ni poubelles ni centres de recyclage.
On jette des déchets par terre.
Les jeunes n'ont rien à faire.
On ne voit personne.
La police ne vient jamais.
Il n'y a aucun travail.
Beaucoup de gens sont au chômage.
le camion
la criminalité
la circulation
la zone piétonne
les distractions (f)
les embouteillages (m)
les heures d'affluence (f)
les transports en commun (m)
le quartier
la maison individuelle
la maison jumelle
l'HLM (habitation à loyer modéré) (f)

bruyant
dangereux
pollué
propre
rapide
sale
tranquille

Resources

CD4, tracks 22–23
Cahier d'exercices, page 88
Grammaire 3.13

Starter 1

Aim
To revise negative expressions.

Ask students working in pairs to come up with as many negative expressions in French as they can, giving them **ne ... pas** as a model. They must also give an English translation of the expressions.

Answers
d, b, a, c, e, g, h, f

1 Quels sont les problèmes à Nulleville? Écoutez et mettez les phrases dans le bon ordre.

Listening. Students listen to a boy describing his home town of Nulleville and put the eight sentences (which appear as captions to pictures) in the order the topics are mentioned in the recording.

Audioscript 22

Bienvenue à Nulleville où j'habite! C'est vraiment horrible ici et il y a plein de problèmes. Par exemple, les jeunes n'ont rien à faire, donc ils s'ennuient pas mal. Avant, il y avait des distractions. Il y avait un club des jeunes et un cinéma. Mais le club des jeunes est fermé depuis un an et il n'y a plus de cinéma. Les transports en commun sont nuls aussi. Il n'y a qu'un seul bus par jour pour aller au centre-ville. Par conséquent, tout le monde y va en voiture, donc il y a trop de circulation et certains jours, on ne peut pas respirer à cause de la pollution. En revanche, le dimanche, c'est trop tranquille et on ne voit personne. Les gens qui habitent ici sont pauvres aussi parce qu'il n'y a aucun travail et beaucoup de gens sont au chômage. De plus, la ville est sale. Il n'y a ni poubelles ni centres de recyclage, donc on jette les déchets par terre. Mais le pire, c'est la criminalité. La nuit, il y a souvent des vols, mais la police ne vient jamais – ils s'en fichent, quoi. Moi, j'en ai assez! Je ne veux plus habiter ici.

Expo-langue: negatives

Use this grammar box to cover negative constructions. There is more information on p. 214 of the Student Book.

R In pairs: students take it in turn to prompt with a negative expression in English and to respond with the French version.

2 Trouvez les phrases qui vont avec celles de l'exercice 1, puis copiez les paires de phrases.

Reading. Students complete the eight descriptions of Nulleville using the texts in exercise 1.

Answers

1. Mais parfois, c'est trop tranquille. Par exemple, le dimanche, on ne voit personne.
2. Le pire, c'est la criminalité. La nuit, il y a souvent des vols, mais la police ne vient jamais.
3. Les transports en commun sont nuls: il n'y a qu'un bus par jour pour aller au centre-ville.
4. Ils s'ennuient ici parce que les jeunes n'ont rien à faire.
5. Il y a trop de circulation et certains jours, on ne peut pas respirer à cause de la pollution.
6. Avant, il y avait des distractions. Mais maintenant, le club des jeunes est fermé et il n'y a plus de cinéma.
7. La ville est sale aussi puisqu'il n'y a ni poubelles ni centres de recyclage, donc on jette les déchets par terre.
8. Les habitants sont pauvres car il n'y a aucun travail, donc beaucoup de gens sont au chômage.

3 Écrivez des phrases positives en adaptant les phrases des exercices 1 et 2.

Writing. Students imagine that investment has been found to make Nulleville a more desirable place to live. They write eight sentences describing the new positive aspects of the town, adapting the sentences in exercises 1 and 2. Point out that this is a good opportunity to use the negative expressions featured in the **Expo-langue** box.

Starter 2

Aim

To practise using language to describe local problems. To practise using negative expressions.

Write up the following jumbled sentences and ask students to put them in order.

1 **n'ont faire jeunes rien à les**
(Les jeunes n'ont rien à faire.)
2 **personne dimanche on le voit ne**
(Le dimanche on ne voit personne.)
3 **de gens il n'y travail donc a aucun beaucoup sont chômage au**
(Il n'y a aucun travail donc beaucoup de gens sont au chômage.)
4 **il poubelles recyclage ni centres de ni n'y a**
(Il n'y a ni poubelles ni centres de recyclage.)
5 **jour bus il a qu'un par n'y**
(Il n'y a qu'un bus par jour.)

4 Écoutez. Quel est le problème? Pour chaque personne, écrivez la bonne lettre. (1–6)

Listening. Students listen to six people describing the place they live in and identify the problem mentioned by each from the list given (a–f).

Audioscript 23

1 *Le problème dans mon village, c'est qu'il n'y a aucune gare et très peu d'autobus, donc si on n'a pas de voiture ou si on ne conduit pas, il est très difficile de se déplacer.*

2 *Je ne sors jamais la nuit dans le quartier où j'habite. Il y a toujours une bande de jeunes au coin de la rue et il y a souvent des voitures volées ou du vandalisme, mais la police ne fait rien.*

3 *J'habite pas loin d'une grande usine de produits chimiques et l'air est très pollué. C'est mauvais pour la santé et ma sœur, qui est asthmatique, est souvent malade de ça.*

4 *C'est bien d'habiter à la campagne, mais comme on est loin de la ville, on ne collecte ni nos bouteilles vides ni nos vieux journaux, donc pour les recycler, on doit les transporter au centre nous-mêmes.*

5 *Ma maison se trouve au bord d'une grande rue et le matin, il y a plein de voitures et de gros camions qui font beaucoup de bruit. C'est dangereux pour les enfants qui doivent aller à l'école à pied.*

6 *Il y a très peu pour les jeunes dans mon quartier. Il n'y a qu'un café où on peut jouer au baby-foot ou au flipper. La boîte où on allait danser n'est plus là.*

Answers
1 c **2** f **3** e **4** b **5** a **6** d

5 À deux. Parlez de votre ville, de votre quartier ou de votre village. Adaptez les phrases en bleu et complétez le dialogue.

Speaking. In pairs: students talk about where they live (their town/area/village, as appropriate). A framework, with the phrases they need to change highlighted, is supplied for support.

6 Lisez l'article. Pour chaque phrase en dessous, écrivez P (Positive), N (Négative) ou P/N (Positive/Négative).

Reading. Students read the newspaper article in which three people describe where they live. They note whether the opinions voiced by each (on each of three topics mentioned, **a–c**) is positive (**P**), negative (**N**) or a mixture of both (**P/N**).

Answers
1 **a** P **b** N **c** N
2 **a** P **b** P **c** P/N
3 **a** P **b** P/N **c** N

7 Écrivez un paragraphe sur les avantages et les inconvénients de votre ville, de votre quartier ou de votre village.

Writing. Students write a paragraph on the advantages and disadvantages of their town, area or village.

+ Display one or two students' texts, asking the class to comment on why you have chosen these as good answers.

Plenary

Put students into teams. Explain that each member of the team needs to say a sentence featuring one of the negative expressions in the unit. The same expression cannot be used twice, or the team is disqualified. A correct answer wins a point. Give students some time to discuss which order they will answer in and to think about their sentences. The team with the most points wins.

Cahier d'exercices, page 88

1

Answers

Moi, j'habite une maison très moderne et confortable dans la banlieue. C'est bien parce qu'il y a beaucoup à faire pour les jeunes; par exemple, il y a un club des jeunes, un cinéma et un centre sportif tout près. Quand on veut aller en ville, il y a un bus qui passe souvent. Je dois dire que les transports en commun sont super.
Ce qui est bien ici, c'est que l'air n'est pas pollué. Il y a deux ans, on a fait une zone piétonne, donc il n'y a plus de voitures ou de gros camions et il n'y a pas d'embouteillages. On peut y trouver de la tranquillité. Avant, c'était bruyant tout le temps, mais maintenant, c'est complètement calme. En plus, il y a des espaces verts où les enfants peuvent jouer en toute sécurité.
Le mieux, c'est qu'il n'y a pas beaucoup de chômage. Il y a du travail pour tout le monde, ce qui est bien pour la vie de famille.
Dans le quartier, il y a des poubelles et un centre de recyclage où on peut mettre les bouteilles, les journaux, les boîtes, etc. ce qui est très bon pour l'environnement. C'est super, Superville!

2

Answers

1 vieux **2** pas beaucoup à faire **3** très loin **4** nul **5** du bruit **6** bruyant **7** le pire **8** le chômage **9** mal **10** sale

3

Answers

Example
Moi, j'habite une maison très vieille et pas du tout confortable dans la banlieue. C'est pas bien parce qu'il n'y a pas beaucoup à faire pour les jeunes; par exemple, il n'y a pas de club des jeunes, de cinéma ou de centre sportif tout près. Quand on veut aller en ville, il n'y a jamais de bus. Je dois dire que les transports en commun sont nuls.
Ce qui est mal ici, c'est que l'air est très pollué. Il n'y a aucune zone piétonne, donc il y a beaucoup de voitures et de gros camions et il y a toujours des embouteillages. On ne peut jamais y trouver de la tranquillité. Avant, c'était calme tout le temps, mais maintenant, c'est toujours bruyant. En plus, il n'y a plus d'espaces verts où les enfants peuvent jouer en toute sécurité.
Le pire, c'est qu'il y a beaucoup de chômage. Il n'y a aucun travail pour tout le monde, ce qui est mal pour la vie de famille.
Dans le quartier, il n'y a pas de poubelles ou de centre de recyclage où on peut mettre les bouteilles, les journaux, les boîtes, etc. ce qui est très mal pour l'environnement. C'est nul, Mauvaiseville!

2 Bonne route?

(Student Book pages 164–165)

Main topics and objectives

- Describing breakdowns and accidents
- Coping with unknown language in texts

Key language

Ma voiture est tombée en panne.
Elle ne démarre plus.
J'ai un pneu crevé.
La batterie est à plat.
Les freins/Les phares ne marchent pas.
l'autoroute (f)
la route nationale
direction (Paris)
à (10) kilomètres de
environ
à peu près
Il/Elle roulait ...
trop vite
lentement
tout à coup
il/elle a couru
il/elle a dérapé
il/elle a freiné
il/elle a heurté
il/elle est entré(e) en collision avec
il/elle était blessé(e)
il/elle était coincé(e)
glissant
le/la camioneur/euse
le/la chauffeur/euse
le/la motocycliste
le/la piéton(ne)
le passage clouté
le permis de conduire
le rond-point
le trottoir
l'ambulance (f)
la ceinture de sécurité
la moto
les sapeurs-pompiers (m)

Resources

CD4, tracks 24–26
Cahier d'exercices, page 89

Starter 1

Aim
To practise checking texts for errors.

Write up the following and give students working in pairs three minutes to list all the errors they can find (underlined here for reference only).

- Ma voiture est <u>tombé</u> en panne. <u>Peuvez</u>-vous envoyer un <u>mecanicien</u>, s'il vous plaît?
- Quel est <u>la</u> problème, madame?
- Les freins ne <u>marche</u> pas.
- <u>Tu peux</u> me donner <u>ton</u> nom, madame?
- C'est Élodie Lambert.
- Et vous êtes <u>ou exactment</u>, madame?
- Je suis sur l'A26, direction Calais, <u>a</u> quinze kilomètres de Calais.

1 On a un problème de voiture! Mettez la deuxième partie du dialogue dans le bon ordre.

Reading. Students read a gap-fill dialogue in which a man is reporting a car breakdown to a garage. The garage owner's side of the dialogue is given in the correct order, the man's in jumbled order. Students decide the order of the man's statements to assemble the dialogue in its correct form.

Answers
For reference only: students check their own answers using the recording in exercise 2.
c, e, b, f, a, d

2 Écoutez et vérifiez.

Listening. Students listen to check their answers to exercise 1.

Audioscript 24

- *Allô, Dépanneurs Duclerc. Je peux vous aider?*
- *Bonjour. Ma voiture est tombée en panne et j'ai besoin d'un mécanicien, s'il vous plaît.*
- *Comment vous appelez-vous, s'il vous plaît?*
- *Jean-Luc Bourget. B-O-U-R-G-E-T.*
- *Et quel est le problème, Monsieur Bourget?*
- *Je ne sais pas exactement. La voiture s'est arrêtée tout à coup et elle ne démarre plus.*
- *Où êtes-vous exactement, monsieur?*
- *Sur l'A13, entre Rouen et Le Havre, direction Le Havre, à dix kilomètres environ de Rouen.*
- *Et c'est quelle marque de voiture?*
- *C'est une Peugeot bleu foncé.*
- *Bon, on va envoyer un mécanicien. On sera là dans vingt minutes à peu près.*
- *D'accord. Merci beaucoup. Au revoir.*

3 Écoutez. Copiez et complétez la grille. (1–4)

Listening. Students copy out the grid. They listen to the four conversations in which people are reporting car breakdowns and fill in the details in the grid.

Give students time to look at the pictures and read the captions before playing the recording.

Audioscript 25

1 – *Allô, oui, Garage Georges Martin.*
– *Bonjour. Ma voiture est tombée en panne. Pouvez-vous m'aider, s'il vous plaît?*
– *Quel est votre nom, s'il vous plaît, madame?*
– *Prévost, Marie Prévost.*
– *P-R-É-V-O-S-T? C'est ça, madame?*
– *Oui, c'est ça.*
– *Et quel est le problème avec la voiture, madame?*
– *Ce sont les freins. Les freins ne marchent pas. Je ne sais pas pourquoi.*

– Vous êtes où en ce moment, madame?
– Je suis sur la Nationale 175, direction Caen, juste après la sortie Pont-L'Évêque.
– Et vous avez quelle marque de voiture?
– C'est une Renault Clio rouge.
– Bon, restez là, madame. Le mécanicien arrivera dans quinze minutes environ.
– Merci beaucoup. Au revoir.

2 *– Allô, c'est bien le service dépanneur?*
– Oui, monsieur, c'est ça. Je peux vous aider?
– C'est que je suis en panne sur l'autoroute. Pouvez-vous envoyer un mécanicien, s'il vous plaît?
– Oui, bien sûr, monsieur. Quel est le problème?
– Je crois que c'est la batterie. Elle est à plat. La voiture ne veut pas démarrer.
– Et c'est quelle marque de voiture, monsieur?
– C'est une Citroën noire.
– Pouvez-vous me donner votre nom, s'il vous plaît, monsieur?
– C'est Vincent Lambert. L-A-M-B-E-R-T.
– D'accord, Monsieur Lambert. Et vous êtes où, exactement?
– Je suis sur l'A26, direction Calais, à quinze kilomètres de Calais à peu près.
– Pas de problème, monsieur. Je serai là dans trente minutes.
– C'est très gentil, merci. Au revoir.
– À bientôt, monsieur.

3 *– Allô, SOS Dépanne. Je vous écoute.*
– Bonsoir. Je m'appelle Marie-Claire Rémy. J'ai un problème avec ma voiture.
– Pouvez-vous épeler votre nom, s'il vous plaît, madame?
– Oui, c'est Rémy. R-É-M-Y.
– Merci, madame. Et qu'est-ce qui ne va pas avec la voiture?
– C'est que les phares ne marchent pas. Il commence à faire nuit et je dois aller à Paris ce soir.
– Bon, vous avez un problème avec les phares. Et vous êtes sur quelle route, madame?
– Je suis sur l'A1, entre Lille et Paris, juste après la sortie pour Calais.
– Et vous avez dit direction Paris, madame?
– Oui, direction Paris. Ma voiture est une Toyota grise.
– D'accord, Madame Rémy. On va vous envoyer une mécanicienne. Elle sera avec vous dans une demi-heure environ.
– Merci bien. Au revoir.

4 *– Allô, Garage Aubert.*
– Bonjour. J'ai un problème avec ma voiture. Je ne sais pas si vous pouvez m'aider.
– Quel est le problème, monsieur?
– J'ai un pneu crevé, mais je ne peux pas enlever le pneu. Il est tout à fait coincé.
– Vous êtes où en ce moment, monsieur?
– Je suis sur la Nationale 2, pas loin de Lagny, direction Roissy.
– Pas de problème, monsieur. On est à dix minutes de là. Vous avez quelle marque de voiture?
– J'ai une Renault Mégane blanche.
– Et comment vous appelez-vous, s'il vous plaît, monsieur?
– Rachid. R-A-C-H-I-D. Saïd Rachid.
– D'accord, Monsieur Rachid. Un de nos mécaniciens sera là aussitôt que possible.
– Merci beaucoup. Au revoir.
– Au revoir, monsieur.

Answers

	nom	problème	où?	voiture
1	*Mme Prévost*	Les freins ne marchent pas.	*N175 direction Caen, juste après la sortie Pont-L'Évêque*	Renault Clio rouge
2	M. Lambert	La batterie est à plat.	A26 direction Calais, à quinze kilomètres de Calais	Citroën noire
3	Mme Rémy	Les phares ne marchent pas.	A1 entre Lille et Paris, juste après la sortie pour Calais	Toyota grise
4	M. Rachid	Le pneu est crevé et coincé/il ne peut pas l'enlever.	Nationale 2, pas loin de Lagny, direction Roissy	Renault Mégane blanche

Starter 2

Aim
To revise the perfect tense.

Write up the following and ask students to give the perfect tense forms of the verbs as indicated.

voir – je
courir – tu
freiner – il
se faire mal – nous
venir – elles
aller – on
monter – ils
faire – vous
s'arrêter – elle

4 À deux. Adaptez le dialogue de l'exercice 1. Utilisez les détails ci-dessous.

Speaking. In pairs: students make up three dialogues with the prompts supplied, adapting the dialogue in exercise 1.

5 Écoutez et lisez les histoires d'accidents de la route. Devinez le sens des mots en bleu. Puis vérifiez dans la section vocabulaire.

Listening. Students listen to two accounts of road accidents, reading the text at the same time. Using the relevant strategies, they try to work out the meaning of the words in blue in the texts and then check their answers in the Vocabulaire section at the back of the Student Book.

Audioscript 26

1 *La semaine dernière, j'ai vu un accident horrible au grand rond-point en ville. Il y avait beaucoup de circulation et il pleuvait, donc la route était glissante. Tout à coup, un chat a couru sur la route, devant un camion qui roulait assez lentement. Le camionneur a freiné, mais il a dérapé et son camion est entré en collision avec une voiture. La chauffeuse de la voiture s'est fait mal à la tête et au bras. De plus, elle était coincée et ne pouvait pas sortir de sa voiture. Heureusement que j'avais mon portable et j'ai téléphoné tout de suite aux sapeurs-pompiers et à une ambulance, qui sont venus immédiatement.*

2 *Hier soir, il y a eu un accident devant une boîte de nuit au centre-ville. Un groupe de jeunes gens attendaient au passage clouté pour traverser la rue. Soudain, une moto a tourné au coin de la rue. Le motocycliste roulait beaucoup trop vite, sa moto est montée sur le trottoir, et il a heurté plusieurs piétons et une voiture. Le chauffeur de la voiture portait sa ceinture de sécurité et il n'a pas été blessé, mais le motocycliste et trois jeunes ont été transportés à l'hôpital. Heureusement que personne n'a été tué. Il paraît que le motocycliste avait bu et qu'il n'avait pas de permis de conduire. Quel idiot!*

Answers

rond-pont – roundabout
glissante – slippery
roulait – was driving
lentement – slowly
a freiné – braked
a dérapé – skidded
coincée – stuck
sapeurs-pompiers – fire brigade
passage clouté – zebra crossing
moto – motorbike
le trottoir – the pavement
a heurté – struck/hit
piétons – pedestrians
ceinture de sécurité – seat belt
blessé – injured
personne n'était tué – no one was killed
permis de conduire – driving licence

6 Choisissez un des textes de l'exercice 5 et écrivez un résumé en anglais.

Reading. Students choose one of the texts in exercise 5 and write a summary of it in English.

7 Écrivez une description de l'accident à droite. Adaptez les textes de l'exercice 5.

Writing. Students use the picture prompt to write a description of an accident. They should use the texts in exercise 5 as a model. Possible opening sentences are supplied for support.

Plenary

Ask students to look at the first text in exercise 5 again and to tell you which tenses are used in it and why, summarising when the perfect and the imperfect are used.

Ask a volunteer to read out his/her response to exercise 7 and get the rest of the class to feed back on whether past tenses have been used accurately.

Cahier d'exercices, page 89

1

Answers

1 L'accident s'est passé le 2 juillet 2001.
2 Non, Laurent était en vélo.
3 Le chauffeur avait 15 ans.
4 La voiture a heurté Laurent parce qu'il roulait trop vite et il avait trop bu.
5 Laurent est handicapé et est en chaise roulante.
6 Le chauffeur avait trop bu et il était trop jeune d'avoir un permis de conduire.

2

Answers

Between 1st June and 31st May 2003, researchers recorded 6,350 deaths on the road, not to mention serious injuries. However, there was a reduction of 18.2% of deaths. Nevertheless, the majority of victims are young adults who lack experience.
Some people think that having a high spec car allows them to drive more quickly; however the braking distance increases hugely with speed, whatever type of vehicle you have.
It's a fact that too many people drive quickly and true that the authorities put up speed cameras to punish people who cheat. I approve of the idea that the authorities are taking measures, but I think that they're too strict.

3 L'environnement va mal!

(Student Book pages 166–167)

Main topics and objectives

- Discussing the environment
- The present and future tenses

Grammar

- Irregular present tense verbs
- The future tense

Key language

Il faut ...
éteindre la lumière
baisser le chauffage central
acheter des produits bio/verts
recycler
Il ne faut pas ...
gaspiller de l'énergie
laisser le robinet ouvert
utiliser trop d'emballages
détruire la couche d'ozone
empoisonner la terre
utiliser trop les voitures
le carton
le frigo
le gaz d'échappement
le journal
le recyclage
le sac en plastique/toile
le verre
la boîte

Resources

CD4, tracks 27–28
Cahier d'exercices, page 90
Grammaire 3.9

Starter 1

Aim
To revise regular verbs in the present tense.

Write up: **penser, attendre, choisir**. Tell students working in pairs to write out all the present tense forms of these verbs as quickly as they can. The pair to finish in the quickest time is the winner, though you will check their answers and add three seconds for each error.

1 Écoutez et lisez. Trouvez les deux bonnes images pour chaque personne qui parle. (1–4)

Listening. Students listen to four people giving their opinions on what is wrong with the environment and read the texts at the same time. For each speaker they identify the two relevant pictures.

Audioscript 27

– *Pourquoi l'environnement va-t-il mal?*

1 *On gaspille de l'énergie et de l'eau. Par exemple, on n'éteint pas la lumière quand on quitte une pièce, on ouvre les fenêtres sans baisser le chauffage central et on laisse le robinet ouvert quand on se brosse les dents. Tout ça est mauvais pour l'environnement.*

2 *Nous jetons nos déchets dans de gros trous dans la terre et nous utilisons trop d'emballages. Par exemple, quand tu achètes des bonbons, ils sont emballés dans du plastique. Si tu achètes un frigo ou une télé, c'est encore pire: des masses d'emballage en plastique que tu ne peux pas recycler.*

3 *Les gens utilisent trop leurs voitures. Les voitures produisent des gaz qui causent de la pollution et qui contribuent au réchauffement de la terre. Cette pollution détruit aussi la couche d'ozone qui nous protège contre les rayons du soleil.*

4 *Si vous achetez des produits non-bio ou pas verts au supermarché, vous ne pensez pas à l'environnement. Les fruits et les légumes bio sont cultivés sans utiliser des produits chimiques qui empoisonnent la terre. Il y a aussi des produits verts, comme la lessive ou le liquide vaisselle, qui sont mieux pour l'environnement.*

Answers
1 d, g **2** c, h **3** a, f **4** b, e

Expo-langue: irregular present tense verbs

Use this grammar box to cover **éteindre, ouvrir** and **produire**, which are irregular in the present tense.

2 Copiez et complétez le vocabulaire en utilisant les textes de l'exercice 1.

Reading. Students copy out and complete the nine vocabulary items with their translations, filling in the gaps in French or English as appropriate.

Answers
1 l'énergie **2** lumière **3** baisser, heating **4** robinet, leave **5** d'emballage, use **6** couche d'ozone, destroy **7** la terre **8** bio **9** produits

R Ask students comprehension questions in French on the texts in exercise 1.

3 Écrivez six règles pour la protection de l'environnement. Utilisez *il faut* ou *il ne faut pas*.

Writing. Students write six rules to help protect the environment using the expressions **il faut** and **il ne faut pas**. An example is given.

Starter 2

Aim

To use grammar knowledge to work out how sentences fit together.

Write up the following gap-fill sentences, plus the answers in jumbled order (given in correct order for reference below).

1 Ils ______ du verre et des boîtes.
2 J'éteindrai la lumière quand je ______ la pièce.
3 Elle ______ le robinet quand elle se brosse ses dents.
4 ______ le chauffage et ______ un pull!
5 Il ______ plus de produits bio.
6 Nous ______ d'utiliser des produits verts.

recycleront
quitterai
ferme
baissez
mettez
achètera
essayerons

4 On parle de ce qu'on fait pour protéger l'environnement. Pour chaque phrase, écrivez Marie, Luc, Zoé ou Thierry.

Listening. Students listen to four people talking about what they do to protect the environment and read the four speech bubbles. They identify the speaker - Marie, Luc, Zoé or Thierry - for each bubble.

Audioscript 28

- *Marie, que fais-tu pour protéger l'environnement?*
- *Je suis surtout consciente de l'environnement quand je fais mes courses. Je regarde bien pour voir si c'est bio ou si c'est marqué comme bon pour l'environnement, par exemple, si le paquet ou la bouteille sont faits en carton ou en verre recyclé.*
- *Et toi, Luc, qu'est-ce que tu fais?*
- *Quand j'ai un voyage à faire, j'essaie de me déplacer par les transports en commun. Par exemple, quand je vais en ville, je prends le bus, et quand je vais à Paris pour voir mon père, je prends le train. Et s'il s'agit d'un trajet plus court, comme aller au collège, j'y vais à pied ou à vélo.*
- *Zoé, tu fais quoi pour l'environnement?*
- *Je ne mets que très peu de déchets à la poubelle. Toutes mes bouteilles vides, mes vieux journaux et magazines, je les emporte au point de recyclage du quartier. Je recycle aussi autant d'emballages en carton que possible, par exemple, les paquets de céréales, les boîtes de pizzas, etc.*
- *Et finalement Thierry. Tu penses à l'environnement aussi?*
- *Ah oui, tout le temps! Je me douche au lieu de me baigner parce que ça consomme moins d'eau, j'éteins la lumière ou la télé quand je sors de la pièce et je mets un pull quand il fait froid au lieu de monter le chauffage central!*

Answers

1 Thierry **2** Marie **3** Luc **4** Zoé

5 C'est au présent ou au futur? Pour chaque phrase, écrivez P ou F.

Reading. Students read the eight sentences and decide for each whether it refers to the present (P) or the future (F).

Answers

1 F **2** F **3** P **4** F **5** P **6** F **7** F **8** P

Expo-langue: the future tense

Use this grammar box to remind students that **aller** has an irregular stem in the future tense. For more examples of verbs with irregular future stems, see the Verb tables on pp. 219–221.

The box also covers the use of the future tense in sentences with **quand** clauses, where a present tense is used in English.

\+ Ask students to make a list of 10 verbs with irregular future stems.

6 Copiez les phrases de l'exercice 5 en les changeant du présent au futur, ou du futur au présent.

Writing. Students write out the sentences in exercise 5, changing all the present tenses to future tenses and vice versa.

Answers

1. J'achète plus de produits bio.
2. Je recycle du verre et des boîtes.
3. J'éteindrai la lumière quand je quitterai la pièce.
4. Je ferme le robinet quand je me brosse les dents.
5. J'utiliserai les transports en commun.
6. Je baisse le chauffage et je mets un pull.
7. Je vais au collège à vélo.
8. J'essayerai d'utiliser des produits verts.

7 À deux. Qu'est-ce que vous faites pour l'environnement? Qu'est-ce que vous ferez plus tard?

Speaking. In pairs. Students discuss what they do for the environment and what they are going to do in the future, taking it in turn to ask the questions and to respond. A sample exchange is given.

Go to www.heinemann.co.uk/hotlinks and enter the express code 7898T for a link to a website containing tips on how to protect the environment.

Plenary

Write up the following:

When I go shopping, I will buy some apples.

I will invite Luc to my party when I see him tomorrow.

Ask students to translate these into French and to summarise the rule for verbs after **quand** when you are referring to the future. Then get them to make up some examples of **quand** sentences like this.

Cahier d'exercices, page 90

1

Answers

veille: standby
suremballage: too much packaging
jetables: throw-away
piles: batteries
ampoules: pills

2

Answers

Pupil's own answers

3

Answers

Example:
J'éteindrai les lumières et les appareils électriques.
Je porterai un pull pour ne pas mettre le chauffage trop fort.
Je prendrai une douche rapide.
Je n'utiliserai de l'eau chaude que quand c'est vraiment nécessaire.
J'éviterai de gaspiller du papier.
Dans les magasins, je ferai attention aux produits que j'achèterai.
Je trierai mes déchets.
Je jeterai les piles, etc. séparément des autres déchets.
Pour les petits trajets, j'y irai le plus souvent à vélo ou à pied.
Pour partir en vacances, je prendrai le train.

4 Avant et après

(Student Book pages 168–169)

Main topics and objectives

- Talking about environmental projects
- Using direct object pronouns in the perfect tense

Grammar

- Agreement in the perfect tense with **avoir** (direct object pronouns)

Key language

Je me douche au lieu de me baigner.
Je partage la voiture avec trois autres.
J'ai recyclé mon portable.
On a installé des containers pour le verre.
On a construit un petit parc.
On a créé un espace vert/une zone piétonne.
On recyclera/utilisera/éteindra ...
On ne gaspillera pas ...

Resources

CD4, tracks 29–30
Cahier d'exercices, page 91
Grammaire 1.7

Starter 1

Aim
To revise language for discussing the environment.

Ask students working in pairs to write a list of six things they did that were good for the environment last week. They can make this up, if necessary.

1 Mettez l'histoire d'Écofille dans le bon ordre.

Reading. Students read the episodes of the story of Écofille, looking at the accompanying pictures, and put them in the correct order.

Answers
g, a, f, c, e, d, b, h

2 Écoutez et vérifiez.

Listening. Students listen to the recording to check their answers to exercise 1.

Audioscript 29

Tout d'abord, je me suis douchée au lieu de me baigner parce qu'avec une douche, on consomme moins d'eau qu'avec un bain. Puis, après avoir pris mon petit déjeuner, je me suis brossée les dents. J'ai fait ça sans laisser le robinet ouvert pour économiser de l'eau. Malheureusement, là où j'habite, les transports en commun sont nuls, donc je suis allée au collège en voiture. Mais je l'ai partagée avec trois autres. C'est mieux pour l'environnement s'il y a plusieurs personnes dans une voiture. Tout de suite après les cours, j'ai dû faire les courses pour ma mère. Bien sûr, je n'ai acheté que des produits bio ou verts. Au supermarché, je n'ai pas pris de sacs en plastique, mais j'ai utilisé des sacs en toile. J'ai fait ça parce que les sacs en plastique qu'on jette à la poubelle ne sont pas biodégradables. Après avoir fait les courses, je suis allée au magasin Oxfam parce que j'avais reçu un nouveau portable comme cadeau d'anniversaire de mes parents. Au lieu de jeter mon vieux portable à la poubelle, je l'ai recyclé en le donnant à Oxfam et il sera utilisé dans un pays en voie de développement.

Expo-langue: agreement in the perfect tense with *avoir*

Use this grammar box to remind students that when a direct object pronoun is used with **avoir** verbs in the perfect tense, the past participle must agree with this pronoun.

There is more information on p. 208 of the Student Book.

3 Écrivez les six choses qu'Écofille a fait pour l'environnement.

Writing. Students write six sentences about the things Écofille has done for the environment. The first is given as an example.

Answers
1 *Elle s'est douchée au lieu de se baigner.*
2 Elle s'est brossée les dents sans laisser le robinet ouvert.
3 Elle a partagé la voiture avec trois autres.
4 Elle n'a pas acheté que des produits bio ou verts.
5 Au supermarché, elle n'a pas pris de sacs en plastique.
6 Elle a recyclé son vieux portable.

➕ Ask students to use the same structures to come up with six different things Écofille did for the environment, e.g. Elle **est allée à la piscine à pied** au lieu d'y **aller en voiture**.

4 À deux. Qui a fait plus pour l'environnement la semaine dernière? Il faut exagérer!

Speaking. In pairs: students discuss what they did for the environment last week. The aim is to outdo their partner in environmental-friendliness, so emphasise that they should be inventive in their answers. A sample exchange is given.

Starter 2

Aim
To practise using pronouns.

Write up the following and ask students working in pairs to translate them into French.

1 The car? I shared it.
2 The bags? I recycled them.
3 The boys? I saw them.
4 The shopping? I did it.
5 The Oxfam shop? I went there.
6 The vegetables? I bought some.

5 Quel était le problème environnemental avant? Qu'est-ce qu'on a fait pour changer la situation? Copiez et complétez la grille en français. (1–5)

Listening. Students copy out the grid. They listen to five people talking about environmental problems they suffered in the past and what happened to change the situation. Students fill in the details in the grid.

Audioscript 30

1 *Dans la ville où j'habite, il y avait beaucoup trop de circulation, surtout des poids lourds, mais il y a trois ans, on a créé une zone piétonne au centre-ville, ce qui est beaucoup mieux pour l'environnement.*

2 *La rue où se trouve mon appartement était toujours très sale parce que tout le monde jetait des déchets par terre, mais l'année dernière, on a installé des poubelles et maintenant, c'est beaucoup plus propre.*

3 *Dans mon quartier, il n'y avait pas d'espaces verts et les enfants jouaient dans la rue, ce qui était très dangereux. Donc les habitants ont écrit des lettres à l'administration locale et cette année on a construit un petit parc où les enfants peuvent jouer en sécurité.*

4 *Dans ma famille, on gaspillait beaucoup d'énergie. Quand on quittait une pièce, on n'éteignait pas la lumière et on laissait souvent la télé ou l'ordinateur en marche quand on ne les utilisait pas. Alors, j'ai laissé de petites notes partout dans la maison: «N'oublie pas d'éteindre la lumière», «N'oublie pas d'éteindre la télé». Maintenant, toute ma famille pense à économiser de l'énergie.*

5 *Au collège, on ne recyclait rien. Tout le monde jetait ses boîtes de coca vides, ses magazines, etc., à la poubelle. Mes copains et moi, nous sommes allés voir la directrice pour lui demander d'installer des containers pour le verre, le plastique, le papier au collège et elle a accepté de le faire. Maintenant, tous les élèves – et les profs aussi – recyclent beaucoup plus et on est vraiment un collège «vert»!*

Answers

	problème	**action**
1	*circulation*	*zone piétonne*
2	rue sale	poubelles
3	pas d'espace verte (pour les enfants)	petit parc
4	gaspillait l'énergie	petites notes (pour ne pas oublier)
5	pas de recyclage	installer des containers

 This covers the pronunciation of **e**, **è** and **é**.

6 Qu'est-ce qu'on a fait pour l'environnement dans votre ville/votre village/votre quartier? Interviewez votre partenaire. Utilisez les idées ci-dessous ou vos propres idées.

Speaking. Students interview a partner on what has been done for the environment in their town/village/area. They should take it in turn to interview and respond, using either the prompts supplied or their own ideas.

7 Écrivez une lettre en français à votre copine Sophie. Répondez à ces questions:

Writing. Students write a letter about their local environment to Sophie, a French friend, which should include answers to the questions listed.

☑ Draw students' attention to the tip box, which highlights the need to look very carefully at the tenses used in questions like these and respond appropriately. This is a key exam skill.

Plenary

Ask students to summarise how direct object pronouns are used in the perfect tense, giving examples and spelling out the past participles.

Then write up the following words. Using what they know about accents, ask students to predict the pronunciation.

mémé, monégasque, Isère, mégère, trèfle, chicorée, chimpanzé, chaudière

Cahier d'exercices, page 91

1

Answers

1 elle a pris un bain; elle n'a pas éteint la lumière et elle a augmenté le chauffage; elle est allée au collège en voiture; elle n'a fait aucun effort pour acheter les produits respectueux de l'environnement; elle a gaspillé du papier
2 elle se douchait; elle bassait le chauffage après sa douche; elle allait à pied avec ses copains; elle utilisait les deux faces
3 Pupil's own answers

2

Answers

Possible answers:
Tu fais beaucoup pour l'environnement?
Non, je ne fais pas beaucoup pour l'environnement.
Qu'est-ce que tu faisais avant?
Je me douchais et je baissais le chauffage après ma douche. J'allais au collège à pied avec mes copains et je ne gaspillais du papier; j'utilisais les deux faces.
Et hier, qu'est-ce que tu as fait?
Hier, j'ai pris un bain et j'ai augmenté le chauffage parce que j'avais froid. Je suis allée au collège en voiture. Quand j'ai fait les magasins, je n'ai fait aucun effort pour acheter les produits repectueux de l'environnement. J'ai gaspillé du papier quand j'ai fait mes devoirs.
Tu voudrais changer et faire des choses qui aidera l'environnement?
Non, pas vraiment!
Et dans le futur, qu'est-ce que tu feras?
Je continuerai à faire ce que je veux!

5 À la une

(Student Book pages 170–171)

Main topics and objectives
- Understanding news stories
- The passive

Grammar
- The passive

Key language
le désastre
le feu
l'ouragan (m)
la fuite
l'incendie (f)
l'inondation (f)
la sécheresse
la conservation
l'arbre (m)
la forêt
le paysage
la côte
la mer
la pétrole
la vie marine
un manque de pluie
depuis dix mois
sec/sèche
plusieurs
des centaines (f) de
les dégâts (m)
les espèces en voie d'extinction (f)
détruit(e) par
dévasté(e) par
inondé(e) par
menacé(e) de
tué(e) par

Resources
CD4, track 31
Cahier d'exercices, pages 92–93
Grammaire 3.12

Starter 1

Aim
To introduce vocabulary to describe news events.
To use strategies to work out new words.
Use exercise 1 as the Starter for this lesson.

1 Lisez les extraits et trouvez le gros titre correspondant à chacun.

Reading. Students read the five newspaper extracts (**1–5**) and match them to the appropriate headline (**a–e**).

☑ Tell students to read the tip box before they start, as this gives support on tackling new vocabulary in the texts.

Answers
1 c **2** e **3** d **4** a **5** b

2 Trouvez l'équivalent en français.

Reading. Students reread the texts in exercise 1 and find the French for the twelve English expressions listed.

Answers

1	inondations graves	**7**	dégâts sérieux
2	incendies de forêt	**8**	centaines de/d'
3	sécheresse	**9**	d'une puissance incroyable
4	ouragan	**10**	détruit(s) par le feu
5	une fuite de pétrole	**11**	a déjà tué
6	marée haute	**12**	inondé par la mer

Expo-langue: the passive

Use this grammar box to introduce the passive. There is more information on p. 214 of the Student Book.

3 Réécrivez ces phrases sans le passif.

Writing. Students rewrite the five sentences to avoid the passive.

Answers
1 Une fuite de pétrole a menacé la côte. **2** Le manque de pluie a détruit le paysage. **3** La mer a inondé le village. **4** L'eau a fait des dégâts. **5** L'ouragan a devasté la ville.

Starter 2

Aim
To practise understanding the passive.

Write up the following, jumbling the order of the second column, and ask students to find the correct ending for each sentence.

1 La ville est détruite par	**l'inondation.**
2 Le paysage est	**menacé par la sécheresse.**
3 Des dégâts ont été	**faits par l'ouragan.**
4 Le village	**sera dévasté par la mer.**
5 Les oiseaux	**seront tués par la fuite de pétrole.**

4 Écoutez. On parle de quel désastre? (1–4)

Listening. Students listen to four conversations about disasters and identify the topic of each from **a–d**.

Audioscript 31

1 *– Les plages de la région sont noires et je ne sais plus combien d'oiseaux ont étés tués.*
– Oui, et on a trouvé des centaines de poissons morts dans la mer. La pêche sera gravement affectée par la pollution aussi.
– Tu as raison. Puis le tourisme sera affecté. On ne pourra ni faire de la natation ni faire de la voile. C'est un désastre écologique et économique.

2 *– J'avais très peur, tu sais. Tout le rez-de-chaussée était inondé et l'eau est montée jusqu'au premier étage.*
– Est-ce qu'il y a eu beaucoup de dégâts?
– Ah oui, c'est la dévastation totale. Les meubles, les tapis
– tout a été complètement détruit. Après tout ça, je n'ai plus envie d'habiter près de la mer. On va déménager.

3 – Je n'ai jamais vu un temps comme ça. Quel vent! Plein d'arbres dans la forêt ont été détruits et pas mal de maisons aussi.
– Oui, le vent était incroyable. Il était si fort que la voiture de notre voisin s'est retournée et il l'a trouvée au milieu de son jardin!
– Et quelle pluie aussi! J'espère qu'il n'y aura plus de temps comme ça.

4 – As-tu vu les infos de vingt heures à la télé?
– Ah, oui! Quelle horreur! Notre belle forêt est dévastée! Beaucoup de gens ont dû quitter leurs maisons à cause du feu.
– J'ai vu la fumée de mon appartement. Le ciel était noir, comme si c'était la nuit et les flammes étaient énormes. Plusieurs sapeurs-pompiers ont été transportés à l'hôpital à cause de la fumée et de la chaleur.

Answers
1 c **2** a **3** d **4** b

5 Imaginez que vous êtes un présentateur ou une présentatrice du journal télévisé. Inventez un reportage sur un désastre dans votre région. Si possible, enregistrez-le en audio ou en vidéo.

Speaking. Students imagine they are a news presenter and make up a news report on a disaster in their region. If possible, give them the opportunity to record it on audio cassette or video.

6 Écrivez votre reportage, avec un gros titre aussi.

Writing. Students write a newspaper report of the disaster they covered in exercise 5, including a headline for it.

7 Copiez le texte et remplissez les blancs avec les mots en dessous.

Reading. Students copy the gap-fill text and fill in the gaps from the words provided.

Answers
1 animaux **2** menacés **3** ont **4** tables **5** forêt **6** détruit **7** Afrique **8** ans **9** plus **10** devenir

✓ ✚ Ask students to research an endangered animal (or another environmental issue which interests them) on the French version of the World Wildlife Fund website. Go to www.heinemann.co.uk/hotlinks and enter the express code 7898T for a link. Tell them to gather information which they could use when preparing for the speaking part of the exam. Remind them that they should still concentrate on using the core structures in the Student Book, but being able to broaden a discussion by introducing additional detail like this will impress examiners.

Plenary

✓ Ask students to imagine they are giving advice to students just about to start preparing for their GCSE in French. Can they come up with six tips on how to do well in the exam? Write up suggestions and encourage students to copy the list down and keep as a final checklist to help with revision.

Cahier d'exercices, page 92

1

Answers
Any 3 facts from the account.

2

Answers

touché(es) – affected	réfugié(s) – refugees
dénombre – count/noted	évacué(es) – evacuated
déplacé(s) – displaced	île(s) – islands
privé(es) – deprived	infiltré(es) – infiltrated
dizaine(s) – tens	produits – products

3

Answers

morts – deaths	grâce aux dons – thanks to the aid
blessés – injured	inondées – flooded
détruites – destroyed	récifs de corail – coral reefs
privées – deprived	abîmés – ruined
plusieurs dizaines – several tens	

4

Answers

ont été détruites	avaient été évacuées
ont pu être reconstruites	ont été abîmés
ont été déplacées	ont été touchés
ont été inondées	ont été infiltrées

Cahier d'exercices, Grammaire, page 93

Answers

1 down avait
2 down peut
3 down pouvait
4 down recyclez
5 down see **11 across**
10 down faut
12 down utilisera
15 down suis douché
17 down devrait
19 down jetait
20 down est entré
6 across est arrivée
7 across détruit
8 across recyclent
9 across ira
11 across pleuvait **& 5 down** était
13 across acheterez
14 across éteins
16 across voudrais
18 across mettras
21 across utilisent
22 across pourrions

Contrôle continu: Un problème environnemental (Student Book pages 172–173)

Topic revised

- writing about environmental problems

1 Copiez les phrases en bleu dans le texte et trouvez l'équivalent en anglais ci-dessous.

Students copy out the phrases in blue in the text and match them to the correct English version (from **1–14**).

Answers

il y a quelques jours
9 a few days ago
j'ai été choqué par ce que j'ai vu
10 I was shocked by what I saw
sur l'herbe
11 on the grass
c'était dégoûtant
4 it was disgusting
des morceaux de verre
12 pieces of glass
je vais proposer à mes copains
5 I'm going to suggest to my friends
nettoyer cet endroit
7 to clean up this place
on ramassera tous les déchets
13 we will collect all the rubbish
on se soucie de l'environnement
1 we care about the environment
les grenouilles
6 frogs
un panneau qui dirait «ne pas déranger les animaux et les oiseaux»
8 a sign which says 'Do not disturb the animals and the birds'
regulièrement
2 regularly
ses environs
14 its surroundings
un site pittoresque qui attirera beaucoup de gens
3 a picturesque spot which attracts lots of people

2 Pour chaque phrase, écrivez V (Vrai), F (Faux) ou PM (Pas Mentionné).

Students reread the text. They then read the ten statements and decide whether each is true or false or not mentioned in the text.

Answers

1 F **2** F **3** V **4** PM **5** V **6** F **7** V **8** PM **9** V **10** F

3 Écrivez une lettre à un journal sur un problème environnemental.

Using the text and the **Boîte à outils** section to help them, students write a letter to a newspaper about an environmental problem.

À l'oral (AQA edition)

(Student Book page 185)

Topics revised

- getting help when your car breaks down
- talking about the environment

1 Your car has broken down in France and you telephone a garage to ask for help. Your partner will play the part of the garage receptionist and will speak first.

Roleplay. Students practise calling a garage for help when their car breaks down, taking it in turn to play themselves/the garage receptionist.

2 Prepare a ninety-second presentation called *L'environnement et moi.*

Presentation. Students prepare a ninety-second presentation on their opinion of the environment and what they do to protect it. A sample cue card is supplied for students to refer to when preparing their own prompts.

3 Possible conversation questions:

These are key questions to practise for the speaking exam, taken from the module as a whole. Students can practise asking and answering the questions in pairs.

☑ Draw students' attention to the tip box for techniques in handling questions like question 1. Also encourage students to try and work in some of the colloquial expressions listed in the **Tu parles!** section.

À l'oral (Edexcel edition)

(Student Book page 185)

Topics revised
- getting help when your car breaks down
- talking about the environment

1 You are travelling by car with your family in France when your car breaks down. You telephone a garage. Your partner will play the part of the garage owner and will begin the conversation.

Roleplay Type C. Students practise calling a garage for help when their car breaks down, taking it in turn to play themselves/the garage owner.

2 Presentation and general conversation

Presentation. Students prepare a one-minute presentation on their opinion of the environment and what they do to protect it. A sample cue card is supplied for students to use for ideas and to refer to when preparing their own prompts.

Possible conversation questions. These are key questions to practise for the speaking exam, taken from the module as a whole. Students can practise asking and answering the questions in pairs.

☑ Draw students' attention to the tip box for techniques in handling questions like question 1. Also encourage students to try and work in some of the colloquial expressions shown in the box.

À l'oral (OCR edition)

(Student Book page 185)

Topics revised
- getting help when your car breaks down
- talking about the environment

1 Your car has broken down in France and you telephone a garage, to ask for help. Your partner will play the part of the garage receptionist and will speak first.

Roleplay Type 2. Students practise calling a garage for help when their car breaks down, taking it in turn to play themselves/the garage receptionist.

2 Prepare a one-minute presentation called *L'environnement et moi.*

Presentation. Students prepare a one-minute presentation on their opinion of the environment and what they do to protect it. A sample cue card is supplied for students to refer to when preparing their own prompts.

3 *L'environnement:* possible conversation questions

These are key questions to practise for the speaking exam, taken from the module as a whole. Students can practise asking and answering the questions in pairs.

☑ Draw students' attention to the tip box for techniques in handling questions like question 1.

À toi

(Student Book pages 204–205)

- Self-access reading and writing

1 Lisez le texte. Puis mettez les phrases en anglais dans l'ordre du texte.

Reading. Students read the text on the environment. They then read ten statements in English and put them in the order these are mentioned in the text.

Answers

b, f, g, i, c, e, j, a, d, h

2 Écrivez une phrase pour chaque conseil de l'exercice 1 en utilisant *il faut, on devrait* ou *on pourrait*.

Writing. Students write a sentence summarising each of the five pieces of advice given in exercise 1. They should aim to include the expressions **il faut, on devrait** and **on pourrait**.

3 Créez un poster pour protéger l'environnement. Donnez au moins cinq conseils (avec des images) qui ne sont pas dans le texte de l'exercice 1.

Writing. Students create a poster showing what should be done to protect the environment. They should include at least five pieces of advice (including pictures) which are not covered in the text in exercise 1.

Draw students' attention to the tip box, which points out that it is the **vous** form which should be used here.

4 Copiez le texte dans le bon ordre.

Reading. Students reassemble the lines of Claire's text, copying it out in the correct order.

Answers

Je m'appelle Claire. Dans ma ville, il y avait une rivière qui /
était pleine de déchets. Il n'y avait plus de poissons à cause de /
la pollution et c'était trop sale pour les oiseaux. Donc, mes /
copains et moi, nous y sommes allés pour la nettoyer. On /
a trouvé dans l'eau plein de bouteilles et de boîtes, qu'on a /
recyclées, un chariot de supermarché (qu'on a rendu au magasin) – et un /
vieux vélo (que mon frère a réparé et qu'il a vendu!). On a planté /
des arbres aussi, pour combattre la pollution. Maintenant, /
la rivière est propre et on peut aller à la pêche. Un jour, j'ai même vu /
une petite grenouille plonger dans l'eau. Je suis fière de /
ce que nous avons fait pour notre ville et pour l'environnement.

5 Imaginez que vous êtes Claire. Répondez aux questions en français.

Reading. Students imagine that they are Claire (from exercise 4) and answer the questions in French from her perspective.

Answers

1. La rivière était pleine de déchets.
2. Il n'y avait pas de poissons à cause de la pollution.
3. Mes copains et moi, nous y sommes allés pour nettoyer la rivière.
4. Nous avons/On a recyclé les bouteilles et les boîtes.
5. Mon frère a réparé le vieux vélo.
6. Nous avons/On a planté des arbres pour combattre la pollution.
7. Je sais que l'eau est propre maintenant parce que j'ai vu une petite grenouille plonger dans l'eau.
8. Je suis fière de ce que nous avons fait pour notre ville et pour l'environnement.

6 Regardez les images et écrivez un paragraphe sur ce que vous avez fait pour l'environnement. Adaptez le texte de l'exercice 4.

Writing. Students write a paragraph on what they did for the environment, using the picture prompts supplied and adapting the text in exercise 4.